Low-Cholesterol Cookbook

FOR

DUMMIES®

by Molly Siple, MS, RD

WILEY

Wiley Publishing, Inc.

Low-Cholesterol Cookbook For Dummies®

Published by
Wiley Publishing, Inc.
111 River St.
Hoboken, NJ 07030-5774
www.wiley.com

Copyright © 2005 by Wiley Publishing, Inc., Indianapolis, Indiana

Published by Wiley Publishing, Inc., Indianapolis, Indiana

Published simultaneously in Canada

For general information on our other products and services, please contact our Customer Care Department within the U.S. at 800-762-2974, outside the U.S. at 317-572-3993, or fax 317-572-4002.

For technical support, please visit www.wiley.com/techsupport.

Wiley also publishes its books in a variety of electronic formats. Some content that appears in print may not be available in electronic books.

Library of Congress Control Number: 2004115692

ISBN: 0-7645-7160-5

Manufactured in the United States of America

10 9 8 7 6 5 4 3 2 1

1B/RQ/RR/QU/IN

WILEY

Dedication

To my stepfather, Milton Otis Shaw, for all his kindness.

About the Author

Molly Siple, MS, RD, is also the author of *Healing Foods For Dummies.* She writes a nutrition column that appears in *Natural Health* magazine and she has taught nutrition at the Southern California School of Culinary Arts in Pasadena, California.

She is the coauthor, with Lissa DeAngelis, of *Recipes for Change,* which was a finalist nominee for the International Association of Culinary Professionals' Julia Child Cookbook Awards in the Health and Special Diet category. Ms. Siple also founded a successful catering business in New York City.

Author's Acknowledgments

Here's a big thank you to Wiley Publishing for giving me the opportunity to write this book. First, thank you to the acquisitions editor, Natasha Graf, for signing off on my receiving the assignment and having the project start so quickly. And what would my days of writing have been like without the bright and cheery e-mails I'd open first thing in the morning from my brilliant project editor, Natalie Harris, who could always see the big picture? Much thanks also to Emily Nolan, a recipe tester who really knows her stuff and pointed out my glitches, and to Tina Sims, copy editor, who asked me clever questions and sometimes performed surgery on my sentences. I also much appreciate the work of Patty Santelli, general reviewer and nutritional analyst, for her thoughtful insights into the technical aspects of the text.

Special thanks also goes to Deborah Morley, a budding chef herself, who took time from her culinary studies to help me test recipes. And what a pleasure to have Lissa DeAngelis calling to give me company as I wrote and answering my cooking questions. But the biggest thank you of all goes to my partner in all things, Victor Watson. While I wrote the book, you ran my errands, hunted up research studies in the library, shopped for the food for testing the recipes, let me know quite clearly when the results were too bland, fed me when I had no time to cook, and, in general, let me feel loved as you cheered me on.

Publisher's Acknowledgments

We're proud of this book; please send us your comments through our Dummies online registration form located at www.dummies.com/register/.

Some of the people who helped bring this book to market include the following:

Acquisitions, Editorial, and Media Development

Project Editor: Natalie Faye Harris

Acquisitions Editors: Mikal E. Belicove, Natasha Graf

Senior Copy Editor: Tina Sims

General Reviewer and Nutritional Analyst: Patty Santelli

Recipe Tester: Emily Nolan

Senior Permissions Editor: Carmen Krikorian

Editorial Manager: Christine Meloy Beck

Editorial Assistants: Courtney Allen, Melissa Bennett

Cover Photo: © Dennis Gottlieb, FoodPix

Illustrator: Elizabeth Kurtzman

Cartoons: Rich Tennant, www.the5thwave.com

Composition

Project Coordinator: Maridee Ennis

Layout and Graphics: Joyce Haughey, Stephanie D. Jumper, Barry Offringa, Lynsey Osborn, Jacque Roth, Brent Savage, Julie Trippetti

Proofreaders: Dwight Ramsey, Brian H. Walls, TECHBOOKS Production Services

Indexer: TECHBOOKS Production Services

Special Help

Elizabeth Rea

Publishing and Editorial for Consumer Dummies

Diane Graves Steele, Vice President and Publisher, Consumer Dummies

Joyce Pepple, Acquisitions Director, Consumer Dummies

Kristin A. Cocks, Product Development Director, Consumer Dummies

Michael Spring, Vice President and Publisher, Travel

Brice Gosnell, Associate Publisher, Travel

Kelly Regan, Editorial Director, Travel

Publishing for Technology Dummies

Andy Cummings, Vice President and Publisher, Dummies Technology/General User

Composition Services

Gerry Fahey, Vice President of Production Services

Debbie Stailey, Director of Composition Services

Contents at a Glance

Recipes at a Glance

Baking recipes

Bean and legume recipes

Breakfast recipes

Fruit recipes

Hors d'oeuvre recipes

Pasta and grain recipes

Poultry recipes

Pork recipes

Red meat recipes

Salad recipes

Sauce and spread recipes

Seafood recipes

Soup recipes

Vegetable recipes

Table of Contents

Introduction

The first place to start in controlling cholesterol and lowering your risk of heart disease is in your lifestyle, in particular, changing and improving on what you eat. Sound hard? Don't despair. My advice is easy to swallow, as I'm sure you'll find when you sample the recipes in this book.

Good nutrition is still the foundation of health. Nutrients in food go to work in amazing ways, on the cellular and molecular level, to restore normal body function. The vitamins and minerals in the foods I tell you about in this book help your body lower the bad cholesterol, raise the good kind, and protect your arteries from damage. And that's just the beginning of the long list of everything they do. Of course, you've already taken the right first step in deciding to pick up this cookbook. Getting healthier starts in the kitchen!

Throughout this book, the dishes I've developed for you are geared to the needs of someone with cholesterol that's moderately elevated. You may have special needs and concerns that will require adjustments to the recipes. Work with your doctor or other health professional to tailor your diet as required. You may also need medication to treat your condition. But again, that's a matter between you and your doctor.

About This Book

The *Low-Cholesterol Cookbook For Dummies* gives you a good overview of an effective way to control cholesterol, backed up by my own experience as a nutritionist as well as scientific studies. The basics are there, about fat and cholesterol in foods, and how to put together meals that give you healthy amounts. I also load the pages with information on all the various nutrients that lower the "bad" LDL cholesterol or raise the "good" cholesterol. And you hear all about soluble fiber that soaks up cholesterol and escorts it out of your body. To make this book is as up-to-date as possible, I also touch on some newly recognized risk factors for heart disease that tie in with managing cholesterol.

Each chapter covers a category of food, such as vegetables or fish. You find out the basics of cooking these and also which ones best suit a cholesterol-controlling diet. Use these recommendations to write your grocery shopping lists. The recipes pages are also packed with useful health advice; the introductions to the recipes are filled with nutrition information on what you're about to cook.

But let's get to the good part: the recipes. First, they're delicious so you'll want to eat them even if they weren't good for you. And as I created each dish, I made a special effort to feature the most nutritious, fresh, and natural foods that also help manage cholesterol. Recipe ingredients and procedures are kept as short and simple as possible, but without sacrificing flavor. With certain recipes you have the chance to shop for special ethnic ingredients I thought you'd find intriguing. Throughout the book, I also try to make a few jokes here and there, especially in the section titles, to amuse myself and you.

Conventions Used in This Book

The recipes in this book are very complete, but they may not spell out every detail of prepping and cooking the food. For example, certain steps and techniques in cooking are standard no matter what you're preparing. In addition, in this book, I require specific types of ingredients and also want to make sure that you adhere to a few of my other cooking preferences. Take a quick look at the following list for points that apply to all the recipes:

- ✔ Organic foods are not required, because I figure you have enough to think about in shifting to a more heart-healthy diet. But by all means, buy organic when you can, to spare your body added toxins. Or at least wash produce in one of the products that removes toxins from fruits and vegetables.

- ✔ Fruits and vegetables are washed under cold running water before using.

- ✔ Pepper is freshly ground pepper. Invest in a pepper mill and give it a few cranks when you want pepper bursting with flavor.

- ✔ Fresh herbs are specified in many of the recipes for their bright, authentic flavor. But you can still make a recipe if you don't plan to use these by substituting dry herbs, using one-third the amount of fresh.

- ✔ Dairy products are lowfat.

- ✔ Eggs are large unless otherwise indicated.

- ✔ Canned goods are the low-sodium or no-added-salt versions.

- ✔ Food products never contain any partially hydrogenated oils.

- ✔ Water is filtered water.

- ✔ Keep pots uncovered unless I tell you to put on the lid.

Some other points about the recipes are also useful to keep in mind:

- ✔ Most of the recipes are written for four servings, an easy number to multiply or divide if you're feeding a crowd or you need just two servings for you and a friend.

- ✔ The nutrient information given at the end of each recipe is the amount of those items in a single serving. Have a larger serving size, and you need to increase these numbers.

- ✔ If you can't find the exact ingredient that a recipe calls for in a specific amount, don't worry. A little more or less of an item won't ruin the dish, and — who knows — if you tinker slightly with the ingredients, you may invent something that you like even better.

- ✔ The preparation time estimated for each recipe includes cutting veggies and assembling ingredients and measuring them. Doing this before you start cooking also makes the whole process more efficient. You won't be surprised that you're out of olive oil just at the moment you need some.

- ✔ The temperature for all recipes is in Fahrenheit.

Here are some non-recipe conventions to keep in mind when reading this book:

- ✔ *Italic* is used for emphasis and to highlight new words or terms that are defined.

- ✔ **Boldfaced** text indicates the action part of numbered steps.

- ✔ `Monofont` is used for Web addresses.

- ☼ This little tomato indicates that the recipe is vegetarian. You see it in on the "tabs" in front of the recipe names in the recipe chapters.

What You're Not to Read

You don't have to read every single word I've written. The material in the regular paragraphs I do recommend. These sections tell you the basics about the subject of controlling cholesterol. But you don't have to read items marked with the Technical Stuff icon, which, although interesting, may give you more details and facts than you want or need.

Reading sidebars is also optional. They provide supporting material on the subject of heart disease but they aren't absolutely essential for finding out how to manage cholesterol. And if you're already a pro at cooking, certainly skip over any cooking advice that you find obvious. But don't worry, I won't tell you how to boil water.

Foolish Assumptions

As I tested the recipes — and I did cook all of them right in my own home kitchen — I pictured you standing there right next to me, following the cooking procedures and sampling the results. I tailored the recipes to suit a certain kind of cook, who I imagine to be like this:

- ✔ You're fairly handy in the kitchen. You know how to clean mushrooms without being told, and stuffing a chicken is no big deal. But making a galantine of chicken (a simmered and boned, stuffed chicken glazed in aspic — oh please!) is beyond your scope, which is okay, because elaborate cooking techniques are nowhere to be found in this book.

- ✔ You know how to shop for food. At least you know your way around a supermarket. But the few times you wandered into one of the new natural foods supermarkets, you saw all sorts of ingredients you never heard of. You also have never ventured into or even come across one of those neighborhood ethnic food shops that look untidy but hold an array of culinary treats. I purposely include special ingredients, such as date sugar, Italian prosciutto, and oil-cured olives in various recipes to lead you into these unique stores.

- ✔ Uninteresting food isn't worth the trouble of preparing it, according to you. You want dishes with personality and flavors that get your attention. It's fine if a food is good for you, but it better have pizzazz.

- ✔ Fiddling with recipes is normal for you when you're trying out a dish. Be my guest! I realized that I couldn't possibly know how much garlic or onion you like, for example. I settled on amounts of ingredients that seemed good to me and to the palates of occasional tasters. (Be forewarned. I currently don't like lots of garlic, have no interest in soy sauce, and think ginger is great in just about everything.)

- ✔ You realize that putting some time into cooking at least one nutritious meal per day is an important part of taking care of your health and controlling cholesterol. But you're not signing on for hours of fussing in the kitchen. A recipe that lets you get in and out in an hour or less is what you're after, or you at least prefer a dish you can throw together and cook without watching the pot.

How This Book Is Organized

Beginning with the introduction, this book is organized around a way of eating and various foods proven to control cholesterol. The book is arranged in seven major parts, and each part is divided into chapters that address specific subjects. The following sections describe the main themes in each part.

Part I: Starting Out Right to Control Your Cholesterol

These five chapters tell you what to eat and why. I present the way of eating that this cookbook embodies, a diet that features nutritious whole foods, cuts back on saturated fat, and balances carbohydrates with healthy oils. I also pack the pages with information on the nutritional components of the recommended foods and how they affect health in terms of biochemistry. I provide shopping lists of the best foods to eat.

You also get some tips on what to order in restaurants. If you're like most people, you intersperse cooking with eating out, and when you do, you can refer to Chapter 4 to find out about the healthy foods you can order. And in Chapter 5, I give you help, should you need it, to set up your kitchen and get ready to cook.

Part II: Mastering the Beneficial Breakfast

Breakfast deserves its own section because it's usually the least nutritious meal of the day. Oats are in the spotlight, of course, as a source of soluble fiber, but I also tell you about other breakfast grains. In the protein chapter, I call on my experience as a nutritionist to write about the saturated fat and cholesterol in many breakfast foods and steer you in the direction of eating a little fish before the sun is high in the sky. I also sort out all the talk about whether eggs are healthy and help you decide how many are fine to eat per week. Chapter 8 tackles the issue of wanting breakfast but having no time to make it and gives you ways to make sure you eat something healthy.

Part III: Making Your Day with Heart-Healthy Starters

All beginner cooks, this part is especially for you because you really can't go wrong making soup or salads. These foods are forgiving, so if you want to add ingredients or change some amounts, you certainly can. I make sure to include lots of cholesterol-controlling foods in these recipes. These dishes also give you a good way of eating red meat, because a little goes a long way in soups and salads. I also include a chapter that gives you a chance to have some fun by putting together party foods — all sorts of healthy items that dress up easily for company.

Part IV: Having Your Poultry, Fish, and Meat

Find out how to include animal protein in your diet without overdosing on saturated fat and cholesterol. It's all about knowing which cuts are the leanest and controlling portion sizes. I give you some good reference material you can use as a guide on these matters, as well as recipes that taste rich and leave you feeling well fed. If you like fish, with their ever-so-healthy oils, I give you a preferred fish shopping list and guidelines on how frequently to eat seafood. Then you can start cooking up some oh-so-tasty dishes.

Part V: A Harvest of Cholesterol-Controlling Veggies, Beans, and Grains

This part lets you explore many enticing ways to cook plant foods, which are naturally low in saturated fat and cholesterol. Read the how-tos on buying, storing, and prepping grains, beans, and vegetables so you can become more confident about cooking these foods. As a result, you'll probably also be more likely to eat them more often. I also give you a shopping list of the top 10 vegetables that are good for you. You'll see that the healthiest vegetables come in a rainbow of colors. I also detail bean cookery and give a chart on grain cooking times.

Part VI: Savory Accompaniments and Sweet Finishes

This part gives you the chance to mix up some yummy sauces and create extra-special desserts. I fill you in on which spices and herbs are best with which foods. You join me on a sodium hunt, and I give you a list of high-sodium processed foods. I offer some great fruit desserts, pointing out along the way which fruits are best for the arteries and why. I even rank fruit in terms of their effect on blood sugar. I finish by turning on the oven to do some baking, using healthy whole-foods ingredients.

Part VII: The Part of Tens

This last part covers two important topics: healthy beverages to enjoy and ways to save money when you're stocking your kitchen with all these quality foods. The information in each chapter is presented as a list of ten points.

Icons Used in This Book

Throughout the book, you can find icons that mark the vital information in low-cholesterol cooking. Here's a listing of what they mean:

Read through the tips in this book for useful shortcuts and information for food preparation, cooking, shopping, and more.

This icon alerts you to things you should avoid eating or that need to be handled in a specific way, or possible complications that come up while you're watching your diet or preparing certain foods.

This icon points out general suggestions about shopping, cooking, and eating that are good to keep in mind.

This text gives you the lowdown on nutrient and vitamin details and scientific studies and findings. You don't have to read this information to use the recipes in the book, but you may find it interesting.

Where to Go from Here

The nice thing about using a *For Dummies* book is that you can open it to any chapter and find all that you need to know about a certain topic without having to flip to other sections. You may very well have picked up this book right now simply because you're hungry and all you want to do is make yourself a salad. Then what you want is Chapter 10. After all, this is a cookbook, and people usually head for the recipes.

However, at some point, perhaps while you munch your salad, I do suggest you poke your nose into the first three chapters, especially Chapter 1. This opening chapter gives you a complete overview of the main themes of the book. Also at least skim over the recommended foods in Chapters 2 and 3. Then you won't just be the reader. You'll be the expert!

Part I
Starting Out Right to Control Your Cholesterol

"Cholesterol numbers are like golf scores, the lower the better – right? Well, I think we bogeyed the entree and birdied the dessert."

In this part . . .

This part gives you a good overview of a proven way of eating to control cholesterol. I tell you about all sorts of delicious foods that lower cholesterol in specific ways and explain why soluble fiber and all sorts of other ingredients are good for your heart. I also explain how items you may have been warned about, such as nuts, red meat, and even certain shellfish, can have a place in a cholesterol-lowering diet. In addition, I help you figure out what to order in restaurants. Finally, I offer advice on how to set up your kitchen to cook in healthy ways, and I suggest some basic cholesterol-lowering ingredients to shop for so you can start trying some of the recipes.

What? You're interested in only the recipes? At least look through Chapter 1, which includes the essence of all the major points in the book.

Chapter 1

Conquering Cholesterol Is Easier (and More Pleasant) Than You Think

. . . .

In This Chapter

▶ Sorting out kinds of cholesterol

▶ Increasing the good cholesterol and lowering the bad

▶ Reducing heart disease risk factors

▶ Developing a way of eating to control cholesterol

▶ Linking cholesterol to carbohydrate intake

▶ Having firsts but not seconds

▶ Introducing the recipes

. . . .

The heart goes about its business, beating 100,000 times a day, and you probably hardly give it a thought, until perhaps you have your cholesterol checked and find out it's too high. Then suddenly caring for this precious piece of yourself takes center stage.

In fact, you need to take care of your heart even if your cholesterol levels are normal. And that's the reason I wrote this cookbook — to give you a tool for controlling cholesterol and keeping your heart healthy with good nutrition.

This chapter starts with a brief description of cholesterol. I then introduce you to a healthy way of eating and discuss types of foods that you should include in a heart-healthy diet. I describe other risk factors for heart disease and explain how the same foods that lower cholesterol help these conditions too. Next, I give a warning about portion control. Finally, I discuss the recipes and their inspiration.

Doing the numbers

The American Heart Association offers these general guidelines to assess cholesterol levels. When you have a cholesterol test, compare the results with these figures. A level of the "good" HDL cholesterol lower than 40 mg/dL is low and increases the risk for heart disease. Cholesterol levels are measured in milligrams (mg) of cholesterol per deciliter (dL) of blood.

Total Cholesterol Level	Category
Less than 200 mg/dL	Desirable
200-239 mg/dL	Borderline high
240 mg/dL and above	High

LDL Cholesterol Level	LDL Cholesterol Category
Less than 100 mg/dL	Optimal
100-129 mg/dL	Near optimal/above optimal
130-159 mg/dL	Borderline high
160-189 mg/dL	High
190 mg/dL and above	Very high

Cholesterol Doesn't Grow on Trees

The liver produces cholesterol, whether it's your liver or the liver of a chicken or cow. Only animal products, such as eggs, meat, and dairy foods, contain cholesterol. Plants don't have livers and they don't contain any cholesterol, which is one reason why a cholesterol-controlling diet features plants.

The body manufactures cholesterol by hooking 15 two-carbon acetates (vinegars) end to end, and after some other steps, a 27-carbon cholesterol molecule is formed. But here's what's really interesting — those two-carbon acetates can come from several sources, including fatty acids, protein, sugars, and starches. Alcohol can also provide acetates for the production of cholesterol!

Normally, your body produces less cholesterol when more is consumed. However, in some people, their blood level of cholesterol increases when they consume more cholesterol. Individual responses to dietary cholesterol vary widely.

Cholesterol can be dangerous because if it accumulates on artery walls it can block the flow of blood to the organs, including the heart. This blockage results in a disease called *atherosclerosis,* a major cause of heart attacks and stroke.

What we call cholesterol circulating in the blood is actually a lipoprotein. A *lipoprotein* is a package of cholesterol, protein, and fat that the liver assembles and releases into the bloodstream. For more details about cholesterol and the heart, take a look at *Controlling Cholesterol For Dummies,* by Carol Ann Rinzler and Martin W. Graf, MD, published by Wiley.

There are many different types of lipoproteins, but the two you hear most about are low-density lipoproteins (LDL) and high-density lipoproteins (HDL).

LDL hauls out cholesterol from the liver and it's this cholesterol that deposits in arterial walls and initiates the formation of plaques which can narrow the artery. Most often a blood clot at the site where the artery has narrowed blocks the flow of blood and triggers a heart attack. (That's why it's called the bad cholesterol.) HDL carries cholesterol back to the liver for conversion into bile acids and excretion via the intestinal track. (In this way, HDL earns its nickname, the good cholesterol.)

Therefore, the purpose of a cholesterol-controlling diet is not just to lower total cholesterol, but also to lower LDL and raise HDL.

 If you don't know your cholesterol levels and plan to have them checked, you may need to have more than one test because cholesterol levels can fluctuate. If your total cholesterol is more than 200, wait a month and take the test again. If the results of the two tests are within 30 mg/dL, average them. If the difference is greater than 30 mg/dL, take a third test and average the three.

Eating to Produce the Right Mix of Cholesterols

The goal of controlling cholesterol with diet is not just to keep the total cholesterol within normal range. You also want to choose foods that have been shown to lower LDL cholesterol and elevate HDL, and avoid foods that do the opposite.

Lowering LDL levels

One of the most forceful messages from the medical community about lowering cholesterol that has come through loud and clear over the years is to reduce the intake of saturated fat and dietary cholesterol because they raise cholesterol. However, as research has progressed, this recommendation has altered slightly. Dietary cholesterol is now considered less of a factor in elevated cholesterol than saturated fat, and a new factor — trans fatty acids — has been added.

Restricting saturated fat intake

All the well-known diets for reducing heart disease— including those of Dean Ornish and the American Heart Association — give high priority to restricting intake of saturated fat. Research leaves no doubt that the percent of calories from saturated fat dramatically increases the risk of heart disease.

In its year 2000 dietary guidelines, the American Heart Association (AHA) recommends limiting saturated fat content to 10 percent of calories for the general population with normal cholesterol levels. It also recommends reducing saturated fat intake further, to 7 percent of calories, for individuals with elevated cholesterol levels or cardiovascular disease. (However, whether it's best to replace saturated fat with carbohydrates or other kinds of fat is now being questioned. I cover this topic in the section "The Eating Plan for Controlling Cholesterol," later in the chapter.)

Major sources of saturated fat in the diet are full-fat dairy products, fatty meats, and tropical oils.

Watching dietary cholesterol

Foods high in cholesterol are not the culprits they were once thought to be. Research is showing that cholesterol-rich foods that are also relatively low in saturated fat, such as egg yolks and shellfish, raise LDL cholesterol levels only minimally and far less than saturated fat.

Researchers at Harvard School of Public Health and Brigham and Women's Hospital in Boston examined the association between egg consumption and incidence of cardiovascular disease in a study published in the Journal of the American Medical Association in 1999. Data came from a population of over 100,000 men and women health professionals. Results of the study showed that eating up to one egg a day had no significant association with the risk of coronary heart disease or stroke. This was true even for individuals with elevated cholesterol.

The American Heart Association now gives the okay to eggs in the diet, even though an egg contains about 213 mg of cholesterol. However, the guidelines still limit cholesterol to a maximum of 300 mg/dL a day for the general population and below 200 mg/dL for persons with an LDL level above specific target levels, and for those who have diabetes and/or cardiovascular disease. Of course, if you consume cholesterol-containing foods such as dairy products and meat, along with an egg for breakfast, you're very likely to surpass the recommended ceiling on cholesterol.

It's always a good idea to limit how much high-cholesterol food you eat. One benefit of limiting items such as red meat is that these also contain a lot of saturated fat. Be sure to work with your doctor and regularly have your cholesterol checked to tailor your diet to the amount of cholesterol you find your system can manage.

When deciding whether to consume a food that contains cholesterol, consider what else you're eating that day.

Avoiding trans fatty acids

Trans fatty acids, predominantly found in partially hydrogenated vegetable oils, elevate LDL cholesterol almost as much as saturated fat, molecule for molecule. They also raise triglycerides, blood fats associated with increased risk for heart disease. (Chapter 3 gives you an even longer list of the harmful effects of trans fats.)

Trans fatty acids are found in partially hydrogenated vegetable oils, which are an ingredient in a great number of food products. Check labels the next time you go to the grocery store, and you'll find these oils in breakfast cereals, salad dressings, all sorts of baked goods such as muffins, pie crusts, breads and cookies, instant hot chocolate, and frozen dinners.

The most effective way to avoid trans fatty acids is to feature in your meals natural ingredients such as fresh fruits and vegetables rather than processed foods. Cooking your own meals using unrefined oils also helps keep trans fats off your plate. The recipes in this book let you bake your own muffins and even crackers, as well as prepare healthful dressings and sauces and all sorts of main courses free of trans fats.

Any time you eat deep-fried foods such as french fries or fried chicken, at home or out, you're taking in some trans fats which form in the hot oil.

Choosing ingredients that lower LDL

As you plan your meals and experiment with recipes, include foods that have been shown to lower LDL cholesterol. Many common ingredients contain components that can significantly lower your risk for heart disease. The following information can help you select foods that are good for you:

- ✔ Polyunsaturated fats lower LDL cholesterol levels. Sunflower and corn oils contain these fats, but these oils are highly processed, so try to avoid them. A better choice is safflower oil, which you can buy unrefined. (See Chapter 3 for more about why processed oils are less healthful than unrefined oils.)

- ✔ Omega-3 fatty acids, a type of polyunsaturated fat, in fish lower LDL levels and benefit the heart in other ways too, such as reducing the tendency of the blood to clot.

- ✔ Monounsaturated oils, when substituted for saturated fats, can lower LDL, reduce the likelihood of LDL oxidation, and stabilize or even raise HDL cholesterol levels. In addition, monounsaturated fats don't raise triglyceride levels. To get monounsaturated fat in your diet, stock up on avocados, almonds, and extra-virgin olive oil.

- ✔ Soluble fiber, to a lesser extent, also lowers cholesterol by helping eliminate it from the body. Chapter 2 gives you a list of foods that contain soluble fiber.

Soy protein also has beneficial effects when substituted for animal protein and may be particularly useful for individuals at high risk for heart disease.

Aiming for more antioxidants

If LDL cholesterol oxidizes, it's more likely to deposit in your arteries and contribute to the formation of plaque. Fortunately, nature provides a wealth of nutrients that can reverse this process, and the recipes in this book are full of these nutrients. Foods high in antioxidants are also the most colorful, so the dishes look great!

A free radical contains an electron that's missing a mate and therefore goes in search of one, darting here and there. When a free radical comes in contact with LDL cholesterol, it steals an electron from it, thereby "oxidizing" the cholesterol. Antioxidants come into play when they intercept free radicals, reacting with them and trapping them. In this way, antioxidants prevent cholesterol from oxidizing.

The most well-known antioxidants are beta carotene, vitamin E, and vitamin C. Several minerals, including selenium, also play a role in preventing oxidation. Numerous phytochemicals, pigments in plants, function as antioxidants, too. (These compounds are in the plant to protect it from sun damage, but when you eat the plant, you reap the benefits!)

Research is showing that you can't pop an antioxidant pill and expect results. An analysis that appeared in the journal *The Lancet* in 2003 combined data from seven vitamin E trials and beta-carotene studies. Researchers tested the effects of taking supplements of these antioxidants on coronary heart disease, and found that supplementation of antioxidants did not reduce fatalities due to heart disease.

It appears that eating real food is the way to reap the benefits of antioxidants that can lower your risk of heart disease. This was the conclusion of an analysis of data from the Health Professionals Follow-up Study and the Nurses' Health Study. Consuming eight or more servings per day of fruits and vegetables rich in the antioxidant vitamin C reduced the risk of coronary heart disease by 20 percent compared with eating less than three servings of these foods a day.

Consuming several antioxidants together, as you find them in fruits and vegetables, provides you with a bonus of antioxidant power because antioxidants work in concert, bolstering each other's activities.

Raising HDL levels

Although lowering LDL levels is an important goal in preventing heart disease, raising HDL levels is also an important primary preventive action. About

30 percent of people with coronary heart disease have low HDL cholesterol levels while their LDL cholesterol level is normal. In fact, according to *The Johns Hopkins White Papers* on heart attack prevention, increasing HDL may be as important as lowering LDL in preventing heart attacks.

Quitting smoking, exercising more, and losing weight raise HDL cholesterol. Research shows that certain dietary changes can also produce results:

- ✔ Replacing saturated fat with monounsaturated fat increases HDL levels. Substituting saturated fat with carbohydrates can decrease HDL levels.

- ✔ Eating foods with a lower glycemic index, an indicator of a food's ability to raise blood sugar levels, is associated with higher levels of HDL. Low glycemic index foods also reduce triglycerides.

- ✔ If you drink at all, consume a moderate amount of alcohol. All types are beneficial, but red wine is a good choice because of its antioxidants. (See Chapter 21 for more on healthy beverages.)

Please don't start drinking just because red wine can be beneficial for your health. If you do begin, first consult with your doctor about risks that may apply to you.

Figuring the ratio of total cholesterol to HDL

Another way to assess your risk of heart disease is by knowing the ratio of total cholesterol to HDL. Let's say your total cholesterol is 200 and your HDL cholesterol is 40. Dividing 200 by 40 gives you 5, making the ratio between total cholesterol and HDL cholesterol 5:1. A ratio has been proven consistently reliable in predicting risk of future heart disease.

To calculate this ratio, divide your total cholesterol by the amount of HDL. In round numbers, a ratio of 5:1 or higher is considered risky. A ratio below 3.5:1 is ideal.

To help tip the ratio in your favor, here's how to eat:

- ✔ Eat enough fat and the right kinds, meaning monounsaturated oils and foods that contain omega-3 fatty acids, such as avocados and almonds. Lowfat diets tend to lower HDL levels more than LDL levels, making the ratio between the two worse.

- ✔ Regularly consuming garlic is well established by scientific research as a means of raising HDL levels and dropping LDL levels. Take one to three cloves of garlic in any form — raw, cooked, or as an extract in supplement form. Raw onions have also been shown to raise HDL levels.

✔ Beans are beneficial because of their low glycemic index and their fiber content, increasing HDL levels slowly over time while reducing LDL levels more quickly. (See Chapter 16 for recipes and more information about beans.)

✔ Avoid trans fatty acids because they increase the ratio of LDL to HDL.

✔ Curb foods with a high glycemic index and avoid simple, refined sugars.

✔ Lose weight.

Replacing saturated fat with carbohydrates results in a decline in total cholesterol and LDL cholesterol but also a decrease in HDL cholesterol.

Paying Attention to Risk Factors

While preventing high cholesterol is an important action to take to ward off heart disease, paying attention to other risk factors also will serve you well. The development of heart disease involves many factors. The more risk factors a person has, the greater the chance of developing coronary heart disease such as atherosclerosis.

High blood pressure and being overweight can raise risk and both are addressed in this cookbook. Chapter 3 gives you some tips on lowering high blood pressure with a diet that contains plenty of fruits and vegetables and whole grains. And the way of eating that the recipes offer can help you reach a healthy weight. The dishes are made with nutritious ingredients that satisfy hunger so you won't need extra food to feel well-fed.

Being overweight or obese, 20 percent above ideal body weight, increases the risk of heart disease. One way of measuring weight is the body mass index (BMI), a figure that considers weight and height. According to data from the National Health and Nutrition Examination Survey, as BMI rises, LDL cholesterol levels and blood pressure also increase. In addition, HDL cholesterol levels decline. To find out your BMI, go to www.consumer.gov/weight-loss/bmi.htm.

There are two more useful indicators of the risk of heart disease, namely homocysteine and inflammation. Homocysteine and inflammation may be new to you, but as time goes by you'll probably be hearing more about them from your doctor. (You could bring up these topics first.) The medical world, taking a fresh look at the research, is now taking both of these conditions seriously.

Having a look at homocysteine

Homocysteine is an amino acid, a component of protein, associated with an increased risk of coronary heart disease. Elevated homocysteine appears to have similar effects on blood vessels as high levels of the "bad" LDL cholesterol, compounding damage. Homocysteine promotes the growth of smooth muscle cells in the arteries, thereby making them narrower, and inhibits the growth of cells that help protect against the development of atherosclerosis. It's thought that the body responds to these changes by depositing cholesterol to mend the damage to the arteries.

Dampening inflammation

Atherosclerosis is now considered to be an inflammatory disease, like arthritis. The arterial walls become inflamed. This inflammation is not like the kind when you cut your finger and it swells and turns red. This is chronic inflammation and produces no obvious symptoms. The test for inflammation measures the amount of a molecule called *C-reactive protein* (CRP) in the blood. People with high CRP levels tend to go on to develop coronary heart disease and have a heart attack. A study published in the journal *Circulation* in 2003 concluded that CRP in the blood may directly contribute to the formation of blood clots which can cause heart attacks.

Having both elevated cholesterol and a high CRP level in the blood increases the risk of a heart attack severalfold.

To have your CRP blood level measured, ask for the high sensitivity CRP (hs-CRP) version of the test which can detect small differences in CRP that may translate into large differences in the risk. Or assess your risk at this Web site, sponsored by the National Institutes of Health: hin.nhlbi.nih.gov/atpiii/calculator.asp?usertype=prof.

Extra benefits in cholesterol-controlling foods

All these various risk factors, just like elevated cholesterol, can be controlled by diet and often with the very same foods! I made sure these ingredients showed up in the recipes in this book so you'd be getting the biggest dose of beneficial nutrients for the calories.

Take a look at Chapter 2 for lists of recommended foods. There's a section on what to eat to reduce homocysteine. The entire range of homocysteine-lowering vitamins is present in green leafy vegetables, citrus fruits, fish, and dairy products. Another section tells you about all the foods with flavor, such as onions, garlic, ginger, and the spice turmeric, which dampen inflammation.

Lowering Cholesterol for Very High Risk Patients

The National Cholesterol Education Program (NCEP) of the National Heart, Lung and Blood Institute provides guidelines for physicians to use in the management of cholesterol based on what other risk factors a patient may have for developing heart disease. These risk factors include high blood pressure, smoking, a family history of heart disease, diabetes, and metabolic syndrome, a constellation of risk factors. (See the section in this chapter "Watching carbs and cholesterol" for a full description of metabolic syndrome and how it relates to heart disease and cholesterol.)

In July 2004, the NCEP announced in a report published in the journal *Circulation* a lower, more cautious LDL target level of 70 mg/dL, based on clinical trials, for patients at very high risk for heart disease, down from the former target of 100 mg/dL. In addition, although acceptable levels of LDL cholesterol remained the same for high-risk and moderately high-risk individuals, the LDL threshold at which drug therapy may be given to these patients was lowered.

The report emphasized the importance of intensive use of nutrition, physical activity, and weight control, but it also opened the door to wider use of cholesterol-lowering medication. If you have high cholesterol, now you're probably more like to hear from your physician that you need medication. This may indeed be right for you, something you and your doctor can figure out, but make sure you combine drug treatment with changes in lifestyle too. Tackle the healthy eating presented in this book. Run around the block and earnestly lose weight. As your cholesterol comes down thanks to these natural means, there will come a day when you just may be able to go off the medication. Then keep up your healthy habits.

A copy of the NCEP update can be found online at www.nhlbi.nih.gov/guidelines/cholesterol/index.htm. In addition, a 10-year heart attack risk calculator can be found at hin.nhlbi.nih.gov/atpiii/calculator.asp?usertype=prof.

The Eating Plan for Controlling Cholesterol

If you want to change your way of eating to control cholesterol, you can start by using the same principles that I used when I developed the recipes for this book. Cook with whole foods, natural ingredients as nature made them and not refined or processed. Rely on and ingredients that provide healthy fats, including polyunsaturated and monounsaturated fats and essential omega-3 fatty acids, soluble fiber, and nutrients that help control cholesterol and maintain heart health. Incorporate plenty of vegetables, fruits, nuts, beans, whole grains, fish, and poultry in your menus. Remember that lean meats, reduced-fat dairy foods, and eggs are also permissible in a low-cholesterol diet, but in smaller quantities.

The recipes in this book feature carbohydrates that have only a moderate effect on blood sugar levels, such as pearled barley and brown rice. (For more on this subject, take a look at *Low-Carb Dieting For Dummies,* by Katherine B. Chauncey, PhD, published by Wiley.) Saturated fat is present only in small amounts, and cholesterol content is limited. You can adapt many of your recipes to follow these same heart-healthy cooking guidelines.

The ingredients in the recipes in this cookbook are also found in the traditional diets of Italy, Greece, and other countries bordering the Mediterranean. Heart disease rates are low in this region, and researchers have concluded that this way of eating, the now widely publicized Mediterranean Diet, is the prime reason.

A growing body of research coming out of Boston also gives support to this approach to diet. Walter C. Willett, MD, and the Harvard School of Public Health, where he is chairman of the department of nutrition, co-developed a way of eating based on the results of three very large studies. These are the Nurses' Health Study, with 121,700 participants; the Health Professionals Follow-Up Study, which includes 52,000 men; and the Nurses' Health Study II, a survey of 116,000 younger women. The studies were the joint effort of the Harvard School of Public Health and the Harvard Medical School and Brigham and Women's Hospital. In total, researchers tracked the food intake and health of over 250,000 men and women.

Here's what the data revealed:

✔ Replacing saturated fat with carbohydrates did not significantly lower the risk of coronary heart disease.

✔ Substituting polyunsaturated or monounsaturated fat for saturated fat was associated with a large reduction in risk of coronary heart disease.

✔ There was an increased risk of coronary heart disease when carbohydrates were substituted for either monounsaturated or polyunsaturated fats. The risk of coronary heart disease increases for individuals who are overweight and sedentary.

✔ Having a high trans fat and low polyunsaturated fat intake tripled the risk of heart disease as compared with low trans fat and high polyunsaturated fat intake.

✔ Total fat consumption was not associated with a risk of coronary heart disease.

✔ Higher nut consumption was associated with a lower risk of coronary heart disease.

Switching fats versus going lowfat

In the 1960s and 1970s, research in the United States was beginning to demonstrate that lowering saturated fat intake and cholesterol could lower serum cholesterol. People followed this advice and replaced the saturated fat with the polyunsaturated kind. At the same time, rates of heart disease declined, undoubtedly at least partly because of this change in diet. Then in the 1980s, the message blurred. Reducing total fat, whatever the sort, became the focus. Carbohydrates as well as unsaturated fats began to take the place of the ousted saturated fat.

The benefits of a diet rich in healthy fats rather than one that is low in fat were clearly demonstrated by the Lyon Diet Heart Study, which began in 1988 and involved more than 5 years of follow-up. French researchers selected heart patients who had had a first heart attack and assigned participants either a Mediterranean-style diet or a Western-type diet low in total fat. Participants on the Mediterranean diet consumed more olive oil, fish, vegetables, and fruits than those on the lowfat diet. They also received supplements of omega-3 fatty acids, which help prevent heart disease and manage cholesterol levels. In this study, cholesterol levels were monitored. Researches noted that with the Mediterranean diet, high cholesterol levels continued to be an indicator of a greater risk of heart disease.

As the Lyon study progressed, the Mediterranean-style diet began to prove much more effective at preventing additional heart problems than the lowfat diet. Of those consuming the Mediterranean diet, 14 individuals had a second heart attack or fatal heart problems compared with 44 patients on the lowfat diet. In fact, the benefits of the Mediterranean diet were so pronounced that after two and a half years, the trial was stopped so that the patients on the lowfat plan could benefit from what had been learned and switch to a more healthy way of eating.

In a report of these results, published in the journal *Circulation* in 1999, the researchers admit that for any diet to be truly effective, it must be "gastronomically acceptable" to ensure compliance. No problem there! The Mediterranean diet includes the delights of Greek, Italian, and French Provençal cooking. For a sample, try the recipe for Garlic Lima Beans in Chapter 16, the Grilled Scallops and Vegetables Marinated in Herbs in Chapter 13, and Roasted Chicken with Marinated Olives, Rosemary, and Oranges in Chapter 12.

Figuring out what's best for you

The healthy fats approach to diet affords some leeway; varying amounts of healthy fats are permitted. The percent of fat is not strictly fixed, and consequently, neither is the percent of protein or carbohydrates. However, a reasonable division of calories to aim for is 30 to 35 percent of calories from fat,

50 to 55 percent of calories from carbohydrates, and 15 percent of calories from protein. You can experiment with more or less protein to see how you feel, while monitoring your weight and checking your cholesterol.

Talk with your doctor about any particular risk factors for heart disease that you may have. Diet recommendations and recipes in this book are meant to be a guide to be adapted to individual needs.

Watching carbs and cholesterol

Cholesterol problems can originate in a condition known as *metabolic syndrome* or *Syndrome X*. The phenomenon of Syndrome X was first recognized by Gerald Reaven, MD, an endocrinologist and professor emeritus of medicine at Stanford University, who initiated a series of studies that lead to its discovery.

Levels of sugar (glucose) in the blood and levels of insulin, a hormone that facilitates the storage of sugar in cells, remain high. The name for this condition is insulin resistance. Eventually the overproduction of insulin stimulates the liver to produce high amounts of VLDL cholesterol. These are "very low density lipoproteins," which are small, and dense, and convert to LDL cholesterol, the bad kind. At the same time, the production of the good HDL cholesterol declines. And in addition, triglycerides (blood fats) increase. Insulin resistance can also cause elevated blood pressure and disturbances in blood clotting. If this weren't enough, high levels of insulin and glucose in the blood also can damage the lining of the coronary arteries, making the accumulation of plaque more likely. This collection of health problems is metabolic syndrome.

To find you if you have metabolic syndrome, have a glucose tolerance test and check your levels of HDL cholesterol and triglycerides, your blood pressure, and your weight.

The dietary treatment of metabolic syndrome involves reducing carbohydrate intake and those foods that quickly raise blood sugar levels. (Reavan himself has developed a diet to treat Syndrome X. The diet consists of 40 percent calories from fat, with 5 to 10 percent saturated, 45 percent from carbs, and 15 percent from protein, plus a limit of 300 mg of cholesterol a day.)

You can tell the likely effect a food will have on blood sugar by knowing its *Glycemic Index* (GI). This is a measurement that compares carbohydrates in terms of their effect on blood glucose levels. Low GI foods receive a rating of 55 or less. Intermediate foods are in the range of 56 to 69. And high GI foods are 70 and above. The GI rating that a food receives depends upon how quickly it is digested and absorbed. Corn flakes are a high GI food and whole grain barley is low. In creating the recipes in this cookbook, I made a point of featuring ingredients with low GI ratings.

Exploring the Recipes in This Book

A diet for controlling cholesterol, as with any diet, begins with preparing food at home, and that's where the recipes in this book come in. After all, this is a cookbook!

The recipes in this book are designed for everyday cooking when time and energy are limited. They don't require that you be an expert cook to turn out something tasty. As long as you know how to do such basic tasks as stir, chop, and stick something in the oven, you'll do just fine. And while I recommend working with quality cookware, you don't need anything as specialized as a pasta maker or a tortilla press.

Relying on whole foods and traditional cuisines

All sorts of familiar and appetizing dishes fit quite naturally into a cholesterol-controlling way of eating. If you want a recipe for pretend fettuccine or odd nonfat cheesecake, this isn't the book. The recipes in this book are normal dishes made with natural ingredients.

Foods made with cholesterol-controlling ingredients can be as tasty as everyday eats and as elegant as gourmet dishes. There's no reason to suffer through anything less.

The reason these dishes are so healthy is that they're made with ingredients that are unprocessed and unrefined, with all their parts — what are known as *whole foods*. Such foods have a full complement of fiber and nutrients, many of which play a role in controlling cholesterol and maintaining heart health. A reliance on whole foods also limits your intake of trans fatty acids.

Wonderful sources of inspiration for whole foods cooking are the traditional cuisines from around the world. Dishes rely on local and seasonal foods. The recipes in this book bow to the various Mediterranean cultures, making the circuit from Morocco to Spain, France, Italy, and Greece. Asian flavors show up too with such recipes as the Steak Stir-Fry with Chinese Vegetables recipe in Chapter 14. I also give you the makings for an Indian dinner, a regular in my household, with the recipe for Chicken Tandoori with Yogurt-Mint Sauce in Chapter 12 and the Red Lentil Dal with Caramelized Onions in Chapter 16.

Don't worry. I'm not going to send you out for kefir, cuttlefish, or elk. You can find most ingredients right in your usual market. Some of the original recipes were high in saturated fat and cholesterol, so I've adapted these to suit a cholesterol-lowering diet. I also include some Western fare, such as the Chicken Gumbo with Okra in Chapter 9 and the Buffalo Meatballs in Chapter 14.

Adapting the recipes to your taste

Please put your own twist on the recipes if it suits you. Few of the specified amounts are written in stone. As you make your way through a recipe, and presumably taste your way through it, too, you'll know what to add or subtract to suit your taste. Boost the chile content if you think a dish is too mild. Skip the cilantro if you hate it. Substitute asparagus for string beans if that's the vegetable you have on hand. The recipes are meant to set a direction for your cooking, but you're still in charge. Just don't destroy the health benefits of the dish by dumping in more fat or sugary ingredients or deep-frying a dish that's meant to be baked!

The recipes use various ingredients that start out lower in fat, such as turkey sausage versus pork sausage, or an ingredient that has some of its fat removed, such as 2 percent milk.

If your physician prescribes that you follow a leaner diet, just lower the fat content of recipes further. For instance, use soy sausage instead of turkey and cook with 1 percent milk. You may also want to fiddle with the carbohydrate and protein content. Just be sure to use healthy ingredients, such as whole grains and lean meats, to keep the dish heart friendly.

Making your own recipes more heart healthy

After you try out some of the recipes in this book, it should be easy to take some of your own tried-and-true recipes and adapt them for your new cholesterol-controlling way of eating. Here's how to start:

✔ Use vegetables and fruits that supply soluble fiber such as carrots, green beans, strawberries, and apples.

✔ Make sure that a dish is full of color by adding red, orange, purple, and yellow fruits and vegetables to give yourself more antioxidants and phytonutrients.

✔ Prepare a main-course dish with fish instead of meat.

✔ Garnish with nuts.

✔ Replace some or all of the refined flour with whole-grain flour. At a minimum, add some vitamin- and mineral-rich wheat germ to white-wheat flour to return what was removed in processing the wheat. (For more info about flours, see Chapters 17 and 20.)

✔ Always cook with unprocessed oils, rather than refined cooking oil and products made with partially hydrogenated oil. Favor oils that contain monounsaturated fats and omega-3 fatty acids. (Chapter 3 tells you about these oils.)

✔ Skip all the white sugar, and if the recipe won't work without it, make something else.

Chapter 2

Favorite Foods for Controlling Cholesterol

• •

In This Chapter

▶ Getting more fiber in your diet

▶ Adding antioxidants

▶ Discovering phytonutrients and minerals that lower cholesterol

▶ Putting anti-inflammatory foods on the front burner

▶ Cooking with the freshest and most colorful foods

• •

The world is full of foods you can eat and still watch your cholesterol. This chapter and the next one present a discussion of these types of foods and explain how they keep your heart healthy.

The edibles featured in this chapter also help your heart in other ways. Find out what foods to cook to reduce high blood pressure and to lose weight. Discover ingredients that counteract new risk factors as well, such as elevated levels of homocysteine, chronic inflammation, and insulin resistance, which add to the stress placed on the heart, making controlling cholesterol all the more important.

In the following sections, you find out about high-fiber foods and why you need some soluble fiber in your meals. I introduce you to sources of antioxidants in all their glory, including the amazing and colorful phytonutrients, a whole new field of study. Then there are the anti-inflammatory foods, the ingredients that lower elevated homocysteine and those friendly, gentle carbs that keep insulin levels normal, thereby controlling cholesterol. (See details of the other risk factors for heart disease in Chapter 1.)

All the recipes in this book feature these ingredients. Read on to begin writing your special cholesterol-controlling grocery list, which you can use on your very next trip to the market.

Making Friends with Fiber

Fiber sounds so bland and boring. Being told to eat more fiber sounds as appealing as being served a salad made with hay! But fiber is actually the great stuff in plant foods that gives them their crunch and texture. All you need to remember is to eat more plant foods and cook with them more often.

Because of the modern diet of processed foods, many people are malnourished when it comes to fiber. For instance, grains lose most of their natural fiber in the refining process. The average person takes in only about 15 grams of fiber per day, far short of the 25 to 30 grams or more of total fiber recommended.

Guidelines for lowering cholesterol always include having enough fiber. Nutrition research supports this advice. In research conducted at Harvard School of Public Health and published in the *American Journal of Clinical Nutrition* in 1999, an analysis of 67 controlled studies found that consuming sufficient fiber can lower both total cholesterol and the "bad" LDL cholesterol. While trimming fat and cholesterol produces more dramatic results, eating enough fiber, especially the soluble kind, is part of the picture. As fiber intake increases, coronary artery disease declines.

Sponging up cholesterol with soluble fiber

Soluble fiber, which earns its name because it dissolves in water, is especially effective in lowering the "bad" LDL cholesterol. Types of soluble fiber include the following:

- **Gum:** This type of soluble fiber, found in oatmeal and dried beans, aids in lowering cholesterol. Guar gum, a gummy substance obtained from legume-family plants, is used as a thickener in commercial food products. It reduces cholesterol and triglycerides (blood fats).

- **Mucilage:** A viscous substance found in plants, it's in dried beans, brown rice, sesame seeds, and oat bran. Such foods deserve to be part of your daily meals.

- **Pectin:** This is the same pectin your great-grandmother used to thicken her jams and jellies. Pectin sops up cholesterol and bile acids in the intestinal tract. As it passes through the body, pectin takes these with it. Be sure to regularly eat apples, carrots, beets, bananas, cabbage, oranges, dried peas, and okra to increase your pectin intake.

- **Lignins:** Choose vegetables such as carrots, green beans, peas, tomatoes, and potatoes to increase your intake of lignins. This soluble fiber is also in peaches and strawberries, as well as Brazil nuts. Lignins bind with bile acids to lower cholesterol.

In the small intestine, soluble fiber dissolves and forms a gel that surrounds and traps bile acids. Bile acids are essential for the digestion of fat and are made out of cholesterol. When the soluble fiber escorts bile out of the body, the liver, in order to make more bile, uses up more cholesterol, pulling it from the blood. Voilà! Cholesterol levels decline. You benefit from the law of supply and demand.

Writing a soluble fiber shopping list

Don't be put off by the slithery texture of foods such as okra or nopales cactus, a common ingredient in Mexican cooking. The part that feels slippery is the soluble fiber. You find soluble fiber in many less gelatinous foods as well. Be sure to eat the following foods regularly:

- ✔ **Fruits:** Apples, pears, bananas, strawberries, peaches, apricots, oranges, grapefruit, plums, and prunes

- ✔ **Vegetables:** Carrots, cabbage, potatoes, Brussels sprouts, beets, broccoli, spinach, okra, green beans, tomatoes, sweet potatoes, and nopales

- ✔ **Legumes:** All beans, lentils, and peas

- ✔ **Nuts and seeds:** Brazil nuts and sesame seeds

- ✔ **Whole grains:** Oats, barley, and brown rice

Remember when oats were the new wonder food for preventing heart disease, because of the soluble fiber they contain? Take a look at Table 2-1, and you see that oats aren't the only game in town. Of course, I'm not suggesting that you have a bowl of beans for breakfast. (As you can see in the table, the amount of fiber given is for 100 grams of each food.)

Table 2-1	Soluble Fiber in Legumes Compared to Oatmeal
Food, 100 grams	*Total Soluble Fiber, in Grams*
Kidney beans	1.1
Lima beans	0.4
Black-eyed peas	0.4
Green peas	0.3
Cooked oatmeal	0.7

Getting a day's worth of soluble fiber

According to the Harvard study referred to earlier in the chapter, consuming 3 grams of soluble fiber per day, the equivalent of 3 apples or 3 bowls of oatmeal, can reduce total cholesterol by 2 percent and the risk of coronary artery disease by 4 percent. But to really make an impact on cholesterol levels, for a

5 to 10 percent drop, you need to eat 2 cups of cooked beans or 1 cup of cooked oat bran every day. The good news is that increased fiber has a more dramatic effect on individuals with high cholesterol, helping those who need it most.

The American Dietetic Association recommends a daily intake of soluble fiber of between 5 and 10 grams. To consume 7½ grams of soluble fiber, you need to eat 1 serving of bran flakes cereal; 1 orange; 1 pear; 1 serving each of kidney beans, green beans, and avocado; a potato with the skin; and 1 slice of whole-grain bread. If you choose the right foods throughout the day, the grams of soluble fiber can add up.

Total fiber counts, too

Total fiber in food is the sum of both kinds, soluble and insoluble. Insoluble fiber is mostly indigestible cellulose, which you find in the skin of vegetables and fruit, and in the bran sheath that covers cereal grains. When you eat a stalk of celery, you're chomping on cellulose. And eating a whole pear, including the skin, or whole-wheat bread rather than white increases your intake of insoluble fiber. Insoluble fiber promotes regularity and also binds with toxins, speeding their elimination from the body. However, insoluble fiber does not lower cholesterol.

Consuming enough total fiber helps maintain a healthy heart by preventing problems beyond cholesterol. This is true for all age groups. A study published in the *Journal of the American Medical Association* in 2003 found that cereal fiber reduced the risk of cardiovascular disease in men and women 65 and older.

Here are some of the benefits of a high-fiber diet:

- Fiber can help in weight loss by filling you up without adding calories.

- Fiber can prevent high blood pressure. A large, four-year study published in the journal *Circulation* in 1993, which addressed hypertension in over 30,000 men, ages 40 to 75, found that the fiber in fruit helped prevent hypertension in over 10 percent of cases. Similar results were also found for women.

- High-fiber carbohydrate foods help control cholesterol by slowing the absorption of food into the system and thereby helping keep insulin levels normal. Elevated levels of insulin in the blood can lead to high cholesterol. (See Chapter 3 for more details.) In the Coronary Artery Risk Development in Young Adults (CARDIA) Study, conducted by Children's Hospital of Boston, in four large cities in the United States, researchers followed the diet and health of nearly 3,000 young adults over ten years. Analysis of the data revealed that fiber intake predicted insulin levels, weight gain, and other heart disease risk factors more accurately than did intake of total or saturated fat.

The fine print on fiber

According to the U.S. Department of Agriculture, if a label claims that a food product is a "good source" of fiber, it must contain at least 2.5 grams of fiber per serving. A food "high in fiber" provides 5 grams or more. To make sure that you eat enough fiber, buy cereals, breads, and crackers with at least 3 grams of fiber per serving.

You can tell that a product has some soluble fiber when the label states that it is heart healthy because of fiber. To make this claim, the product must contain at least 0.6 grams of soluble fiber per serving.

One type of insoluble fiber, lignins, lowers cholesterol. They work like soluble fiber and bind with bile acids. An abundant source of lignins is flaxseeds, but you also find them in carrots, peas, green beans, Brazil nuts, whole grains, strawberries, potatoes, tomatoes, and peaches.

To give yourself the recommended minimum of 25 grams of fiber a day, you need to eat 2 apples, 1 pear, ½ cup chili beans, and 3 slices of whole-grain bread — not much, really, in a day's worth of eating. A lowfat vegetarian diet provides even more, as much as 50 to 60 grams of fiber.

Arming Yourself with Antioxidants

You have good reason to cook with ingredients that contain lots of antioxidants. While you go about your day, these little guys are busy in the byways of your arteries, preventing problems before they start. Antioxidants are substances that prevent oxidation, a type of chemical reaction that, in some instances, can do harm to body tissues and substances like cholesterol. In fact, one of the major theories of the aging of the body is that it's all about oxidation. Oxidation occurs when electrons (tiny parts of molecules) go dashing about your insides, reacting with anything they meet up with and doing some damage. But antioxidants can come to the rescue. They intercept free radicals, including cholesterol, and trap them, preventing them from oxidizing.

Various studies focusing on the standard antioxidants — vitamin C, vitamin E, and beta carotene — found that taking supplements of antioxidants just isn't enough. The results of a combined analysis of several of these studies, which appeared in 2003 in the journal *The Lancet* confirmed this. The researchers found that supplementing with the antioxidants vitamin E and beta carotene did not reduce fatalities due to heart disease.

Antioxidants in foods are the most effective in protecting the heart. So vegetable haters, it looks like you're stuck. Eating more veggies and other plant foods is the only way out.

Antioxidants to the rescue

To increase your antioxidant intake, put these foods on your shopping list, with an emphasis on those that provide vitamin C and vitamin E. These provide the most ammunition for fighting heart disease.

✔ **Vitamin C:**

- **Vegetables:** Red peppers, broccoli, Brussels sprouts, cabbage, alfalfa sprouts, and tomatoes
- **Fruits:** Papayas, guavas, kiwis, lychees, oranges, grapefruit, mangoes, cantaloupe, watermelon, and strawberries

✔ **Vitamin E:**

- **Grains:** Millet, oats, whole wheat, and cornmeal
- **Nuts:** Almonds, Brazil nuts, hazelnuts, and peanuts
- **Seeds:** Sunflower
- **Fish:** Shrimp, haddock, mackerel, herring, and salmon
- **Unrefined cooking oils:** Safflower oil and extra-virgin olive oil

✔ **Beta carotene:**

- **Vegetables:** Sweet potatoes, carrots, winter squash such as butternut and acorn, pumpkin, spinach, kale, and red peppers
- **Fruit:** Cantaloupe, mangoes, apricots, persimmon, plantains, and papayas

The action of vitamin E is helped along by the trace mineral selenium. A quick way to have your daily fix is to eat a couple Brazil nuts, which are loaded with this mineral. But I really mean only a couple, because Brazil nuts also have plenty of saturated fat. You find selenium, in lower amounts, in whole grains, common vegetables such as cabbage and mushrooms, sesame and sunflower seeds, and in fish, poultry, and meats.

Calling all antioxidants

Besides the several vitamins that function as antioxidants, compounds called *phytonutrients* also have antioxidant power. These phytonutrients make up a huge new cast of characters within the world of nutrition. Scientists are in the process of discovering and figuring out the many ways these compounds protect us from disease. Here's a little peek inside this new world of nutrition.

Phytonutrients also block cancer, which I discuss in more detail in my book *Healing Foods For Dummies* (published by Wiley). Look at that book, too, for tons of suggestions on healthy eating.

An array of antioxidants shows up in plant foods because plants also need these clever compounds to protect them from free radical damage. As plants convert sunlight to life-giving energy — the process of *photosynthesis* — this chemical activity generates huge amounts of free radicals. It's easy to spot some of the foods that contain antioxidant phytonutrients because many phytochemicals are also pigments. For instance, carotenoid phytonutrients color sweet potatoes a golden orange, and another group of phytonutrients, anthocyanins, put the pink in pink grapefruit.

Crowing about carotenoids

Carotenoids are one of the two main classes of the pigments in plants. They are various yellows, oranges, and reds and consist of a group of over 600 compounds, including beta carotene, a form of vitamin A. However, only about 50 are in the foods you eat, and you can absorb only about half of these. It's probably no surprise that carrots contain carotenoids, but they're also found in winter squash such as hubbard and turban, sweet potatoes, mangoes, cantaloupe, pumpkins, apricots, and bananas.

Carotenoids are hiding in green vegetables such as spinach, but masked by the green of chlorophyll.

Praising anthocyanins

The other main category of plant pigments, besides the carotenoids, is the anthocyanins, pronounced with the accent on the "cy." Anthocyanins range from reddish-blue crimsons and magentas to violet and purplish blue indigo. Various studies have taken a close look at the antioxidant activity of anthocyanin pigments in such foods as cranberries and pomegranates. Results suggest that these compounds protect against heart disease in several ways, from preventing the oxidation of LDL cholesterol, to helping prevent blood clots and breaking down plaque after it has formed.

Rich food sources of anthocyanins include raspberries, red grapes, pomegranates, plums, blueberries, and blackberries.

Heat damages anthocyanins. To enjoy the maximum benefits, eat anthocyanin-rich foods raw. Have a bowlful of the Strawberry-Blueberry Sundae in Chapter 8, made with fresh raw berries and yogurt.

Looking at more antioxidant phytonutrients

Besides these pigments, many other compounds in plant foods supply you with antioxidant power:

- ✔ Catechins in dark chocolate are powerful antioxidants. (Yes, chocolate is a health food!) Milk chocolate has fewer catechins, and white chocolate has none. Catechins are also found in tea leaves.

- ✔ Quercetin in apple skins neutralizes a particularly damaging form of free radical. Onions, mangoes, apricots, sour cherries, sweet potatoes, and berries also contain quercetin.

> ✔ Hesperetin in oranges, limes, and lemons revives vitamin C after it's quenched a free radical, so your Cs can quench more free radicals.
>
> ✔ Flavonoids, a large class of compounds, many of which have antioxidant activity, also prevent blood from clotting. In the Zutphen Elderly Study, a 5-year study involving over 800 men, conducted in the Netherlands, intake of flavonoids in regularly consumed foods such as tea, onions, and apples lowered the risk of fatal heart disease.

No supplement delivers the range of beneficial nutrients that are in the average piece of fruit.

Testing foods for antioxidant content

So which foods have the most antioxidant punch from all these different compounds? Researchers at Tufts University in Boston figured out a way to measure this and scored various foods in ORAC units. ORAC is short for oxygen radical absorbance capacity. The higher the number, the more antioxidant power a food has. In the following table, blueberries have the most ORAC units, but there's no limit to ORAC units possible. For instance, 3.5 ounces of prunes have an ORAC score of 5,770 because they are dried fruit and they have a concentration of nutrients. To ensure a good intake of antioxidant nutrients, aim to take in 3,500 ORAC units a day in the fruits and vegetables you eat. Table 2-2 shows how different fruits and vegetables rate, according to the USDA Agricultural Research Service.

Table 2-2	Antioxidant Power in Common Foods per 3.5-Ounce Serving		
Fresh Fruits	*ORAC Units*	*Vegetables and Legumes*	*ORAC Units*
Blueberries	2,400	Kale	1,770
Blackberries	2,036	Spinach, raw	1,260
Cranberries	1,750	Brussels sprouts	980
Strawberries	1,540	Alfalfa sprouts	930
Raspberries	1,220	Broccoli florets	890
Plums	949	Beets	840
Avocado	782	Red bell peppers	731
Oranges	750	Kidney beans	460
Red grapes	739	Onions	450
Cherries	670	Corn	400

Your body: An antioxidant factory

The body itself produces two powerful antioxidants, glutathione and alpha-lipoic acid, both of which support heart health. Alpha-lipoic acid in turn facilitates the production of glutathione. Alpha-lipoic acid is soluble in both water and in fatty tissues, making it a particularly powerful antioxidant in preventing heart attacks and stroke. Did I mention that alpha-lipoic acid also helps prevent wrinkles?

The body makes most of these antioxidants from common components such as amino acids in the food you eat, but as you age — wouldn't you know it? — production of these invaluable antioxidants declines. Fortunately, you can also add to your supply by eating foods that contain them:

✔ Glutathione: Asparagus, avocados, potatoes, spinach, okra, strawberries, white grapefruit, peaches, oranges, cantaloupe, and watermelon

✔ Alpha-lipoic acid: Spinach, broccoli, tomatoes, potatoes, peas, and Brussels sprouts

If you follow a low-carb diet and cut out fruits and many vegetables from your diet, you're denying yourself more than just the sugars in these nutrient-dense foods. You're also denying yourself the many colorful phytonutrients in these foods that support heart health.

Phytonutrients That Lower Cholesterol

Phytonutrients, also sometimes called phytochemicals, are compounds manufactured by plants. These consist of a broad range of compounds, some of which are pigments, while others provide flavors and scents and deter bugs from eating the plants. Many phytonutrients function as antioxidants. But that's not all these marvelous compounds can do. Some phytonutrients lower cholesterol. No one is recommending that you rely on phytonutrients alone to control cholesterol, but cooking with foods that contain these compounds is a good habit when it comes to choosing what to eat. Here are some phytonutrients that lower cholesterol:

✔ **Beta-sitosterol:** Beta-sitosterol has a structure similar to cholesterol. This phytonutrient competes with cholesterol for absorption and comes in first! The result is lower levels of cholesterol in the bloodstream. Sterols that manufacturers add to butter substitutes designed to lower cholesterol act in the same way. Peanut butter contains lots of beta-sitosterol, and oranges, cherries, bananas, and apples also contain some. Ponder this information as you nibble on the Grilled Marinated Chicken with Creamy Peanut Sauce in Chapter 12.

✔ **Inulin:** This is a fiberlike carbohydrate in raisins. During digestion, inulin ferments in the intestinal tract, producing short-chain fatty acids that help lower cholesterol. Inulin forms as the grapes dry in the process of making raisins, but it is not in the fresh fruit.

✔ **D-glucaric acid:** This is a cholesterol-lowering compound present in grapefruit, Granny Smith apples, cherries, apricots, and oranges.

✔ **Sulfur:** Sulfur compounds in onions are thought to be the reason that these tasty vegetables raise HDL cholesterol. The prescription for sulfur is half an onion a day, preferably raw.

✔ **Lycopenes:** Lycopenes in tomatoes significantly lowered LDL cholesterol in a small study conducted at the University of Toronto and published in the journal *Lipids* in 1998. Participants consumed tomatoes in the form of juice and spaghetti sauce. Mangia!

Mineral Allies That Control Cholesterol

Besides antioxidants and an array of phytonutrients, minerals come to your aid for fighting cholesterol. Are you beginning to get the idea that you need to eat plenty of fresh, minimally processed foods to make sure you have good reserves of these nutrients? Refined and process food items, which have had nutrients removed, are hardly up to the task of controlling your cholesterol. Here are minerals to watch in your diet:

✔ **Copper:** Copper lowers elevated cholesterol, according to a report from the USDA's research center in Grand Forks, North Dakota. Conversely, copper deficiency can lead to high cholesterol, according to a study in the *Journal of Nutrition in the Elderly.* Copper may also help prevent heart rhythm disorders (arrhythmias) and high blood pressure. Wouldn't you know, copper also functions as an antioxidant. The best food sources of copper are whole-grain products, almonds, green leafy vegetables, and legumes, the same foods known to lower cholesterol. Most seafood is also a good source. How about some Sweet and Spicy Refried Black Beans from Chapter 16 to accompany the Halibut with Cilantro-Lime Salsa in Chapter 13?

Taking zinc supplements longer than a month will deplete copper reserves.

✔ **Manganese:** When manganese is deficient, it can lead to lower levels of the "good" HDL cholesterol, according to animal studies conducted at the University of Maine. Lack of manganese may also promote the binding of LDL cholesterol to artery walls, increasing the risk of heart disease. Whole-grain cereals, nuts, seeds, and green vegetables are sources of manganese. Processing of food removes a good portion of its manganese. Do have a bowl of Cherry-Studded Three-Grain Porridge in Chapter 6.

✔ **Chromium:** In combination with niacin (vitamin B3), it lowers cholesterol in one out of two people with high cholesterol. Good sources of chromium are mushrooms, beets, whole-wheat bread, and beef. The Beet, Pear, and Belgian Endive Salad in Chapter 10 is waiting!

B-ing careful about homocysteine

A bonus of eating all the foods that help control cholesterol is that you also give yourself certain B vitamins that lower homocysteine. *Homocysteine* is an amino acid that the body uses to make protein. It is thought to have a damaging effect on the lining of the arteries, similar to the effect that LDL cholesterol has. (See Chapter 1 for more on this compound.)

Homocysteine causes no problems at normal levels, but researchers have found a close association with elevated blood levels of homocysteine and the likelihood of clogged arteries. The body needs the B vitamins to convert homocysteine to other things, so that it doesn't accumulate and reach high levels. Consuming sufficient amounts of these nutrients can control homocysteine levels and reduce homocysteine when it is elevated.

Here are the B vitamins you need and the foods that provide them:

✔ **Folic acid:** Lentils, beans, orange juice, green leafy vegetables, strawberries, asparagus, oatmeal, and all whole-wheat products such as breads and flour. Folic acid is also now added to all commercial breads.

✔ **Vitamin B6:** Whole grains such as brown rice, beans, spinach, mangoes, walnuts, tuna, turkey, beef, and pork.

✔ **Vitamin B12:** Tuna, trout, salmon, shellfish, beef, pork, lamb, and yogurt.

Studies show that vegetarians in particular can be deficient in folic acid and B12 and that they can have higher levels of homocysteine.

Intercepting Inflammation

Atherosclerosis is an inflammatory disease, involving chronic low-grade inflammation of the arteries. Plaque in arteries is separated from the blood by a fibrous "cap." Inflammation can degrade this protective cap. Then the plaque can rupture, and a blood clot may form, cutting off the flow of blood to the heart. The combination of inflammation and elevated cholesterol increases the risk of heart attack many times over as elevated cholesterol levels promote the formation of plaque and inflammation makes plaque more dangerous.

Various stresses, including food allergies, toxins in the environment, and a diet low in antioxidants, can trigger chronic inflammation. But to prevent inflammation there are also many actions you can take:

✔ Avoid processed foods.

✔ Opt for organic produce and meats whenever you can.

✔ Stay away from food additives and products such as artificially flavored beverages.

✔ Use a purifier for your drinking water.

✔ Wash dishes with nontoxic, all-natural detergents.

Certain foods can also directly cause inflammation because substances in these are the raw material from which inflammatory compounds are made. Arachidonic acid, found in meat and egg yolks, is one such compound. Polyunsaturated oils that contain omega-6 fatty acids (described in Chapter 3) also generate the formation of arachidonic acid as well as others that promote inflammation.

To control inflammation, cut back on red meat, egg yolks, and vegetable oils Instead, emphasize those foods that inhibit and prevent the formation of inflammatory compounds. You have loads of delicious items from which to choose:

- **Fish:** Favor especially those native to cold water, such as salmon and tuna.
- **Nuts and seeds:** Flaxseeds and walnuts are your best bets.
- **Seasonings:** Garlic, ginger, and turmeric contain anti-inflammatory compounds.
- **Vegetables:** Both onions and mushrooms dampen the heat.
- **Fruit:** Cooling compounds are in berries, apples, mangoes, and apricots.

Cooking with the Best

Bet you can't wait to start cooking with all these good-for-you ingredients now that you know how they care for your heart. Turn to the recipes in any of this book, and you find plenty of ways to prepare these recommended foods. Start with fresh ingredients, and you end up with gorgeous flavor and dishes full of healthy fiber and plenty of antioxidants.

Swallowing some vitamin pills and taking supplemental fiber just aren't the same as eating foods that naturally provide these things . You need real edibles that haven't been processed or refined. Such whole foods contain a full complement of nutrients, in the right mix as nature intended. As research now shows, antioxidants for instance work together. They're not as effective when acting alone.

For a gourmet touch, make an effort to use fresh herbs whenever possible, adding them to the recipes in the book to suit your taste. Use Figure 2-1 to help you spot the ones you're looking for at the market. The common, less expensive herbs, like cilantro and basil, are sold in large bunches, while the dearer kinds come in little plastic boxes.

Figure 2-1:
Identifying
fresh herbs
to use in
recipes.

Chapter 3

Looking at Those Foods You've Been Warned About

Talk about diet and cholesterol usually focuses on all the foods you shouldn't eat. You can almost see the wagging finger when the subject of eggs or meat comes up and hear the "tsk, tsk" over high-fat foods. But the truth is not as simple as this. Such edibles affect different people in different ways, and some forbidden foods have redeeming virtues.

This chapter gives you ways to judge cholesterol-containing foods so you can have some of them in your meals. Fats are considered in terms of varying quality rather than being all lumped together. You find out about the ones you absolutely need to consume to keep your heart healthy and your cholesterol in check. I also put your possible worries about nuts and the fat they contain into perspective. Use the suggestions of allowable foods in this chapter to write your own shopping list. A cholesterol-controlling diet has more give in it than you might expect!

Calming Down about High-Cholesterol Foods

So what about eggs and other animal sources of protein? Can you ever eat them again if you're watching your cholesterol? The answer of course is yes, if you do it the right way. Here's how to approach such foods.

The American Heart Association has long recommended a ceiling on cholesterol intake of 300 milligrams a day. This is a good ballpark number for controlling cholesterol, but individual tolerance for cholesterol can vary.

Normally, as a person consumes more cholesterol, the liver compensates by producing less. But other factors, such as a high intake of fat or sugar, or rarely exercising, can be at the root of the elevated cholesterol.

Looking at the bigger picture

Certainly you should be generally aware of the total amount of cholesterol you consume in the three meals you eat each day. But to totally avoid a food simply because it is high in cholesterol is the wrong way to go. Foods such as eggs and meats are very nutritious and don't deserve to be banished. You simply need to eat these in reasonable portions and make sure that the foods you have them with contain little or no cholesterol.

Having an egg for breakfast once in a while is fine if the rest of the day you eat foods low in cholesterol and saturated fats, and meals abundant in fruits, vegetables, whole grains, lean meats, poultry, and fish. Eating this way also gives you healthy oils and plentiful nutrients for reducing the risk of heart disease.

The Savory Steak Salad with Broiled Tomato Dressing in Chapter 10 combines a small portion of meat with lots of vegetables — a mix of high- and no-cholesterol ingredients. And the single egg in the Apple-Sour Cream Crumble in Chapter 19 owes no apologies, earning its place by holding the crumble together.

Just because a dish contains no cholesterol doesn't give you permission to eat all you want. Angel food cake and meringues are made with only egg whites and no yolks, but that doesn't make them health foods. They're still made with refined flour and white sugar, but they're a better choice than a buttery yellow cake made with lots of egg yolks. (For handy suggestions on healthy ways to include eggs at breakfast, turn to Chapter 7.)

A risky combination: Cholesterol and saturated fat

Saturated fat intake is more predictive of heart disease than the amount of cholesterol a person consumes. It's true that dietary cholesterol may increase levels of unhealthy LDL cholesterol. This is the form of cholesterol which can deposit in arterial walls, initiating the formation of plaques and lead to a heart attack, in contrast to the "good" HDL cholesterol which prevents plaques from forming. (For more details about how these two basic forms of cholesterol function, see Chapter 1.) But saturated fat has an even greater impact on blood cholesterol levels. So a useful way to judge high-cholesterol foods is to see how much saturated fat they also contain.

Food labels make it easy to find out how much cholesterol and saturated fat is in food products because they list amounts. You'll see information such as "Cholesterol 30 mg" (that's milligrams), and "Saturated Fat 4.5 g" (that's grams). The label also tells you how much cholesterol and saturated fat a single serving of the food provides, expressed as a percent of target healthy amounts. These amounts are based on an allowable 300 mg of cholesterol per day and a maximum of 10 percent calories from saturated fat.

However, what if you're aiming at consuming less cholesterol and saturated fat than this? For example, the American Heart Association's special diet for lowering cholesterol limits cholesterol to 200 mg and saturated fat to no more than 7 percent of total fat intake. Then the numbers on the label would under-estimate the percent of daily intake in a serving as it applies to how you're trying to eat. Better to stick to the actual milligrams of cholesterol and grams of fat to judge a product. (Chapter 5 also offers help on the intricacies of reading labels.)

For foods that don't come with a label that details nutritional content, such as meats, poultry, and produce, refer to nutrition charts, which give you the missing information. I put together Table 3-1, showing items I thought you'd be curious about. It gives you some telling figures for cholesterol and saturated fat content in an assortment of common foods that are usually associated with cholesterol worries, for better or for worse. In terms of saturated fat, eggs and shellfish aren't so bad. A small study conducted by Rockefeller University and Harvard School of Public Health and published in the *American Journal of Clinical Nutrition* in 1996 found that substituting shrimp, a food high in cholesterol but low in fat, for beef or other high-fat foods in the diet did not adversely affect cholesterol levels.

Table 3-1	Cholesterol Content and Saturated Fat in Common Foods	
Food Item	*Cholesterol in mg*	*Saturated Fat in Grams*
Whole egg	213–274	1.7
Egg yolk	213–274	1.7
Egg white	Trace	0.0
T-bone steak (3.5 ounces)	84	10.2
Ground beef, extra lean (3.5 ounces)	82	6.3

(continued)

Table 3-1 *(continued)*

Food Item	Cholesterol in mg	Saturated Fat in Grams
Canadian bacon (2 slices)	28	1.3
Cured bacon, pan fried (3 pieces)	16	3.3
Beef liver, braised (3.5 ounces)	389	1.9
Chicken breast without skin (3.5 ounces)	85	1.3
Chicken leg without skin (3.5 ounces)	93	2.7
Cheddar cheese (1 ounce)	30	6.0
Cream cheese (1 ounce, 2 tablespoons)	31	6.2
Parmesan, grated (1 tablespoon)	4	1.0
Feta cheese (1 ounce)	25	4.2
Whole milk, 3.7% fat (8 fluid ounces)	35	5.6
Lowfat milk, 2% fat (8 fluid ounces)	18	2.9
Buttermilk, cultured (8 fluid ounces)	9	1.3
Butter (1 teaspoon)	11	2.5
Shrimp, 12 large (3 ounces)	130	0.3
Scallops, 6 large (3 ounces)	28	0.1
Olive oil (1 tablespoon)	0.0	1.8
Safflower oil (1 tablespoon)	0.0	1.2
Coconut milk, canned (1 tablespoon)	0.0	2.7
Brazil nuts, 8 medium nuts (1 ounce)	0.0	4.6
English walnuts, 14 halves (1 ounce)	0.0	1.6

Getting the Fat Story Straight

Now with the low-carb dietary movement in full swing, fat has been given a pardon. But quantity of fat still counts, and what kind of fat you eat is enormously important. This section introduces you to the various types of fat as well as a man-made version known as trans fatty acids.

When low-carb diets raise cholesterol

Proponents of low-carb diets insist that this way of eating doesn't raise cholesterol. On these diets, people are encouraged to replace starchy foods and sweets with protein foods. Lean meats and fish and lowfat dairy products are wisely recommended in low-carb diets such as the South Beach Diet, but some people embrace the advice about eating more protein and start loading up on red meat and cheese, which are high in cholesterol as well as saturated fat.

Certain individuals can manage such an increase in dietary cholesterol; their bodies produce less cholesterol in response, resulting in no change in their original cholesterol levels. But for individuals who are sensitive to dietary cholesterol, and have no need for additional saturated fat, dramatically increasing the intake of cholesterol and saturated fat can cause cholesterol to rise rapidly to dangerously high levels. The take-home message is, if you follow a low-carb way of eating, be sure to have your cholesterol levels monitored regularly to know if the foods in your low-carb diet are giving you high cholesterol.

Some fatty foods are actually an essential part of ways of eating that are associated with lower cholesterol. You're about to find out which fatty foods these are.

Introducing the fatty cast of characters

All fats are not created equal. Most fats are a combination of the three basic types — saturated, polyunsaturated, and monounsaturated — but in different proportions. When in doubt about the makeup of an oil you have in your kitchen, refer to Figure 3-1, which tells you at a glance the makeup of many of the most common cooking oils. Each oil has a different effect on cholesterol levels. Cook with those high in monounsaturated and polyunsaturated fatty acids to control cholesterol.

Every molecule of fat is composed of a glycerol backbone and three chains of fatty acids (carbon and hydrogen atoms linked together). The difference between any two fats is the composition of these chains. Some have more hydrogen atoms than others. When a chain has all the hydrogen atoms it can hold, it's considered saturated. When one hydrogen atom is missing, the fat is monounsaturated, and when two or more hydrogen atoms are missing, the fat is — you guessed it — polyunsaturated. When a fatty acid chain contains fewer hydrogen atoms than it is able to hold, the fat becomes liquid at room temperature.

Saturated fats

Saturated fat generally is solid at room temperature. Butter is mostly saturated fat, which is why it comes in sticks and not in a bottle. It can also remain solid inside you. You find saturated fat in the following foods:

- Meats and poultry
- Dairy foods such as cheese, milk, yogurt, and butter
- A few plant foods, notably coconut oil and palm oil

Eating excess saturated fats can raise levels of the unhealthy LDL cholesterol and total blood cholesterol levels.

Polyunsaturated fats

Polyunsaturated fats are generally liquid at room temperature. There are two kinds of these fats, the omega-6s and the omega-3s. For heart health, a diet needs to provide the right proportion of each. (See the section, "Embracing essential fatty acids" in this chapter.) Primary sources are the following:

- Vegetables oils such as sunflower, safflower, and corn oils
- Fish and shellfish
- Nuts and seeds

Consuming polyunsaturated oils reduces LDL cholesterol levels, thereby helping to lower total cholesterol level.

Monounsaturated fats

Monounsaturated fat is the mainstay of the well-studied Mediterranean diet associated with a lower risk of heart disease. Good sources include these foods:

- Olives and olive oil
- Almonds
- Avocados

Monounsaturated fats lower the "bad" LDL cholesterol levels, reduce the likelihood of LDL cholesterol oxidation (which makes it easier for plaque to accumulate in arteries), and stabilize or even raise the "good" HDL cholesterol levels.

A compatible family of fats

These three basic forms of fat — saturated, polyunsaturated, and monounsaturated — all belong in your diet. The question is how they will share the turf. For instance, the 2001 National Cholesterol Education Program (NCEP) guidelines, in its Therapeutic Lifestyle Diet designed to lower LDL cholesterol, recommend reducing total fat to between 25 percent and 35 percent of total calories, with monounsaturated and polyunsaturated fats making up the majority of the calories. Saturated fat is to be kept to less than 7 percent of calories in order to reduce cholesterol, particularly LDL cholesterol.

Different fats used in cooking contain about the same amount of calories. One tablespoon of butter provides 108 calories, and one tablespoon of olive oil contains 119 calories.

These proportions should cause no problems to you as a cook. Any recipe with 30 percent calories from fat will taste rich and delicious. However, if you eat out a lot, you're likely to be eating dishes with far higher fat content if you're not careful. Figure 3-1 compares the fat content of different fat sources.

| Cholesterol mg/Tbsp ☐ | Saturated Fat ■ | Polyunsaturated Fat ■ |
| Other Fats ☐ | Monounsaturated Fat ☐ | |

		Saturated Fat	Other Fats	Monounsaturated Fat	Polyunsaturated Fat
Canola oil	0	6%		31% ←1%	62%
Safflower oil	0	9%		78% 1%→	12%
Sunflower oil	0	11%		69%	20%
Corn oil	0	13%		62%	25%
Peanut oil	0	13%		33% 5%	49%
Olive oil	0	14%	9%	77%	
Soybean oil	0	15%		61%	24%
Chicken fat	11	30%		22% ←1%	47%
Lard	12	41%		12%	47%
Beef fat	14	51% 4% ←1%			44%
Palm oil	0	51%	10%		39%
Butter (fat)	33	54% 4% 12%			30%
Coconut oil	0	77% 2%→		15%	6%

Figure 3-1: Comparing the dietary fats.

Fat is the flavor carrier in food. If you attempt to follow a very fat-restricted diet, making food tasty is much more of a challenge. I find that the lowest I can go and still keep foods such as soups and stews appealing is about 15 percent calories from fat.

A twist in the plot: Trans fatty acids

A century ago, food manufacturers looking for a way to make liquid vegetable oil solid at room temperature came up with the process known as hydrogenation. For an idea of what hydrogenation involves, take a look at the fatty acid chains in Figure 3-2. When vegetable oil, an unsaturated fat that's missing hydrogen atoms, is hydrogenated, hydrogen atoms are added back so that a more rigid structure forms.

Thanks to the advent of hydrogenation, a new product came into the world in 1911, Crisco shortening, made with hydrogenated fats. By the 1930s, food manufacturers began to use hydrogenated fats in products on a large scale. The advantages to both producer and customer were that a product such as margarine or shortening acts like butter but is less expensive. Hydrogenated fats also have a long shelf-life.

But hydrogenated fats have a problem. Hydrogenation causes an unnatural twist in the fat molecule. The name for these misshapen characters is trans fatty acids.

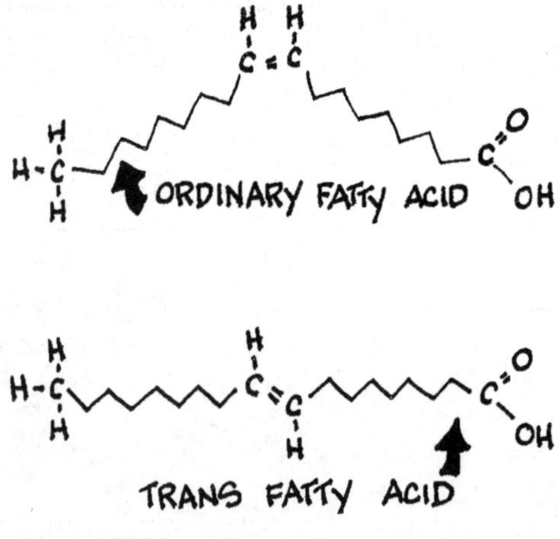

Figure 3-2: Ordinary and trans fatty acid chains.

Trans fats can still participate in the many important functions that fat normally performs throughout the body, but their behavior is defective. They impair the functioning of cell membranes and the immune system and have an impact on hormone synthesis. In addition, in terms of heart health, trans fats make platelets in the blood stickier, increasing the likelihood of a clot in a small blood vessel, leading to heart attack or stroke. They also interfere with the body's ability to regulate blood pressure and the muscle tone in the walls of the arteries. These deformed molecules also raise total cholesterol, and they increase the unhealthy LDL cholesterol while lowering the good HDL cholesterol. This combined effect on the ratio of LDL to HDL cholesterol, an important indicator of the risk of heart disease, is double that of saturated fat.

According to a paper on trans fatty acids and heart disease published in 1993 in the journal *Epidemiology,* trans fats raise total and LDL cholesterol less than saturated fat, but more than monounsaturated and polyunsaturated fats. Weighing in on the amount of trans fatty acids safe to have in the diet, the Institute of Medicine, a branch of the National Academy of Sciences, recommends a tolerable upper limit of zero. While total elimination may not be possible, the Western diet has lots of room for improvement: Trans fatty acid intake makes up as much as 2.5 percent of total calorie intake. In the Mediterranean diet, associated with heart health, trans fats contribute only 0.5 percent of calories.

If you have always assumed or heard that margarine is better for you than butter, take a look at Table 3-2. While butter gives you lots of saturated fat, it spares you some trans fats.

Table 3-2	Trans Fat Content of Margarines and Butter
Product	*Percent of Trans Fatty Acids*
Hard, stick margarine	16–36%
Soft margarines	10–30%
Butter	2–9%

When you try to cut out trans fats from your diet, you have to stop eating the huge number of processed and packaged foods that contain hydrogenated fats, including baked goods such as breads, cakes, and cookies, as well as many breakfast cereals. Because such foods are typically also full of white flour and various sugars, you'll be doing your body a big favor by saying no to these items.

Check the labels of the products on the shelves of your kitchen right now. See how many food products contain hydrogenated oils and, consequently, trans fatty acids. When you see any of these items listed on the label of a product, you know that the food contains trans fatty acids:

✔ Partially hydrogenated vegetable oil, such as corn or soybean oil

✔ Hydrogenated vegetable oil

✔ Shortening

Trans fats are in other foods too, including the following:

- ✔ Crackers
- ✔ Fast foods fried in oil, such as doughnuts and French fries
- ✔ Butter-flavored oil poured over your movie popcorn

The United States Food and Drug Administration is requiring that, beginning in January 2006, food manufacturers list the trans fat content of food products immediately below saturated fat on all labels.

Embracing essential fatty acids

Polyunsaturated fats are divided into two groups: the omega-6 fatty acids and the omega-3s. Another name for these acids is *essential fatty acids (EFAs)*. They are workhorses, doing all sorts of important jobs in the body. The EFAs provide the raw material for building cell walls and help in the conversion of food into energy. They make up a major portion of your brain. And that's only the beginning of the long list of their many functions.

Processed oils: Shadows of their former selves

Most of the oils you find at the supermarket, such as canola, corn, and soybean oils, are processed and refined. Safflower oil typically is also refined, although you can buy an unrefined version. Even olive oil, except for the unrefined extra-virgin kind, is processed.

These oils are put through a long and complicated procedure to give them shelf-life. This treatment removes vitamins such as beta carotene and vitamin E, antioxidants that protect cholesterol from oxidative damage, and minerals such as calcium, magnesium, iron, and copper, all of which play a role in heart health.

Refining also eliminates natural substances such as lecithin, a fat emulsifier, and (get this) phytosterols, which actually *block* cholesterol absorption from the intestines! Similar compounds, stanol esters, are added to vegetable

oil spreads that the manufacturers promote as a means of lowering cholesterol. But in unprocessed oils, phytosterols are a natural part of the package, although in much smaller amounts than in the specially designed spreads. In addition, chemical solvents are also used in processing, and traces may remain in the final oil. Then when the oil is finally deodorized, the high temperatures (464 to 518 degrees Fahrenheit, for 30 to 60 minutes) generate the formation of trans fatty acids.

All in all, processed oils are foods of low quality. They are sources of healthy monounsaturated and polyunsaturated fatty acids, but in terms of nutrients, they're virtually the equivalent of refined white sugar, which has no nutrients at all, only calories.

Essential fatty acids also play a vital role in preventing heart disease. The omega-6 fatty acids may even slow down the production of cholesterol. The omega-6s and the omega-3s also work together, in opposing ways, to keep the circulatory system healthy.

The body uses essential fatty acids to make hormone-like compounds, called prostaglandins. One type of prostaglandin the omega-6s produce, called Series 2 prostaglandins, makes the blood stickier and promotes inflammation. Balancing these effects, the omega-3s generate different prostaglandins that block the actions of the Series 2. The omega-6 fatty acids also promote high blood pressure, but the omega-3 fatty acids in fish oil counteract this effect by lowering elevated blood pressure. Omega-3-rich fish oils also help keep arteries more fully open and help prevent an irregular heart beat.

When omega-3 fatty acids replace saturated fat in the diet, they lower cholesterol levels in the blood.

Not consuming enough essential fatty acids in daily meals can increase the risk of heart disease.

Trouble in paradise: Overconsumption of omega-6 fatty acids

The amount of omega-6 fatty acids in the diet in relationship to the omega-3s is very important for heart health. Since earliest times, mankind evolved on a diet that provided the omega-6 and omega-3 fats in a ratio of about 1:1. Even 100 years ago, before the advent of processed oils, the ratio had changed little and was perhaps 2:1. However, these days, the modern Western diet consists of EFAs in a ratio of 10:1 to as high as 20–25:1, in favor of the omega-6s. This ratio can encourage blood clots, inflammation, and elevated cholesterol.

Increasing the intake of omega-3s

The great majority of people eating a diet of refined and processed foods are omega-3 deficient. Another reason for the lack of omega-3s was the push for eating lowfat and nonfat foods so popular just a few years ago. At that time, physicians warned patients off butter and recommended vegetable oils instead. Unfortunately, most commercial vegetable oils contain a predominance of omega-6 fatty acids. Few people also increased their intake of omega-3s to maintain the proper EFA balance.

There is a good chance you need to eat more of the following EFA-rich foods:

- Oily, cold-water fish such as salmon, sardines, mackerel, and herring
- Walnuts
- Flaxseed oil
- Wild game

Butter wannabes

Margarine and products known as vegetable oil spreads are often recommended for lowering cholesterol because they're made with oils that are low in saturated fat. The various types differ in nutritional benefits, and if you take flavor into consideration, no single one is perfect.

Here are some points to keep in mind if you want to cook with these products:

✔ Avoid margarines made with hydrogenated fats.

✔ Vegetable oil spreads made with a mix of essential fatty acids can be fine if you spread them on toast, but in a skillet they may dissolve into a watery mess.

✔ Xanthan and guar gums, added for body, can give some brands a weird gelatinous texture.

✔ Butter substitutes function well as an ingredient in homemade baked goods, but watch out for those with an aftertaste because this may come through the other flavors in your cake. In Chapter 20, the Chewy Oatmeal Cookies with Currants give you a chance to bake with a vegetable oil spread.

✔ Even products that are free of trans fats and nonhydrogenated are usually made with processed oils. You can find a few products made with organic oils.

Some vegetable oil spreads are made with stanol esters proven to lower cholesterol. These compounds are made from soybeans or pine tree pulp and are plant versions of cholesterol. They block the absorption of cholesterol in the digestive track. These products are legally considered a food but act like a drug. Clinical trials have shown that for people with elevated cholesterol, consuming these products can reduce cholesterol by 7 to 10 percent, when coupled with a diet low in fat. Two to three servings a day are needed for maximum effect.

Chewing the fat about healthy oils

So which fats are best for cooking and for health, when you consider flavor as well as nutritional composition? If you want to cut back on saturated fat and trans fats, the final list of acceptable oils (which do not include the poor-quality processed oils) is quite short. I recommend the following cooking oils, which are the ones I use in the recipes in this book:

✔ **Extra-virgin olive oil:** Use as a primary cooking fat and for salad dressings.

✔ **Unrefined safflower oil:** Use in cooking and baking, when you want a mild flavor.

✔ **Unrefined sesame oil and gourmet oils such as almond and hazelnut:** These oils are good as flavor condiments.

✔ **Canola oil:** This oil is a very good source of monounsaturated fats and omega-3 fatty acids, and it's low in saturated fat. However, use this product only occasionally, because all canola oil is refined.

If you can trust yourself to use only a little bit, cooking with a smidgeon of butter for its flavor is just fine as long as you're not eating a lot of saturated fat in other foods. If you do buy butter, buy organic to avoid residues of toxic pesticides that tend to accumulate in the fat component of dairy products.

Nibbling on Nuts — in Moderation

I have good news for you! You can eat nuts. In fact, having some nuts as a snack and using nuts in your cooking can actually be good for the heart. Less than an ounce of plain nuts a day can lower total and LDL cholesterol.

An ounce of nuts is usually about a handful — 14 walnuts, 18 medium cashews, and 22 almonds.

In clinical studies, diets that contained walnuts or almonds decreased cholesterol. The Nurses' Health Study, sponsored by the Harvard School of Public Health and Brigham and Women's Hospital in Boston, found that women who ate more than 5 ounces of nuts a week had a significantly lower risk of heart disease than those women who rarely ate nuts. Figure 3-3 shows nuts that are recommended in a healthy diet.

Nutrition in little packages

Replacing saturated fat with the monounsaturated fats and essential fatty acids in nuts is likely an important factor in their beneficial effects. Other reasons may be the high amounts of protein, fiber, vitamin E, magnesium, and potassium they contain.

Nuts are also rich in the amino acid arginine. The body uses arginine to produce nitric oxide, a relaxing compound that can dilate blood vessels. Nitric oxide has an effect similar to that of nitroglycerin.

Eating nuts rather than donuts to prevent heart disease

All sorts of new research are proving that eating nuts can lower the risk of heart disease. One such study is the Adventist Health Study that involved over 31,000 individuals and was conducted over six years by Loma Linda University and published in the *Archives of Internal Medicine* in 1992. Those who consumed nuts more frequently than four times a week had fewer fatal heart attacks than those who ate nuts less than once a week. In this same study, nut eaters were found to weigh less than those who rarely ate these delicious snacks. So what are you waiting for?

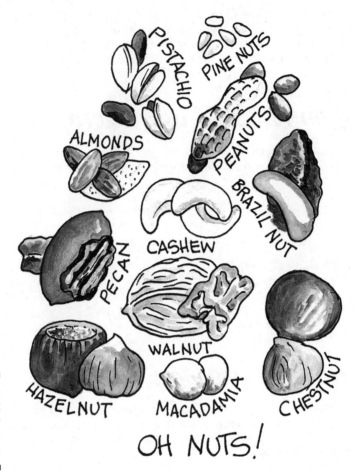

Figure 3-3:
Nuts that are okay to eat in a healthy diet.

Stock up on the following nuts and nibble away:

- ✔ Walnuts
- ✔ Almonds
- ✔ Cashews
- ✔ Pecans
- ✔ Brazil nuts, in small amounts

Peanuts also have their benefits, but they don't go on the A list because they are usually salted and may also be dipped in sugar. And peanut butter is usually made with hydrogenated oils. But plain roasted peanuts and nonhydrogenated peanut butter without trans fats are just fine.

Bringing Cholesterol-Controlling Foods into Your Kitchen

The first step in filling your kitchen with heart-healthy foods is to take a hard look at the items you normally buy and do some editing. Hunt through your fridge and freezer and explore the dark recesses of your cabinets. Consider the foods you have on hand and go from there.

Taking inventory of the foods you have on hand

You may already be on the right track when it comes to cooking with healthy foods. But you probably have room for improvement. Check what ingredients you have on hand and toss out old stand-bys that don't serve your health. Here are some questions to ask as you poke around your kitchen:

- Are the produce drawers in your refrigerator nearly empty?
- Do you see vegetables that are red, yellow, and green?
- Is there a colorful display of fruit on the kitchen counter?
- Are the breakfast cereals, breads, and crackers made with whole grains?
- Have you accumulated a stockpile of cookies, cakes, and candies?
- What oils do you have on hand for cooking and are they unrefined?
- Where are the walnuts?

You get the idea. Look for whole, minimally processed fresh foods. See if you've stocked up on good sources of soluble fiber, nutrients, and healthy fats recommended in this chapter and in Chapter 2.

When you cut out foods that contain trans fats, hydrogenated oils, and loads of salt, you give yourself a bonus because these are typically found in processed and fast foods that are missing important nutrients.

Rewriting your standard grocery list

Add these healthy foods to your shopping list, and you'll be thanking yourself for years to come:

- Beans of all sorts
- Blueberries

- ✔ Extra-virgin olive oil
- ✔ Flaxseed oil
- ✔ Rolled oats
- ✔ Spinach
- ✔ Turkey
- ✔ Walnuts
- ✔ Whole-grain bread
- ✔ Wild salmon

Of course, dozens of other foods benefit the heart (as you see in the recipe chapters), but these food items are a good place to start.

Chapter 4

Controlling Cholesterol When Eating Out

Sometimes you don't feel like cooking, or you simply don't have the time to fuss in the kitchen, which in reality may be quite often. According to the National Restaurant Association, 46.4 percent of the annual household food dollar is spent on restaurant meals and snacks, an average expenditure of $2,276 per household, or $910 per person. At the same time, healthy options on menus are also on the rise. So, you can still watch your cholesterol if you know how to spot the more nutritious foods on the menu. Eating out can even be a health strategy in itself: Relax, reduce stress, and let someone else do the cooking!

This chapter walks you through ordering breakfast, lunch, and dinner in a variety of restaurants. You certainly can find good-for-you foods when faced with these restaurants' menus, remembering the dishes and ingredients recommended in this book and my coaching on what to order. This chapter also gives you several tips on how to keep yourself well nourished when traveling for business and on vacation. Even away from home you can continue to eat many of the foods that help you control cholesterol.

I don't cover much about ordering in upscale restaurants and five-star hotels because the kitchens in these places turn out such a wide variety of foods that you can always find something healthy and the management is open to special orders. The challenge is finding something good for body and heart at your local eatery. Read on.

Having Breakfast in the Usual Joints

Coffee shops and diners make a business of selling breakfasts made to order and served quickly, with eye-opening coffee poured the moment you sit down. If you have breakfast out once in a while, don't worry too much about what you eat. Enjoy the treat — go ahead and order the French toast and share an order of bacon. Then the rest of the day, trim your fat intake and fill up on whole grains, fruits, vegetables, legumes, fish, and lean meats. But if you eat breakfast in restaurants all the time, like many people do as part of their work schedule or by preference, then taking a hard look at breakfast menus is essential for your health.

Breakfast menus are a mixed bag. You can usually find simple, nourishing foods like fresh fruit and hot cereal. However, many typical breakfast dishes have their drawbacks. Menu items such as pancakes, waffles, French toast, English muffins, Danish pastry, and donuts are made with white flour and sugar, foods lacking in fiber and nutrients important for heart health. The pancake syrup served is corn syrup with maple flavoring and has never been near a maple tree. Breakfast meats like bacon and sausage are high in saturated fat and loaded with salt. However, by keeping your meal simple and unadorned, you'll do just fine. Have a bowl of oatmeal with lowfat milk and a sliced banana, or yogurt and fresh fruit plus some crunchy rye toast. Granted, your breakfast may not be as entertaining as you may prefer, but then, you're not at a party.

If you're tempted to order pancakes and strips of sizzling bacon, instead ask for Canadian bacon, lower in fat than regular bacon; a whole-wheat English muffin for the whole grain; and a half grapefruit. Such a meal is satisfying and far better for your health. And promise yourself you'll cook a healthier version of pancakes and bacon at home, using a whole-grain pancake mix such as the one you find in Chapter 6, served with lowfat turkey sausage.

Choosing healthy morning eats

You can have most of the standard breakfast foods as long as you choose the healthy versions. The following sections give you specifics about the most heart-friendly items in each category.

Cereals

Have a cold cereal such as Shredded Wheat or All-Bran, one not loaded with sugar, which unfortunately is true of most breakfast cereals out there. Top the cereal with lowfat or nonfat milk.

Beware of granolas, which may contain as much fat and as many calories as a dessert.

In the category of hot cereals, oatmeal tops the list for its cholesterol-lowering soluble fiber, but keep these two points in mind:

✔ You want the regular, old-fashioned kind that digests slowly and keeps blood sugar from rising rapidly. Don't order instant oatmeal, which is the grain chopped up into little bits and which has a very high glycemic index, which can lead to weight gain and be bad for your heart. (Chapter 1 has more information about glycemic index.)

✔ Stay away from oatmeal products that are flavored because they're sure to be loaded with added sugar.

Cream of rice and grits are also good choices, better than cream of wheat, because they add a variety of grains to your diet.

Eggs

Have poached eggs for high-quality protein prepared without fat. When an egg is poached, the white of the egg protects the yolk, the only part of the egg that contains cholesterol and keeps the cholesterol from oxidizing. Oxidized cholesterol is the kind that is more likely to lead to an accumulation of plaque, narrowing the arteries and setting the stage for a heart attack or stroke.

Stay away from scrambled eggs because the yolk and cholesterol come in direct contact with a very hot cooking surface and easily oxidizes. Frying eggs also exposes the yolk to direct heat. And need I say that eggs Benedict cloaked in buttery hollandaise sauce is off limits!

And if you've made up your mind that you'll never again eat egg yolks because you know they're high in cholesterol, you can always have the waiter ask the cook to make you an egg white omelet. However, in my opinion, egg white omelets need some jazzing up, because egg whites are bland and your omelet now doesn't have the satisfying fat that the yolk provides. Also order some Canadian bacon or a bit of smoked fish, such as salmon, to put together a tasty breakfast that also gives you enough energy to last until lunch.

Muffins and toast

Order rye toast for a grain that contains phytonutrients, a class of substances that have many health benefits including acting as antioxidants. To watch your fat intake, tell your server you want the toast dry, not slathered in the kitchen spread, but with butter on the side that you can add if you wish.

Think twice before you order a healthy-sounding bran muffin. It's likely to be very high in sugar and fat despite all that fiber. In fact, virtually all muffins normally served in restaurants are just cake in another form. A regular white-flour bagel is preferable, as it's likely to be lower in fat and not made with sugar. You also may want to ask whether the restaurant serves whole-wheat bagels or whole-wheat English muffins.

Potatoes

Spuds are a source of potassium, which helps lower blood pressure. But have the home fries, likely to be made with fresh potatoes and onions, rather than hash browns. Such potatoes are often frozen products that restaurants buy in bulk, and they may contain partially hydrogenated oils, which can increase blood levels of cholesterol.

Breakfast meats and fish

For the taste of pork, have Canadian bacon, which is lower in total fat and saturated fat than regular cured bacon. If you want fish, make smoked salmon or lox (brine-cured cold-smoked salmon) your first choice. Savor this on half a toasted bagel with all the trimmings — raw onions that thin the blood and counteract inflammation, fresh sliced tomatoes with heart-protective lycopenes, and olives with their healthy monounsaturated fats. And if you happen to be in the Midwest or South, remember to order such regional breakfast fish dishes as catfish in biscuits — if the fish isn't deep-fried — and grouper omelets.

Fresh fruit

Instead of getting your fruit from juice, ask for one of the following:

- ✔ A grapefruit half (which most restaurants always like to decorate with a maraschino cherry in the middle)
- ✔ A slice of refreshing cantaloupe or honeydew melon
- ✔ A bowl of soluble-fiber-rich canned prunes
- ✔ Sliced bananas
- ✔ A bowl of strawberries

If the only fruit offered on the menu is canned fruit or you decide you want the canned prunes, it's fine to order canned fruit to put some fruit in your diet. Eat the fruit and just skip the sugary juice. (Having a dose of sugar at every meal can lead to a condition known as metabolic syndrome and increase the risk for cardiac disease. For more details about the association between these ailments, see Chapter 1.)

Whole fruit provides fiber and more nutrients than fruit juice and does not contain added sugars.

Condiments

When choosing condiments, favor salsa over catsup. That way, you avoid some sugar and give yourself tomatoes, which contain antioxidants; onions, which raise the "good" HDL cholesterol; and chile peppers, which help prevent blood clots.

Also choose a little butter rather than margarine, which is likely to contain trans fats.

Beverages

If you need your morning caffeine, order black or green tea for the phytonutrients these drinks contain. (See Chapter 2 for more info about phytonutrients.) These beverages can also help you wean yourself from the need to consume large amounts of caffeine to get going. Black tea contains about a third less caffeine than coffee, and green tea contains only half the amount in black tea. Caffeine stresses the adrenals glands and the heart muscle as the chemistry it triggers sends your body into high gear.

Black and green teas also contain phytonutrients that help keep blood vessels functioning normally, reduce chronic inflammation (which is now considered a risk factor for heart disease), and function as antioxidants, preventing the "bad" LDL cholesterol from shifting to its dangerous oxidized form. (Chapter 21 gives you details on the health benefits of these teas.)

But if only a cup of java will do, then limit how much you have to one or two cups total for the day. As I explain in Chapter 21, research is showing that drinking a lot of coffee can raise cholesterol. And if you're one of the millions of people who line up in the morning at trendy coffee places for an order of gourmet coffee, be smart about the beverage you choose. Have cappuccino made with lowfat milk to reduce saturated fat and skip those sweet concoctions, often laced with stuff like caramel syrup, that these joints are always inventing. These beverages can add hundred of calories to your daily intake before you've even had your first meal.

Instead of having a rich coffee drink, save the calories and fat for actual breakfast foods and have your coffee as plain as possible.

Uncomplimentary breakfasts: Eating in the hotel lobby

You're on the road, spend the night in a hotel, and wake up hungry. Making your way to the hotel lobby, you find the free breakfast buffet that comes with the price of the room. The table holds an array of sweet rolls, sugar-coated cereals, white toast, orange juice, and packets of jelly, margarine, and non-dairy creamer for your coffee. What a way to start the day!

A meal of these breakfast foods will certainly get your blood sugar up and running, but this menu is not one you need for heart health. When faced with the hotel-motel buffet, concentrate on the healthier foods that sometimes show up:

- Have the whole-wheat toast, which is, in part, made with whole grains. Smear it with a little grape jelly if you want something sweet, but not the margarine, which contains trans fats.

- Grab the shredded wheat — which has no sugar and is a whole grain — before someone else does.

✔ Rather than fruit juice, take the whole fruit, usually apples or bananas. These fruits give you fiber and won't be as likely to cause your blood sugar to spike. (Few hotel guests take these, so you won't have much competition here.)

✔ Have your morning caffeine in the form of tea, a source of antioxidants.

If you'd rather not risk relying on the hotel breakfast buffet to supply you with a complete and healthy breakfast, here are some suggestions for taking your breakfast along with you when you travel:

✔ Oranges, grapes, apples, and bananas travel well, but peaches don't. Dried fruits, such as dates, apple rings, and halves of apricots, also travel well.

✔ Pack some lowfat cream cheese to give yourself fat and protein to get you through your first morning meeting. Have this with crunchy, whole-grain crackers.

✔ Bring along a small jar of nut butter, and have this with whole-grain bread and baked goods, including those made with the recipes in Chapters 6 and 20. This mini-meal can supply you with enough fuel to last until lunch.

If the hotel breakfast buffet fails the healthy-foods test and you forgot to pack any nutritious foods, slip around the corner to the local diner and order some of the recommended breakfast foods listed in this section.

Nourishing Yourself on Your Lunch Break

Of all the eating-out scenarios, the noontime workday meal presents the most challenges if you're watching your cholesterol. You have limited time to eat and have to rely on whatever restaurants are within walking or short driving distance of your workplace. Consequently, you'll be eating at the local coffee shop, a sandwich counter, a deli, or a casual chain or franchise restaurant. You can find many heart-healthy foods on the menus of these eateries. Here are some suggestions:

✔ Make soup your first choice at lunch. They can't deep-fry it or add much sugar, so when you eat soup for lunch, you're already way ahead of the game. The broth still contains all the vitamins and minerals of the various ingredients that have cooked in it in the process of making the soup. Many soups give you at least a serving of vegetables, a good step toward your daily quota. Served hot, soup is a satisfying mini-meal on chilly days. And many soups are bulky, filling you up but with fewer calories. Good choices are bean, lentil, tomato, and mixed vegetable soups.

✔ Lunching on crispy salad is a fine choice. The makings are usually low in fat (not counting the dressing of course!), and the vegetables are raw and full of nutrients. Salads contain fiber foods that help steady blood sugar. Ingredients such as onions and garlic thin the blood. Colorful salads in particular give you a variety of heart-protective antioxidants.

✔ Grilled chicken atop a mixed greens salad makes a lean, complete meal.

Avoid salads that feature fatty meats, fried noodles, cheese, and lots of oily croutons, like chef's salad, Chinese chicken salad, and Caesar salad.

✔ Choose the fruit salad with lowfat or regular fat cottage cheese.

✔ Try a tostada, a huge taco shell filled with lots of lettuce plus beans, tomato, sweet peppers, and shredded chicken. Oh, and don't eat the shell, which is deep fried in oil and loaded with fat. And tell the waitress to hold the cheese.

✔ You can always request whole-wheat bread instead of white. Eating two slices give you two servings of whole grains, a good way to lower your risk of heart disease. (Chapter 17 tells you all about the health benefits of whole grains.) Or request rye bread or pumpernickel, also made with a good proportion of rye flour, to increase the variety of grains in your diet.

✔ Enjoy sandwiches spread with mustard rather than mayonnaise to cut fat and calories. You can also request your sandwich dry and order a small side of lowfat salad dressing to spread on the bread.

Business lunches with guys don't have to include steak and fries

Somewhere between the martini lunch and when real guys decided not to eat quiche, food for men became irrevocably associated with all that's meaty and fat. Business meetings are held in restaurant-bars that specialize in buffalo chicken wings and ribs. Serious man's food is the order of the day. It takes an independent male indeed to buck this tide. What do you do in such a situation?

Plan ahead and show your alpha-male leadership. Know in advance exactly what you're going to order so that you won't be tempted to go along with the gang. In a clear, loud voice, order the grilled fish. Have that salad, dressing on the side, and the others will see that you plan to be in the saddle a long time. And know that you have company, even though they may not be sitting at your table. Plenty of men, pre- and post- heart attack, have heard the message from their cardiologists, and nutritionists like me, and have decided not to mess around with their health.

Men who eat healthy lunches and skip dessert also earn a fast pay-off while their companions load up on heavy food: They find it easier to stay awake and clear-headed during the afternoon meetings, while their competition is likely to be dozing off.

✔ Fish oils lower cholesterol and the risk of heart disease, so having fish for lunch is a great idea. Fish is also a protein food that can provide you with energy for several hours, especially important if you have a busy afternoon ahead. Here's what to look for on menus in specific types of restaurants:

- **Coffee shops:** Canned tuna and canned salmon are the usual offerings. A tuna salad sandwich is a better choice than egg salad or roast beef to control cholesterol, but the best way to have your tinned tuna or salmon is unadorned as part of a green salad. Dress this with vinaigrette rather than mayo. If such a salad is not on the menu, ask whether the cook can assemble this for you.

  Instead of eating fish with tartar sauce, made with fatty mayonnaise, enjoy fish, as the English do, with a savory brown sauce or a sprinkling of malt vinegar. This acidic condiment nicely complements the oiliness of fish.

- **Casual dining restaurants:** Many of these establishments offer fish dishes prepared with health in mind. The menus may include items such as lowfat grilled whitefish with mango salsa, grilled catfish and cod, and salads topped with broiled salmon.

- **Delis:** Smoked and marinated fish — salmon, whitefish, and herring — are standard items. Enjoy some on a piece of rye or a bagel, with some coleslaw on the side. You also may see cream cheese mixed with smoked salmon, which is delish but high in saturated fat from the cheese.

- **Fast food places:** Fish sandwiches in fast food restaurants sound like a healthy lunch to order, but typically the fish is deep-fried and covered in batter, not a heart-healthy choice at all.

- **Taco stands:** If you're fortunate enough to have these in your area, make sure to order a fish taco, a mix of white fish, tomato, raw onion, and cilantro inside a folded, soft corn tortilla, a naturally healthy combination that's big on flavor.

Putting the "break" back into lunch break

The midday meal is called a lunch "break" for a reason. It should also be a time for rest. One way to give yourself respite is to lunch at what's known as casual dining restaurants. Healthy items to order include a soup and salad combo, broiled or grilled fish, chicken stir-fry, spaghetti marinara, turkey and garden burgers, bean soups, and side orders of vegetables. Have hot or iced tea and skip dessert. And remember, if you do order a typical dinner item at midday, be sure to ask for the lunch-size portion so you don't load up on calories and need an afternoon nap.

Ordering for the shy and unassertive

When you're in a restaurant, requesting something special is perfectly acceptable, especially for reasons of health. You're the customer, and it's fine if your waiter doesn't love you. Besides, many restaurants these days have a policy of accommodating health-conscious guests. If you sometimes feel timid, like I do, press on and speak up! Here are some things you can request to eat more nutritious foods and cut calories.

- A substitution of one food for another, replacing potato salad with fresh fruit, or onion rings with plain, cooked vegetables

- Lunch or dinner composed of only healthy appetizers and vegetable side dishes

- Several vegetable side dishes with your entree

- An appetizer-size serving of an entree

- Your meal cooked with a minimum amount of fat

- A two-egg omelet made with one yolk

- Salad dressing and gravy on the side

- A half-order

- A doggie bag, so you can eat part of your meal now and save the rest for another meal

- No mayo and no cheese

- A glass of ice cubes and a cup of herbal tea if you want iced tea without caffeine

- Information about the following: what kind of fat or oil the food you want to order is made with, whether the major ingredients are fresh or prepackaged and frozen, and how the dish is prepared

Doing Dinner

Finding healthy foods on dinner menus is usually fairly easy. From the soups and salads to the poultry and fish, you can assemble a delicious meal and still control cholesterol. Just don't order too much and then eat it all simply because you're paying for it.

If you know in advance that a restaurant's menu is a minefield of deep-fried foods, suggest another restaurant to your family or friends. You don't want to go to a place where everyone is chomping down on fried chicken and you're eating a green salad and baked filet of sole.

Going American

Because I'm so interested in food, I love to try the cooking of other cultures, but then comes the day when plain old American food tastes just great. Then I want to head for the nearest diner, family restaurant, or hotel dining room for some familiar dishes. If I'm there on the right day, I might get to have some bean soup! The menu almost always includes green salad, roast chicken, and some basic vegetables like carrots and baked potatoes, which are fine to eat as long as you don't add butter and sour cream. Instead, choose lowfat sour cream or lowfat yogurt.

Such restaurants typically serve loin pork chops and sometimes filet mignon, a lean meat, and both are good choices when you're watching your fat intake if the cuts are well-trimmed. Grilled and broiled fish such as salmon and filet of sole are also standard healthy items that suit a cholesterol-conscious diet. These big, well-stocked kitchens usually can also assemble a vegetable plate on quick notice, giving you a way to have a vegetarian meal even if no vegetarian main course is offered on the menu. And for dessert, order fresh fruit.

Beverages are often an important part of such meals, but beware when the server comes to take your drink order. Drinks are a good way to swallow loads of calories without taking notice, especially in margueritas, sangria, and sake. Instead, try having a plain iced tea, mineral water, or a single glass of red wine, which can help keep the heart healthy. If you do want to imbibe, at least give yourself some nutritious fruit juice at the same time. Order tequila and orange juice or a mix of cranberry juice, club soda, and vodka. If you decide to skip the cocktail, however, treat yourself by having a bite of someone else's dessert!

Fast food is made with highly processed ingredients that are also low in nutrients. Even recent attempts to introduce grilled chicken sandwiches and healthier salads don't compare with the healthier versions you can find in the average coffee shop or diner. And if you want a reality check on the consequences of consuming burgers and fries, check out the Web site www.super sizeme.com, about the award-winning film, *Super Size Me*. A fit and healthy youngish man decides to eat fast food every meal for a month and also stops all exercise to find out how this lifestyle affects his health. He gains lots of weight, his cholesterol soars, and his system takes a full year to recover from the damaging effects of his experiment.

Diners without borders: Exploring restaurants

Go for it! Step into that dimly lit Indian restaurant. Sidle up to a sushi bar. Pop into that new Peruvian place around the corner (something that I keep promising myself I'll do very soon). These restaurants offer traditional dishes, the time-tested, nourishing foods that have sustained peoples over the centuries. Typically, ethnic dishes include a wide variety of ingredients, including legumes, nuts, seeds, exotic vegetables and fruits, and unusual grains, spices, and herbs. Recipes for these dishes evolved as cooks found ways to prepare whatever foods were available locally, both wild and cultivated. Such dishes often contain good amounts of plant foods, which are high in fiber and phytonutrients, a trustworthy formula for creating heart-healthy meals.

Chapter 5

Gearing Up for Healthy Cooking

In This Chapter

▶ Finding healthy foods in supermarkets and natural foods stores
▶ Deciphering the food labels
▶ Getting ready to start cooking

A s you shift to a healthier way of eating to control cholesterol, revising how you shop for food and how you prepare it comes with the territory. This chapter guides you through the changes you may need to make in your marketing habits and even how you cook. Whether you're an expert or a timid beginner, you still may need to stock up and even tool up to begin preparing more healthy meals.

The following sections give a guided tour of supermarkets and natural food stores to show you where you can buy cholesterol-controlling foods. I also help you sort out what food labels really say. And I suggest some kitchen items to help you save time and labor and facilitate lowfat cooking. Of course, you can probably manage by following your usual cooking routine, but making some changes may make preparing healthy meals so much easier and increase the likelihood that you'll eat them.

Gathering Healthy Ingredients

Begin a new era of treating yourself well by having on hand only those foods that support heart health and control cholesterol. Imagine a kitchen containing only fresh, quality ingredients so that whatever you choose to eat is good for you. You can have such a kitchen by following the advice in this chapter.

You can find many of the recommended foods in your regular supermarket, but you may also need to visit natural foods stores and perhaps ethnic food shops for certain special items. You're about to discover a whole new way of shopping for food that is both satisfying and entertaining.

Rediscovering your supermarket

You're about to take a virtual tour of the food store where you usually shop. Your current routine may take you to the deli section first to pick up luncheon meats and cheese, and then to the freezer section for handy frozen vegetables and ice cream. But you can just as easily make your way to more nutritious foods. Here's how.

Shopping around the edges of the store

While the aisles in grocery stores are filled with row upon row of boxed, bottled, and canned foods, mostly processed or refined food products, the perimeter of supermarkets is where fresh and natural food is displayed. Make the edges of the markets your turf! Here's where you'll find the majority of foods with the most nutrients.

- ✔ Head for the produce section for fresh vegetables and fruits of the season, making sure to buy a variety of produce and things you haven't eaten for a while. How about some berries, spinach, kale, asparagus, artichoke, avocado, mangoes, and sweet potatoes?

- ✔ While you're in the produce department, treat yourself to fresh herbs. Also be sure to stock up on such flavoring staples as onions, fresh garlic, chiles, and gingerroot.

- ✔ In the refrigerator section, look for milk and plain yogurt with lowered fat content, as well as lowfat and gourmet cheeses. Whenever possible favor organic brands to avoid the traces of pesticides and growth hormones present in standard dairy products.

- ✔ In the dairy section, look for vegetable oil spreads to use on toast instead of butter. Unlike butter, they contain no cholesterol and are also lower in saturated fat. Other names that manufacturers give these products are "natural oil blend" and "buttery spread."

- ✔ Cart home a carton of orange juice that contains some pulp.

- ✔ Check the meat section for turkey breast (a handy way to buy lowfat protein), pork loin, and frozen boneless, skinless chicken breasts.

- ✔ Purchase fresh fish fillets and whole fish if you trust the quality. Otherwise, shop at a dedicated fish store. (Chapter 13 gives you guidelines on shopping for fish.)

- ✔ The deli section isn't off limits! Select reduced-fat turkey sausage, Canadian bacon, smoked salmon, marinated herring, and soy versions of breakfast meats.

✔ When you do buy eggs, favor brands that state on the label that the eggs contain higher amounts of omega-3 fatty acids, a type of fat that helps prevent the formation of clots and inflammation. (See Chapter 1 for an explanation of how inflammation plays a role in the development of heart disease.) You also can usually find cartons of 100 percent egg whites in this section. (For more on omega-3s, check out Chapter 3.)

Touring the aisles

Supermarket aisles do harbor some healthy foods, such as whole-grain items and dried beans. Make a point of strolling down the aisles of the market where you shop and take a fresh look at what's available. You're sure to find many of the recommended items on the following list:

✔ In the cereal section, pick up some rolled oats.

Stay away from all the instant hot cereals because they quickly raise blood sugar.

✔ Pick up some brown rice, wild rice, bulgur wheat, barley, kidney beans, and lentils.

Don't buy beans where you suspect turnover is slow. They're likely to be dried out and take forever to cook. Canned beans are an alternative but only if they aren't covered with a sweet sauce. Check the ingredient list on the label for added sugars.

✔ You may want to bring home a bottle of extra-virgin olive oil, although it's cheaper by the gallon, sold in this quantity in specialty Italian markets. (For more tips on being thrifty when it comes to food, take a look at Chapter 22.)

Most oils sold in supermarkets are refined, so you don't want to buy them. Refined oils are easy to spot; they're packaged in transparent containers and all have the same light color.

✔ Look for all-fruit spreads that contain no added sugar.

Buy real maple syrup, the kind that comes from trees, not pancake syrup made from corn.

✔ Poke around the baked goods section for whole-grain English muffins, bagels, breads, and crackers and don't forget to buy some corn tortillas, also a whole-grain product.

✔ Buy almonds, walnuts, and peanut butter if you can find a brand that doesn't include hydrogenated oils.

Heading for the natural foods store

If you haven't shopped for "health food" for a few years, you're in for a treat. The once typically small and cluttered health food shop that had a faint smell of medicinal herbs is being replaced by glamorous food emporiums that offer a vast range of fresh produce, meats, and fish, as well as a wealth of nutritious packaged and frozen items. And organic is the rule rather than the exception.

In natural foods stores, you can find exotic and gourmet health food fit for a queen — and her pocketbook — but fortunately, these stores also still carry many tried and true staples. Many items that you probably can't find at the supermarket you're sure to locate here. (But that's not to say that your regular supermarket won't sell some of these. Times have changed, and many standard markets are beginning to offer healthy alternatives in response to customer demand.) Here are some tips to help you with your shopping:

- Natural foods stores offer the full range of unrefined and minimally processed cooking oils, from extra-virgin olive oil to unrefined safflower and sesame seed oils. You also find gourmet walnut and almond oils.

  Buy oils that have the word "unrefined" on the label. "Expeller pressed" oil is better than refined but still not of the very highest quality. To produce expeller-pressed oils, the nuts or seeds are mechanically pressed, rather than using chemical solvents for extraction. However, after extraction, an expeller pressed oil may still be refined.

- Look for flaxseed oil found in the refrigerator section of the store. (You need to store it in your fridge, too.) This oil is sold in opaque containers to protect the fragile fats from being damaged by light. The nature of flaxseed oil causes it to go rancid quickly. Purchase the small, 8-ounce bottle so you can use it all within a month.

- Vegetarian versions of common foods abound, usually based on soy. Look for canned soy chili, soy hot dogs, and soy ice cream.

- Spend a few minutes exploring the bulk bins that contain a variety of whole grains, flour, legumes, nuts, seeds, oat bran, and dried fruits, such as cherries and cranberries. This is the thriftiest way to buy such ingredients, and you can scoop up just the amount you need. These staples are likely to be fresh because of high turnover.

- Natural foods stores offer all sorts of whole-grain breads made with exotic grains such as kamut, amaranth, and spelt as well as wheat-free and gluten-free loaves. Also check out whole-grain pastas made with brown rice, spelt, quinoa, whole wheat, and buckwheat. Some pastas also contain spinach and Jerusalem artichoke.

Buckwheat noodles, called soba noodles, are good with Chinese sesame sauce, which is made with sesame paste, soy sauce, rice wine vinegar, honey, sherry, fresh cilantro, and chili oil. This dish is good topped with toasted peanuts.

✔ All sorts of whole-grain breakfast cereals that don't contain trans fatty acids and lots of added sweeteners are available in these stores. Some are made with unusual grains such as spelt, quinoa, and kamut. Try them all and never be bored with breakfast again.

✔ Natural foods stores offer a full range of natural sweeteners, including date sugar, pure maple syrup, stevia (a sweet herb), and raw honey, which still contains pollen, honeycomb, living enzymes, and propolis, a compound with antibacterial and antioxidant properties.

✔ You find poultry and meats that are free of residues of growth hormones and antibiotics, as well as many brands of organic beef, pork, and poultry. An advantage of the new and improved natural foods stores is that they offer a terrific variety of cuts.

✔ The freezer section contains such useful items as organic frozen dinners, organic vegetables, and organic sorbet. You also find frozen whole soybeans, called edamame.

Organic produce: Clean greens and more

The Environmental Working Group, an advocacy organization, makes available on its Web site, www.ewg.org, lists of the fruits and vegetables most contaminated with pesticides. The site tells you which are the most contaminated and also provides a handy wallet guide on shopping for produce that you can download and take with you to the market. Go to the Quick Index drop-down menu and click on Organic Food. Take a look at the section titled "Shopper's Guide to Pesticides in Produce."

The site reports that the following fruits and vegetables, listed in alphabetical order, are the most contaminated and best to buy organic: apples, bell peppers, celery, cherries, imported grapes, nectarines, peaches, pears, potatoes, red raspberries, spinach, and strawberries.

These fruits and vegetables, also listed in alphabetical order, are the 12 least contaminated: asparagus, avocados, bananas, broccoli, cauliflower, corn, kiwi, mangoes, onions, papayas, pineapples, and sweet peas.

The lists are based on data assembled by the USDA Pesticide Data Program.

To limit your intake of pesticides from produce, follow these guidelines:

✔ Eat a variety of fruit and vegetables.

✔ Wash all produce. (Take the extra step of using special rinse products now available in stores.)

✔ Buy organic produce whenever possible.

Figuring Out Food Labels

Food labels focus on fat, cholesterol, and sodium — all things that concern people who are trying to prevent heart disease. The label tells you how much of these substances is in a given serving, stated in grams and as a percent of the amount recommended per day. Such information can be very useful when trying to decide whether a food fits into a cholesterol-controlling diet. If you see that a 1-cup serving of canned chili gives you 13 percent of your Daily Value for cholesterol or that a serving of a single cookie from a box contains 17 percent of your daily allotment of saturated fat, you're well-armed to make an informed decision. You may decide that foods high in substances you want to limit in your diet are fine to eat occasionally because you plan for the rest of the day to balance these with foods that are low in cholesterol and fat. Or, when you check the numbers, you just may decide to eat something else.

The label also tells you the number of milligrams of cholesterol in a serving. The percent of recommended daily intake is also given, based on a limit of 300 mg per day. But be aware that if you follow the new recommendations for persons at high risk for heart disease and are limiting your intake to 200 mg per day, then the percent on the label will overstate the amount you can have. Labels can be misleading in other ways as well. Here are some examples:

- ✔ A food low in cholesterol and/or fat may be high in sugar.

- ✔ Lowfat does not necessarily mean low-calorie.

- ✔ Simply because a food is low in cholesterol doesn't mean it is necessarily good for you.

Labeling nutrition facts

The amounts of fat and so forth listed in Nutrition Facts, a standard part of every food label, are based on specific numbers that may not reflect the way you eat. The suggested intake is based on a concept called the Daily Value. This is the amount of fat, carbohydrate, protein, cholesterol, sodium, and certain nutrients the U.S. Food and Drug Administration (FDA) recommends for health. The amounts are based on the Recommended Dietary Allowance, but an outdated version of these. Furthermore, the recommended amount of carbohydrates, protein, and fat is based on a 2,000-calories-a-day diet. This hypothetical eating plan is defined as 30 percent calories from fat, 60 per cent calories from carbohydrates, and only 10 percent calories from protein. Figure 5-1 shows a typical Nutrition Facts food label.

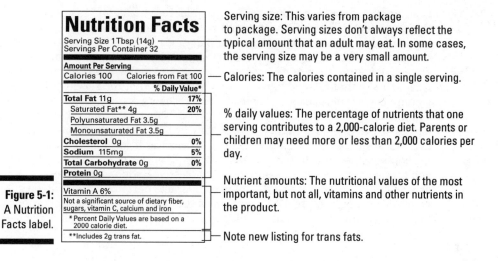

Figure 5-1:
A Nutrition
Facts label.

Serving size: This varies from package to package. Serving sizes don't always reflect the typical amount that an adult may eat. In some cases, the serving size may be a very small amount.

Calories: The calories contained in a single serving.

% daily values: The percentage of nutrients that one serving contributes to a 2,000-calorie diet. Parents or children may need more or less than 2,000 calories per day.

Nutrient amounts: The nutritional values of the most important, but not all, vitamins and other nutrients in the product.

Note new listing for trans fats.

The way of eating that this formula represents can help you lower cholesterol depending upon the kinds of fat, carbohydrates, and protein you eat. However, this isn't the only eating scheme that works. As I explain in this book, one that allows more fat and protein of the right kinds can also help control cholesterol. And if you're following a diet other than the one the label is based on, then the percentages of fat and so forth allowed will not apply to you, over- or understating how much of these you should have.

But suppose that you're on a diet that matches the one on the label. The following tells you how much actual fat, saturated fat, carbs, and protein you can have in a day:

- ✔ Thirty percent calories from fat is 67 grams of fat. (One tablespoon of oil contains a total of 14 grams of fat.)

- ✔ Ten percent calories from saturated fat is 22 grams of saturated fat. (One tablespoon of butter contains 7.5 grams of saturated fat.)

- ✔ Sixty percent calories from carbohydrates is 300 grams of carbs. (One slice of bread contains 13 grams of carbohydrate.)

- ✔ Ten percent calories from protein is 50 grams of protein (Three and a half ounces of skinless, boneless chicken breast contain about 30 grams of protein.)

As you see, this formula doesn't give you a lot of grams of saturated fat to play with. And the new diet recommendations for people at high risk of heart disease restrict saturated fat intake even further, to 7 percent of total calories. This cuts grams of saturated fat per day to 15½ grams.

In addition, the serving size given for a product may lead you to conclude that a product is better for you than it is. The serving size is often surprisingly small, so when the label tells you that one serving gives you just 5 percent of your daily allotment of fat, don't sigh with relief. You're probably going to eat more than one serving. I just checked my own shelves and found a can of soup that is ½ cup per serving and noticed that the serving size stated on a box of crackers is a measly two crackers.

Similar to the Nutrition Facts labels on food products, the nutritional information at the end of each recipe in this book gives the actual amount of various nutrients per serving. It tells you the number of grams of fat, carbohydrate, and protein and the specific amounts of cholesterol, sodium, and dietary fiber as well. When you decide on the number of grams of these various dietary components you want to aim for in your meals, use these recipe tabulations to help you add up your tally for the day.

Studying the label lingo

Labels geared to the health-conscious market are usually better at announcing what the food inside does *not* contain, but you need to read all the info on the labels, especially if you're watching your cholesterol. The Food and Drug Administration has developed various terms that can be very useful when you're scouring the store for special diet foods. The following sections give you the basic vocabulary.

"Free" for all: Looking for the absence of a substance

Look for the word "free" on the label when you want to avoid a certain substance, such as fat or cholesterol, but still enjoy the food it's usually in. And be forewarned that you sometimes have to pay a little extra for such "free" specialty foods.

- ✔ **Fat free:** The product has less than ½ gram (0.5 g) of fat per serving. Manufacturers are allowed to round this to zero for a single serving.

- ✔ **Saturated fat free:** The product has less than 0.5 grams of saturated fat. When a serving contains this amount or less, manufacturers are permitted to round this amount to zero.

- ✔ **99% fat free:** Every 100 grams of food has 1 gram or less of fat.

- ✔ **Cholesterol free:** The product contains less than 2 milligrams of cholesterol per serving. This value is rounded to zero.

- ✔ **Sodium free:** The food has less than 5 milligrams of sodium per serving and can be rounded to zero.

The lowdown on "low"

"Low" is a lovely word when you see it on items such as dairy products, because it tells you that inside is all that creaminess but with much less fat than the food originally contained. The words "reduced" and "light" also tell you that fat and calories have been cut but to a lesser extent than "low" versions of the product.

- ✔ **Lowfat:** The product contains 3 grams of fat or less per serving.

- ✔ **Low in saturated fat:** One serving has 1 gram or less of saturated fat.

- ✔ **Reduced fat:** The food's fat has been reduced by at least 25 percent compared with the amount it originally contained.

  Estimate how much fat is still left before you call "reduced fat" a good deal.

- ✔ **Light or lite:** The product contains 33 percent fewer calories or 50 percent less fat per serving compared with the amount the original food contained.

- ✔ **Low-calorie:** The food has 40 calories or less per serving.

- ✔ **Lean:** This term applies to meat and poultry only and means that the food has less than 10 grams of fat, less than 4 grams of saturated fat, and less than 95 milligrams of cholesterol per serving.

- ✔ **Low-cholesterol:** Per serving, the food contains 20 milligrams or less of cholesterol and 2 grams or less of saturated fat.

  Don't get too excited when a label announces that what's inside is cholesterol free. Plant foods naturally don't contain any cholesterol, so the fact that a cooking oil or a cookie made with sugar and flour doesn't contain any cholesterol either is no big deal.

- ✔ **Low-sodium:** This term indicates that a product contains 140 milligrams or less of sodium per serving.

- ✔ **Very low-sodium:** The food has 35 milligrams or less of sodium per serving.

All of these terms apply to just one serving of a product, which sometimes can be pretty dinky. You may need to multiply the amounts by 2 or 3 to match what you really ate.

Preparing to Cook

Even if you're someone who cooks with spontaneity and passion, bringing a semblance of order to the process can't hurt. Having all the ingredients and cooking tools ready to go in advance helps prevent a kitchen crisis and leaves you free to enjoy the pleasures of cooking. (In French cooking, the name for this divine state of preparedness is *mise en place.*) Why should TV chefs have all the fun, with their vast support staffs setting up everything in advance? Here's the drill:

- ✔ Put on your apron, roll up your sleeves, and check that clean dish towels and paper towels are within arm's reach.

- ✔ Warn everyone not to anger the cook and resolve to stay calm while cooking. A study in the *Journal of the American College of Cardiology* found that expressing anger accelerates the progression of atherosclerosis (hardening of the arteries).

- ✔ Clear your work surface of clutter and have a cutting board ready to use.

  Keep items you use often close to where you usually use them. Store cookware you rarely use — perhaps that pasta machine — in the back of the cupboard or on a high shelf.

- ✔ Choose a recipe if you haven't already done so, and take a quiet moment to thoughtfully read through the entire recipe you plan to cook. You can avoid surprises and perhaps better organize your cooking procedure.

- ✔ Assemble all the ingredients called for in a recipe. For accuracy, give your full attention to measuring key ingredients, such as baking soda or spices.

- ✔ Wash and prepare produce and cut fruit and vegetables according to recipe instructions. Trim meats, and wash and prepare poultry. (Depending upon the recipe, sometimes preparing certain ingredients while others are cooking is a more efficient approach.)

- ✔ Keep a pan of sudsy dishwater nearby or fill the sink basin with soapy water, where you can put dirty bowls, mixing spoons, and the like as you finish using them. You'll have a jump-start on cleaning up the kitchen and have your equipment ready to use again if you need it for another step in the recipe.

After you're done cooking and the delicious results are yours to enjoy, sit down at a table to eat your meal slowly in order to fully appreciate this chance to nourish yourself.

Part II
Mastering the Beneficial Breakfast

The 5th Wave   By Rich Tennant

"Frank's learning to adapt to low-cholesterol meals. Still, I have to watch him around the suet block next to the bird feeders."

In this part . . .

The three chapters in this part focus on breakfast, a meal that typically can be full of foods that raise cholesterol. But don't worry — you discover lots of clever ways to start your day with heart-healthy dishes that are so tasty they're destined to become part of your morning routine.

I explain why some carbohydrates are ideal for controlling cholesterol. I help you make sure that you have some protein while you limit your saturated fat. And yes, I help you unscramble all the advice out there about eating eggs. This part concludes with ideas for quick breakfast recipes to make sure you can always give yourself a meal that keeps you going until lunch and that also controls cholesterol.

Chapter 6

Greeting the Morning with Healthy Carbs

Breakfast can be the most challenging meal of the day when you need to eat in a way that controls cholesterol. So many standard breakfast items are loaded with sugar and fat and are missing nutrients that help keep the heart in working order. The first meal of the day, some say the most important, has been replaced by snacking on something sweet, plus a cup of strong coffee.

In this chapter, I take a fresh look at breakfast foods based on grains, identifying those items that are the most nutritious and revising such standard offerings as French toast and pancakes. You can still enjoy these treats and take care of your arteries simply by adjusting the usual recipes.

Even if you're cutting back on carb intake, whole grains kept in proportion to protein and fat still merit a place at the breakfast table for the role they can play in maintaining heart health. Sweet flavorings, too, can be included when they're wholesome ingredients enjoyed in small amounts.

Sorting Out Starches and Sweets

Whether you're picking up something quick for breakfast at the deli counter, breakfasting at a fancy restaurant with white linen tablecloths, or touring the aisles at a supermarket, avoiding baked goods and cereals made with refined grains and sugars takes some diligence. Sweet rolls, pancakes, waffles, bread, and many hot and cold cereals are mostly comprised of these ingredients that can lead to high blood sugar, weight gain, and eventually heart problems when they become your usual breakfast. They also shortchange you by providing calories without a comparable amount of nutrients. But the good news is that nutritious-carb baked goods are showing up more and more often.

Adding whole carbs while reducing refined carbs

Avoiding all the white flour and white sugar that's offered to you every day takes commitment, because the white foods are so prevalent. You need to be a sleuth and read those package labels closely (see Figure 6-1 for white flour substitutes). Planning what you'll eat for the day ahead of time also helps keep you from resorting to these products. Making changes to your daily meals in steps is a fine approach. You stand to benefit if you manage to replace even half of the refined carbs you normally eat. Here are some actions to take:

 ✔ When you go grocery shopping, search out whole-wheat bagels, English muffins, and whole-grain and multigrain breads. More and more manufacturers are providing these alternatives. Also, request whole-wheat and whole-grain breads when you're eating out.

 ✔ Look for cereals made with whole grains and not made with partially hydrogenated vegetable oils and added sugars. Read the label and you find that by these standards, Grape-Nuts cereal is a winner.

 ✔ Be aware of the many forms of added sugar and their names. Many commercial cereals contain several forms of sugar that can really add up:

  • Corn syrup and corn sweeteners

  • Fructose and high-fructose corn syrup

  • Dextrose and dextrin

  • Fruit juice concentrate

  • Evaporated cane juice

✔ Have a big enough breakfast at home so you're not hungry when you leave the house and are tempted to eat from the snack cart at work or stop for a fast food breakfast. Assemble what you plan to eat for breakfast the night before so it's ready to prepare quickly in the morning.

✔ Carry nutritious snack foods with you when you're away from home. That way, when you feel a little hungry, you don't cave in and buy something starchy and sweet, the usual sort of snack food you find. Bring along almonds, fresh cherries, grapes, or crunchy vegetables and a bit of yogurt dip.

I realize that avoiding white flour and white sugar is easier said than done. If you need motivation, just remember: Cutting out the array of breakfast pastries is one of the most effective dietary steps you can take to maintain your health.

Figure 6-1: The large variety of grains out there means you aren't limited to refined white flour.

Ode to oats

Oats are one of the few grains that manufacturers leave as is, bringing oats to market still unrefined with germ and bran intact. Several years ago, this homey breakfast staple suddenly became a must-have health food for its ability to lower cholesterol. The fanfare has died down some, and other foods such as legumes now share the spotlight, but a bowl of oatmeal still ranks as one of the healthiest choices for breakfast.

Oat bran gives you soluble fiber, the kind that lowers cholesterol. Oats also are a good source of vitamin E, folate, iron, copper, and zinc, and they're very high in manganese and protein. According to one study, published in the *American Journal of Clinical Nutrition* in 2002, oats are far better than wheat for lowering cholesterol and for improving blood lipids and lipoprotein profiles. Researchers at Colorado State University had 36 men, ages 50 to 75 years, consume two large servings of oat cereal or wheat cereal daily for 12 weeks. For those eating oats, levels of LDL cholesterol declined without lowering HDL cholesterol or raising triglycerides. But for those consuming the wheat cereal, LDL cholesterol, the ratio of LDL to HDL cholesterol, and triglycerides all increased (see Chapter 1).

The requirements for soluble fiber are between 5 and 10 grams a day. Table 6-1 shows how oat bran as a source of soluble fiber compares with some other foods.

Table 6-1	Amount of Soluble Fiber in Oat Bran Compared with Other Foods
Food	*Soluble Fiber in 3.5 ounces*
Oat bran	7.4
Dried split peas	1.6
Strawberries	0.8
Cooked rolled oats	0.8

According to the American Dietetic Association, to experience the cholesterol-lowering effect of soluble fiber, consuming 3 grams a day is required. In terms of oatmeal, here's how much you need to eat to obtain this amount:

> ✔ 1½ cups cooked oatmeal, made with ¾ cup dry oats
>
> ✔ ¼ cup dry oat bran, sprinkled on foods or cooked
>
> ✔ ½ cup dry oatmeal plus ⅛ cup oat bran, cooked

If eating a cup and a half of oatmeal each day doesn't appeal, you can sneak oatmeal, oat flour, and oat bran into your meals in other ways. For example, you can include them in recipes for muffins, pancakes (see the recipe for Buttermilk Pancakes with Pecan-Maple Syrup in this chapter), and meat loaf. Oatmeal cookies count, too! (See the Chewy Oatmeal Cookies with Currants recipe in Chapter 20 for an especially nutritious version.)

How sweet it is: Watching your sugar intake

If you're not careful, your breakfast can include more sweet foods than any other meal of the day. No wonder Americans eat over 150 pounds of sweeteners per person per year. Sweet breakfasts give you a running start on the nearly half pound of sugar you must consume each day to reach this mammoth amount. Sure, this estimate of sugar intake is probably exaggerated, but individuals eating a Western-style diet are definitely taking in too much.

If you want to figure out how much sugar is in a food product, check the label for the number of grams of sugar it contains per serving — 4 grams equals 1 teaspoon of granulated white sugar.

Keeping artificial sweeteners out of the pantry

The recipes in this cookbook are designed to give you ways to prepare dishes made with natural, unrefined and unprocessed foods. Artificial substances are avoided whenever possible. Man-made sweeteners and sugar substitutes are not called for in any of the recipes.

These chemical substances are used to replace real foods, such as maple syrup and honey, and they do cut calories. However, the way of eating presented in this book, with its emphasis on plant foods and lean meats, already provides you with a way to do this. In addition, portion control (another good way to cut calories) is one of the cornerstones of this cholesterol-controlling diet (see Chapter 1). There are also safety concerns with artificial sweeteners, which, although they have not proven to be clearly harmful, have not been proven to be completely safe either. Used in cooking, they can also impart an aftertaste. For many reasons, stick with the real stuff.

Natural sweeteners to keep on your pantry shelf

You can still include sweet somethings in your breakfast by using more wholesome kinds. Try these natural sweeteners, each with special benefits:

- **Maple syrup:** The natural sap of the maple tree, this syrup contains calcium, potassium, magnesium, manganese, phosphorus, and iron, as well as trace amounts of B vitamins. Maple is also just the right flavor to complement so many breakfast foods.

- **Honey:** You need less honey to sweeten a dish because honey is sweeter than table sugar. Hunt for artisanal honeys with special flower flavors at farmers markets. Some honeys even have medicinal properties, such as Manukka honey, which is antibacterial.

- **Date sugar:** This form of sugar is dried dates that have been ground. Like dates, date sugar is loaded with nutrients such as niacin, potassium, and calcium. Buy this whole food sweetener in natural food stores and try it sprinkled on the Cranberry Fruit Pudding in this chapter.

- **Stevia:** This plant compound is 200 to 300 times sweeter than sugar and contains virtually no calories. It's available in liquid form and in crystals in health food stores and an increasing number of markets. Stevia is considered safe in small doses, which is all you'll ever need. South Americans have used stevia for centuries, and the Japanese sweeten all sorts of commercial pickled and preserved foods with this herb.

Stevia has a slightly earthy aftertaste, and if you use too much, it can taste bitter.

For information on the quantity of honey and maple sugar needed to replace white sugar, see Chapter 20, about baked desserts.

Carb- and Cholesterol-Friendly Breakfast Recipes

Sample these whole grain recipes for a treat. They taste more like gourmet specialties than like sober health food. The fruit pudding is so yummy that it also works as a dessert. And enjoy the baked apples, cloaked in mango chutney, for a change of pace.

✽ Cherry-Studded Three-Grain Porridge

Let this porridge be your inspiration for other versions. I chose millet and roasted it for its popcorn flavor, and I used barley and oats for their soluble fiber. Dried cherries, sold in natural foods stores, contain powerful antioxidants. Serve this mix of hot cereals for weekend breakfasts and enjoy leftovers on weekdays when you're short of time. To reheat the porridge, scoop some into a bowl, pour a little milk over the cereal to loosen it up, and give the cereal a zap in the microwave for 1 minute. Top with a little honey or maple syrup if you'd like.

Preparation time: *30 minutes*

Cooking time: *45 minutes*

Yield: *4 servings*

¼ cup millet	⅓ cup dried cherries
¼ cup pearl barley	¼ cup rolled oats
3½ cups water	2 tablespoons oat bran
¼ teaspoon salt	

1 Put the millet in a bowl of water and briefly swish it around to remove excess starch. Pour out the water, repeat the rinsing, and pour out the water again. (Any remaining moisture on the grains will evaporate in toasting.) Distribute the millet in a skillet on medium heat. Stir frequently with a wooden spoon until the grains dry and begin to give off a sweet, toasted scent, about 2 minutes. Remove the skillet from the heat and transfer the millet to a small bowl.

2 Put the barley in a bowl of water and briefly swish it around to remove excess starch. Pour out the water, repeat the rinsing, and pour out the water again. (The barley does not require toasting.)

3 Put the water and salt in the skillet used to toast the millet and place over medium high heat. Bring the water to a boil. Add the millet, barley, and dried cherries. Turn the heat to low and simmer the grain mixture, partially covered, 15 minutes. Stir the grains once or twice during the process.

4 Add the oats and oat bran and continue to cook the grains on low for 30 minutes, stirring frequently. Add hot water when necessary for desired porridge consistency. Serve warm.

Go-With: *Serve with your choice of Canadian bacon, smoked salmon, a butter substitute such as Earth Balance butter sticks, or toasted nuts and flaxseed oil for a nutritional home run.*

Per serving: Calories 241 (From Fat 18); Fat 2g (Saturated 0g); Cholesterol 0mg; Sodium 150mg; Carbohydrate 49g (Dietary Fiber 6g); Protein 7g.

🍑 Buttermilk Pancakes with Pecan-Maple Syrup

These elegant pancakes supply soluble fiber in the oat flour and bran and also give you a small serving of nuts. The recipe also calls for wheat germ, a highly nutritious part of wheat, which is removed when the grain is refined. I added this ingredient because the recipe includes 1 cup all-purpose flour, which is wheat flour that's been refined. This way, you have the lightness and delicate flavor of refined wheat flour plus the nutrients.

Preparation time: *20 minutes*

Cooking time: *15 minutes*

Yield: *4 servings*

½ cup chopped pecans	*¼ teaspoon salt*
½ teaspoon unrefined safflower oil	*2 tablespoons oat bran*
¾ cup maple syrup	*1 tablespoon wheat germ*
¼ cup orange juice	*1 egg*
1 cup unbleached, all-purpose flour	*1¾ cups buttermilk (see the tip at the end of the recipe)*
½ cup oat flour	
1½ teaspoons baking powder	*2 tablespoons unrefined safflower oil, plus extra for greasing the griddle*

1 Make the syrup: Heat the pecans and safflower oil in a small skillet over medium-high heat, stirring frequently, until you can smell the pecan's fragrance, 2 minutes. Add the maple syrup and orange juice and stir to combine. Set aside.

2 To make the batter, sift together twice the all-purpose flour, oat flour, baking powder, and salt. Add the oat bran and wheat germ to the flour mixture and mix with a fork. In a smaller bowl, whisk the egg. Add the buttermilk and safflower oil to the egg and whisk to combine. Gradually whisk the egg mixture into the dry ingredients, just until no lumps remain.

3 Heat a nonstick skillet or griddle over medium heat. Dip a folded paper towel in safflower oil and lightly coat the cooking surface. Spoon about ¼ cup batter into the skillet for each pancake. Cook for 2 minutes, or until a few bubbles form on the top of the pancake and the underside is golden brown. Using a spatula, flip the pancakes over and cook an additional 1½ minutes, until they're just cooked through.

4 To make another batch, first lightly re-oil the cooking surface. Keep the pancakes and ovenproof serving plates warm in a 250-degree oven. Serve with the warm pecan-maple syrup.

Note: *For thicker pancakes, reduce the buttermilk to 1¼ cups.*

Per serving: *Calories 567 (From Fat 197); Fat 22g (Saturated 3g); Cholesterol 57mg; Sodium 423mg; Carbohydrate 83g (Dietary Fiber 5g); Protein 13g.*

☙ Cranberry Fruit Pudding

I've packed this pudding with fruit that's good for the heart. Raisins contain a compound that lowers cholesterol, cranberries contain antioxidants, and the apples and prunes provide soluble fiber. Such pudding, comfort food from England, is usually made with cream and lots of sugar. This recipe is far lighter and topped with date sugar, which is simply dried, ground-up dates. Enjoy warm or cold the next day, with milk or yogurt.

Preparation time: *20 minutes*

Cooking time: *45 minutes*

Yield: *8 servings*

8 pitted prunes, chopped

½ cup dried cranberries

½ cup ruby or dark raisins (Pavitch brand preferred)

1 cup water

2 medium-size baking apples, such as Granny Smith or Rome, cored and chopped (about 3 cups)

1 banana, sliced

¼ cup sliced raw almonds

4 slices multigrain bread, diced (bread that contains oats preferred)

1 cup 2 percent milk

½ teaspoon vanilla

1 teaspoon allspice

2 tablespoons date sugar (see the tip at the end of the recipe)

1 Preheat the oven to 400 degrees. Put the prunes, cranberries, and raisins, along with the 1 cup water, in a medium-size pot. Bring to a boil and remove from the heat.

2 Stir in the apples, banana, almonds, and bread. Transfer the bread mixture to a greased 8-x-8-inch baking pan.

3 In a small bowl, combine the milk, vanilla, and allspice. Pour the milk mixture over the fruit and bread. Sprinkle the top of the pudding with the date sugar.

4 Bake for 40 minutes, or until the apples have softened and the pudding is firm and golden brown. Enjoy it warm immediately or serve it cold the next day, with milk or yogurt.

Tip: *You can find date sugar in natural foods stores.*

Per serving: *Calories 187 (From Fat 26); Fat 3g (Saturated 1g); Cholesterol 2mg; Sodium 82mg; Carbohydrate 40g (Dietary Fiber 4g); Protein 4g.*

Baked Apples with Mango Chutney

These baked apples turn into a mini-meal of carbohydrate, fat, and protein after you fill them with sausage. Using veggie sausage makes the dish lighter but equally appealing. Be sure to use a good cooking apple, such as Golden Delicious, Granny Smith, or Rome. Decorate the apples, cutting away narrow strips of the apple skin. Use a citrus stripper, a special tool with a stainless-steel notched edge that cuts ¼-inch-wide strips.

Specialty tool: *Citrus stripper*

Preparation time: *15 minutes*

Cooking time: *45 minutes*

Yield: *4 generous servings*

½ cup mango chutney	4 tart cooking apples
1 tablespoon maple syrup	4 ounces turkey sausage or soy veggie sausage (Yves brand recommended)
1 cup water	

1 Preheat the oven to 350 degrees. Put the mango chutney, maple syrup, and water in a shallow 8-x-8-inch baking dish just large enough to hold the apples. Stir the glaze with a fork to combine. Set aside.

2 Core each apple almost through to the bottom. Enlarge the cavity until it is about 1 inch wide. Using a citrus striper, cut lines through the apple skin at intervals, starting at the stem end and running from top to bottom. The apples will end up with 5 or 6 stripes.

3 Stuff the sausage into the openings, dividing it evenly among the 4 apples and mounding it on the apple tops. Drizzle a teaspoon of glaze over the exposed sausage.

4 Put the baking dish in the oven. Begin basting the apples after 10 minutes and several times during baking. Bake the apples until the apples are tender and the glaze has thickened, about 45 minutes.

5 Remove the apples from the oven and allow them to sit 5 minutes. Spoon any remaining glaze in the dish over the apples. Serve warm.

Tip: *A loaf pan is handy for baking small to medium-size apples, the narrow width helping to hold the apples upright and in place.*

Go-With: *Serve the apples with sautéed polenta. You can purchase polenta ready-made, and then all you need to do is slice and sauté. (See Chapter 8 for more about ready-made polenta.)*

Per serving: Calories 178 (From Fat 15); Fat 2g (Saturated 0g); Cholesterol 9mg; Sodium 196mg; Carbohydrate 40g (Dietary Fiber 5g); Protein 5g.

⌒ *Baked French Toast with Blueberry Sauce*

This French toast is made with fewer yolks and less fat than the usual French toast, but it still tastes like you're having breakfast in Paris.

Preparation time: *15 minutes*

Cooking time: *20 minutes*

Yield: *4 servings*

2 eggs

2 egg whites

1 cup 1 percent milk

½ teaspoon vanilla

2 drops lemon extract

8 slices day-old bread, cut in half on the diagonal (whole-grain or multigrain preferred)

Unrefined safflower oil for coating the skillet

¾ cup plus 1 tablespoon blueberry or apple juice

1 tablespoon cornstarch

12 ounces fresh or frozen blueberries, thawed

2 tablespoons maple syrup

1 In a large shallow dish with sides, whisk the eggs and egg whites. Add the milk, vanilla, and lemon extract and whisk to combine.

2 Working in batches, place some of the bread triangles in the egg mixture and let the bread soak for 2 minutes. Turn the slices over and let sit until the bread is saturated. Repeat with all the bread slices until all the bread has soaked.

3 Lightly oil a nonstick skillet or a nonstick griddle pan with the safflower oil. In batches, cook the bread triangles in a single layer over medium heat. Cook for 5 minutes, turn the slices over, and cook an additional 5 minutes, or until the French toast begins to brown. Transfer cooked French toast to a platter and cover loosely with aluminum foil to keep warm while you continue to cook the remaining soaked bread.

4 Meanwhile, using a fork, combine 1 tablespoon of the fruit juice and the cornstarch in a small bowl. Set aside.

5 In a small pan, warm the blueberries, fruit juice, and maple syrup until the liquid simmers. Add the cornstarch mixture and continue to simmer the sauce, stirring frequently, until it thickens, about 3 minutes.

6 Serve the French toast immediately, topped with the blueberry syrup.

Per serving: *Calories 308 (From Fat 50); Fat 6g (Saturated 2g); Cholesterol 109mg; Sodium 351mg; Carbohydrate 54g (Dietary Fiber 6g); Protein 13g.*

Chapter 7

Starting Your Day with Protein

· ·

In This Chapter

▶ Controlling blood sugar and cholesterol with protein

▶ Cracking the egg controversy

▶ Getting your protein from fish, lowfat breakfast meats, or nuts

▶ Making protein-filled breakfast dishes

· ·

Recipes in This Chapter

🍳 Egg-White Scrambled Eggs with Tomato and Feta

▶ Mexican Eggs and Canadian Bacon

🍳 Coddled Eggs with Sautéed Mushrooms

🍳 Hash Browns with Veggie Bacon

▶ Scandinavian Mustard-Dill Herring

🍴 🍸 🍳 🌶 🥕

*I*ncluding protein turns breakfast into a complete and satisfying little meal, but it also can add saturated fat and cholesterol. The trick is to factor the meat and eggs you have for breakfast into your plans for lunch and dinner. That way, you can still start the day well fed without compromising your cholesterol intake for the rest of the day.

This chapter discusses many protein choices, with a thoughtful look at eggs and how to best cook this optimally nutritious food. You're tempted with savory breakfast fish and also breakfast meats.

Best of all, in the following pages, you find several winning breakfast recipes. One is a refresher course on poaching eggs, and another gives you the chance to sample eating corn tortillas, as I sometimes do, for breakfast. The ingredients have your heart health in mind, and they don't sacrifice flavor.

Making a Point of Eating Protein

Do yourself a favor and make sure to have some protein at breakfast. Protein foods such as fish, dairy products, nuts, breakfast meats, and eggs also contain some necessary fat to give you lasting energy. (Believe it or not, a little fat in the diet is important, but remember that moderation is the key!) If you start the day with just a piece of dry toast and a cup of black coffee, you may crave a Danish pastry by 10 a.m. That's because the body converts the toast carbohydrates to energy in about an hour and a half and then runs out of fuel. But protein takes longer to metabolize, at least two hours, so it takes over when the toast energy konks out. The fat, which burns the slowest, provides energy next, after about three hours. There, you've made it to lunch!

Now, you may not think you need a serious breakfast. No farmer's buffet of bacon and eggs and more for you. After all, you don't plan to perform heavy labor, and you're not tending cattle. But there are good health reasons not to eat a skimpy and carb-only breakfast. A habit like that can increase the risk of heart disease, in several ways:

- ✔ Having a breakfast that's all sugar and starch may lead to weight gain when a morning snack becomes a necessity.

- ✔ Feeling hungry can fill your morning with stress; as your brain tunes out, fatigue takes over, and consequently, things start to go wrong. Stress is a known factor for heart disease.

- ✔ An all-carb breakfast can raise cholesterol, at least in certain individuals. A breakfast that's all sugar and starch, such as pancakes floating in maple-flavored corn syrup, quickly overloads the system with carbohydrates. Such assaults, over time, can lead to a cluster of problems, including insulin resistance, elevated triglycerides, and elevated cholesterol.

Considering Eggs: Not the Villains They're Cracked Up to Be

Eggs contain a significant amount of cholesterol, which increases with the size of the egg. Small eggs contain about 157 mg, medium eggs 187 mg, large eggs 213 mg, and extra-large and jumbo eggs up to 290 mg. Given that the American Heart Association recommends that healthy people with normal cholesterol consume a maximum of less than 300 mg of cholesterol per day, eating one egg whatever the size will take a large bite out of this daily quota. And, following the Association's guidelines of 200 mg of cholesterol per day for patients with high LDL cholesterol and/or cardiovascular disease, only one small and medium egg per day can be worked into the diet. If you have an egg at breakfast, then you need to avoid virtually all sources of cholesterol (animal foods) the rest of the day.

When eggs are called for in most recipes, including those in this book, you can assume this means large eggs, which provide an average amount of volume. If you want to reduce the cholesterol content, substitute a smaller egg, like in the Coddled Eggs with Sautéed Mushrooms recipe in this chapter; then simply add more mushrooms. However, use some caution in baking recipes, because reducing the egg content can ruin the recipe.

The relationship between egg consumption and heart disease isn't as simple as the tidy rules in this chapter suggest. First, no study has ever shown that healthy people who eat more eggs have more heart attacks than those who eat fewer eggs. A case in point: In a study published in 1999 in the *Journal of the American Medical Association,* Harvard researchers who followed the eating habits of almost 120,000 healthy men and women over many years found that those individuals who ate up to one egg a day had no higher risk of heart disease or stroke as people eating less than one egg a week.

Eggs also contain nutrients that lower the risk of heart disease, in particular folate, vitamin B6, and vitamin B12. These are known to lower elevated blood levels of homocysteine, a risk factor for heart disease, as described in Chapter 1. And the yolk contains cholesterol and vitamin E, an antioxidant nutrient that helps protect the cholesterol from oxidation. Vitamin E also makes the cholesterol less "sticky" and therefore less likely to make plaque accumulate in the arteries. In addition, eggs contain a particular fat that lowers the absorption of cholesterol from the GI track into the system, according to an animal study conducted at Kansas State University and published in the *Journal of Nutrition.*

Still, if your cholesterol is elevated, are eggs for you? The answer is yes if you limit cholesterol from other sources. And of course, the egg white, which contains no cholesterol, is fine to eat anytime.

While eggs start out as a high-quality ingredient before people get their hands on them, cooked eggs can be anything but a health food. Saturated fat often gets into the act, in the form of butter, bacon, or cheese, in dishes meant for gourmet brunches and in fast food breakfast items.

Cholesterol in the egg yolk becomes oxidized during the cooking process to a greater or lesser extent, depending upon how the egg is cooked. You want to keep this oxidation to a minimum because oxidized cholesterol in particular can lead to narrowed arteries. Exposure to oxygen, light, and heat oxidizes the cholesterol. This is what happens when you scramble eggs. You break the yolk and maximize its exposure to the air, light, and the hot cooking surface. Frying an egg is only slightly better because the yolk is still exposed to high heat.

Eating egg whites is no yolk

Eating only the egg whites lets you avoid the cholesterol, which is all in the yolks, but gives you only part of the protein, vitamins, and minerals. However, if you do have good reason to avoid the cholesterol in eggs, start with actual eggs and crack open some yourself, separating the whites from the yolks. (See the accompanying illustration.) You can also find just egg whites at the supermarket, in the dairy section. Buy the purest form and avoid products made with lots of added substances, such as artificial flavor and color. Then sample the Egg-White Scrambled Eggs with Tomato and Feta recipe in this chapter.

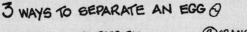

3 WAYS TO SEPARATE AN EGG

① CRACK THE EGG IN HALF, OVER A BOWL... ..AND PASS THE YOLK FROM 1 SHELL TO THE OTHER, ALLOWING THE WHITE TO GRADUALLY FALL INTO THE BOWL BELOW.

② CRACK THE EGG AND BREAK THE EGG INTO YOUR CUPPED HAND HELD OVER A BOWL. GENTLY, RELAX FINGERS, ALLOWING THE WHITE TO SPILL THROUGH INTO THE BOWL BELOW.

③ USE AN EGG SEPARATOR! PLACE IT OVER A SMALL BOWL OR GLASS. CRACK THE EGG OPEN AND LET IT FALL INTO THE CENTER.

THE WHITE WILL SLIP THROUGH THE SLOTS AND THE YOLK WILL STAY IN THE SEPARATOR.

To minimize the oxidation that occurs as an egg cooks, use a cooking method that doesn't require high heat and keeps the yolk encased in the white. Here are three classic ways of preparing eggs that protect the yolk:

- ✔ **Soft-cooking** an egg in its shell protects the yolk from light and air.

- ✔ **Poaching** an egg involves placing a whole egg in liquid and cooking it gently just below the boiling point. A visual sign that a safe temperature has been reached is when the surface of the poaching liquid begins to show slight movement.

> ✔ **Coddling** is a method of cooking eggs that involves placing the egg in an individual container that is covered and set in a larger pan of simmering water, which is placed on the stovetop or in the oven at very low heat. The warmth of the water bath slowly cooks the egg.

Instead of cooking an omelet with some filling, have poached eggs instead, garnished with the filling. (See the recipe for Mexican Eggs and Canadian Bacon in this chapter.)

Expanding Your Breakfast Protein Options

Don't think that toast, cereal, and eggs are the only foods you can eat for breakfast. Take a tip from the Japanese and Scandinavians, who start the day with fish. Try out some soy products, those breakfast "meats" that look and almost taste like the real thing, with your toast or cereal. And don't forget nuts, so good on top of yogurt or sprinkled over pancakes along with the syrup.

Adding some fish

Anytime is a good time to eat some fish, even as you have your first cup of coffee. The oils in fish are good for the heart in so many ways — from reducing triglycerides and normalizing cholesterol levels to preventing blood clots. However, all these reasons may not be enough to convince you to bite down on a herring early in the morning. If you need more convincing, why not sample the following fish. This list starts with mild fish and builds up to the stronger stuff.

✔ Smoked sable, soft-textured and mild-flavored, sold in delicatessens

✔ Smoked trout, available packaged in the deli section of some supermarkets

✔ Wild Alaskan smoked salmon, the top choice for flavor and omega-3 content

✔ Kippered herring, a hearty favorite of Scotsmen that you may want to try once you get your feet wet with some other fish

✔ Marinated herring in wine with raw onions (see the Scandinavian Mustard-Dill Herring recipe later in this chapter for a recipe that uses a variation of this product)

Bagels and dark, dense rye breads and pumpernickel go well as a neutral background for the richness of the fish. But watch your portion sizes. A half bagel or one slice of bread will do!

Enjoying lower-fat breakfast meats

Sometimes nothing but a piece of crisp bacon or salty breakfast sausage will do as an accompaniment to eggs or waffles, yet such meats can be very high in saturated fat. To solve this dilemma, look for brands of sausage that contain reduced fat, especially turkey sausage. Choose Canadian bacon, which has only a third of the saturated fat you find in regular bacon. And of course, be sure to have only modest portions of these tasty treats.

Soy look-alikes are another option. You need to buy a few different kinds and give these a taste test to find the ones that only minimally remind you of cardboard. I found a brand of soy bacon that cooks up into a very edible treat, especially when combined with fresh, natural ingredients. These products are flavorful and low in fat, contain no cholesterol, and can be very useful in cooking. But remember, soy masquerading as meat is still a highly processed food and not as nutritious as the original soybean.

Giving the nod to nuts

You could do worse than a peanut butter sandwich on whole-grain bread for breakfast. Peanuts as well as other nuts are a concentrated food source of protein, healthy fats and many nutrients. And nuts are also a rich source of the B-complex vitamins, vitamin E, calcium, iron, potassium, magnesium, phosphorus and copper. (For more about the healthy fats in nuts and preferred kinds of nuts to eat, take a look at Chapter 3.) For starters, consider the possible ways of adding peanuts to your diet:

- ✔ Hunt for fresh ground peanut butter, sold at health food stores.
- ✔ Buy only brands of peanut butter that do not contain partially hydrogenated oil, a source of trans fatty acids, which you should avoid.
- ✔ Sprinkle some nuts in pancake and waffle batter before you start the cooking.
- ✔ Scatter nuts on hot cereal, cold cereal, and breakfast fruit-and-yogurt sundaes.

Hearty Recipes for Breakfasts with Protein

The following recipes give you the chance to sample tasty scrambled eggs made with only egg whites and to try your hand at poaching eggs. I also invite you to sample some fish for breakfast when you make the recipe for herring. You may find the flavor of herring a bit too pungent for breakfast, but give it a chance. Such food is a breakfast staple in Scandinavia. And finally, treat yourself to hash browns that also include some soy protein — a meal in itself — a great way to start the day.

Egg-White Scrambled Eggs with Tomato and Feta

Use this quick and easy recipe as a template for making egg-white scrambled eggs. The key is to include ingredients that have exceptional flavor and be sure to add some fat. Egg whites, which are lean and bland, need some help. I tested this recipe adding a fresh August tomato I bought at a farm stand, but at another time of year I can use Roma or cherry tomatoes. The feta cheese, which is so salty and pungent you need only a small amount, balances the acidity of the tomato. Other pairings, such as asparagus and cheddar cheese, work as well.

Preparation time: *5 minutes*

Cooking time: *3 minutes*

Yield: *1 serving*

2 teaspoons unrefined safflower oil	*⅓ cup egg whites, sold in a carton*
1 tablespoon scallions, cut crosswise into ¼-inch slices	*Pepper*
	2 teaspoons feta cheese
⅓ cup diced, seeded fresh tomato	

1 In a small skillet, heat the oil over medium heat. Add the scallions and tomato to the oil long enough to coat them and then add the egg whites. Cook for about 2 minutes, stirring regularly, until the whites start to become firm. Season to taste with pepper.

2 With the heat off, crumble the feta cheese on top of the scrambled egg mixture and cover to melt the cheese a little. Serve immediately.

Per serving: *Calories 152 (From Fat 96); Fat 11g (Saturated 2g); Cholesterol 6mg; Sodium 208mg; Carbohydrate 5g (Dietary Fiber 1g); Protein 10g.*

Mexican Eggs and Canadian Bacon

Try this breakfast dish, a version of huevos rancheros, for a taste of how the day begins in Mexico — with poached eggs nestled in heart-healthy tomato salsa. In this recipe, the eggs are poached the night before to save you time in the morning. Canadian bacon is added to boost the protein.

Preparation time: *15 minutes*

Cooking time: *15 minutes*

Yield: *4 servings*

2 teaspoons white vinegar

½ teaspoon salt

4 eggs

8 slices Canadian bacon

1 cup fresh salsa, drained (available in produce and deli sections of markets), or a good brand of commercial salsa

4 corn tortillas, 6-inches in diameter

1 Fill a deep, small skillet with an inch of water, add the vinegar and salt, and bring to a boil. Lower the heat so that the water barely bubbles. One at a time, break the eggs into a small bowl and slip into the water. Cover the skillet, or start to spoon the water over the eggs. Cook until the white has just set and the yolk has filmed over, 3 to 5 minutes.

2 Remove each egg with a slotted spoon and drain on a paper-towel-covered plate. Keep the eggs warm by covering the plate loosely with aluminum foil.

3 In a nonstick skillet, cook the Canadian bacon until brown, cooking 2½ minutes on each side. Meanwhile warm the salsa in a small pot and heat the tortillas. An easy method of heating the tortillas is to microwave several tortillas stacked on a plate and covered with a paper towel. As you add each tortilla to the stack, dip your fingertips in water and flick some water on the tortilla so that it will steam when heated. Microwave on medium no more than 1 minute to prevent the tortillas from becoming chewy.

4 Assemble each serving by placing 1 tortilla on a warmed plate. Spread almost ¼ cup salsa over the tortilla. On top of this, place 2 slices of the bacon, slightly overlapping. With a slotted spoon, remove 1 egg from the pot and place on top of the bacon. Garnish the eggs with a tablespoon of salsa. Serve immediately.

Tip: *Poached eggs can be cooked the night before and stored, covered, in the refrigerator. To warm the poached eggs, bring water to a gentle simmer in a medium-size pot. Trim any ragged edges from the eggs and, using a slotted spoon, gently lower each into the water. Reheat for 1 minute.*

Go-With: *Nopales, the paddles of the cactus plant, are a great source of soluble fiber, the kind that lowers cholesterol. Look for canned nopales in gourmet and specialty markets. The taste is even better in fresh paddles. Shave off the thorns with a vegetable peeler, cut the flesh into small strips, and simmer in water until tender, about 15 minutes. Nopales taste something like string beans.*

Per serving: *Calories 229 (From Fat 87); Fat 10g (Saturated 3g); Cholesterol 240mg; Sodium 1,118mg; Carbohydrate 16g (Dietary Fiber 2g); Protein 19g.*

⏲ Coddled Eggs with Sautéed Mushrooms

Coddling gently cooks eggs at a moderate temperature and lets you carefully time the cooking of the yolk, to keep it slightly runny and less oxidized. The mushroom-parsley base provides a simple mix of just a few flavors to appeal to a delicate morning appetite, and the mushrooms are also one of the best sources of chromium, a mineral that helps your body manage sugars. Cook the eggs in 3-inch, ovenproof ramekins or use egg coddlers, special containers with tight-fitting lids.

Specialty tools: *Four 3-inch ovenproof ramekins or egg coddlers*

Preparation time: *10 minutes*

Cooking time: *30 minutes*

Yield: *4 servings*

1 teaspoon butter	*2 teaspoons unrefined safflower oil for coating the ramekins*
4 ounces button mushrooms, trimmed and diced	*4 large eggs*
1 tablespoon finely chopped fresh parsley	*4 tablespoons 2 percent milk*
Salt and pepper	

1 Preheat the oven to 350 degrees. Using the corner of a paper towel dipped in oil, wipe the inside of each ramekin to coat the bottom and sides with oil to help prevent the cooked eggs from sticking.

2 Melt the butter in a small skillet set over medium heat and add the mushrooms and parsley. Sauté, stirring occasionally, until the mushrooms soften, 7 minutes. Season to taste with the salt and pepper. Divide the mushroom mixture among 4 ramekins.

3 Crack the eggs, one at a time, into a small bowl and carefully slip each egg into a ramekin. (Cracking the eggs into a bowl first is helpful in case any egg yolks break.) Add 1 tablespoon of the milk to each ramekin. Season with pepper to taste.

4 Cover each filled ramekin with a square of aluminum foil. Set the ramekins in a shallow baking dish and add hot tap water to the dish so that it comes halfway up the sides of the ramekins. Bake for 20 minutes for softly set eggs or longer if you prefer firmer eggs. (After you remove the eggs from the oven, they continue to cook for a minute or two.)

5 Remove the ramekins from the hot-water bath and pat dry. Remove the foil and serve immediately.

Per serving: *Calories 109 (From Fat 65); Fat 7g (Saturated 3g); Cholesterol 246mg; Sodium 314mg; Carbohydrate 3g (Dietary Fiber 0g); Protein 8g.*

☽ Hash Browns with Veggie Bacon

I've received enthusiastic compliments on these savory, lowfat potatoes from people who would never agree knowingly to eat bacon made out of soy.

Specialty tool: *Food processor*

Preparation time: *15 minutes*

Cooking time: *30 minutes*

Yield: *4 servings*

2 large potatoes, Russet or Idaho, peeled	*5 slices soy bacon*
½ medium yellow onion	*¼ teaspoon summer savory*
2 scallions	*Salt and freshly ground black pepper*
1 red bell pepper	*2 tablespoons extra-virgin olive oil*

1 Shred the potatoes by hand, using a metal grater, or use a food processor fitted with a grating disk. This should yield 4 cups of somewhat firmly packed, shredded potatoes. Transfer to a bowl filled with salted water. Set aside for 10 minutes.

2 Trim the yellow onion and cut into thin slices to yield ½ cup. Trim and chop the scallions. Trim the red bell pepper, remove the seeds, and slice into thin strips. Chop the soy bacon. Put all these ingredients in a large bowl. Add the summer savory.

3 In a medium-size skillet, sauté the onion, scallions, red pepper, soy bacon, and summer savory in 1 tablespoon of the olive oil 7 minutes, or until softened. Season with salt and pepper to taste. Set the vegetable mixture aside in a large bowl.

4 Drain the potatoes in a sieve. Holding the potatoes over the sink, tightly squeeze to remove excess moisture. Place on a paper towel to remove additional moisture so the hash browns are more likely to hold together and become crispy. Transfer the potatoes to the bowl containing the vegetable mixture. Toss all ingredients to combine.

5 Put the other tablespoon of oil in a medium (9-inch) nonstick skillet. Add one-half of the potato mixture to the pan. Using a spatula, press down on the vegetables to pack the ingredients. Cook on medium heat for 10 minutes, or until the potatoes begin to turn brown on the bottom.

6 Using a spatula, cut a pie-shape wedge in the potato mixture and turn over to brown the other side. Proceed to cut additional wedges until all the mixture has been turned over. If needed, add more oil during this process. Continue to cook until the vegetables are cooked and the potatoes are brown on the bottom. Season with salt and pepper to taste.

7 Repeat Steps 5 and 6 with the second half of mixture. Enjoy, served hot from the skillet.

Per serving: Calories 251 (From Fat 65); Fat 7g (Saturated 1g); Cholesterol 0mg; Sodium 359mg; Carbohydrate 37g (Dietary Fiber 6g); Protein 11g.

Scandinavian Mustard-Dill Herring

Here is the way Norwegians, Swedes, and Danes start the day — with a helping of marinated herring, an excellent source of omega-3 fatty acids and monounsaturated fats. Herring also contains a generous amount of vitamin D, necessary for the absorption of calcium; vitamin B-12, which helps keep homocysteine levels in check (see Chapter 1 for more about homocysteine); and selenium, the trace mineral that works in tandem with the important antioxidant, vitamin E. To make this dish, you begin with a jar of pickled herring, normally served as an hors d'oeuvre with drinks. The version I bought to test this recipe also contained sliced onions, which make an appetizing addition to the mixture. Onions have an anti-inflammatory effect that protects the heart.

Preparation time: *15 minutes*

Yield: *4 servings*

1 jar (12 ounces) herring in white wine sauce	*2 tablespoons reduced-fat mayonnaise*
1 tablespoon minced fresh dill	*1 teaspoon lemon juice*
1 tablespoon coarse-grained mustard	*Salt and pepper*
3 tablespoons lowfat sour cream	

1 Empty the jar of herring into a sieve and drain. Hold the sieve under the tap and gently rinse the fish with running water to remove the sharp flavor of the marinade.

2 Transfer the herring to a cutting board and cut the fish into narrow strips. Pat dry with paper towels.

3 In a medium-size bowl, put the dill, mustard, sour cream, mayonnaise, and lemon juice. Mix thoroughly to combine. Stir in the herring. Season with salt and pepper to taste and serve with slices of dense rye bread or toasted bagels.

Per serving: Calories 157 (From Fat 118); Fat 13g (Saturated 3g); Cholesterol 13mg; Sodium 277mg; Carbohydrate 4g (Dietary Fiber 0g); Protein 5g. (Analysis does not include bread.)

Chapter 8

Having Breakfast in a Jiffy

In This Chapter

▶ Incorporating fruit in your morning meal

▶ Looking at the benefits of nuts

▶ Preparing quick and easy breakfast dishes

Toast and coffee is a quick breakfast, but it doesn't offer many nutritional benefits. To start your day off with a healthy meal that will see you through until lunch, you need more than that. This chapter gives you some ideas on quick and easy breakfasts. I show you how certain pick-up-and-eat foods, such as fruit and nuts, and morsels such as last night's dessert, can be the basis for ways to reinvent breakfast. Begin to think outside the box — the cereal box that is — and you'll be surprised how many breakfast food options you have.

Eating even a small amount of nutritious food at home is far better for you and your heart than swinging by a fast food place for a high-calorie, high-sodium, refined-foods meal on your way to work. Having a nourishing breakfast at home also helps reduce the allure of a mid-morning pastry snack from the vending machine.

If having suspect breakfast foods has been your way of life, simply switching to eating a wholesome breakfast will give you more lasting energy and may even help you lose weight. You'd be surprised how little time it takes to prepare a good breakfast, if you plan ahead.

Grabbing a Piece of Fruit

Research shows that making the effort to eat more fruit, as well as vegetables, can lower the risk of heart attack as well as stroke. This is the conclusion of a National Health and Nutrition Examination survey conducted by Tulane University School of Public Health and the National Institutes of Health, published in the *American Journal of Clinical Nutrition* in 2002. Consuming as little as 3 or more portions of fruits and vegetables a day reduced the risk of fatal heart attack or stroke compared with individuals who ate less than 1 serving of fruit or vegetables a day. (The U.S. Department of Agriculture recommends a minimum of 5 daily servings of fruit and vegetables as a general guideline for Americans.)

Make fruit at breakfast a habit, an easy way to increase your fruit intake.

Thank heavens for the banana, the eat-on-the run breakfast food that comes in its own natural package. But don't stop there when looking for breakfast fruits. Stock up on all the delectable, sweet fruits in the market that are an essential part of a healthy diet. Make a habit of eating fruit that supplies you with soluble fiber, the kind that lowers cholesterol, starting with apples and pears. Peaches, plums, and bananas are also a good source. And be sure to choose the most colorful fruit because the pigments also function as nutrients (see Chapter 2). For instance, golden-reddish-orangey fruit, such as cantaloupe, persimmons, and apricots, are a great source of beta carotene, an antioxidant that protects cholesterol and arteries. And when you have a choice at the market, buy pink grapefruit, blood oranges, and dark purple grapes rather than less richly colored versions.

Squeeze a little fresh lemon or lime juice over melon to spark the flavor.

Treat yourself to a kiwi, just the right amount for a breakfast portion. It's full of vitamin C, which your body must have in order to convert cholesterol into bile acids that can then be eliminated from the system. Other great sources of vitamin C, besides citrus (which you know all about by now), are berries, melons, and tropical fruit such as guava, papayas, and mangoes. What, you don't buy mangoes because you don't know how to get at them? Check out Figure 8-1, which shows you how to avoid the mango's single, enormous seed while you cut off all the part you want to eat. Wait until you see a slice of diced mango with the skin turned inside out. Very fancy!

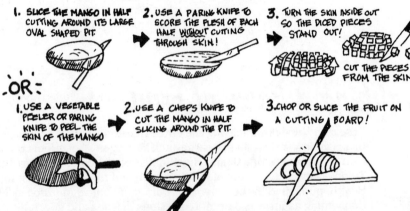

Figure 8-1:
Two
different
ways to cut
a mango.

Go for a variety of fruit to make sure you benefit from a range of nutrients. If you haven't had, for instance, fresh pineapple for a while, it's time!

Raw fruit is much better than cooked. Heat significantly damages the antioxidant capacity of fruit.

Berry, berry good for you

Berries, fruit that sports the colors of royalty, are great for breakfast, handy to eat by the spoonful, on their own, or on top of cereal. But these fruits also have a lot more going for them. The pigments themselves are powerful antioxidants. When you consume colorful berries, these nutrients go to work, protecting your "bad" LDL cholesterol from oxidation so that plaque is less likely to accumulate in arteries. (Chapter 2 tells you more about these heart-healthy colors.) Berries also contain phytonutrients that dampen chronic inflammation, which can contribute to coronary artery disease.

Fresh berries can be very expensive, especially when you buy them as specialty items out of season. However, considering the nutrients they provide, they're a bargain. Many markets also sell frozen berries, often less expensive and still full of nutrients, as the berries are frozen soon after harvesting. Be sure to skip the frozen berries that come in heavy, sugary syrup, to avoid excess and empty calories.

Whenever possible, buy organic berries, fresh and frozen. Berries are high on the list of produce that is a source of pesticides in the diet. And at minimum, be sure to gently but thoroughly wash berries. Do this just before eating. Washing berries and then storing them causes them to become waterlogged.

Here are some berries to put on your breakfast menu:

- **Blueberries** have more antioxidant power than any other fruit or vegetable, containing over two dozen phytonutrient pigments that join forces to quench free radicals. Blueberries also provide modest amounts of vitamin C, folate, potassium, and vitamin A. You find fresh blueberries in markets from May to October.

- **Blackberries** have almost as much antioxidant activity as blueberries. They're also a fairly good source of vitamin C, folate, vitamin E, potassium, and magnesium and an excellent source of manganese. Shop for fresh blackberries May through September.

- **Strawberries** contain about a third less of the antioxidant pigments as the berries that are bluer, but they still have more than other kinds of fruit. They also provide vitamin C and some folate and potassium. Although strawberries are available in stores year-round, for the best flavor, enjoy them fresh in their peak season, April to June.

✔ **Raspberries** are a close fourth for antioxidant power and, like other berries, are a good source of vitamin C and folate. They also provide more fiber than most other fruits. Fresh raspberries are sold year-round, but peak harvests are in June and early September.

To store delicate berries, such as raspberries, place unwashed berries in a single layer in a shallow pan lined with paper towels, and store them in the refrigerator.

Whole fruit versus juice

Don't rely on fruit juice as your prime source of this major food category. Whole fruit is the only source that gives you all the fiber and nutrients you need, in the right combination. By comparison, juice is processed fruit, missing fiber and some nutrients. (Turn to Chapter 2 for details about specific fruits and what they provide.)

Sliced oranges are more nutritious than orange juice. Both are a good source of vitamin C, but orange slices also give you valuable fiber and bioflavonoids, vitamins found in the pith and membranes of the orange. Bioflavonoids are especially concentrated in that white, soft stem that runs through the core. Bioflavonoids strengthen capillary walls.

When you want orange juice, squeeze your own. It's likely to include some pulp along with pith and membranes, or buy the home-style kind that contains a mixture of pulp and pith. Orange juice is a great choice when you want fruit juice because it's a good source of potassium and B vitamins.

Instant fruit combos

For something a little different to start your day, cut up a couple kinds of fruit, add some nuts or an herb, and toss them together. Choose contrasting flavors, textures, and colors. Or combine a fruit with a small piece of cheese. Here are some ideas to get you started:

✔ Strawberries and bananas

✔ Blueberries and pears

✔ Yellow apple, red grapes, and almonds

✔ Peaches and mint

✔ Applesauce and a wedge of lowfat cheddar cheese

Concord grape juice is a terrific source of antioxidants (see Chapter 2) and flavonoids, the nutrients given credit for the heart-healthy effects of red wine. Now research shows that consuming the nonalcoholic version of grape juice is also a good idea. Consuming just two cupfuls a day can be beneficial, as shown in research conducted at the University of Wisconsin Medical School in 1999. When 15 adults with coronary artery disease consumed 12 to 16 ounces of purple grape juice daily for two weeks, researchers observed a significant reduction in the susceptibility of LDL cholesterol to oxidize and an improvement in the elasticity of arteries. Atherosclerosis, also known as hardening of the arteries, is less likely to develop in such an environment. In addition, grape juice slows the activity of blood platelets, reducing the risk of a blood clot.

Be sure to read carefully the labels of commercial fruit juice before you take some home. Here's a checklist of what to look for and avoid:

✔ Select products that are made of 100 percent juice.

✔ Avoid juice that contains high-fructose corn syrup, an added sweetener that provides calories but not nutrients.

✔ Stay away from bottled juices that are labeled "fruit drink." They look like the real thing (in which the pigments are also antioxidants), but the juice drinks contain artificial colors that do not function as nutrients.

If you come across 100 percent cherry juice or 100 percent pomegranate juice, give these luxury juices a try. These fruits come to market only in certain months, cherries from May through August and pomegranates in November and December, and when they're out of season, the juice is a smart alternative. Both richly colored juices help prevent heart disease. A study published in the *American Journal of Clinical Nutrition* in 2000 documents several ways in which the antioxidant activity of pomegranate juice blocks the development of atherosclerosis. And the reddish-blue pigments in cherries have been shown to have an anti-inflammatory effect. Chronic inflammation of the arteries (see Chapter 1) can contribute to the build-up of plaque. And drinking these juices is a lot easier than dealing with the cherry and pomegranate seeds in the fruits.

The body absorbs fruit juice readily, causing a rapid rise in blood sugar. A spike in blood sugar can lead to an increase in risk factors for heart disease. (See Chapter 1 for more information.) To counteract this, have only small amounts of fruit juice at a time, about a half cup, especially if you're not consuming solid food at the same time. If you want more liquid, dilute the juice with water or seltzer. Also, drink fruit juice slowly, so it takes the same amount of time to consume as if you were slowly eating the actual piece of fruit.

As a general rule, ¾ cup of juice equals about 1 piece of fruit.

Starting Your Day the Nutty Way

People have been told so long to stay away from fat that many have cut way back on the amount of nuts they eat and feel guilty when they do have a few almonds or peanuts. Indeed, fat contributes 73 percent to 90 percent of the calories in nuts. Yet nuts deserve to be staples in your kitchen because they supply protein, healthy fats, and many nutrients. (See Chapters 3, 6, and 19 for details. I'm really in to nuts if you couldn't tell.)

By the way, seeds such as sunflower and sesame are also loaded with nutrients. They contain all the major building blocks (proteins, unsaturated fats, and a wide range of vitamins and minerals) of the plant they have the potential to sprout. Edible seeds, such as sesame, sunflower, and pumpkin, provide B complex vitamins; vitamins A, D, and E; calcium; iron; potassium; magnesium; and zinc. In particular, sunflower seeds contain up to 50 percent protein, and sesame seeds are high in calcium. Enjoy them raw, dried, roasted, or cooked and eaten as snacks or tossed into salads, soups, and baked goods.

Unhulled seeds have a long shelf life, kept in a cool, dry place in a tightly covered container, but hulled seeds need to be stored refrigerated, in a tightly covered container, and used up in a couple weeks.

Exploring the benefits of nuts

Peanuts, almonds, and English walnuts are the most frequently consumed nuts, with hazelnuts, cashews, and pistachios next in popularity. Nuts are just what the heart needs, for the following reasons:

- ✔ The commonly favored nuts — peanuts, almonds, and walnuts — are good for you because they're high in polyunsaturated fat and low in saturated fat. Walnuts are a premier source of omega-3 fatty acids, another good thing.

- ✔ Many nuts are very high in monounsaturated fats, the cornerstone of the Mediterranean diet, which is associated with a lower risk of heart disease: Peanuts contain 49 percent; almonds, 65 percent; English walnuts, 23 percent; and hazelnuts, 78 percent.

- ✔ In a small study, conducted in conjunction with the University of Toronto and St. Michael's Hospital in Toronto and published in the journal *Circulation* in 2002, snacking on almonds had positive results for healthy individuals with elevated cholesterol: Participants consuming just 1 ounce of almonds per day experienced significant reductions in the unhealthy LDL cholesterol and an improvement in the LDL:HDL ratio. Even greater improvements in cholesterol levels were seen in those consuming 2½ ounces of almonds a day, and these individuals also had a reduction in oxidized cholesterol.

✔ Most nuts contain a good amount of *arginine,* an amino acid that that the body uses as a building block to manufacture nitric oxide. Nitric oxide is a potent compound that dilates blood vessels, helping to prevent a blockage in arteries that could trigger a heart attack.

✔ Most nuts are rich in a compound that widens arteries and inhibits clot formation.

✔ Nuts are excellent sources of magnesium, copper, folic acid, potassium, and vitamin E.

Adding an ounce of prevention to your breakfast

You benefit from eating nuts even when you have just a small amount. In the Nurses' Health Study, begun in 1976 in association with the Harvard School of Public Health and Brigham and Women's Hospital, 1 ounce of nuts was considered a serving, not much if you really start nibbling. Yet women who ate more than 5 servings a week had a significantly lower risk of coronary heart disease than women who rarely ate nuts (see Chapter 3). So make this amount part of your daily breakfast regimen. Nuts taste great on all sorts of breakfast foods, from hot and cold cereal to yogurt sundaes. (See the Strawberry-Blueberry Sundae recipe in this chapter.) Of course, the benefits don't increase indefinitely as you eat more nuts. They are still very fatty foods, so enjoy them in moderation.

One ounce of nuts is a small handful, about 6 walnut halves, 14 almonds, or enough peanut butter to smear on a piece of toast, about 2 tablespoons.

Maybe you prefer to get your quota of daily nuts from nut butter. If so, browse through the nut section of a natural foods store, and you can find a luxurious assortment of nut butters, including delectable roasted almond and cashew. Or stay with classic peanut butter, but be sure to read labels. Don't buy a peanut butter if the ingredient list includes added sugars or partially hydrogenated oils.

If the oil has separated and is sitting on the top of the nut butter, don't pour it off. This oil is a good source of polyunsaturated fatty acids (see Chapter 3). After you stir the oil into your nut butter, store the jar in the refrigerator, and the oil won't separate.

Preparing Breakfast in Your Sleep (Well, Almost)

Even if you wake up in a fog, some breakfasts are so quick and easy to put together that you can still give yourself something decent to eat. Here are some suggestions:

- ✔ Try canned kidney beans (not sugary baked beans) on rye toast. Warm the beans in a small pot set over medium heat, stirring occasionally, and spoon the heated beans over the toast. Beans on toast is a time-honored British breakfast favorite and is jolly good. Having a cup a day of cooked beans can raise your HDL level and lower your LDL level, because beans are a low glycemic index carbohydrate and contain fiber, particularly soluble pectin (see Chapter 2 for more on pectin).

- ✔ Start the day with whole rolled oat porridge that you cooked the night before. The oats taste fine the next morning if you heat them in the microwave. If you're committed to eating rolled oats for their soluble fiber every day, this strategy lets you bring them to the table in record time, day after day.

Stay away from instant hot breakfast cereals, which rapidly raise blood sugar.

- ✔ Whip up a shake in a blender. Start with 2 large serving spoons of lowfat yogurt and add a cup of fruit, a couple tablespoons of soy protein, and ¼ cup fruit juice.

- ✔ If you don't want bread, spread nut butter on slices of apple and pear.

Quick-and-Easy Breakfast Recipes

In addition to the recipes presented here, other recipes in this cookbook are quite acceptable for breakfast. After exploring the delicious recipes here, take a look at all the dessert recipes in Chapters 19 and 20. Instead of being tempted by Danish pastry, have a slice of nutritious Banana-Date Tea Loaf (see Chapter 20) instead. Even the Chewy Oatmeal Cookies with Currants (also in Chapter 20) are an acceptable breakfast along with your cup of coffee. If a serving is fine for dessert after supper, it also can fit into a cholesterol-controlling diet 12 hours later!

☕ Ready-Made Waffles with Walnut-Pear Sauce

Use sauces to dress up ready-made grain items, such as the frozen waffles in this recipe. This timesaving product is ideal for quick breakfasts, and the sauce gives you a means of adding special, healthy ingredients.

Preparation time: *2 minutes*

Cooking time: *5 minutes*

Yield: *1 serving*

¼ cup chopped walnuts

½ cup pears, cored and diced

1 teaspoon grated fresh gingerroot

2 tablespoons pure maple syrup

2 frozen waffles, preferably plain flavor

1 Put the walnuts in a small skillet over medium heat and toast, stirring occasionally, until they begin to brown and become aromatic, about 5 to 6 minutes.

2 Immediately add the pears and gingerroot and stir to combine. Add the maple syrup and cook the mixture for 30 seconds, reducing the maple syrup somewhat. Remove from the heat.

3 Toast the waffles. Serve topped with the Walnut-Pear Sauce.

Per serving: *Calories 525 (From Fat 229); Fat 25g (Saturated 3g); Cholesterol 16mg; Sodium 524mg; Carbohydrate 71g (Dietary Fiber 6g); Protein 9g.*

Polenta Rounds with Basil Tomato Sauce

The classic way of preparing polenta is to add it to a pot of boiling water and stir the mixture continuously for the better part of an hour, adding more hot water if necessary, until the grain has absorbed the liquid and is thoroughly cooked. Polenta has superior flavor, which can be yours to enjoy at breakfast if you make the polenta the night before. Follow the instructions on the package and pour the cooked, thick polenta into a loaf pan. Then when you're ready for breakfast, just cut off a slice. Alternatively, buy one of those handy tubes of polenta, packaged in see-through wrapping, that you can find in supermarkets in the grain section of the aisles. Cut off slices of the ready-made polenta to make this recipe.

Preparation time: *5 minutes*

Cooking time: *10 minutes*

Yield: *4 servings*

4 teaspoons extra-virgin olive oil

1 package (24 ounces) ready-made polenta, cut into 8 to 10 slices

1 can (15 ounces) stewed tomatoes, cut into small chunks if necessary

¼ cup loosely-packed fresh basil leaves, cut into strips

Salt and pepper

1 Using 2 large skillets, set over medium-high heat, add 2 teaspoons of olive oil to each. Arrange one-half of the polenta slices in each skillet and cook until the undersurface begins to brown, about 7 minutes. Lower the heat slightly if the oil begins to spatter.

2 Meanwhile, put the stewed tomatoes and basil in a small saucepan. Cook, covered, over medium heat to desired consistency. Season with salt and pepper.

3 Using a spatula, turn over the polenta slices and cook an additional 5 minutes.

4 To serve, distribute polenta slices on serving plates and spoon the heated tomato sauce over each serving.

Tip: I recommend using the plain-flavored ready-made polenta rather than the sun-dried tomato version, which can have an overly pungent, artificial taste.

Tip: If you like your polenta crispier, you can cook it for as long as 12 to 14 minutes per side, depending on the heat distribution in the pan.

Per serving: Calories 196 (From Fat 41); Fat 5g (Saturated 1g); Cholesterol 0mg; Sodium 977mg; Carbohydrate 35g (Dietary Fiber 4g); Protein 4g.

Savory Fish and Egg White Scramble

Consuming as little as 1 ounce of fish a day was associated with a 50 percent lower risk in fatal coronary heart disease, according to a 20-year follow-up study of men conducted in the town of Zutphen in the Netherlands and published in the *New England Journal of Medicine* in 1985. This egg recipe gives you a tasty way to get this benefit in your breakfast. Whole-egg omelets aren't recommended on a cholesterol-controlling diet, because the high heat oxidizes the cholesterol in the egg yolk, making it sticky and more likely to promote the formation of plaque on artery walls. All-egg-white omelets don't have this problem. And mixing them with fish adds a richness that the missing yolk once provided.

Preparation time: *2 minutes*

Cooking time: *5 minutes*

Yield: *1 serving*

1 ounce white fish, smoked trout, or fish such as halibut, left over from last night's dinner	*Leaves of 1 sprig parsley, chopped*
1 teaspoon unrefined safflower oil	*Whites of 2 large eggs, or 6 tablespoons 100% liquid egg whites (see the tip at the end of the recipe)*
Pepper	

1 Crumble the fish into small bits. Heat the safflower oil in an omelet pan and add the fish. Heat the fish on medium heat for 2 minutes, stirring occasionally. Season with pepper to taste.

2 Add the parsley and pour the egg white over the fish. Gather the whites around the fish as they begin to set. After about 2 minutes, using a spatula, flip the egg mixture and cook an additional minute. The egg is cooked when it becomes opaque but still has the tenderness of custard. Serve immediately.

Tip: *You can find 100 percent liquid egg whites in the refrigerator section of supermarkets.*

Vary It! *For an elegant touch, as the omelet is cooking, toast thin rye bread cut from a square loaf. Then cut the toast into 4 equal triangles to create toast points as a garnish for the dish.*

Per serving: *Calories 131 (From Fat 60); Fat 7g (Saturated 1g); Cholesterol 22mg; Sodium 152mg; Carbohydrate 1g (Dietary Fiber 0g); Protein 16g.*

☙ Strawberry-Blueberry Sundae

What a fun way to eat foods that are good for you — layered in a sundae. Try this recipe to taste how berries, yogurt, cereal, and sliced almonds all come together. Then invent your own breakfast dessert. Be sure to use Grape-Nuts, one of the few cereals without added sweeteners or partially hydrogenated oils. The prime ingredients in this product are whole wheat, a nutritious whole grain, and barley, a source of soluble fiber.

Preparation time: *5 minutes*

Yield: *1 serving*

4 strawberries, hulled and cut in half	*¼ cup blueberries*
6 tablespoons plain lowfat yogurt	*1 tablespoon sliced almonds, preferably toasted*
¼ cup Grape-Nuts cereal	

1 Place 2 halved strawberries in the bottom of a parfait glass or a stemmed water glass that flares at the top.

2 Add 3 tablespoons of the yogurt and top with the cereal.

3 Add the blueberries and the remaining 3 tablespoons yogurt.

4 Top with the remaining 2 halved strawberries and sprinkle with the almonds.

Per serving: *Calories 255 (From Fat 62); Fat 7g (Saturated 2g); Cholesterol 6mg; Sodium 244mg; Carbohydrate 42g (Dietary Fiber 6g); Protein 11g.*

☙ Meal in a Muffin

The purpose of this recipe is to include as many healthy ingredients as possible to produce a highly nourishing morsel. The soy flour and egg whites provide protein, the oat flour and bran supply soluble fiber, and the walnuts and safflower oil give you essential fatty acids. For a nutritious breakfast on the run, pick up one or two of these muffins in the morning as you head out the door.

Preparation time: *20 minutes*

Baking time: *35 minutes*

Yield: *12 muffins*

1 cup whole-wheat flour

½ cup oat flour

½ cup soy flour

2 teaspoons double-acting baking powder

½ teaspoon baking soda

½ teaspoon allspice

¼ teaspoon salt

3 tablespoons oat bran

½ cup walnuts, chopped

1½ cups lowfat plain yogurt

White of 1 large egg or 3 tablespoons 100 percent liquid egg white

3 tablespoons unrefined safflower oil

2 tablespoons honey

4 tablespoons 100 percent fruit spread

1 Preheat the oven to 375 degrees.

2 Sift together in a large bowl the wheat flour, oat flour, soy flour, baking powder, baking soda, allspice, and salt. Add the oat bran and walnuts and stir to incorporate.

3 Put the yogurt, egg white, safflower oil, and honey in a bowl and stir to combine.

4 Make a well in the center of the flour mixture and pour in the yogurt mixture. Stir to moisten the flour and thoroughly mix.

5 Place paper muffin cup liners in a muffin baking tin. Spoon some of the batter, which will be stiff, into each muffin cup, filling it two-thirds full. Place a teaspoon of the fruit spread on top in the middle, pressing it into the batter. Cover with a second spoonful of batter, distributing the batter equally among the muffins.

6 Bake the muffins until the tops are golden brown, about 35 minutes.

Tip: *If you prefer a sweeter, richer-tasting muffin, substitute blackstrap molasses or maple syrup for the honey and add ¼ cup raisins or chopped dates.*

Vary It! *If you don't eat wheat, make these muffins with flour made from spelt, an ancient form of wheat that for many people is less allergenic. It behaves the same as modern wheat in baking.*

Per serving: Calories 160 (From Fat 61); Fat 7g (Saturated 1g); Cholesterol 2mg; Sodium 193mg; Carbohydrate 21g (Dietary Fiber 3g); Protein 6g.

Part III
Making Your Day with Heart-Healthy Starters

The 5th Wave   By Rich Tennant

GOURMET LOW CHOLESTEROL COOKING

"Henry! Your apple's ready!"

In this part . . .

As I recipe tested the soups, salads, and party foods
in this part, I pictured you right there with me. Now
it's your turn to do the cooking, but I'm still here in the
chatty sections in and around the recipes.

I give you guidelines for making stock and suggest special
cholesterol-lowering ingredients to toss into the pot as
you prepare the various soups. I help you assemble salads
in the same way. I explain why you want to favor the most
colorful ingredients (that means they're full of phytonutrients) and offer advice on turning out some gorgeous
dishes. The final chapter in this part gives you recipes
designed for entertaining. (Yes, you can control your
cholesterol and have good party fare at the same time!)
I waltz you through prepping crunchies and munchies
that your heart — and your guests — will love.

Chapter 9

Preparing Soup, Simple and Hearty

In This Chapter

▶ Starting out right with richly flavored stock

▶ Adding cholesterol-controlling ingredients

▶ Serving meal-in-a-pot soups

▶ Inventing soups with ready-made foods

*I*f you can boil water, you can make soup. Think of soup as just water with a few added ingredients. Making soup is simple — precise measuring not required. And it doesn't take as much time and effort as you might expect because you don't have to watch the pot!

This chapter includes everything from simple first-course soup offerings to soups that are a meal in themselves. These soups are short on fat and long on flavor and leave room for invention. Do some experimenting. You can't go wrong with soup!

There's nothing wrong with canned soup in a pinch. For a quick lunch, a bowl of canned lentil soup is a better for the heart than a slice of pizza. But be sure to buy low-sodium soups if you're sensitive to sodium, which can elevate blood pressure. Also favor lowfat and fat-free items to reduce calories and always avoid soup products made with hydrogenated oils that behave like saturated fat in the body. Check the ingredient list on labels for contents.

Begin at the Beginning: Developing a Tasty Stock

A *stock* is a liquid in which certain ingredients have been cooked and then strained out. The goal is to make sure that the flavor of the added ingredients transfers to the stock. But that's not all that ends up in the liquid. Vitamins and minerals also migrate from the ingredients to make a healthy, nutritious brew. Bones contribute calcium, needed to maintain a normal heartbeat; carrots contribute beta carotene, an antioxidant; and onions provide the phytonutrient quercitin, which dampens inflammation (see Chapter 1). And stock that is well skimmed is an excellent substitute for fat in certain dishes, providing concentrated flavor without the calories. For instance, instead of sautéing vegetables, such as sliced zucchini or string beans, in oil, cook them in a small amount of savory stock.

Add a teaspoon of apple cider or other types of vinegar to stock ingredients to extract more minerals from the bones during cooking.

Beef stock, too, is very handy when you want the robust flavor of meat in a soup or casserole dish, but without the saturated fat. In making beef stock, start with beef shank or chuck and marrow bones, and be sure to first brown both in the pot to develop rich flavor.

Fish stock has more limited uses, destined only for fish dishes, but in these, a full flavored stock can guarantee that the fish you're cooking turns out as satisfying as one covered in cream sauce. To make fish stock, start with fish trimming and add some vegetables, such as onion, carrot, and celery, and seasonings like parsley, bay leaves, and peppercorns, plus white wine and a squeeze of lemon juice. Simmer for one hour. All these various stocks are valuable ingredients when cooking for low cholesterol.

Supermarkets sell canned chicken and beef broth. A broth is made by cooking poultry or meat in water, while a stock is made with other ingredients, such as vegetables. Canned broth successfully replaces homemade stock in recipes, especially when you add some flavorful vegetables and herbs.

Read on to find out how to make various stocks that are very tasty while relatively low in fat. Use these in the cholesterol-controlling soup recipes in this chapter or serve stock as a light and appetizing starter to a meal.

Creating vegetable stock

This light, fresh-tasting stock can add complexity to the flavors of bean and vegetable soups and is essential when preparing vegetarian recipes. To make vegetable stock, start with finely chopped vegetables, which will cook quickly. Bring to a boil in water and simmer for ½ hour or more, until the vegetables are very tender. Use vegetable stock in dishes with short cooking times to keep the flavor of stock from deteriorating. For instance, vegetable stock is a good choice for the cooking liquid when preparing rice.

Onions, carrots, and celery are a must for making vegetable stock and are standards in chicken and beef stock as well. You can also add other vegetables, but do so with care.

Think twice before adding veggies that will dominate flavor or color the stock. The taste of cabbage is just what you want in borscht, but probably unwelcome in pea soup. Add the following veggies with caution: cabbage, broccoli, cauliflower, spinach, parsnips, turnips, asparagus, beets, and garlic.

A good vegetable stock also calls for sprigs of fresh herbs such as parsley, thyme, a small bay leaf, and a single clove. Other options include marjoram, chervil, or a slice of fresh ginger. The French romantically call this little bunch of herbs a *bouquet garni.*

Virtually any stock, including vegetable, can benefit from the addition of the rich flavor of mushrooms. Use whole mushrooms or just the trimmed stems from mushrooms you've prepared for another dish. Better yet, use dried ones, which are easy to keep on hand because they store for months. Instead of the pricey dried mushrooms sold in upscale supermarkets, look for bargain black mushrooms in Chinese markets. These mushrooms are dried shiitakes, shown in studies to lower cholesterol because of a specific amino acid they contain that helps speed up the processing of cholesterol in the liver.

Fresh-made vegetable stock can provide a savory and robust setting especially suited for grains, beans, and a recipe's featured vegetables. The following procedures are all designed to ensure that you cook with the tastiest vegetables, developing and extracting their flavors to the max.

✔ **Use vegetables that are mature but not old and, ideally, in season.**
  Check Chapter 15 for information about what to look for when you shop
  for fresh produce.

✔ **Sauté or roast vegetables before adding them to the pot.** Cook the vegetables until they begin to brown to ensure rich flavor and deepen the color of the stock.

✔ **Purée vegetables before adding to the water.** When you *purée* vegetables, you finely mash them to a smooth, thick consistency. Press well-cooked vegetables through a sieve or purée them by using a blender or a food processor fitted with a metal blade.

✔ **Begin cooking vegetables and meats in cold water.** This method draws juices from these foods and extracts the most flavor.

✔ **When straining out vegetables from a finished stock, press them against the sieve with the back of a spoon.** By pressing the vegetables, you can release more of the juices. The final broth will be less clear but more flavorful.

○ *Roasted Vegetable Stock*

Roasting vegetables to be used in stock adds another prep step that requires little effort. But the flavor pay-off is big, reducing the need for salt and fat in the final dish.

Preparation time: *15 minutes*

Cooking time: *1½ hours*

Yield: *3 quarts (12 servings of 1 cup each)*

2 large onions, quartered but not peeled	*5 sprigs parsley*
4 carrots, peeled and roughly cut	*2 sprigs fresh thyme*
2 celery stalks, roughly cut	*10 peppercorns*
2 parsnips, peeled and roughly cut	*½ cup white wine (optional)*
6 cloves garlic, peeled (optional)	*2 quarts (8 cups) water, plus 4 additional cups water*
2 tablespoons extra-virgin olive oil	

1 Preheat the oven to 400 degrees. Place the onions, carrots, celery, parsnips, and garlic (if desired) in a 9-x-12 inch roasting pan. Drizzle with the olive oil and put the pan in the oven.

2 Roast, shaking the pan occasionally and turning the ingredients once or twice until the vegetables are nicely browned, about 45 minutes.

3 Using a slotted spoon, transfer all the ingredients to a stockpot. Add the parsley, thyme, peppercorns, white wine, if desired, and 2 quarts of the water.

4 Add a cup or two of water to the roasting pan and, using a large spoon, mix it around, loosening the bits of vegetables that have stuck to the bottom. Pour this mixture into the stockpot along with the remaining water.

5 Bring the contents of the stockpot just about to a boil, partially cover, and adjust the heat so the mixture sends up a few bubbles at a time. Cook until the vegetables are soft, 30 to 45 minutes.

6 Strain, pressing the vegetables to extract as much juice as possible. The stock is now ready to use in other recipes, such as the liquid for cooking grains or as the base for a soup.

Tip: Stock keeps fresh 1 to 2 days, but you can extend its refrigerator life if you boil it after 2 days to destroy any bacterial growth. If there is a layer of fat on top of the stock, don't skim it until you're ready to use the broth. The fat helps protect the stock. You can also freeze stock, which will keep 4 to 6 months at 0 degrees. Pack it in recipe-size quantities, using small containers so they can be filled nearly to the top. In this case, remove the fat before storing, as it tends to turn rancid even at very low temperatures.

Per serving: Calories 24 (From Fat 20); Fat 2g (Saturated 0g); Cholesterol 0mg; Sodium 3mg; Carbohydrates 1g (Dietary Fiber 0g); Protein 0g.

Preparing chicken stock

You can derive a certain amount of satisfaction when you know that you have homemade chicken stock on hand, a nicety of a well-stocked kitchen. When you're in the mood for soup, you already have a basic ingredient, one you can trust for quality and content. Now please believe me when I say that making your own chicken stock isn't a big deal. You can make stock just in the process of cooking chicken, which if you're like me, you do at least once a week.

Basic Chicken Stock

This recipe makes use of the classic ingredients of chicken stock. But in actuality, only the onion and bay leaf are essential in a savory chicken broth.

Preparation time: 15 minutes

Cooking time: 1½ hours

Yield: 3 quarts (12 servings of 1 cup each)

1 whole 3- to 4-pound chicken, rinsed	1 sprig fresh thyme or a pinch of dried thyme
1 onion, roughly cut, not peeled	1 small bay leaf
1 carrot, roughly cut	Several sprigs fresh parsley
1 small stalk celery, roughly cut	1 teaspoon salt
1 teaspoon apple cider vinegar	3½ quarts (14 cups) water

1 To shorten the cooking time, cut the chicken into parts.

2 In a stockpot, combine the chicken, onion, carrot, celery, vinegar, thyme, bay leaf, parsley, and salt. Add the water.

3 Bring almost to a boil, partially cover the pot, and adjust the heat so the mixture sends up a few bubbles at a time. Cook for 1½ hours, until the stock is richly flavored.

4 Using tongs, remove the chicken from the pot and set aside. Strain the stock, pressing on the vegetables to extract as much juice as possible. Taste and add more salt if necessary.

5 Refrigerate the stock overnight so the broth congeals and the fat rises to the top. Before using the stock, use a spoon to skim the chicken fat from the surface and discard.

Vary It! To make beef stock, substitute meaty beef bones, such as shank, shin, or short ribs. Add a couple parsnips, a few sprigs more parsley, a couple cloves, 10 peppercorns, and more water if necessary. Cook for at least 3 hours.

Per serving: Calories 13 (From Fat 7); Fat 1g (Saturated 0g); Cholesterol 3g; Sodium 198mg Carbohydrates 0g (Dietary Fiber 0g); Protein 1g.

Chicken broth from scratch

Gourmet cooks can prepare a chicken broth, using a whole chicken, along with vegetables and herbs. You cook these ingredients for three hours or more and then discard the ingredients now robbed of their flavor and nutrients. An extra-rich chicken broth is the result. But if you can't bear to throw out what looks like food and you need a chicken stock in quicker time, there's an alternative. Try the recipe for Basic Chicken Stock, which yields stewed chicken, too.

Minimizing the saturated fat to lower cholesterol

Poultry and meats contain saturated fat, but you can prevent most of it from ending up in your stock. Follow these three easy tips to cut the fat and your cholesterol.

- ✔ Start with less fat in the first place, trimming the fat on all meats.

- ✔ In cooking stock, take care that the liquid doesn't reach a full boil. All that bubbling makes it easier for the molecules of fat to mix with the molecules of water. Fat that is dispersed like that is difficult to remove.

- ✔ When the stock is finished cooking, you can follow the process shown in Figure 9-1 to remove any excess fat.

Figure 9-1: Cutting fat from your soup stock.

You can also keep some frozen homemade stock on hand and use it to replace salt or butter for a more heart healthy recipe. Simply follow these easy steps:

1. **Reduce a stock until it's highly concentrated.**

2. **Freeze it in an ice cube tray.**

3. **Transfer the stock cubes to a freezer bag.**

4. **To enhance the flavor, pop a couple of cubes into the dish you're preparing — they replace ½ teaspoon of salt.**

Basing Your Soup on Heart-Healthy Ingredients

Select one of the cholesterol-controlling foods presented in Chapter 2 and build a soup around it. Add stock, flavorings, and a little garnish. This is the way I invented the recipe for carrot soup in this section. Or, you can cook up some standard soup favorite, such as onion soup or lentil soup, which feature some of the recommended vegetables and legumes. I also include yummy recipes for each of these.

You can also add heart-healthy foods not part of the original ingredients and not ruin the flavor. Vegetable soup welcomes lentils and beans. Root vegetables, barley, and rice enhance turkey soup. These add-ons and others can make a good-for-you soup even healthier for your heart and add an amusing twist to an old recipe.

Featuring soluble fiber

All manner of legumes — beans, lentils, and peas — contain soluble fiber, as do certain grains and vegetables. Check the list of soluble fiber foods in Chapter 2 and consider these intriguing options you may have overlooked as ingredients for your soups:

- Apples
- Barley
- Brown rice
- Cannellini beans
- Lentils, red or green
- Lima beans
- Nopales (cactus paddles)
- Okra
- Pears
- Soybeans, whole fresh
- Sweet potatoes

Onion soup to the rescue

Would you ever have imagined that savory, soul-satisfying onion soup is health food? Well it is, thanks to the ability of compounds in onions, which have an anti-inflammatory effect on tissues. That's good news because it's now becoming evident that inflammation plays a role in the development of heart disease. You didn't know that? For details about how this works, see Chapter 1. Although classic French onion soup relies on butter and a generous topping of cheese, the version in this chapter relies on olive oil, red wine (which provides antioxidants), garlic (which also dampens inflammation), and less of the cheese typically called for, mellow Gruyère.

Tucking in some vitamins and minerals

Folic acid, vitamin B6, and vitamin B12 keep homocysteine in check, another factor in heart disease now coming to the fore. Whole grains supply B6 and folate and also add texture. Next time you're cooking soup, toss in a small handful of one of these ingredients:

- Barley
- Brown rice
- Buckwheat
- Millet
- Quinoa

Poultry and meats are good sources and include vitamin B12, too!

Antioxidants are known to help prevent the accumulation of plaque in arteries. One of them, beta carotene, is also a pigment, the color orange. Increase your intake of orangey foods by preparing soups with the following ingredients:

- Carrots
- Dark leafy greens such as kale — the green in the chlorophyll covers over the orange beta carotene, but it's there
- Orange sweet potatoes (instead of boniato, a pale sweet potato that has a thin, light yellow skin and pale yellow flesh)
- Orange winter squash, such as Hubbard, turban, and acorn
- Sweet red pepper

Bad news/good news about lowfat sour cream

In producing lowfat sour cream, manufacturers add guar gum and other substances to replicate the mouth feel of full fat. Unfortunately, the resulting sour cream can feel more like JELL-O gelatin than butter. However, the *guar gum,* a thickener made from legumes, is also a great source of soluble fiber known to lower cholesterol.

Try the recipe for Curried Carrot Soup with Fresh Ginger that follows and savor the beta carotene in this golden orange potage. The soup is garnished with fresh gingerroot. In case you don't know how to tackle prepping one, see the step-by-step guide in Figure 9-2. To store leftover gingerroot, put it in a sealed plastic bag and keep it in your freezer until you need it again.

Blending creamless cream soup

The ingredients you leave out are also important in making a soup that fits into a cholesterol-controlling diet. Ingredients such as cream, very high in saturated fat, need replacing.

This section tells you how to prepare a creamy vegetable soup that doesn't contain any cream. The secret is to blend the vegetables until they're nearly smooth but still a little chunky and then add some mashed potatoes. In this section's recipe for Curried Carrot Soup with Fresh Ginger, the potato starch thickens the mixture, and because of the potato's off-white color, the soup even looks a little creamy!

I experimented with some broccoli and worked out a ratio of vegetable, potatoes, and stock that produces the right texture for a satisfying creamless cream soup: 4 cups vegetables, ½ cup mashed potatoes, and 2 cups stock. For my trial run, I used the chicken stock I made from the dinner trimmings that I describe in this chapter's section on chicken stock. I stored it in the refrigerator overnight and scraped the congealed fat off the top before adding the stock to the pot.

Here is the procedure to follow.

1. **Start with 4 cups of cooked vegetables, such as steamed broccoli, and blend it in a food processor fitted with a metal blade until nearly smooth.**

   If you overprocess the vegetable, it becomes frothy, and the final soup feels like a broccoli milkshake in your mouth. I know from experience.

2. **Put 2 cups of chicken stock in a large soup pot, add the blended vegetables and ½ cup mashed potatoes, and whisk to combine.**

3. **Warm over medium heat for 15 minutes.**

4. **Season with salt and pepper and serve.**

Of course, you can add other seasonings and ingredients, but this is the basic recipe. I served my creamless cream of broccoli soup garnished with a drizzle of Chinese hot sesame oil, and it was divine. No one missed the cream.

Of course, the soup is still healthy with the sesame oil. All soups, including creamless cream soups, need some fat. Without any fat, the broccoli mixture is nothing but a vegetable purée. To its credit, fat is a flavor carrier and provides some needed calories. Without a little fat, a vegetable soup can be bland, and after you've eaten it, you'll soon be hungry again.

Gourmet guilt-free soup recipes

These soups are proof that a healthy soup can also be a real culinary treat. They're easy to make, and they're deliciously artistic in addition to being healthy. They have enough substance to be popular with guests as well.

Leek and Mixed Vegetable Soup

Eating a minimum of 5 servings a day of fruit and vegetables is recommended for general good health. Lunching on vegetable soup is an easy way to start. This forgiving mixture of vegetables accepts all sorts of heart-healthy additions — leftover vegetables from last night's dinner, a handful of cooked beans, or some cooked brown rice or barley. Or enjoy it as is, a range of colorful vegetables and nutrients, tied together by the delicate flavor of leek — a soothing rainy-day dish with a hint of spring.

Preparation time: *10 minutes*

Cooking time: *25 minutes*

Yield: *4 servings*

6 cups chicken stock (see the Basic Chicken Stock recipe in this chapter or use canned, low-sodium fat-free chicken broth and omit salt seasoning)

1 leek, top trimmed, cut horizontally in ½-inch pieces and thoroughly washed to remove sand

1 carrot, cut horizontally in ½-inch pieces

1 celery stalk, cut horizontally in ½-inch pieces

1 zucchini, quartered lengthwise and quarters cut horizontally in ½-inch lengths

1 yellow summer squash, quartered lengthwise and quarters cut horizontally in ½-inch lengths

1 small potato, peeled and diced

3 sprigs parsley, stems removed

1 tablespoon extra-virgin olive oil

½ teaspoon salt

¼ teaspoon pepper

Pinch of red pepper flakes

1 Place all ingredients in a large pot and bring to a boil.

2 Lower the heat to medium and cook for 20 minutes, or until the vegetables are soft.

3 Serve the soup immediately, with a slice of whole-grain bread and a small wedge of quality cheese on the side.

Vary It! *For a soup with fuller flavor, at the beginning of the cooking process, add ½ teaspoon dried herbs, such as thyme, oregano, or basil, or a combination of these.*

Tip: *To give the vegetables in your soup some dignity, give each type a uniform cut rather than serving a hodgepodge of produce. You'll feel well fed while eating lean.*

Per serving: *Calories 119 (From Fat 44); Fat 5g (Saturated 1g); Cholesterol 5mg; Sodium 619mg; Carbohydrates 16g (Dietary Fiber 3g); Protein 4g.*

Curried Carrot Soup with Fresh Ginger

This satisfying soup is full of heart-healthy ingredients, including carrots, which provide soluble fiber to control cholesterol, and gingerroot, a blood thinner, which prevents blood clots. The recipe calls for curry powder, which comes in two basic forms, standard and Madras, which is the hotter version used in this recipe.

Special tool: *Food processor*

Preparation time: *30 minutes*

Cooking time: *1 hour and 15 minutes*

Yield: *4 servings*

1 large yellow onion, coarsely chopped

2 tablespoons extra-virgin olive oil

3-inch piece of gingerroot, peeled and finely grated (see Figure 9-2)

1 tablespoon Madras curry powder

2 pounds medium carrots (8 to 10), peeled and sliced horizontally into ½-inch pieces

1 large russet potato, peeled and diced

8 cups chicken stock (see the Basic Chicken Stock in this chapter or use low-sodium, nonfat canned chicken broth and omit salt seasoning)

½ teaspoon salt

¼ teaspoon pepper

¼ cup lowfat sour cream

1 In a large soup pot over high heat, sauté the onion in the oil for 5 minutes, stirring occasionally. When the onion begins to give up its moisture and reduce in volume, lower the heat to medium.

2 Add to the onion all but 1 tablespoon of the ginger and the curry powder. Continue cooking the mixture until the onion is tender and translucent, 5 to 7 minutes.

3 Add the carrots and potato to the onion mixture and cook for 15 minutes, stirring occasionally, until some of the potato pieces begin to brown slightly.

4 Add the chicken stock to the vegetables and bring to a boil over high heat. Lower the heat and simmer, uncovered, 30 to 40 minutes.

5 Remove the pot from the heat to purée, allowing the soup to cool a few minutes before proceeding.

6 With a ladle, scoop some soup into a food processor fitted with a metal blade or into a blender. Mix in batches, taking care in handling the hot liquid. Pour the puréed soup into a bowl.

7 Return the puréed soup to the pot. Season with salt and pepper. Warm the soup over medium heat.

8 While the soup is reheating, combine the sour cream with the reserved ginger. Serve the soup immediately, with a dollop of ginger sour cream as a garnish.

Per serving: Calories 280(From Fat 90); Fat 10g (Saturated 2g); Cholesterol 12mg; Sodium 840mg; Carbohydrates 42g (Dietary Fiber 8g); Protein 8g.

Figure 9-2:
The proper steps for mincing gingerroot.

Onion Soup with Shortcuts

The classic recipe for French onion soup requires at least an hour to sauté the onions until they turn a rich brown, and then you must melt the cheese that normally covers the entire top of the soup under a broiler. For that step, you need ovenproof soup bowls, which I don't own and you probably don't either. In this speedier version, you first bake the onions, shortening sautéing time, and you place a more modest garnish of cheese in the bottom of the soup bowl. You then pour the hot soup in over the cheese, which melts. *Voilà!* You're finished cooking and ready to enjoy all the same flavors as the classic version, but with less fat and no new bowls.

Preparation time: *15 minutes*

Cooking time: *1 hour and 50 minutes*

Yield: *6 servings*

6 yellow onions (about 3 pounds)

4 tablespoons extra-virgin olive oil

6 garlic cloves, sliced

¼ cup red wine

4 cups beef broth, (if canned, use the low-sodium and fat-free variety) (see the tip at the end of the recipe)

2 cups chicken broth (see the Basic Chicken Stock recipe in this chapter or use canned, low-sodium fat-free chicken broth)

Salt and pepper

6 slices whole-grain bread, cut ⅓-inch thick

¾ cup loosely packed grated Gruyère cheese

1 Heat the oven to 375 degrees. Place the whole onions, with the skins on, in a roasting pan for an hour, until the vegetable begins to soften. Remove from the oven and allow to cool for 5 minutes.

2 Peel the onions, cut them in half vertically, and cut each half horizontally into thin slices.

3 Heat the olive oil in a large saucepan over medium heat. Add the sliced onions and garlic. Sauté on medium heat until brown and caramelized, but not burned, stirring occasionally, about 20 minutes.

4 Add the wine and simmer until the wine is reduced to a glaze, about 3 minutes.

5 Gradually mix in the beef broth and chicken broth, scraping up browned bits from the bottom of the pan.

6 Turn the heat to medium-high and bring just about to a boil; then lower the heat so the soup sends up a few bubbles at a time. Season to taste with salt and pepper. Simmer the soup until the flavors blend, about 15 minutes. The soup can be prepared to this point and refrigerated, covered, and served the next day. Reheat the soup before continuing.

7 Meanwhile, toast the bread and place 1 slice in each of 6 soup bowls. Top with 2 tablespoons of the cheese. Or use a toaster oven and sprinkle the cheese on the bread and let the cheese melt as the bread toasts. Ladle the soup over the toast and serve immediately.

Tip: *If using canned beef broth and/or canned chicken broth, omit the salt seasoning.*

Per serving: Calories 264 (From Fat 134); Fat 15g (Saturated 4g); Cholesterol 16mg; Sodium 639mg; Carbohydrates 23g (Dietary Fiber 4g); Protein 11g.

☙ *Lentil Soup Scheherazade*

In a heart-healthy diet, lentil soup is one of the staples. Lentils are a lowfat source of protein and contain soluble fiber that has been proven to lower cholesterol. Here's a Middle Eastern version, made with coriander, lemon, and spinach — the deep green of the leaves breaking up the beige-brown of the lentils. Along with the soup, serve a plate of slices of feta cheese and black and green marinated olives as accompaniments. Also provide wedges of lemon, called for in the recipe, so diners have the option of adding a squirt of lemon juice to the soup to accent the flavor.

Preparation time: *15 minutes*

Cooking time: *1 hour and 10 minutes*

Yield: *6 generous servings*

1½ cups brown lentils	½ cup fresh parsley
8 cups water	¼ teaspoon black pepper
1 medium-size yellow onion, diced	⅛ teaspoon hot red pepper flakes, or to taste
5 cloves garlic, peeled and minced	Salt
1 can (6 ounces) tomato paste	1 lemon, cut into wedges
1 teaspoon ground coriander	Feta cheese
1 bunch (¾ pound) spinach, stems removed and coarsely chopped	Olives

1 Place the lentils and water in a large soup pot and bring to a boil, covered. Reduce the heat to medium-low and cook the lentils for 30 minutes.

2 Add the onion, garlic, tomato paste, and coriander to the lentils. Cook the lentil mixture on medium-low for an additional 30 minutes. The lentils will begin to dissolve and the soup become thick.

3 Add the spinach, parsley, black pepper, and pepper flakes. Continue to cook the soup for another 10 minutes on medium-low, to wilt the spinach and combine the flavors.

4 Season to taste with salt and serve with lemon wedges, feta cheese, and olives on the side. Because this soup thickens on standing, to reheat the soup, add a little water.

Per serving: *Calories 209 (From Fat 7); Fat 1g (Saturated 0g); Cholesterol 0mg; Sodium 151mg; Carbohydrates 37g (Dietary Fiber 14g); Protein 16g.*

Making Soup into a Meal

Turn to soup when you need a timesaving, complete meal in a pot. You can give yourself some protein, some carbohydrate, and some healthy fat just as if you sat down to a three-course meal. Because it's bulky, soup also lets you fill up sooner, on fewer calories. Try the following lunch suggestions in this section and the hearty soups that you can call dinner.

Inventing soup-and-sandwich combos

Many upscale department stores once had dining rooms where customers could elegantly lunch while watching a fashion show and fortifying themselves for more shopping. A standard item on the menu was a cup of soup and a half sandwich, just enough to satisfy your hunger and help you fit into the clothes you were about to buy. This combo is offered on many restaurant menus today and still makes a great lunch — the soup warming, the half sandwich filling. Here are some suggested combinations that feature ingredients that are good for your heart (you can find instructions for all the soup recipes in this chapter):

- Mock Squash Soup and sliced turkey breast with cranberry relish on whole-wheat bread
- Onion Soup with Shortcuts and egg salad on French bread
- Beet Soup and lean sliced beef with horseradish on rye bread
- Corn and Sweet Red Pepper Chowder and salmon salad on pumpernickel
- Creamless cream of broccoli soup and sliced chicken breast on whole-grain bread
- Lentil Soup Scheherazade and whole-wheat pita filled with Greek salad made of tomato, cucumber, and lettuce and garnished with feta cheese and olives

Soup recipes with substance

For some customers, a lovely little broth just doesn't do it. When the kids are hungry or you have a guy to feed, your bowl of soup had better look like a real meal. The two recipes in this section, Beef Barley Soup and Chicken Gumbo with Okra, fit the bill. And they both help you control cholesterol and take good care of your heart, providing soluble fiber and a variety of nutritious vegetables.

Beef Barley Soup

Barley is a premier grain for controlling cholesterol because it supplies soluble fiber. The mushrooms are a great source of chromium that helps your body metabolize carbs. And this soup freezes well.

Preparation time: *15 minutes*

Cooking time: *2 hours and 30 minutes*

Yield: *6 servings*

One 1¼-pound beef shin on the bone, trimmed of excess fat	1 teaspoon dried thyme
Salt and pepper	½ cup pearl barley, rinsed
3 tablespoons extra-virgin olive oil	1 cup chopped tomato, or 1 can (14 ounces) diced tomato
1 carrot, diced	1 teaspoon unsalted butter or substitute
1 medium onion, diced	6 ounces button mushrooms, brushed, trimmed, and quartered
1 rib celery, diced	3 tablespoons minced flat-leaf parsley
6 cups water	

1 Season the meat to taste with salt and pepper. Heat 2 tablespoons of the oil in a large soup pot and place the meat in the pot. Over medium-high heat, cook the meat on all sides until seared and well browned, about 15 minutes. Remove the meat and set aside.

2 Add the remaining 1 tablespoon oil to the pan and lower the heat to medium. Add the carrot, onion, and celery and cook until tender, about 10 minutes. To the vegetable mixture, add the reserved meat and the water.

3 Bring to a boil and adjust the heat to maintain a gentle simmer. Cover the pot. Cook the soup for 1½ hours, until the meat is tender.

4 Add the thyme, barley, and tomato. Simmer the soup an additional 30 minutes, until the barley is tender.

5 Meanwhile, in a separate pan, heat the butter over medium-high heat, add the mushrooms, and sauté until golden, about 10 minutes. Add the mushrooms to the soup and simmer for an additional 15 minutes.

6 Remove the meat and cut into small chunks.

7 Skim the fat from the surface of the soup. Return the meat to the soup. Add the parsley. Season to taste with salt and pepper.

Per serving: Calories 215 (From Fat 89); Fat 10g (Saturated 2g); Cholesterol 26mg; Sodium 139mg; Carbohydrates 19g (Dietary Fiber 4g); Protein 14g.

Chicken Gumbo with Okra

Bet you can't remember the last time you ate some okra. It's an essential ingredient in this American classic and gives you a serving of soluble fiber. Another integral ingredient is the filé powder, which has a woodsy flavor and is made of sassafras leaves. Filé flavors and helps thicken the broth. This dish also needs its sausage for the flavor. Use the real thing for sensational taste: smoky andouille pork sausage that the original recipe requires. Before serving, skim the visible fat from the soup and enjoy a few slices of sausage. After all, this meal can be your dinner.

Special tool: *Food processor*

Preparation time: *30 minutes*

Cooking time: *1½ hours*

Yield: *8 servings*

2½ pounds chicken breast, skin removed	2 green bell peppers, cored and seeds removed	2 tablespoons tomato paste
3 quarts chicken stock (see the Basic Chicken Stock in this chapter or use low-sodium, nonfat canned chicken broth and omit salt seasoning)	3 ribs celery	1 pound fresh or frozen okra, cut into ½-inch pieces
	¼ cup unrefined safflower oil	1 tablespoon filé powder
	6 cloves garlic, minced	Hot pepper sauce
	6 ounces andouille or other spicy sausage, thinly sliced	Cayenne pepper
2 medium onions, peeled	1½ cups (14-ounce can) tomatoes, chopped	Salt and black pepper
		Steamed rice

1 In a large pot, poach the chicken breast in the stock over medium heat, uncovered, for 20 minutes, until the meat can be easily pierced with a fork. Remove the chicken and set aside the meat and the stock.

2 Meanwhile, roughly chop the onions, peppers, and celery. In a food processor fitted with a metal blade, finely chop the vegetables.

3 Heat the oil in a large, heavy-bottomed soup pot and add the garlic, onions, peppers, and celery. Cook the vegetables on medium heat for 10 minutes, stirring occasionally, until the onion is soft and translucent.

4 Add the sausage, tomatoes, tomato paste, and the reserved stock to the vegetables.

5 Bring the vegetable and sausage mixture to a boil and then reduce to a simmer.

6 Shred the chicken and add this to the pot, along with the okra and filé powder. Season the soup to taste with the hot pepper, cayenne, and salt and pepper.

7 Simmer the gumbo for 1 hour to combine the flavors. Ladle over steamed rice and serve. This soup tastes even better the next day.

Per serving: *Calories 367 (From Fat 156); Fat 17g (Saturated 4g); Cholesterol 103mg; Sodium 756mg; Carbohydrates 14g (Dietary Fiber 4g); Protein 39g.*

Inventing Soups Starting with Canned and Bottled Ingredients

Canned soup is handy to have around in a pinch. When I remember, I keep favorites such as canned pea soup and bottled borscht on my kitchen shelf. If high blood pressure is a concern, look for brands that offer low-salt versions to avoid the copious amounts of sodium normally in canned soup.

Doctoring canned chicken broth

If you do resort to canned chicken stock in some of the preceding recipes, choose a product that's virtually fat free and low sodium. You can then work with it a bit, adding a healthy fat such as unrefined safflower oil and controlling the added salt. Include some of the vegetables and herbs featured in the two stock recipes and season with freshly ground pepper to make the broth more interesting.

To ready canned chicken stock for use in Chinese cooking, omit the thyme, and add a few slices of fresh ginger, a couple cloves of garlic, 1 scallion, and a tablespoon or two of dry sherry.

A can of this and a bottle of that

Okay, so you don't have time to cook one of the recipes in this chapter from start to finish. You can still enjoy some homemade soup! By combining ready-made ingredients, you'll be surprised what you can come up with. I once gave a Christmas buffet for about 20 friends. They loved the soup I served and asked me what it was. With my eyes cast down modestly, I said it was curried squash soup, a soup I thought sounded homey but gourmet, and then changed the subject. What they were really eating began with a can of puréed pumpkin. This soup is the first item on the following list of soups you can throw together in no time and with little effort.

Try these heart-healthy selections. I offer quantities to give you an idea of the ratio of ingredients, but you can adjust the amounts to suit your taste. It's your call as you have fun experimenting with these soups.

- **Mock Squash Soup:** Using a food processor fitted with a metal blade, purée in batches the following ingredients: a 29-ounce can puréed pumpkin, 6 cups of homemade chicken broth or 1 49-ounce can, 1 pear (peel, stem, and core removed), 1 cup whole milk, 1 tablespoon Madras curry powder (or if you prefer, 1 teaspoon cinnamon and ¼ teaspoon nutmeg), and 1 teaspoon butter. Cook over medium heat for 30 minutes, stirring occasionally, and serve. The pumpkin is a great source of antioxidant vitamin A, and the pear provides soluble fiber.

✔ **Corn and Sweet Red Pepper Chowder:** In a food processor fitted with a metal blade, process an 8-ounce jar of roasted sweet red peppers and a 16-ounce bag frozen white corn until the mixture has the consistency of applesauce. Cook over medium heat, and in 15 minutes you'll have a thick-textured, delicious lunch chowder, and the peppers provide you with antioxidants.

✔ **Salmon Potage:** Purée in a food processor fitted with a metal blade a 14.75-ounce can of salmon (skin and bones removed), 2 cups lowfat milk, and 1 teaspoon dried dill. Warm on medium heat, stirring occasionally. Add pepper to taste. The salmon contains omega-3 fatty acids that lower cholesterol.

✔ **Beet Soup:** Combine over medium heat the following ingredients: a 33-ounce bottle of borscht, 2 cups chopped fresh cabbage, 1 apple (diced), 1 potato (diced), and 1 tablespoon fresh dill. Cook for 30 minutes. Serve in individual soup bowls, each garnished with a tablespoon of lowfat sour cream.

Chapter 10

Super Salads for Everyday Meals

In This Chapter

▶ Looking for the freshest salad ingredients

▶ Adding color to your salads

▶ Fixing fantastic salads and dressings

▶ Converting a salad into a meal

Salads are a great way to give yourself all sorts of ingredients that can keep your heart healthy and control cholesterol. Vegetables, fruits, and beans in salads provide special vitamins and minerals, as well as soluble fiber, and salad oils can help balance the "good" HDL cholesterol and the "bad" LDL cholesterol. These dishes are also your chance to include some raw foods in your diet. In this form, they retain all their original nutrients and take longer to digest, so they tend not to raise blood sugar rapidly and help keep cholesterol at lower levels.

Browse through this chapter to find information on buying and storing produce and the basics on making salad. Experiment with the recipes for side salads, main course salads, and salad dressings. Treat yourself to the best ingredients you can find, particularly because you'll be eating them as is. Make your salads irresistible, and you'll be likely to eat more of these cholesterol-controlling foods.

Making Salads with the Best and the Brightest

Fresh salad fixings contain the most nutrients, which begin to ebb the longer produce sits around in your kitchen. Produce harvested when it is fully ripe is also the healthiest. When fruits and vegetables are picked before they're fully ripe, they don't have a chance to acquire the last uptake of nutrients, particularly minerals.

If you want really fresh produce (and have the time and the inclination), try growing your own produce in pots or in the backyard. For starters, buy potted herbs such as chives and thyme and pinch some off to add to salads.

Much of the produce in stores is picked before it ripens so that it travels well and has a longer shelf life. Such produce doesn't taste as fresh as local produce and may also have been treated with added wax, other preservatives, and chemical ripening agents that local produce does not require.

Shopping for the freshest produce

Search out farmers markets in your area to buy local produce. You find unusual items such as vine-ripened bulbs of fennel, fresh fava beans, patty pan squash, yellow wax beans, Bosc pears, Rainier cherries, and unusual kinds of apples.

Fruits and vegetables are transported an average of 1,200 miles from farm to table, which is why it's advantageous to have a chat with the person managing the produce section in the supermarket where you shop. Ask which items are from your region and which originated from as far away as South America. Of course, during winter months the supply of local produce can be very limited in northern climates, making buying fruits and vegetables from other regions a necessity. Supplement your supply with frozen fruits and vegetables, which are processed soon after harvesting and retain a good portion of their original nutrients.

Think local; think seasonal. Buy fruits and vegetables grown in your area and favor the produce of the season for foods with maximum flavor and nutrients.

Handling fruits and veggies with care

While many fruits and vegetables do just fine in the standard produce compartments of refrigerators, some foods require special care. Here's a quick review of the needs of certain items:

- ✔ Tomatoes don't ripen properly in the fridge, so they won't become juicy and sweet. They require temperatures above 50 degrees Fahrenheit. To ripen tomatoes, leave them sitting on the kitchen counter, not in the sun, and once ripe, eat them within a day or two. Refrigerating tomatoes, even ripe ones, causes them to lose flavor and become mushy.

- ✔ Asparagus should be used as soon as possible after you've bought it and stored it in the refrigerator. Stand stalks upright in a tall container filled with 1 inch of water. Cover the asparagus tops loosely with a plastic bag.

- ✔ Avocados must be ripened at room temperature. After they're ripe, you can transfer them to the vegetable drawer of your refrigerator.

✔ To keep a bunch of herbs fresh, trim the ends off the stems and place in a tall glass of cold water to which you've added a pinch of sugar. Store this in the refrigerator. Trim the ends and change the water as necessary. You can also revive wilted sprigs by moistening the herb with a fine mist of water and chilling the herb briefly.

What color is your produce?

Plenty of research shows that colorful fruits and vegetables are full of phytonutrients, which in many cases are also the pigments themselves and nutrients that are good for you just like vitamins and minerals. But what's also becoming increasingly clear is that combining a variety of phytonutrients at one meal multiplies their beneficial effects. A mix of foods in different colors contains much more antioxidant power, enhances blood vessel protection, and proves more effective at lowering cholesterol. You can read more about the specific phytonutrients in Chapter 2, and Chapter 19 gives you a more detailed view of the rainbow of colors in fruit. Cooking with color is a beautiful way to make meals more nutritious.

The recipe for Colorful Coleslaw that appears in this chapter is a great way to sample one of these nutrient cocktails. Here are some other ways to add colorful fruits and veggies to your salads:

✔ Sweet peppers come in five colors — green, red, orange, yellow, and purple. Buy one of each. Core and slice these, and cook in olive oil flavored with sliced clove garlic. Serve as part of an antipasto.

✔ If you need some citrus in your salad, add pink grapefruit or blood oranges, which have flesh that is red, purple, or burgundy. They are less acidic than regular oranges and have a subtle taste of raspberry.

✔ If you're making slaw, add some purplish-red cabbage along with the green, but do so with caution because raw red cabbage has a peppery taste.

✔ Shred orange carrots and slice red radishes into your standard lettuce salad. Make the salad with red leaf lettuce.

✔ When you want raw onions in a salad, add red onions instead of yellow onions for a touch of color and milder flavor. Red onions are at their best raw, but when cooked, then become watery and lose their color.

✔ Make potato salad with a mix of purple and yellow Yukon Gold spuds.

Add your standard salad ingredients, such as tomatoes, scallions, and mushrooms, as well. Certain nutrients are concentrated in some foods but not in others. When you eat a variety of vegetables, you benefit from a range of nutrients.

Tossing Together Your Basic Salad

Making a salad can be as simple as one, two, three. In fact, two of the following recipes — the Beet, Pear, and Belgian Endive Salad and the Fennel, Orange, and Avocado Salad — feature just three main ingredients. Some fine-tasting oil and vinegar add the finishing touch. The individual flavors of each ingredient are there to be savored separately and also to complement each other.

Leading with lettuce

When creating a salad, start out with an interesting lettuce. The familiar iceberg lettuce does have its uses when you want crunch and something juicy — it's 96 percent water. But I invite you to experiment with other, more interesting kinds of greens to spruce up your next salad. Try these:

- **Arugula:** With its pungent, spicy flavor, this lettuce bites back. It's excellent combined with sweet or bitter greens as the first course for an Italian meal. For a treat, top arugula with a few toasted walnuts and a well-trimmed slice of prosciutto.

- **Belgian endive:** This lettuce is good with a full-bodied dressing, especially a sweet one, which balances the green's slightly bitter taste.

- **Radicchio:** Serve this rather bitter-tasting lettuce raw, braised, grilled, or wilted, perhaps with a splash of vinegar and oil.

- **Red leaf lettuce:** This lettuce has frilly-edged leaves that are delicate in texture and flavor. Enjoy this lettuce mixed with other greens and with a mild dressing.

For really crisp lettuce, wash under cool running water, shake off the excess moisture, blot with paper towels, and refrigerate for about an hour before you use it to make a salad.

Figure 10-1 shows more of the different types of greens and lettuces that are often found in produce sections of grocery stores.

Vitamin K, present in leafy greens and other vegetables, helps the blood to clot. Coumadin, on the other hand, often prescribed for heart patients, is a blood thinner. The two can be safely combined if your intake of foods rich in vitamin K remains steady and you have your clotting times checked regularly. This way, the opposing actions of these two substances can stay in balance.

Please, Eat Your **Greens**!

Bibb
Red Leaf
Loose-leaf
Boston Lettuce
Romaine
Iceberg Lettuce
Cabbage
Arugula
Belgian Endive
Escarole
Curly Endive
Dandelion
Watercress
Radicchio
Spinach
Frisée

Figure 10-1: Different types of greens and lettuces.

Making the best-dressed list

Salad dressings are your opportunity to give yourself cholesterol-controlling vegetable oils to replace saturated fat. This strategy has been shown to reduce the risk of heart disease and control cholesterol. Both the polyunsaturated and the monounsaturated components lower LDL, and the monounsaturates raise HDL as well. (For more on LDL and HDL, flip back to Chapter 1.)

For optimal health, you also want to go one better and use unrefined versions of these, to avoid oils that contain trans fatty acids and have been stripped of nutrients in the refining process.

The way to differentiate between refined and unrefined oils when you go shopping is that the refined oils are basically all the same pale yellow color. They're also flavorless. In contrast, unrefined oil has the color and flavor of the food it was made from, such as the green oil made from olives. Look for the word "unrefined" on the label and always opt for these high-quality oils and avoid refined.

Stocking up on quality oils

You don't need a wide variety of oils for making salad dressing, but you do need the best. Because such oils are unrefined, they all have distinctive flavors. Consequently, you may want to sample different brands until you find the ones you especially like. These are the different kinds of oils to consider:

- ✔ **Extra-virgin olive oil:** Your best choice, for flavor, texture, and health, olive oil contains monounsaturated fats, which lower LDL and raise HDL, just what you want.

  Like tea, olive oil contains polyphenols, antioxidants that can protect LDL from oxidation so that it's less likely to contribute to the formation of arterial plaque. In addition, the monounsaturates in olive oil lower high blood pressure.

- ✔ **Unrefined safflower oil:** You can use this oil in salad dressings although it has a heavier, oilier feel in the mouth. But you still will want some on hand for cooking and baking.

- ✔ **Flaxseed oil:** If you add this oil to any oil and vinegar dressing you're preparing, you boost your intake of omega-3 fatty acids, which are abundant in this oil.

  Flaxseed oil is sold in the refrigerated section of natural foods stores. The oil is packaged in opaque containers so that light doesn't damage the fragile fatty acids. Buy the smallest container possible, 8 ounces. After you open it, you can use it up in a month while it's still fresh.

Treating yourself to specialty oils

Although I strongly recommend that you normally use unrefined oils in your cooking, I make an exception for those refined, gourmet oils that add delectable flavor. These oils can turn you into an instant expert at producing gourmet salads. Enjoy them in their luscious roasted forms. Their flavor is so distinctive that you need only a couple teaspoons' worth. Start with the following:

- **Roasted walnut oil:** It brings a depth and richness of flavor even to simple greens. The oil also contains omega-3 fatty acids, which lower cholesterol.

- **Toasted sesame oil:** This oil imparts an Asian flavor to a salad.

- **Almond oil:** The unique roasted almond flavor is delicious as dipping oil for bread, as well as in salad dressings and baked goods.

- **Hazelnut oil:** This oil adds a depth of flavor when added to salad dressing and, like olive oil, is very high in heart-healthy monounsaturated fat, making up 75 percent of total fat in the nut.

Flavoring your dressing

You build a dressing by starting with oil and then adding other tasty ingredients. Garlic and onions are a good place to start. Research shows that regularly consuming garlic is a means of raising the healthy HDL cholesterol and dropping the harmful LDL cholesterol. Include garlic, raw or cooked, in your meals and aim for 1 to 3 cloves a day. Raw onions have also been shown to raise HDL cholesterol.

The flavor of garlic mashed through a garlic press is about ten times stronger than garlic that's only been minced with a knife. Mashed garlic is also more therapeutic. Crushing releases more *allicin,* a phytonutrient that lowers cholesterol, thins the blood, and widens blood vessels. After you mash the garlic, set it aside for 10 to 15 minutes to allow its medicinal properties to develop.

The first step in making an oil and vinegar dressing is to decide how acidic you like it. (Some people use equal amounts of oil and vinegar and find the bite of the dressing just right. I tend to prefer a 3 to 1 ratio of oil and vinegar for my taste, as you'll find in the recipes in this chapter, but by all means adjust these amounts if you like.) Next, add a small amount of flavorings, such as a little mustard and a pinch of herbs, until you come up with a dressing that hits the spot.

To accurately judge the acidity and flavor of a dressing, instead of sipping dressing from a teaspoon, dip the edge of a lettuce leaf in the dressing and sample this.

Consider adding these ingredients to your dressing for flavor:

- Dijon mustard

- Minced shallots for a mild onion flavor

- Fresh herbs, such as basil and dill

- Vinegars flavored with tarragon, sherry, or chile peppers

Dried herbs have a more intense flavor than fresh herbs, so when a recipe calls for 1 teaspoon of dried and you prefer to use fresh herbs, add 3 teaspoons of the fresh.

When you use one of the less acidic vinegars, such as balsamic or rice wine vinegar, you need less oil to balance the tartness and thereby save calories.

Recipes beyond the regular green salad

The entertaining salads that follow are good on their own but are also useful accompanying salads to serve with dinner. From the coleslaw that follows, a standard side dish with fish, to the spinach, walnut, and grapefruit salad that a friend always serves with Christmas dinner, you'll be glad to have these numbers in your repertoire.

⟳ Colorful Coleslaw

You can tell that this salad is full of antioxidants because it's also full of color, most notably the orange in the carrots and the red in the tomatoes. The cabbage, with its reddish-purple hue, contains *anthocyanins* (powerful phytonutrient antioxidants) and almost twice the vitamin C found in green cabbage. Eating such foods can play a role in controlling cholesterol. In a small study conducted at Western General Hospital in Edinburgh, Scotland, consuming 7 ounces of raw carrot every day for 3 weeks resulted in a significant and lasting reduction in total cholesterol. To prepare this recipe for coleslaw, use a food processor to shred the cabbage and carrots or do it the old-fashioned way and burn some calories as you shred the vegetables by hand using a grater.

Special tool: *Food processor*

Preparation time: *15 minutes*

Yield: *8 servings (1 cup each)*

½ cucumber, peeled	3 tablespoons unrefined safflower oil
4 cups shredded red cabbage	3 tablespoons flavored rice wine vinegar
2 carrots, peeled and shredded	Salt and pepper
2 medium tomatoes, trimmed	

1 Cut the cucumber once lengthwise and cut each piece in half again lengthwise. Dice each cucumber spear into ¼-inch cubes. Put in a large bowl and add the shredded cabbage and carrots.

2 Cut the tomatoes into small ½-inch pieces and add to the other vegetables.

3 In a small bowl, mix together the safflower oil and wine vinegar. Pour the dressing over the cabbage mixture.

4 Toss to combine and season to taste with salt and pepper. Serve for lunch with a sandwich or with fish for dinner.

Per serving: Calories 76 (From Fat 48); Fat 5g (Saturated 0g); Cholesterol 0mg; Sodium 89mg; Carbohydrate 7g (Dietary Fiber 2g); Protein 1g.

☞ Sliced Tomatoes with Avocado Dressing

This recipe provides the full range of healthful oils, including monounsaturates and polyunsaturates as well as omega-3 fatty acids in the flaxseed oil. It also specifies vine-ripened tomatoes because they contain more nutrients and can be more flavorful.

Special tool: *Food processor*

Preparation time: *10 minutes*

Yield: *4 servings*

1 medium avocado

1 shallot, minced (1 tablespoon)

¼ cup olive oil

1 tablespoon fresh flaxseed oil (see the tip at the end of the recipe)

1 tablespoon sherry vinegar

Salt and pepper

1 pound vine-ripened tomatoes, sliced

1 Cut the avocado in half lengthwise. Rotate one half and remove. Use a large spoon or the tip of a knife to remove the seed from the other half. Cut each avocado in half lengthwise and peel the skin. Put the avocado in a food processor fitted with a metal blade.

2 Add the shallot, olive oil, flaxseed oil, and sherry vinegar. Process until smooth. This recipe makes about ¾ cup dressing, enough for 1 pound of tomatoes, plus ¼ cup of dressing left over.

3 Season the dressing to taste with salt and pepper.

4 Arrange the tomatoes on individual salad plates. Garnish each with 2 tablespoons of avocado dressing.

Tip: *Check that the flaxseed oil is still fresh by sampling a bit. It should have a flavor faintly reminiscent of butter.*

Per serving: Calories 244 (From Fat 212); Fat 0g (Saturated 24g); Cholesterol 0mg; Sodium 156mg; Carbohydrate 10g (Dietary Fiber 5g); Protein 2g.

♡ Beet, Pear, and Belgian Endive Salad

This recipe shows you that using the perfect combination of ingredients makes it easy to prepare an elegant dish. This salad gives you juiciness, crunch, sweetness, and the heartiness of a root vegetable, and it comes out a festive magenta color.

Preparation time: *15 minutes*

Cooking time: *1 hour*

Yield: *6 servings as a side salad with dinner, or 2 servings for a lunch main course*

3 beets	3 tablespoons unrefined safflower oil
1 Bosc pear	1½ tablespoons balsamic vinegar
1 head Belgian endive, plus optional 6 additional endive leaves as garnish	Salt and pepper

1 Preheat the oven to 400 degrees. Wash the beets, wrap them in aluminum foil, and put them on a baking sheet. Cook for about 1 hour, until you can easily pierce the beets with a thin-bladed knife. Remove from the oven and cool. Peel the beets, dice them, and place them in a large bowl.

2 Dice the pear and add to the beets. Cut the endive crosswise into ¼-inch slices and add to the bowl.

3 Whisk together the oil and vinegar in a small bowl and pour over the salad.

4 Toss all the ingredients together. Season to taste with salt and pepper.

5 Distribute the salad among individual salad plates or transfer the salad to a serving bowl. Garnish with optional endive leaves, the wider end tucked under the edge of the salad.

Vary It! *Combine equal parts diced beets and diced apples and toss with a lowfat mayonnaise dressing seasoned with mustard and fresh dill.*

Per serving: *Calories 111 (From Fat 64); Fat 7g (Saturated 1g); Cholesterol 0mg; Sodium 149mg; Carbohydrate 12g (Dietary Fiber 5g); Protein 2g.*

☙ Arugula Salad with Barley and Chickpeas

This salad, which has an Italian accent thanks to the arugula and marinated artichoke hearts, makes a popular buffet offering or a tasty dish that goes well with lasagna. It also gives you another way to include barley — a good source of soluble fiber — in your meals. The grain coupled with chickpeas provides a vegetarian complete protein. Cook the pearl barley from scratch or prepare it the night before for dinner and make extra to have this salad the next day for lunch.

Preparation time: *10 minutes*

Yield: *6 servings*

2 cups cooked pearl barley (see the tip at the end of the recipe)

1 jar (12 ounces) marinated artichoke hearts, drained

1 can (15 ounces) chickpeas, rinsed (2 cups)

1 bag (7 ounces) washed salad greens that include arugula, or a mix of arugula and red leaf lettuce

2 tablespoons balsamic vinegar

6 tablespoons extra-virgin olive oil

2 tablespoons lemon juice

Salt and pepper

1 In a large bowl, mix together the pearl barley, artichoke hearts, and chickpeas. Add the salad greens and toss with the barley mixture.

2 Whisk together the vinegar, oil, and lemon juice. Drizzle over the salad and toss.

3 Season to taste with salt and pepper and serve immediately.

Tip: *To prepare barley from scratch, begin with 1 cup of grain and cook according to package instructions. The cooking process takes about 45 minutes and yields 2 cups of grain.*

Per serving: *Calories 225 (From Fat 94); Fat 11g (Saturated 1g); Cholesterol 0mg; Sodium 258mg; Carbohydrate 28g (Dietary Fiber 6g); Protein 6g.*

☞ Fennel, Orange, and Avocado Salad

The oranges in this salad are roughly cut, with the membranes left intact. That way, you get the full benefit of the bioflavonoids, vitamins that strengthen capillary walls, contained in the membranes. The citrus also provides tartness that balances the creamy avocado. And the fennel offers crispness and a refreshing, licorice-like flavor.

Preparation time: *10 minutes*

Yield: *4 servings as a side salad, or 2 servings for a light lunch*

1 small bulb fennel, trimmed	*3 tablespoons extra-virgin olive oil*
1 navel orange, peeled	*1 tablespoon balsamic vinegar*
1 avocado, peeled and pitted	*Salt and pepper*

1 Cut the fennel bulb in half lengthwise and then crosswise in ¼-inch slices.

2 Separate the orange into segments and slice these into ½-inch chunks, including the membranes and the soft white part that runs through the middle of the orange.

3 Cut the avocado into ½-inch chunks. Gently combine the avocado, orange, and fennel together in a large bowl.

4 Mix together the olive oil and the balsamic vinegar in a small bowl and drizzle over the salad. Toss together gently with a wooden spoon to avoid cutting into the soft avocado. Season to taste with salt and pepper and serve.

Tip: To cut the avocado into chunks, first cut the avocado in half lengthwise. Rotate one half and remove from seed. Use a large spoon or the tip of a knife to lift out the seed from the other half. Cut each avocado in half lengthwise and peel the skin. Cut the avocado flesh into chunks.

Per serving: *Calories 195 (From Fat 149); Fat 17g (Saturated 3g); Cholesterol 0mg; Sodium 177mg; Carbohydrate 13g (Dietary Fiber 6g); Protein 2g.*

☜ Spinach and Walnut Salad with Ruby Grapefruit

Spinach is a world-class vegetable in terms of nutrition. It's loaded with vitamins and minerals for heart health: the antioxidants beta carotene, vitamin C, and alpha-lipoic acid; folic acid, which helps lower homocysteine levels; and potassium, which is associated with lower blood pressure. In addition, a large study conducted by the Harvard School of Public Health that focused on fruit and vegetable intake of over 75,000 women who participated in the Nurses' Health Study found that consuming more green leafy vegetables and citrus fruit was associated with a lower risk of stroke. This salad contains both. These benefits aside, wait until you experience the mix of textures and flavors in this salad — the richness of toasted walnuts balanced by the juiciness of tart grapefruit. You'll be asking for seconds.

Preparation time: *20 minutes*

Cooking time: *3 minutes*

Yield: *6 servings as a side salad for dinner, or 2 for lunch*

½ cup walnut halves	3 tablespoons extra-virgin olive oil
1 head Belgian endive, trimmed and washed	1 tablespoon red wine vinegar
1 red grapefruit, peeled	1 small shallot, minced
1½ pounds baby spinach, washed and stems removed	½ teaspoon Dijon mustard
	Salt and pepper

1 In a small nonstick skillet, toast the walnuts over medium heat until they begin to brown and become fragrant, about 3 minutes. Transfer to a bowl and set aside.

2 Slice the endive crosswise in ¼-inch slices. Put the endive in a large bowl.

3 Separate the segments of grapefruit and cut into bite-size chunks. Add the grapefruit, spinach, and walnuts to the bowl with the endive.

4 In a small bowl, whisk together the olive oil, vinegar, shallot, and mustard. Pour over the salad.

5 Gently toss all the ingredients together. Season to taste with salt and pepper.

Tip: *This recipe nicely complements the Beet, Pear, and Belgian Endive Salad in this chapter. Serve both on a buffet.*

Per serving: *Calories 160 (From Fat 110); Fat 12g (Saturated 1g); Cholesterol 0mg; Sodium 195mg; Carbohydrate 10g (Dietary Fiber 4g); Protein 4g.*

Salads That Begin with Protein

Salads, like soups, are forgiving dishes that let you add all manner of extra ingredients. Take advantage of this by including more vegetables, fruits, and nuts in your salads. You can also turn a simple salad into a complete meal just by topping it with lean protein.

Making nutritious salads doesn't have to be hard. Simply tuck in additional healthy tidbits that you probably already have in your kitchen pantry or refrigerator. Here are some possibilities:

- ✔ Open a can of beans, such as kidney, Great Northerns, chickpeas, or cannellini. Drain the beans in a sieve, rinse them with water, and sprinkle them in a salad.

- ✔ Toss in some nuts, such as pecans, walnuts, or sliced almonds, and add some seeds like sesame and sunflower, or even trail mix.

- ✔ Add nopales, prickly pear cactus paddles, which are sold fresh or bottled in Latin markets. The prepared kind comes peeled with the needles removed. Nopales taste like string beans and are an excellent source of soluble fiber.

  To increase soluble fiber, also consider including apples, carrots, green beans, lentils, Brazil nuts, and barley.

- ✔ Add slivers of chicken breast from last night's dinner.

- ✔ Enlist recently leftover cooked vegetables to join the salad.

- ✔ Garnish your salad with a small cluster of purple grapes.

- ✔ Use the bottled artichokes, olives, and marinated sweet red peppers you were saving for guests.

Salad companions

Salad needn't stand alone. If you enjoy your salad with a slice of baguette and butter, try spreading bread, preferably whole-grain, with mashed avocado instead. That way, you avoid the saturated fat found in butter. And because having red wine is good for the heart, why not also enjoy a glass along with your salad?

Avocados earn an A

Don't be afraid of avocados as an addition to a salad. Yes, they're high in fat, but the monounsaturated kind. Like the oil in olives, the fat in avocados protects the arteries. In an Australian study of middle-aged women, eating avocados daily for three weeks improved the ratio of the "good" HDL cholesterol to the "bad" LDL cholesterol more effectively than did a lowfat diet.

Avocados also contain a greater proportion of soluble fiber than most fruit and vegetables, and they're especially rich in a powerful antioxidant, glutathione. They also contain another helpful compound, beta-sitosterol, a plant-based fat that reduces the amount of unhealthy LDL cholesterol absorbed from food and lowers triglyceride levels as well.

You may need to let avocados ripen after you bring them home from the store. I know someone who needed to ripen avocados quickly for her daughter's wedding reception, so she slept with her avocados under an electric blanket the night before the wedding. Here's an easier way to ripen avocados: Put the avocados in a paper bag with an apple, set this on your kitchen countertop, and keep them there for 2 to 3 days.

Hot salads for cool nights

Salads aren't only for eating in the heat of the day. A salad can make a great dinner entree, especially when topped with chicken, fish, or some sort of meat right out of the skillet or fresh off the grill. The sizzle in such foods is just what a quiet leaf of lettuce needs.

One of my favorite dinners in a local restaurant is a mixed greens salad that is made with large grilled scallops and shrimp. The dish also includes mango slices and toasted sliced almonds. This is a great way to include shellfish in a cholesterol-controlling diet. By including them in a salad, you don't need a large serving of these cholesterol-containing foods to feel like you've had a satisfying shellfish dinner.

The advantage of using a salad as the base for animal protein is that a small 3- to 4-ounce serving of beef, chicken, or shellfish can fill you up.

Recipes for main-course salads

The three recipes that follow are meals in themselves, providing servings of protein, plus vegetables and trimmings. Add some whole-grain bread toasted with olive oil and herbs and finish with one of the fruit desserts in Chapter 19 for gourmet eating at home.

Tuna Salad Niçoise

Salad Niçoise is one of the great classic salads, inspired by the produce of summer in Provence, France, and the fish that swim in the Mediterranean Sea. It embodies many of the ingredients that make the Mediterranean style of eating so good for the heart. Classic Salad Niçoise involves the preparation of many ingredients, including hard-boiled eggs, which are omitted here. This recipe is a shortened version of this dish. It's still a satisfying mix of flavors, but it takes less time to prepare. Enjoy this mini-meal for lunch.

Special tool: *Collapsible metal steamer*

Preparation time: *10 minutes*

Cooking time: *5 minutes*

Yield: *1 generous lunch salad*

1 cup 1-inch pieces of green beans, ¼ pound

1 can (6 ounces) chunk light tuna, packed in water

1 tablespoon capers

2 tablespoons extra-virgin olive oil

2 teaspoons balsamic vinegar

2 teaspoons Dijon mustard

Salt and pepper

1 Using a medium-size saucepan with a tightly fitting lid, insert a collapsible metal steamer and enough water to partially fill the area beneath the steamer platform. Add the green beans, cover the pot, and steam about 3 minutes, until the beans are slightly tender and bright green. Transfer the green beans to a sieve and rinse under cold water to stop the cooking and retain the color.

2 Put the beans in a large bowl. Add the tuna and break into small chunks. Add the capers and combine all ingredients.

3 In a small bowl, whisk together the olive oil, vinegar, and mustard. Drizzle over the tuna mixture. Toss lightly with a wooden spoon. Season to taste with salt and pepper.

Vary It! *If you want to make enough of this salad to serve 4 people, here's what to do. Double the amounts of all the ingredients, except for the tuna, by 2, and use 3 cans of tuna. Add 1½ cups sliced steamed red-skin potatoes, 1 bell pepper (trimmed, seeds removed, and sliced), and a handful of cherry tomatoes. Also beef up the dressing with ½ cup of loosely packed basil leaves, chopped, and, if you're not watching your sodium, 6 minced anchovies. Garnish the salad with marinated Greek kalamata olives or olives de Nice, available in gourmet markets.*

Per serving: *Calories 463 (From Fat 265); Fat 30g (Saturated 4g); Cholesterol 43mg; Sodium 1,574mg; Carbohydrate 12g (Dietary Fiber 4g); Protein 39g.*

Mexican Chicken Salad

This festive salad is a great meal to make for family and friends on a weekend afternoon, a good reason to start up the barbecue grill. If you prefer to keep this dish vegetarian, skip the chicken and add more corn and beans. These two foods contain complementary amino acids, the building blocks of protein, that when combined provide high-quality protein.

Special tool: *Blender*

Preparation time: *25 minutes, plus 1 hour to soften the chile peppers and at least 3 hours for marinating the chicken*

Cooking time: *40 minutes*

Yield: *6 servings*

Marinade:

2 dried ancho or Anaheim chile peppers, stems removed

6 large cloves garlic

2 teaspoons ground cumin

Salad:

1½ pounds skinless, boneless chicken breasts

3 ears of corn, husks removed

1 can (15 ounces) black beans, no added salt, drained (2 cups)

6 cups shredded iceberg lettuce

Dressing:

½ cup extra-virgin olive oil

3 tablespoons red wine vinegar

2 tablespoons balsamic vinegar

1 tablespoon fresh cilantro, chopped

Juice of ½ lime

Salt and pepper

1 Place the chiles in a small saucepan. Add water to cover the chiles and bring to a boil. Cover the pot and remove from the heat. Let stand for 1 hour. Reserve 1 cup cooking fluid. Remove the seeds from the chiles and rinse. In a blender, purée the chiles with the garlic, cumin, and the reserved 1 cup cooking liquid.

2 Arrange the chicken breasts in a shallow dish and spread both sides with the chile marinade. Refrigerate, covered, for a minimum of 3 hours.

3 Meanwhile, bring a large pot of water to a boil and add the cobs of corn. Cook on high heat until tender, about 12 minutes. Let cool. Working on a cutting board, slice off the corn with a knife. (You should have about 4 cups of corn.) Collect the corn in a bowl and manually break up any strips into individual kernels. Add the black beans and mix.

4 In a small bowl, whisk together the olive oil, red wine vinegar, balsamic vinegar, cilantro, and lime juice. Season the dressing to taste with salt and pepper. Pour over the corn and bean mixture and toss to combine.

5 Heat a grill or grill pan and cook the chicken breasts until no pink meat remains, about 10 minutes per side, depending on the thickness of the chicken. Cut the chicken across the grain into slices. Season to taste with salt and pepper.

6 To compose the salad on individual plates, first arrange a cup of lettuce. Top with a cup of the corn and bean mixture. On top of this, arrange ½ cup sliced chicken and serve.

Per serving: Calories 384 (From Fat 188); Fat 21g (Saturated 3g); Cholesterol 45mg; Sodium 159mg; Carbohydrate 28g (Dietary Fiber 8g); Protein 24g.

Savory Steak Salad with Broiled Tomato Dressing

You can have steak for dinner on occasion, even though it contains higher amounts of saturated fat because it's a red meat. Just limit the amount of saturated fat you have in other meals that day and limit the portion, which is easy to do when steak is combined with lots of vegetables in a salad such as this one. The dressing for this salad is based on a purée of broiled tomatoes, making it leaner than most oil dressings. Broiling the tomatoes is essential to produce this rustic, full-flavored dressing, a tomato-red sauce flecked with bits of slightly charred and smoky tomato skin. This dressing is also good served warm over grilled chicken and fish or drizzled into a homemade taco.

Special tools: *Collapsible metal steamer, food processor*

Preparation time: *20 minutes, plus 2 hours or more for marinating the flank steak*

Cooking time: *55 minutes*

Yield: *4 dinner-size salads*

3 tablespoons red wine	*½ cup extra-virgin olive oil*
3 cloves garlic, peeled and chopped	*8 button mushrooms, cleaned and sliced*
2 sprigs parsley or other herb, stems removed and chopped	*2 sweet red bell peppers, cored, seeded, and sliced*
1 pound lean flank steak	*½ pound green beans, trimmed*
Black pepper	*2 teaspoons red wine vinegar*
1 pound Roma tomatoes, about 5, trimmed and cut in half horizontally	*Salt*
4 large shallots, trimmed and chopped	*12 leaves red leaf lettuce, washed and torn into pieces*

1 In a shallow baking dish, combine the red wine, 1 clove of the garlic, and the parsley. Stir to combine. Place the steak in the marinade and turn over to coat both sides. Season with pepper. Refrigerate, covered, for 2 hours. Remove the steak 20 minutes before cooking to bring to room temperature.

2 Turn on the broiler. Arrange the tomato halves, cut side up, on a broiler tray and broil 4 inches from the heat for 15 minutes. Turn the tomatoes over about halfway through cooking and allow the skin to blister and slightly char.

3 In a skillet, cook the shallots in 1 tablespoon of the olive oil on medium heat until they just begin to become translucent, about 5 minutes. Add the mushrooms and continue to cook for an additional 3 minutes. Transfer to a bowl, cover to keep warm, and set aside.

4 Add the red peppers to the same skillet along with 1 tablespoon of the olive oil. Cook on medium heat, stirring occasionally, until they begin to soften and brown, about 10 minutes.

5 Meanwhile, place a collapsible metal steamer inside a medium-size pot with a tight-fitting lid. Add just enough water so that it comes to slightly below the bottom of the steamer. Place the green beans in the steamer and cover the pot. Cook on medium heat until the green beans turn bright green and are still a little crunchy, about 10 minutes. Turn off the heat and remove the pot lid.

6 In a food processor fitted with a metal blade, add the broiled tomatoes, red wine vinegar, and the remaining 2 cloves of chopped garlic. Begin puréeing, slowly adding the remaining olive oil by drizzling it through the processor tube. Season to taste with the salt and pepper.

7 Heat a griddle pan or broiler and cook the steak for 4 minutes per side for medium rare. Transfer the steak to a plate, cover loosely with aluminum foil, and let rest 5 minutes for residual cooking and to evenly distribute the juices. Place the steak on a cutting board and slice across the grain.

8 Put the lettuce in a large bowl and drizzle with ¾ cup dressing, setting the remaining dressing aside. Toss the salad. To compose the salad, divide the dressed lettuce among 4 dinner plates. Spoon the shallot-mushroom mixture over each. Arrange the green beans on this and then the sweet peppers. Top with slices of steak. Drizzle a stripe of the remaining tomato dressing across each salad.

Per serving: Calories 505 (From Fat 326); Fat 36g (Saturated 7g); Cholesterol 54mg; Sodium 224mg; Carbohydrate 21g (Dietary Fiber 5g); Protein 26g.

Chapter 11

Mouth-Watering Morsels for Special Occasions

In This Chapter

▶ Creating healthy munchies with satisfying flavor and crunch

▶ Serving dinner in little bites

Party foods, by definition, are full of flavor and not short on fat. They crunch, they dazzle with their good looks, and they're fun to eat. But can such entertaining fare also be heart-healthy and do its part in controlling cholesterol? Yes indeed, because so many of the foods recommended for heart health are already standard party fare. Nuts to nibble, avocado in guacamole, smoked salmon with capers, and olives of all sorts are green-light foods. Making sure they're healthy is just a matter of how you prepare them.

In this chapter, you discover heart-healthy foods with crunch that have not been deep fried, and satisfying nibbles high in the right sort of fats. I also give an assortment of quick and easy recipes for basic party offerings, including a vegetarian pâté and marinated olives. Presentation of food is also part of the drill. Party food at its best is also eye-catching. Read on to find all sorts of suggestions for creating scrumptious party offerings that meet your dietary needs.

Little Bites a Cardiologist Would Love

The hors d'oeuvres and little nibbles that meet the nutritional requirements of a cholesterol-lowering, heart-healthy diet are so numerous they would fill a buffet table. These morsels feature raw vegetables, fresh herbs, healthy fats, chicken, and fish. In addition, these foods are eaten in very small amounts, but many are so tasty that you'll be tempted to make a meal out of them.

Adding crunch to party fare

Healthy foods, perhaps because they're never deep-fried, often lack crunch, leaving you longing for the sound of crispy food and a satisfying chew. Party favorites like potato chips and tacos are full of crunch, while healthier foods, such as grains, nut butters, and vegetables, are quiet foods. The following gives you ways to combine the best of both worlds: the cholesterol-conscious and the crispy.

Crostini

Toast is crunchy, so how about starting with that and making some crostini, which means "little toasts" in Italian. Here's how to prepare crostini:

1. **Adjust the rack of a broiler so that it is at least 4 inches from the heat source and preheat the broiler.**

2. **Cut a slim baguette of French bread (about 2 inches in diameter and sold in specialty bakeries and upscale supermarkets) into thin slices and place on a large baking sheet.**

   Cut slices of bread on the diagonal for a stylish presentation.

3. **Brush the slices on one or both sides with a little olive oil and rub one or both sides with a halved clove of garlic.**

4. **Broil the bread so that one side is lightly toasted.**

5. **Turn the bread over and broil for a minute or two, making sure that the bread does not toast all the way through.**

Use crostini as a platform for other foods. Here are some suggested toppings:

- A smear of tapenade, an olive paste seasoned with capers, anchovies, garlic, and lemon juice and sold in jars
- Goat cheese mixed with fresh herbs, such as basil and parsley, and topped with a sliver of sun-dried tomato
- A spoonful of garlicky, mashed cannellini beans scented with oregano

Homemade baked tortilla chips

Instead of noshing on corn chips fried in who-knows-what kind of oil and loads of salt, enjoy the crunch of home-baked tortilla chips. Start with corn tortillas or whole-wheat tortillas, both made with whole grains, far healthier than white flour tortillas (see Chapter 17 for details). Here's the procedure.

1. **Using a pastry brush, brush each side of a corn tortilla with unrefined safflower oil or lightly spray each side, using an oil sprayer filled with unrefined oil.**

To give the chips a southwest flavor, sprinkle the oiled tortillas with ground cumin or chili powder.

2. **Stack the tortillas and cut them into 8 wedges, as you would a pie.**

3. **Place the wedges in a single layer on an ungreased baking sheet and bake in a preheated 400-degree oven, until they just begin to become golden, 10 to 12 minutes.**

Serve tortilla chips with a bean dip for a dose of soluble fiber. Or use guacamole, which is a great source of folate (see Chapter 2), or classic tomato salsa, which is full of healthy ingredients (see Chapter 18).

Doing the crudité dip

Eating raw vegetables at parties became chic when the veggies took on the name *crudité*, which is French for "raw." They are indeed refreshing, crispy, and full of all the vitamins and minerals nature gave them. But what do you do with all the bits of vegetable after you cut them? The following ideas tell you how to bring order to the chaos.

✔ Start with sticks of carrot, celery, and seeded cucumber, and maybe some blanched asparagus or blanched string beans, and give each vegetable a separate container, such as glass tumblers, colorful ceramic mugs, or small flower vases. Cluster the containers on the serving table, creating a vegetable forest.

✔ Arrange vegetables on a long, rectangular platter or basket lined with kale, and give each vegetable its own row.

✔ Tuck raw vegetables in between the leaves of a full head of Boston lettuce, following the instructions in the recipe, Crudité with Mango Salsa and Creamy Avocado Dip.

Figure on 1 cup of dip for every 20 guests. If you're serving chunky dips, you may need a bit more.

The fat of the matter: Acceptable appetizers

One of the great pleasures of party food is that it's full of hard-to-resist assertive flavors, in part because the food is also full of fat, a flavor carrier. Taking a holiday from diet restrictions, the most careful of eaters will graciously accept the hot cheese puffs and chocolate truffles being offered. But there's no reason you can't enjoy the feel of fat, even if you're watching your cholesterol. You have options.

Nuts and olives

Nuts and olives are two classic cocktail nibbles that are perfectly acceptable heart-healthy foods. In numerous studies, both nuts and olives, the basis of the famed Mediterranean diet, have been linked to a lower risk of heart disease. In addition, the monounsaturated and polyunsaturated fats in these foods help control cholesterol.

So which nuts have the most of these healthy fats and are low in the cholesterol-raising saturated kind? Here are a few that fit the bill:

- ✔ Almonds
- ✔ Filberts
- ✔ Pecans
- ✔ Pistachios
- ✔ Walnuts

One way to include nuts in a party menu is to add walnuts to hummus, pureeing them along with the other ingredients. The rich, mellow flavor of walnuts blends well with the flavors of the other ingredients and walnuts add omega-3 fatty acids, making hummus even more nutritious. Here's how to make this: In a food processor, combine 2 cups chickpeas (one 15-ounce can), ½ cup walnuts, ½ cup tahini sesame paste, ¼ cup fresh lemon juice, and 1 clove garlic, plus water or oil to reach the desired consistency. Season with cumin and salt.

Cheeses

You can save on fat by eating lowfat and nonfat cheeses or having a soy cheese look-alike, but I can't promise you great flavor or texture in all cases. For instance, I'd rather have a shaving of world-class Parmigiano-Reggiano as a garnish for slices of pear topped with a paper-thin slice of prosciutto, than a large wedge of rubbery, nonfat mozzarella any day. But do sample some lowfat cheese and see what you think. For instance, lowfat ricotta can be very satisfying. If you want to cut back on fat intake and still eat cheese, modified products let you keep these creamy-tasting foods in your diet.

When shopping for cheese, be sure to read the label for content of total fat and saturated fat as well as cholesterol. The amounts present vary among producers. Cheeses such as Camembert, Brie, Roquefort, cheddar, and American processed cheese can contain more than 25 percent of your daily quota of saturated fat and about 10 percent of a day's worth of cholesterol. And these amounts are in just 1 ounce, which isn't very much, especially for a devoted cheese eater. Best to stay away from these unless you can stop after one nibble. Feta and mozzarella, the full-fat kind, are lower in fat and cholesterol and better choices.

For the feel of fat on the tongue, use lowfat yogurt and lowfat sour cream, both very palatable, in your hors d'oeuvres.

Caviar

If any food says "special occasion," it's caviar. Because caviar is salted fish eggs, just like chicken eggs, it is a whole food and a balanced source of nutrition. In addition, although fat contributes 61 percent of the calories, caviar, like fish, contains mostly the healthy monounsaturated and polyunsaturated kinds. Admittedly, caviar is high in sodium (containing 240 mg per tablespoon) and in cholesterol (containing 31.3 mg per teaspoon), but you're not likely to be eating a bowlful of caviar anyway.

I give you two ways of serving caviar that give you a smidgeon of this glamorous stuff. On a budget, use black lumpfish caviar, golden whitefish caviar, or salmon red caviar, all sold in little jars in supermarkets. Otherwise, invest in some American farm-raised caviar or the even pricier imported sevruga, osetra, or beluga caviar.

1. **Boil round, red potatoes, the smallest you can find, until they're cooked through and tender.**

2. **Peel the potatoes, slice in half crosswise, and cut some potato off the base of each half, so the potato is steady when placed on a plate.**

3. **Using a melon baller, cut into the flat surface of each potato half and scoop out a little bowl in the middle.**

4. **Fill the hollow of each potato with lowfat sour cream and sprinkle the sour cream with caviar.**

For this elegant hors d'oeuvre, caviar is displayed on pale chartreuse Belgium endive.

1. **Wash a head of Belgium endive and cut it at the base to separate leaves.**

2. **Using a teaspoon, place a small dollop of lowfat sour cream at the wider end of each leaf and then sprinkle caviar on the sour cream.**

3. **Garnish the caviar and sour cream with a tiny sprig of dill.**

4. **On a round serving platter, arrange these like spokes, with the narrow end of the leaf pointing out.**

Tasty recipes to impress your guests

Not only are the following recipes attractive to the eye, but also you and your guests will likely count them among your favorites for regular snacking. The Citrus-Scented Marinated Olives, in particular, are known to be highly addictive. Enjoy!

⟳ Crudités with Mango Salsa and Creamy Avocado Dip

The inspiration for this recipe is a delicious combo dip I buy ready-made, a container with a layer of fresh guacamole topped with a layer of mango salsa. The combination of smooth and spicy is just right. The Creamy Avocado Dip included here is full of healthy monounsaturated fats and high in folic acid, while the Mango Salsa gives you an effortless way to increase your fruit intake. For the crudités, try using only green and white vegetables, like I suggest here, for a designy, high-style look (see Figure 11-1).

Preparation time: _20 minutes_

Yield: _20 servings_

1 head Boston lettuce, with the outside leaves still intact (see the tip at the end of the recipe)

1 large turnip

2 dozen slim spears of asparagus, trimmed and blanched

1 head endive, leaves separated and washed

1 cucumber, peeled, seeds removed, and sliced into spears

_1_ Taking the base of a head of Boston lettuce in one hand, gently open the leaves of the lettuce with the other hand, wiggling your fingers down in between the leaves. (If the lettuce is sandy, submerge the opened head in a sink filled with water and briefly swish to loosen dirt. Drain upside down in an empty dish rack before proceeding.)

_2_ Meanwhile, peel the turnip and cut in ¼-inch rounds. Picture the turnip slice as the earth and cut a small V-shaped wedge at the North Pole and South Pole. Also make two V-shaped wedges at each end of the "equator."

_3_ Bring about an inch of water to boil in a skillet and add the asparagus. Cook until the asparagus is bright green and al dente, about 2 minutes. Remove with tongs, and submerge the asparagus in a bowl of cold water until they have reached room temperature.

_4_ Tuck the turnip slices, asparagus, endive leaves, and cucumber in between the lettuce leaves. Serve with the Mango Salsa and Creamy Avocado Dip.

Vary It! _If you decide your crudité composition is begging for more color, add carrot sticks._

Tip: _If the Boston lettuce on display has had the outside leaves removed, ask the produce manager where you shop to bring you a full and untrimmed head from the cartons of produce stored in the back._

Per serving: _Calories 8 (From Fat 1); Fat 0g (Saturated 0g); Cholesterol 0mg; Sodium 8mg; Carbohydrate 2g (Dietary Fiber 1g); Protein 1g._

Mango Salsa

This recipes lives and dies on whether the mango is sweet with a smooth texture, so chose your mango with care. When ripe, a mango yields to gentle pressure like a ripe avocado, and the stem end has a gentle aroma. Choose plump mangos, avoiding those with bruised or shriveled skin. This nonfat mix of healing fruits and vegetables also goes great with chicken and fish.

Preparation time: 15 minutes

Yield: About 3 cups (60 servings)

1 ripe mango, diced into ¼-inch pieces

1 cup sweet red pepper, cut into ¼-inch pieces

2 tablespoons minced red onion

1 fresh jalapeño chile, or to taste, seeded and minced

1 tablespoon minced cilantro

2 tablespoons lime juice (juice of 1 lime)

Salt

1 Put the mango, sweet red pepper, onion, chile, cilantro, and lime juice in a mixing bowl. Toss gently to combine the ingredients.

2 Season to taste with salt and serve immediately.

Per serving: Calories 16 (From Fat 9); Fat 1g (Saturated 0g); Cholesterol 0mg; Sodium 20mg; Carbohydrate 2g (Dietary Fiber 1g); Protein 0g.

Creamy Avocado Dip

Sour cream dips have just the right tartness to complement the sweetness of fresh, raw vegetables. Cut the saturated fat of the cream by making the dip with lowfat or nonfat sour cream, and as in this recipe, substituting some of the sour cream with avocado to add healthier fats.

Special tool: Food processor

Preparation time: 15 minutes

Yield: About 1½ cups (30 servings)

1 cup nonfat sour cream

¼ teaspoon ground cumin

1 avocado, peeled and cut into chunks

1 small clove garlic, minced

1 tablespoon chopped, fresh cilantro leaves (3 sprigs), plus extra for garnish

Salt and pepper

1 Put the sour cream in a food processor fitted with a metal blade.

2 Add the cumin to the sour cream in the processor, and then add the avocado, garlic, and cilantro. Process until smooth, scraping down the side of the processor bowl if necessary to incorporate all of the ingredients.

3 Season to taste with salt and pepper. Transfer the dip to a small serving bowl and garnish with chopped cilantro. Serve immediately. (The dip can also be prepared earlier the same day you plan to serve it. Press plastic wrap onto the surface of the dip so that no air comes in contact with the avocado in the dip to keep it from turning brown. Refrigerate until ready to serve and add the cilantro garnish right before serving.)

Per serving: Calories 19 (From Fat 9); Fat 1g (Saturated 0g); Cholesterol 1mg; Sodium 31mg; Carbohydrate 2g (Dietary Fiber 0g); Protein 0g.

Figure 11-1:
Boston
lettuce
holding
crudités.

🍎 *Cinnamon and Spice Almonds*

Almonds have more of the monounsaturated fats, the cornerstone of the heart-healthy Mediterranean diet, than any other nut. Scent them with spices, add some raisins, and you've created a healthy treat. The small amount of butter in this recipe imparts its inimitable flavor without adding much saturated fat. When nuts are toasted in this way, they don't absorb much of the cooking oils because they already contain a large amount of fat. Serve this snack with cocktails or after-dinner coffee.

Preparation time: *5 minutes*

Cooking time: *10 minutes*

Yield: *3 cups (24 servings)*

1 tablespoon butter	*1 tablespoon ginger*
1 tablespoon unrefined safflower oil	*1½ teaspoons nutmeg*
3 cups raw almonds	*1½ cups raisins*
1 tablespoon cinnamon	*Salt*

1 In a skillet over medium heat, melt the butter and combine with the oil.

2 Add the almonds and toss to coat with the oil. Sprinkle the almonds with the cinnamon, ginger, nutmeg, and toss to combine ingredients. Toast, stirring occasionally, for 5 minutes.

3 Add the raisins and continue to cook the almond mixture, until the nuts begin to brown, an additional 2 to 3 minutes. Season to taste with salt. Make sure to cool the nuts completely before storing.

Per serving: Calories 151 (From Fat 91); Fat 10g (Saturated 0g); Cholesterol 1mg; Sodium 26mg; Carbohydrate 12g (Dietary Fiber 3g); Protein 4g.

🍅 *Citrus-Scented Marinated Olives*

Put one of these olives in your mouth, close your eyes, and you can taste summer in Provence! Let the Mediterranean flavors transport you. This recipe uses brine-cured olives, but if you want to cut back on salt, ordinary canned olives work fine as well. Use pitted ones so that more of the marinade can find its way into the olives. You can also marinate these olives in olive oil, but I use water here to cut back on calories and create a lighter taste.

Preparation time: *15 minutes, plus 3 days for the olives to marinate*

Marinade time: *3 days*

Yield: *3 cups olives (24 servings)*

1½ cups kalamata olives or other brine-cured olives	*1 tablespoon grated orange peel*
	1 tablespoon grated lemon peel
1½ cups cracked brine-cured green olives	*2 bay leaves*
4 large cloves garlic, smashed	*2 anchovies, minced, or 2 tablespoons anchovy paste*
¼ cup orange juice	
¼ cup fresh lemon juice	*½ teaspoon dried thyme*

1 Combine the olives, garlic, orange juice, lemon juice, orange peel, lemon peel, bay leaves, anchovies, and thyme in a glass jar with a tight-fitting lid.

2 Add enough water to the citrus marinade to cover the olives.

3 Seal the jar with the lid and shake the jar several times to distribute and combine the ingredients.

4 Refrigerate the olives for 3 days, shaking the jar once each day to keep the marinade well mixed.

Go-With: *Serve the olives with goat cheese and a baguette of French bread.*

Per serving: Calories 44 (From Fat 36); Fat 4g (Saturated 0g); Cholesterol 0mg; Sodium 431mg; Carbohydrate 3g (Dietary Fiber 0g); Protein 0g.

Turning Dinner into Hors d'Oeuvres

Amaze your friends with your elaborate hors d'oeuvres by cooking a main course and then serving it to them in little bites! Dinner dishes and accompaniments easily turn into fabulous party morsels, the kind major caterers serve at museum openings. Several of the recipes in this book are ideal for converting into passed hors d'oeuvres. Experiment with the following:

- **Apple Salsa (see Chapter 18):** Enjoy as is, as a dip.
- **Sweet and Spicy Refried Black Beans (see Chapter 16):** Warm this purée and serve it as a dip with home-baked tortilla chips.
- **Turkey Burger (see Chapter 12):** Cook 2-inch patties and serve on tiny biscuits.
- **Chicken Tandoori with Yogurt-Mint Sauce (see Chapter 12):** Start with 1-inch pieces of chicken and proceed with the recipe. Thread one piece on a 6-inch bamboo skewer and serve with Yogurt-Mint Sauce as a dip.
- **Grilled Marinated Chicken with Creamy Peanut Sauce (see Chapter 12):** Start with 1-inch pieces of chicken and proceed with the recipe. Thread one piece on a 6-inch bamboo skewer and serve with Creamy Peanut Sauce as a dip.

Getting some help: Ready-made appetizers

I often serve canned stuffed grape leaves and no one is the wiser. My guests sometimes even ask for the recipe. Offer some of these heart-healthy, ready-made appetizers on their own or add to a few of yours. You find them in supermarkets or natural foods stores:

- Roasted sweet red peppers
- Marinated artichoke hearts
- Smoked salmon
- Sliced veggies from the salad bar, to serve as crudités with a dip
- Stuffed tortellini (serve it on skewers)
- Freeze-dried vegetable crunchies, such as corn, peas, red bell peppers, carrots, and tomatoes, produced with no added fat and sold in natural food stores
- Canned stuffed grape leaves

Party recipes that double as meals

All of the following recipes are hearty and healthy enough to be served as main courses as well as party munchies. You can even turn the Mushroom Pâté into a pasta sauce, as I explain in the recipe introduction. Delicious!

Skewered Scallop Seviche with Avocado

Seviche, popular in Latin America, is raw fish that has been marinated in citrus juice, usually lime. The acid in the fruit "cooks" the fish. Any white-fleshed fish or scallops can be prepared this way. Shellfish has a reputation for being high in cholesterol, but a serving of 4 skewers of these scallops contains only 16 mg of cholesterol.

Special tools: *36 bamboo skewers, 6 inches long*

Preparation time: *20 minutes, plus 4 hours marinating time*

Yield: *9 servings (about 4 skewers each)*

1½ cups fresh lime juice, or enough to cover the scallops	*½ pound tiny bay scallops, about 70, perfectly fresh*
4 sprigs cilantro, stems removed and minced	*2 avocados*
1 tablespoon minced red onion	*1 box (8 ounces) cherry tomatoes, washed*
1 clove garlic, crushed and minced	*Salt and pepper*

1 In a shallow 8-inch square baking dish, combine the juice, cilantro, onion, and garlic.

2 Rinse the scallops. If necessary, remove the tough, stark white hinge that attaches the scallop to the shell. Place the scallops in the lime juice marinade. Cover and refrigerate a minimum of 4 hours, or overnight. The scallops are "cooked" when they're opaque.

3 Cut each tomato in half crosswise. Peel and remove the seed of the avocados and cut them into ¾-inch cubes. The cubes need to be substantial enough so that they don't fall off the skewer. Drain the seviche and season to taste with salt and pepper.

4 Assemble the skewers by threading the components in this order: 1 scallop, 1 cube avocado, 1 scallop, and 1 cherry tomato half. Run the skewer through the center of the face of the tomato where it was cut and then out the top through the skin, so the tomato becomes a cap on the other foods.

5 On a round platter, arrange the skewers of seviche like spokes of a wheel, with the tomato caps at the center. Or use a horizontal tray and place the skewers in a row with the food colors forming stripes.

Per serving: *Calories 31 (From Fat 14); Fat 2g (Saturated 0g); Cholesterol 4mg; Sodium 54mg; Carbohydrate 2g (Dietary Fiber 1g); Protein 3g.*

⌣ Mushroom Pâté

With its hearty texture, rich brown hues, and a dash of sherry, this vegetarian mushroom pâté is much more than a passable substitute for the regular pork and liver versions. Instead, cashews are added as a source of oils. This pâté is such a winner that I experimented thinning it with a little white wine and making it into a pestolike pasta sauce, served with penne. It worked!

Special tool: *Food processor*

Preparation time: *30 minutes, plus 4 hours chilling time*

Cooking time: *20 minutes*

Yield: *12 to 15 servings of 2 tablespoons each*

5 tablespoons unrefined safflower oil

2 large shallots, chopped (½ cup)

2 cloves garlic, crushed and chopped

1¼ pounds fresh shiitake mushrooms, stemmed and coarsely chopped

1 cup roasted salted cashews

1 tablespoon finely chopped fresh basil

1 tablespoon finely chopped fresh parsley, plus sprigs for garnish

2 tablespoons sherry

Salt and pepper

1 In a large, heavy skillet over medium heat, heat 4 tablespoons of the oil and add the shallots, garlic, and mushrooms. Cook until the mixture begins to brown and all the liquid evaporates, stirring frequently, 15 to 20 minutes, depending on the moisture content of the mushrooms. Remove the skillet from the heat.

2 In a food processor fitted with a metal blade, chop the cashews until they have a fine texture. Add the remaining 1 tablespoon oil and continue to process to make a coarse paste.

3 Add the mushroom mixture, basil, parsley, and sherry. Pulse the processor on and off until the pâté has a coarse texture. Season to taste with the salt and pepper.

4 Transfer the mushroom pâté to a small ceramic loaf pan, or a bowl lined with plastic wrap so you can easily pop out the pâté. Cover and chill 4 hours. Serve in the loaf pan, or turn the pâté out of the bowl and garnish with sprigs of parsley. Enjoy on crostini.

Per serving: Calories 85 (From Fat 66); Fat 7g (Saturated 1g); Cholesterol 0mg; Sodium 50mg; Carbohydrate 4g (Dietary Fiber 1g); Protein 2g.

Part IV
Having Your Poultry, Fish, and Meat

In this part . . .

In this part, you discover how to include poultry, fish, and meats in a cholesterol-controlling menu. I give you tips on selecting the right cuts and deciding on portion sizes so that you can limit the saturated fat and cholesterol that animal foods contain. I introduce you to some ways of preparing chicken that are tasty and a little different, and I show you how to use turkey in unexpected ways to turn out some mighty fine chili and tacos.

Then you can dive into the subject of cooking fish, including how to shop for, store, and cook it in ways that enhance its succulence. The seafood chapter includes a checklist of the healthiest fish for controlling cholesterol. The chapter on meats covers beef, pork, lamb, and, on the wild side, buffalo, ostrich, and emu.

Chapter 12

Flocking to Chicken and Turkey: New Ways to Prepare Old Favorites

In This Chapter

▶ Looking at the health benefits of chicken and turkey

▶ Boning up on chicken

▶ Turning your attention to turkey

*J*ust when you think you've eaten your millionth chicken, there are good reasons to eat more. And talk about turkey, which is showing up in all sorts of dishes and in many new forms! This bird, more than the crowning glory of the Thanksgiving table, is now a health food, too. In this chapter, you find the specifics on why chicken and turkey belong in a cholesterol-controlling diet. I also give you basic information and guidelines on shopping for, storing, and cooking poultry. These birds are good cooked so many different ways and with all sorts of seasonings. This chapter also gives you eight scrumptious recipes to let you experiment.

But don't limit your avian intake to these two basic birds. Duck is fine to eat from time to time although its meat is swathed in all that fat under the skin. The total fat and saturated fat in duck meat, eaten without the fat and skin, falls somewhere between the fat in dark meat chicken and flank steak. And the cholesterol content is comparable. Lean slices of breast of duck, glazed with an apricot-brandy sauce can still be yours to enjoy on a special occasion. Or rustle up some ostrich or emu (see Chapter 14), red-meat fowl that is as rich tasting as beef but lower in fat.

Cholesterol-Controlling Benefits of Poultry

The popularity of chicken and turkey is all about their lower fat content; these types of poultry have less fat than red meat and are lower in saturated fat. As a bonus, poultry also supplies vitamins and minerals that are good for the heart.

Crowing over cutting fat

Compared with red meats, poultry can boast having far less fat and fat of a better kind for heart health. Chicken and turkey contain significantly more monounsaturated and polyunsaturated fats than saturated. Furthermore, most of the fat is in the skin, which can be easily removed either before or after cooking.

A quick comparison of the fat in chicken, turkey, and beef in Table 12-1 tells the story. The numbers given are for a single-serving size of 3 ounces, for an accurate comparison of the different foods. Three ounces is equivalent to one half-breast of chicken or one chicken leg.

To control cholesterol, favor light meat chicken and turkey rather than dark meat poultry, which is higher in fat.

Table 12-1 has no column for cholesterol because cooked chicken and turkey have about the same amount of cholesterol, an average of 75 mg per 3-ounce serving, similar to cooked lean beef. White meat turkey contains about 60 mg and dark meat about 70 mg, while chicken contains somewhat more. White meat chicken has 70 mg, while dark meat chicken contains about 90 mg. Cooked ostrich, emu, and duck without the skin have cholesterol in about the same range.

In Table 12-1, the total fat is expressed in grams, and the type of fat is expressed as a percentage of total fat. For comparison, I chose ground beef with a fat content of 15 percent, the minimum amount you need to cook a juicy, satisfying hamburger. I also include a column for omega-3 fatty acid content, a type of polyunsaturated fat that lowers cholesterol. The number tells you the percent of your daily requirement that a serving of these foods delivers.

Table 12-1	Comparison of Fat Content in Chicken, Turkey, and Beef				
Poultry or Meat	*Total Fat*	*Saturated Fat*	*Mono-unsaturated Fat*	*Poly-unsaturated Fat*	*Omega-3 Fatty Acid*
Chicken, whole; roasted	11.6 grams	31%	44%	25%	21%
Chicken, half-breast, bone-less, skinless; broiled	3.03 grams	33%	41%	25%	10%
Chicken, leg, boneless, skin-less; broiled	8.44 grams	31%	42%	27%	27%
Turkey, light meat; roasted	2.74 grams	42%	23%	35%	13%
Turkey, dark meat; roasted	6.14 grams	39%	26%	35%	24%
Turkey, ground; cooked (13% fat)	11.2 grams	29%	42%	28%	19%
Beef, ground; pan-broiled (15% fat)	11.9 grams	46%	51%	3%	2%

These figures put in perspective how much fat you may be getting when you scarf down a plate of fried chicken or one of those macho steaks that drape over the edge of the plate! The advantage of eating home-cooked chicken is that you have some control over the amount of fat you bring to the table. Whether you're cooking chicken soup or roasting a turkey, you have several ways to remove the fat and skim calories at the same time:

✔ Remove the skin from chicken or turkey, either before or after cooking.

✔ When preparing a whole bird, remove all the fat from inside the body cavity before cooking.

✔ Refrigerate chicken broth overnight. The fat will harden in a layer on the surface of the liquid and then you can lift off the fat with a spatula and discard it.

✔ Cook a whole chicken or turkey on a rack set in a baking pan. The fat will drip into the bottom of the pan.

✔ Bake vegetables to be served with the chicken or turkey in a separate dish. Don't bake them in the bottom of the baking pan, where they can absorb the fat that collects.

✔ Use a gravy separator or a baster to remove the fat.

✔ To remove fat floating on the top of room-temperature broth, float an absorbent paper towel, laid out flat on the surface. Once you see it's soaked up fat, have a bowl handy and lift the towel with a spatula and transfer it to the bowl to catch drippings. Repeat if necessary.

If you love chopped chicken liver on your bagel in the morning, think twice. Chicken liver contains about 535 mg of cholesterol per 3-ounce serving.

Vitamins and minerals in pecking order

Of the many B vitamins that poultry contains, one deserves to be at the top of the list: vitamin B6. This nutrient is associated with lower levels of homo-cysteine, an amino acid in the blood that, when elevated, is linked to a greater risk of heart disease. Both chicken and turkey contain high amounts of B6 (see Table 12-2). Two other B vitamins found in smaller amounts in poultry, riboflavin (B2) and vitamin B12, also play a role in keeping homocys-teine levels in check. Chicken and turkey are also an excellent source of niacin (B3), an ally of your heart. In a study coupling niacin with a statin drug, the combination resulted in lower "bad" LDL and higher "good" HDL cholesterol levels.

B vitamins are not destroyed by heat, but as poultry cooks, the meat does lose juices that contain these water-soluble vitamins. To recover these nutri-ents, be sure to use the pan drippings in your final dish. Skim the fat and add a little white wine to produce a light sauce. Serve your chicken au jus and have your B vitamins too!

Poultry is exceptionally high in selenium, a trace mineral needed for normal heart function. The amounts in all cuts of chicken and turkey are high, but dark meat turkey has the most. The numbers in Table 12-2 represent the per-cent of the Recommended Dietary Allowances (RDA) in a 3-ounce serving, in relation to a caloric intake of 2,500 calories per day.

Table 12-2	Percentage of the RDA for Heart-Healthy Nutrients in 3 Ounces of Chicken and Turkey				
	Vitamin B2	*Vitamin B3*	*Vitamin B6*	*Vitamin B12*	*Selenium*
Chicken, whole; roasted	11%	45%	23%	10%	34%
Chicken half-breast, boneless, skinless; broiled	8%	73%	34%	11%	40%
Chicken, leg, boneless, skinless; broiled	18%	39%	25%	12%	37%
Turkey, light meat; roasted	9%	36%	31%	12%	46%
Turkey, dark meat; roasted	17%	19%	20%	12%	59%
Turkey, ground; cooked	11%	26%	22%	11%	54%

Old MacDonald Had Some Chickens — and So Can You

When shopping for chickens, being savvy about what to look for helps guarantee that the final cooked chicken is tasty and tender. Keep in mind how you plan to prepare the bird and the number of people you plan to serve. Then select the kind of chicken you need, a whole bird or parts, and if parts, decide if you need boneless and/or skinless. Knowing how to judge freshness in fresh and frozen chickens is also important, as well as being skilled at handling the raw meat safely in your kitchen to prevent any bacteria it may harbor from reaching other foods.

Shopping for the freshest chickens

Chicken that's labeled "fresh" hasn't just waltzed in from the barnyard. Some chickens may have been raised nearby and then packed with ice cubes before reaching the market by the next day. But most mass-produced, conventional chickens are shipped chilled, in temperatures near freezing. Technically, the meat itself isn't frozen, but the water in the carcass does freeze. Such a chicken may be held for many days before reaching the consumer.

Because of the variety of chicken on the market, being a good judge of quality is very important. The next time you go shopping, take a good look at the poultry, with the following in mind.

- ✔ When buying a whole chicken, look for a bird with a breast that is full in relation to the legs.
- ✔ Chicken skin should look fresh and not be broken, mottled, or transparent.
- ✔ Chicken meat should look clear and unblemished.
- ✔ The breastbone should easily bend. Flexibility shows that the bird is younger, and therefore the meat is more tender and lower in fat.
- ✔ Fresh chicken smells fresh. Before buying a package, give it a sniff.
- ✔ A package of chicken that contains water indicates that the chicken was likely once frozen and then defrosted. If the poultry is purchased and refrozen in a home freezer, it may contain bacteria that developed during the time the chicken was first thawed.

Don't judge a chicken by the color of its skin, which has nothing to do with its quality. The color of chicken ranges from creamy white to yellow, depending upon the breed and whether yellow pigments were added to the feed.

Chilled-out chicks: Buying a frozen bird

Frozen chickens can be tasty, but be sure that you're buying a chicken that was handled properly after it arrived at the store. Both for flavor and safety, you need to be particularly fussy about its condition. Keep the following in mind when buying a frozen bird:

- ✔ The chicken should be rock hard.
- ✔ Frozen liquid inside the package is a sign that the bird has thawed and been refrozen, possibly increasing the likelihood of contamination with bacteria. Avoid these birds.
- ✔ Heavy frost is a sign that the chicken has been stored a long time.
- ✔ The chicken skin should not appear powdery or have discolored patches.

It's time to have a little chat with your butcher if you're not clear whether the chickens for sale have been frozen, thawed and refrozen, or how long ago the frozen birds arrived at the store.

Handling chickens safely

The first consideration in preparing chicken is making sure that it's safe to eat. Unlike red meat, poultry is sold with the skin on, and more bacteria are found on an animal's skin than in the meat. Room-temperature chicken is the Promised Land to toxic bacteria such as salmonella, which, when exposed to air, thrives in the warm and moist environment found on chicken skin and on the surface of chicken cavities. Food poisoning caused by contaminated chicken is extremely common. These bacteria multiply exponentially every 20 minutes. Millions of bacteria can breed within just four hours. Your chicken has no hope of recovery.

The ironclad rule of chicken left unrefrigerated longer than four hours is to throw it out.

Storing chicken

You can take several steps in storing and cooking poultry to greatly reduce the risk of becoming sick from eating spoiled chicken or turkey. When you shop for chicken, bring it home immediately. If you plan to cook chicken the day you buy it, you can keep it in its plastic wrap. If not, unwrap the chicken and remove it from its package. Rinse the chicken, dry it, and rewrap loosely in plastic or wax paper. Stored this way, the chicken will keep well in the refrigerator for 1 to 2 days.

However, cut-up chicken parts, wrapped loosely, stay fresh refrigerated no more than 24 hours. The exception is brands of chicken parts that are sold vacuum-sealed in very thick plastic. These packaged chicken parts can be safely refrigerated for several days.

Whole chickens are sold with the giblets and neck, packaged loose or in a paper packet. Be sure to avoid eating the chicken liver, which is very high in cholesterol. But if you do want to keep these extras, remove them from the chicken and refrigerate them separately for no more than 24 hours.

Preparing chicken

Making sure chicken is safe to eat also includes being extra cautious during preparation. Take these precautions:

- ✔ Wash all utensils, such as cutting boards and knives that come in contact with the chicken. Clean these thoroughly with soap and hot water to prevent cross-contamination that can occur when you use these same utensils to prepare other foods.

- ✔ Wash the kitchen counter and your hands after handling chicken.

- ✔ If a recipe calls for marinating a chicken, after the chicken is cooked, make sure that you don't add any of the uncooked marinade to the final dish. If you do want to use the marinade in a sauce, first heat it in a small pot and bring it to a boil.

Knowing how long to hold 'em

Chicken and turkey have a short shelf life in your fridge. Whole birds and parts, if raw, last two days at most. Raw chicken parts, cut into pieces, have an even shorter time limit of 24 hours. Cooked chicken may be refrigerated safely for 3 to 4 days, but if it has a sauce, the safe storage time is just 2 days. If you want to store a chicken dish with sauce for a longer period of time, freeze it.

Know the telltale signs of foul fowl — a slimy film on the surface of the bird and an unpleasant odor.

Bon voyage! Touring the world with chicken recipes

One thing about poultry, particularly chicken, is that you can take it anywhere, at least in culinary terms. It's at home in all the major world cuisines, featured in traditional dishes and updated in modern variations. Wherever you travel, chicken is on the table, from the sun-drenched lands of the Mediterranean to the Indian continent and Asia.

In the following recipes, you journey to the northern shore of the Mediterranean to sample the flavors of Spain, France, and Italy — oranges, olives, rosemary, thyme, garlic, prosciutto, and basil. Then you move on to Morocco and cook a chicken inspired by the offerings of the spice bazaar. Next you visit India for that country's special tandoori chicken, and finally you come to Thailand for chicken treated to a spicy peanut sauce.

Roasted Chicken with Marinated Olives, Rosemary, and Oranges

This versatile recipe has become a standard in my household. The olives specified are the Citrus-Scented Marinated Olives in Chapter 11. You can also use store-bought kalamata olives, but be sure the brine used for curing them doesn't overpower the flavor of the dish. To temper their taste, soak the olives in water overnight. Give the onions the decorative cut suggested, and this Mediterranean dish looks even more gorgeous.

Preparation time: *20 minutes*

Cooking time: *1 hour*

Yield: *4 servings*

1½ pounds round red potatoes with skins, washed, cut into ½-inch thick slices

1 medium yellow onion, cut lengthwise in quarters (see the tip at the end of the recipe)

5 tablespoons extra-virgin olive oil

Salt and pepper

2 cloves garlic, minced

3 tablespoons fresh orange juice

2 large navel oranges, peeled and thinly sliced

4 skinless chicken breast halves (about 2 pounds)

4 plum tomatoes, halved lengthwise

10 marinated, pitted black and/or green olives (see the Citrus-Scented Marinated Olives recipe in Chapter 11), sliced thin lengthwise

1 teaspoon dried crumbled rosemary, or 1 tablespoon fresh rosemary leaves

1 Preheat the oven to 375 degrees.

2 Put the sliced potatoes and onions in a large bowl. Add 2 tablespoons of the olive oil and salt and pepper to taste. Toss to coat. Arrange the vegetables in a 9-x-12-inch baking dish and place in the heated oven. If you don't have two 9-x-12-inch pans, it's okay to use 9-x-9- or 8-x-8-inch pans for the potatoes and onions.

3 In a small bowl, combine the garlic, orange juice, 2 tablespoons of the olive oil, and salt and pepper to taste. Put the chicken breasts in the bowl used for the vegetables. Add the marinade and turn the chicken to coat.

4 Arrange the orange slices in a second 9-x-12-inch baking dish, making individual beds of overlapping slices for each of the chicken breasts. Place 1 chicken breast on each bed.

5 Arrange the tomatoes around the chicken and drizzle the tomatoes with the remaining 1 tablespoon of olive oil. Sprinkle the olives and rosemary over the chicken and remaining vegetables. Cover the baking dish with aluminum foil. When the potatoes have roasted 15 minutes, put the second chicken in the oven.

6 When the chicken has cooked 20 minutes, remove the foil and cook the chicken uncovered for another 15 minutes. Baste the chicken with the remaining marinade and cook an additional 10 to 15 minutes. If you're unsure that the chicken breasts are done, cut into one with a thin-bladed knife. The center of the breast should be white or slightly pink.

7 Transfer the chicken and roasted vegetables to an oval platter, with a bouquet of fresh rosemary set at one end of the plate, and serve immediately.

Tip: To turn the onion quarters into flowers, follow the directions shown in Figure 12-1. And if you're feeling really inspired, you can create onion chrysanthemums. With a paring knife, making sure not to cut through the root end, cut the onion in half and each half again. Continue until segments are too narrow to cut further. Brush with oil and add to the baking pan. The more onion the better, because onions are anti-inflammatory and blood thinning.

Tip: For a less sweet, spicier taste, the orange slices can be omitted from the recipe. It will still have Mediterranean flavor, but of a different type.

Per serving: *Calories 617 (From Fat 227); Fat 25g (Saturated 4g); Cholesterol 125mg; Sodium 428mg; Carbohydrate 47g (Dietary Fiber 7g); Protein 51g.*

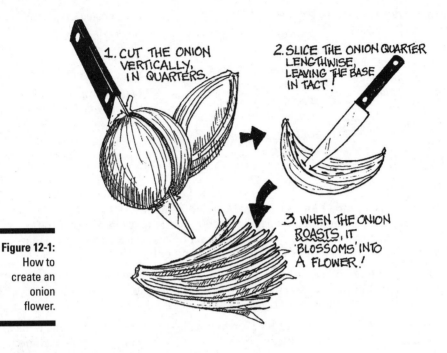

1. CUT THE ONION VERTICALLY, IN QUARTERS.

2. SLICE THE ONION QUARTER LENGTHWISE, LEAVING THE BASE IN TACT!

3. WHEN THE ONION ROASTS, IT 'BLOSSOMS' INTO A FLOWER!

Figure 12-1: How to create an onion flower.

Roasted Chicken Provençal

This recipe gives you a way of cooking chicken parts that results in a bird that's succulent and infused with the flavors of lemon and herbs. Rosemary and thyme are tucked under the skin, which holds the juices in the meat. If you happen to have a source of fresh lavender, you can also add these to this mix of herbs — a very Provençal touch! You don't need to eat the skin after the chicken is cooked, but the skin does seal in flavors while the chicken is roasting.

Preparation time: 15 minutes

Cooking time: About 1 hour

Yield: 4 servings

1 teaspoon dried thyme, or 1 tablespoon finely chopped fresh thyme

1 teaspoon dried rosemary, or 1 tablespoon finely chopped fresh rosemary

1 teaspoon finely chopped fresh lavender (optional)

3 tablespoons extra-virgin olive oil

1 tablespoon lemon juice, plus half a lemon

1 clove garlic, minced

Salt and pepper

1 chicken, 2½ pounds, cut into parts, rinsed and patted dry with paper towels

1 Preheat the oven to 350 degrees. Combine the thyme, rosemary, lavender (if desired), 2 tablespoons of the olive oil, the 1 tablespoon lemon juice, garlic, and salt and pepper to taste in a small bowl.

2 Using your fingers, carefully spread the herb mixture under the skin of the chicken breasts and, if possible, the legs, keeping the skin intact.

3 Place the chicken in a medium roasting pan. Rub the skin with the remaining 1 tablespoon olive oil and, using the lemon half, squeeze some of the juice over the chicken parts. Season to taste with salt and pepper. Put the chicken in the oven and roast for 20 minutes.

4 Squeeze the remaining lemon juice over the chicken. Roast the chicken an additional 40 minutes, basting once or twice. The chicken is done when an instant-read thermometer inserted into the thickest part of the thigh reads 160 to 165 degrees. Or check for doneness by making a small cut in any section, right to the bone. You should see no red whatsoever but a slight tinge of pink is acceptable, as the meat will finish cooking by the time you bring the chicken to the table.

Tip: *To reduce the fat content of this dish, before serving the chicken parts, remove the skin.*

Tip: *To save some change, when a recipe calls for chicken parts as this one does, buy a whole chicken and cut it up yourself.*

Per serving: *Calories 300 (From Fat 164); Fat 18g (Saturated 4g); Cholesterol 97mg; Sodium 239mg; Carbohydrate 1g (Dietary Fiber 0g); Protein 32g.*

Moroccan Chicken with Couscous

Seat yourself on pillows around your coffee table and pretend you're dining in the Kasbah as you savor this roasted chicken filled with couscous and infused with spices. This recipe calls for ras el hanout. You probably don't have a jar of this item sitting on your kitchen shelf, but you can make your own version by following the recipe in Chapter 18. Take the time. You'll know it was worth it when you taste this delish dish.

Preparation time: *30 minutes, plus 10 minutes while the couscous soaks*

Cooking time: *1½ hours*

Yield: *4 servings*

½ cup couscous, preferably whole wheat	*2 tablespoons extra-virgin olive oil*	*Salt and pepper*
⅔ cup water	*Salt and pepper*	*3 to 4 pound chicken, packaged neck and giblets removed, rinsed and patted dry with paper towels*
⅛ cup golden raisins	*1 yellow onion, chopped*	
1 tablespoon homemade ras el hanout (see the recipe in Chapter 18)	*1 stick cinnamon*	*1 teaspoon turmeric*
	1 inch length of gingerroot, peeled and sliced	*2 tablespoons honey*
	½ cup white wine	

1 Preheat the oven to 400 degrees. Put the couscous in a bowl, add the water, and stir to combine. Set aside for 10 minutes while the couscous absorbs the water. Add the raisins, ras el hanout, 1 tablespoon of the olive oil, and salt and pepper to taste. Toss to combine. Stuff the chicken loosely with this mixture and truss the chicken (see Figure 12-2). Rub the chicken with the remaining olive oil.

2 Put the onion, cinnamon, ginger, wine, and salt and pepper to taste in a 9-x-13-inch roasting pan. Place the chicken on top of this mixture.

3 Roast the chicken for at least 1¼ hours depending on the size. Baste the chicken with the pan juices about halfway through if you'd like. Combine the turmeric and honey in a small bowl. When the chicken has cooked 1¼ hours, spread the top with the honey mixture. Cook an additional 20 minutes to allow the honey to caramelize. The chicken is done when an instant-read thermometer inserted into the thickest part of the thigh reads 160 to 165 degrees. Or check for doneness by making a small cut in any section, right to the bone. You should see no red whatsoever, but a slight tinge of pink is acceptable.

4 Transfer the chicken to a platter and let it rest for about 5 minutes before carving. Meanwhile, pour the pan juices into a clear measuring cup and pour or spoon off as much fat as possible. Remove the couscous and set it aside to use as a side dish.

5 Put the pan juices in a blender or a food processor. Add the bits of onion and ginger but not the cinnamon stick. Blend until the mixture is a thick sauce. Reheat in a small pot. Serve the chicken promptly with the sauce and couscous stuffing.

Per serving: Calories 659 (From Fat 280); Fat 31g (Saturated 8g); Cholesterol 134mg; Sodium 426mg; Carbohydrate 47g (Dietary Fiber 6g); Protein 47g.

Trussing a Chicken

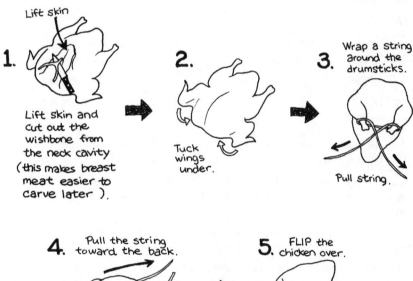

1. Lift skin

Lift skin and cut out the wishbone from the neck cavity (this makes breast meat easier to carve later).

2. Tuck wings under.

3. Wrap a string around the drumsticks.

Pull string.

4. Pull the string toward the back.

Catch the tucked wings underneath the string.

5. FLIP the chicken over.

hook the string under the backbone.

Tie the string into a secure knot.

6. Flip it over, and.... VOILA!

beautiful!

Now make a wish with that wishbone you took out!

Figure 12-2:
Simple steps for trussing a chicken.

Grilled Marinated Chicken with Creamy Peanut Sauce

One of the healthiest items you can order from a Thai restaurant menu is Chicken Sate, grilled chicken served with a sweet and spicy peanut sauce. This recipe gives you a way to make it at home. In a large-scale study, eating more nuts, including peanuts, was associated with an impressive drop in heart disease — so dip into this sauce. It's lusciously creamy and full of healthy, unsaturated fats.

Specialty tools: *About 36 6-inch bamboo skewers, or 18 12-inch bamboo skewers, soaked in water for 30 minutes*

Preparation time: *20 minutes, plus 1 hour to marinate the chicken*

Cooking time: *10 minutes for one batch*

Yield: *6 servings*

3 tablespoons fresh lime juice	*1 cup water*
2 tablespoons minced fresh ginger, about 2 inches gingerroot	*2 pounds chicken tenders*
	Creamy Peanut Sauce
2 cloves garlic, minced	*Lime wedges for garnish*
1 tablespoon honey	

1 In a shallow baking dish, make the lime marinade by combining the lime juice, ginger, garlic, honey, and water.

2 Cut each chicken tender in half lengthwise into strips about 1¼ inches wide. Again cutting lengthwise, slice each strip in half to produce chicken strips that can easily be threaded on a skewer.

3 Place the chicken strips in the lime marinade. Spoon the marinade over the chicken to coat. Cover and refrigerate for 1 hour.

4 Thread the chicken strips on the bamboo skewers. Use 12-inch skewers if you plan to cook the chicken on a barbecue grill and shorter, 6-inch skewers if you need to fit them on a ridged grill pan.

5 Prepare the barbecue or the grill pan by first wiping the surface with vegetable oil and heating to medium high. Cook the chicken 3 to 4 minutes on each side or until cooked through. If you're unsure that the chicken is done, cut into one of the pieces with a thin-bladed knife. The center of the chicken should be white or slightly pink.

6 Serve with the Creamy Peanut Sauce and serve on a platter garnished with wedges of lime.

Creamy Peanut Sauce

Preparation time: *15 minutes*

Cooking time: *5 minutes*

Yield: *2½ cups sauce*

1 cup smooth peanut butter	2-inch length of fresh gingerroot, peeled and chopped
3 tablespoons fresh lime juice	
3 tablespoons soy sauce	½ teaspoon dried crushed red pepper flakes
2 tablespoons honey	1 can (14½ ounces) low-sodium chicken broth, or 2 cups homemade broth

1 Put the peanut butter, lime juice, soy sauce, honey, gingerroot, and red pepper flakes in the bowl of a food processor fitted with a metal blade. Process until smooth.

2 Transfer the peanut mixture to a medium-sized, heavy saucepan. Gradually add the chicken broth while stirring the sauce. Warm on medium heat, stirring as the sauce reduces, until it is the consistency of heavy cream, about 5 minutes.

3 Pour the peanut sauce into a bowl and serve with the grilled chicken.

Tip: You can make this sauce as much as 3 days ahead. Store covered in the refrigerator. Before serving, warm the sauce over medium heat until hot, stirring continuously and thinning with water if necessary.

Per serving: *Calories 460 (From Fat 233); Fat 26g (Saturated 6g); Cholesterol 85mg; Sodium 772mg; Carbohydrate 17g (Dietary Fiber 3g); Protein 43g.*

Chicken Tandoori with Yogurt-Mint Sauce

This dish is one of the great classics of Indian cooking. Tandoori cooking is traditionally done in a tandoor, a small pit lined with clay, which functions as an oven. Poultry and meats are threaded on long skewers that are lowered into the tandoor pit and cooked. At the same time, flat breads, called naan, are slapped onto the walls of the oven where they stick, puffing and baking. With this recipe, you can simulate a version of chicken tandoori, cooked in your own home oven. The cool and creamy yogurt-mint sauce, which Indians call raita, is the perfect complement. Besides their wonderful flavors, the seasonings in this dish are also beneficial in that the active ingredients in the garlic, onion, and turmeric dampen inflammation. And because yogurt is full of friendly bacteria, the raita sauce aids digestion. To short-cut this recipe, buy tandoori paste, a mix of spices sold in Indian specialty stores and gourmet supermarkets. Mix this with the 1 cup of lowfat yogurt and marinate the chicken in this mixture.

Specialty tool: *Food processor*

Preparation time: *25 minutes plus 24 hours for the chicken to marinate*

Cooking time: *30 to 40 minutes*

Yield: *4 servings*

1 medium yellow onion, peeled and coarsely chopped	*¼ teaspoon ground mace*
	¼ teaspoon ground nutmeg
6 whole cloves garlic, peeled and coarsely chopped	*¼ teaspoon ground cloves*
	¼ teaspoon ground cinnamon
1 piece of fresh ginger, 2 inches long, peeled and coarsely chopped	*1 teaspoon salt*
	¼ teaspoon black pepper
3 tablespoons lemon juice	*¼ teaspoon cayenne pepper, or to taste*
1 cup lowfat plain yogurt	*3½ pounds fryer chicken parts, skin removed*
1 tablespoon ground coriander	*Yogurt-Mint Sauce*
1 teaspoon ground cumin	
1 teaspoon ground turmeric	

1 Put the onions, garlic, ginger, and lemon juice in a food processor fitted with a metal blade. Blend until the mixture is a smooth paste, about 1 minute. Transfer to a large bowl. Add the yogurt, coriander, cumin, turmeric, mace, nutmeg, cloves, cinnamon, salt, black pepper, and cayenne. Mix thoroughly.

2 Put the chicken parts in the marinade and turn to coat. Cover and refrigerate the chicken for 24 hours. Turn several times while the chicken is marinating.

3 One hour before cooking, take the marinated chicken out of the refrigerator to bring it to room temperature and ready it for roasting.

4 Heat the oven to 400 degrees. Remove the chicken from the marinade. Place the parts on a wire rack set into a shallow roasting pan lined with foil for easy clean-up. Roast the chicken, basting with marinade halfway through the cooking process. Cook for 30 to 40 minutes, or until the meat is cooked through. The chicken is done when you see clear juices if you make a small cut in the meat near the bone. Serve with the Yogurt-Mint Sauce and naan or pita bread.

Yogurt-Mint Sauce

1 medium cucumber, peeled, seeds removed, and coarsely grated

1½ cups lowfat yogurt

¼ teaspoon ground cumin seeds, roasted

1 heaping tablespoon freshly chopped fresh mint

Salt

Combine the cucumber, yogurt, cumin seeds, and mint. Season to taste with salt.

Per serving: *Calories 423 (From Fat 130); Fat 14g (Saturated 5g); Cholesterol 144mg; Sodium 967mg; Carbohydrate 18g (Dietary Fiber 2g); Protein 53g.*

Chicken Stew with Prosciutto and White Beans

This stew is full of flavor but not fat. It has two lowfat sources of protein: the chicken and the beans. The small amount of saturated fat in the prosciutto, added for its rich, smoky taste, is balanced with the two classic beneficial Italian seasonings, onions and garlic, which thin the blood. Use bottled beans, if you can find them at the store, rather than canned which often have a slight metallic taste.

Preparation time: *30 minutes*

Cooking time: *50 minutes*

Yield: *6 servings*

¼ cup all-purpose flour

¼ cup whole-wheat flour

Salt and pepper

6 chicken thighs with bones, skin removed (about 3 pounds)

2 tablespoons extra-virgin olive oil

1 large onion, diced, about 1½ cups

5 cloves garlic, minced

3 ounces sliced prosciutto, chopped into ½-inch squares

2 cans (14½ ounces each) diced tomatoes

2 cans (14½ ounces each) low-salt chicken broth

¾ cup dry white wine

1 bottle or can (14½ ounces) cannellini or white kidney beans, drained and rinsed

½ cup fresh basil leaves, loosely packed, cut into narrow strips

1 Put the all-purpose flour and whole-wheat flour in a shallow bowl. Season with salt and pepper. Place a chicken thigh in the flour and turn to coat all sides. Set on a separate plate. Do the same with the rest of the chicken meat.

2 Put the olive oil in a heavy, large pot over medium-high heat. Sauté the chicken in the oil, about 3 minutes per side. Using tongs, transfer the chicken to a large bowl.

3 Add the onion and garlic to the pot and sauté until the onion becomes translucent, about 10 minutes. Add the prosciutto, tomatoes, chicken broth, and white wine. Bring to a boil, scraping off any browned bits on the bottom of the pot.

4 Return the chicken and any accumulated juices to the pot. Cover and simmer the stew until the chicken is thoroughly cooked, about 20 minutes. Add the cannellini and basil. Simmer an additional 10 minutes to develop flavors. Season to taste with salt and pepper. Serve immediately and enjoy leftovers the next day too, after the flavors have had a chance to further blend overnight.

Per serving: *Calories 413 (From Fat 161); Fat 18g (Saturated 5g); Cholesterol 108mg; Sodium 799mg; Carbohydrate 26g (Dietary Fiber 6g); Protein 37g.*

Talking Turkey All Year Long

Turkey contains much less fat than red meat and even less fat than chicken (see Table 12-1). It's also an especially good source of vitamin B6 and selenium and also supplies good amounts of riboflavin, niacin, vitamin B12, zinc, and omega-3 fatty acids. (See Chapter 2 for specifics on the benefits of these nutrients.) Shopping for turkey requires a watchful eye to judge quality and a sniff to judge freshness. Careful handling is all-important because, like chicken, turkey is an ideal host for pathogens that cause food-borne illness. Cooked simply, it's delicious, but turkey too is versatile and can be prepared in a variety of imaginative ways.

Watching for the right turkey

The standard supermarket turkey, often sold at bargain prices per pound, can be just as tasty as pricier versions such as kosher turkeys and "wild" turkeys, which, by the way, are really domesticated. (The only way to bring home a truly wild turkey is to go out and shoot the fellow if you could find one.) However, if you prefer to eat birds raised with special feed and those that don't contain residues of antibiotics, then free-range organic turkeys are the right choice. These are increasingly available in markets.

While chicken has become the favored bird because of its handy size, which generally cooks in about an hour and provides 4 servings, most people think of cooking turkey as a hefty undertaking, requiring hours of cooking, best served at Thanksgiving when you have lots of mouths to feed. In fact, turkey is just as easy and convenient to cook as chicken. Roasting a whole bird involves the same procedures, although turkey, which is somewhat drier meat, requires more basting. And these days, most markets offer turkey parts to suit the cooking needs of singles, couples, and today's small families.

Using the best turkey parts

Turkey breast is a great choice because you can have the luxury of eating a turkey sandwich made with unprocessed white turkey meat. Deli turkey meats, on the other hand, are extremely high in sodium and contain chemical preservatives that have been linked to cancer. Turkey breast is sold with and without the bone, and also formed into boneless, turkey breast cutlets. Turkey breast can be substituted for white meat chicken in many dishes such as in the recipe for Chicken Stew with Prosciutto and White Beans and the Grilled Marinated Chicken with Creamy Peanut Sauce in this chapter. You can also use turkey breast, which has rich flavor despite its low fat, to replace veal in recipes for Italian scaloppine.

You also find a wide assortment of other turkey parts, like drumsticks, wings, and thighs. And turkey is sold ground, all light meat or a mix of light and dark meat, which is the higher in fat of the two. Turkey parts are also sold smoked in some upscale markets.

When cooking turkey breast, baste the meat every 15 minutes to keep it moist. To cook a 3- to 6-pound turkey breast, roast it for 45 minutes and then begin testing it for doneness every few minutes, using an instant-read thermometer. The turkey is done when the temperature reaches 160 degrees. Before carving, let the turkey rest 5 to 10 minutes.

Turkey in other forms

Look for turkey sausage and turkey bacon. These products are out there, designed for customers who want to cut fat intake. But check the labels for the amount of total fat and saturated fat in a serving, and also check how large or small a serving is. Some turkey products may contain as much fat as beef. And if you're trying to cut back on salt, also check the sodium content.

Fresh versus frozen turkey

Fresh turkey is more available year-round these days, but you find a lot of frozen turkeys, too. The frozen birds are often very inexpensive per pound, a thrifty purchase if you have a large freezer.

Defrosting a rock-solid, basketball-size bird may look like a daunting task, but if you remember to start defrosting well before you need to cook the bird, it's no problem. Just follow the schedule in Table 12-3.

Table 12-3	Defrosting Times for Whole Turkeys	
Weight	*Defrosting Time In Refrigerator*	*Defrosting Time In Cold Water*
8 to 10 pounds	18 to 24 hours	4 to 6 hours
10 to 12 pounds	24 to 36 hours	8 to12 hours
14 to 18 pounds	36 hours or more	12 to16 hours
18 pounds or more	48 hours or more	18 hours or more

Roasting your big bird: Cooking whole turkeys

Choose the best-sized bird to fit your family and your love of turkey leftovers. (Consult the suggestions in this section about what to do with these.) Cooking a whole turkey does require your attention. The breast meat of a whole roasted turkey can be dry, so you'll need to take some preventive measures.

✔ For a smaller turkey, under 10 pounds, you can start cooking it on its breast and then flip the turkey over on its back for the final cook, 30 to 60 minutes.

✔ For a bird over 10 pounds, just tent the breast with aluminum foil for the last hour of roasting. If you try to flip a big bird, the turkey might go flying!

✔ To stuff the bird, allow ½ to ¾ cup stuffing per pound of turkey and pack it loosely as it will expand during cooking. If your recipe makes more stuffing than the bird will hold, wrap the remaining mixture in foil and bake alongside the bird in the pan during the last ½ hour of roasting.

Be careful not to over-roast your turkey. Follow the cooking time guidelines in Table 12-4.

Table 12-4	Cooking Times for Whole Turkeys at 350 Degrees
Pounds	*Cooking Times*
8 to 12 pounds	4 to 4½ hours
12 to 16 pounds	4½ to 5½ hours
16 to 20 pounds	5½ to 6½ hours
20 to 24 pounds	6½ to 7½ hours

For gravy that is great tasting, when the turkey is half done, heat 1 cup of white wine, making sure you don't boil it, and pour the wine over the turkey. When the turkey is finished cooking, collect the drippings, skimming most of the fat, and proceed to make the gravy, which will have a more gourmet flavor thanks to the wine.

Winging it with leftovers

The beauty of cooking a whole turkey is that it gives you leftovers. Use these as inspiration to work some new dishes into your usual cooking routine. Here are some examples:

✔ Grind your own turkey meat to make turkey burgers, such as the Turkey Burger in the next section.

✔ Use ground turkey meat in a chili, such as the Turkey Chili with Jalapeño and Herbs in the next section.

✔ Make a turkey taco.

Self-defeating turkeys

Self-basting turkeys are an attempt to moisten turkey breast meat while it cooks. One of the major pluses of turkey meat is that it's relatively low in fat, especially the breast. In self-basted turkeys, fat or oil is placed under the breast skin before the bird is packed or frozen. Pop the turkey in the oven, and as the bird heats up, the fat melts and oozes over the turkey, with some added to the meat to make it moist. To avoid these added fats, which may include hydrogenated oils and added flavorings, it's better to baste the turkey yourself with the accumulating drippings in the baking pan. Remember, these contain the B vitamins present in the turkey juices.

Recipes for gobbling up gobblers year-round

You don't have to wait until a holiday to enjoy some turkey. Why not cook up some scrumptious turkey burgers or a pot full of turkey chili for a change rather than using beef. These American standard dishes adapt well to this native bird.

Turkey Chili with Jalapeño and Herbs

This chili is made with turkey breast, which is naturally low in fat; healthy extra-virgin olive oil; and barley and beans, both great sources of soluble fiber. This dish is a far cry from standard beef chilis with their little lakes of fat floating on top, but it still delivers wake-up flavors. The mix of fresh jalapeño, herbs, and spices holds its own. Feel free to turn up the volume with more jalapeño and Tabasco if you want more bite.

Specialty tool: *Food processor*

Preparation time: *20 minutes*

Cooking time: *1 hour and 25 minutes*

Yield: *10–12 servings*

5 tablespoons extra-virgin olive oil

½ cup minced onion

3 cloves garlic, minced

4 teaspoons cumin

1½ pounds ground turkey breast

4 cups chicken broth (homemade or fat-free
and low-sodium canned broth)

⅓ cup barley

1 jalapeño chile with seeds, chopped fine

1 teaspoon oregano

1 teaspoon summer savory

¼ teaspoon cinnamon

1 can (14 ounces) pinto beans, drained and
rinsed

1 can (14 ounces) Great Northern beans,
drained and rinsed

1 can (14 ounces) tomatoes (Glenmuir organic
fire-roasted tomatoes preferred)

Tabasco sauce

Salt and pepper

1 In a large nonstick skillet, heat 4 tablespoons olive oil over medium heat. Add the onion and garlic and cook until tender, about 7 minutes. Add the cumin and stir with a wooden spoon until fragrant, about 30 seconds.

2 To the onion mixture, add the ground turkey. Cook, stirring occasionally, about 10 minutes, until the meat is no longer pink.

3 Add the chicken broth, barley, jalapeno, oregano, summer savory, and cinnamon. Cover and simmer until the barley is almost tender, stirring occasionally, about 45 minutes.

4 Add the pinto beans, Great Northern beans, and tomatoes. Simmer, uncovered, until the barley is tender and the chili is thick, about 20 minutes. Add more stock or water if necessary.

5 Season to taste with the Tabasco sauce and salt and pepper. Serve immediately. (You can also prepare the chili a day ahead and then cover and refrigerate. Heat thoroughly before serving.)

Per serving: Calories 357 (From Fat 94); Fat 11g (Saturated 2g); Cholesterol 74mg; Sodium 885mg; Carbohydrate 27g (Dietary Fiber 8g); Protein 36g. Analysis reflects rinsed and drained beans.

Turkey Burger

You can enjoy a hearty burger but without all the fat when you use ground turkey rather than beef. However, because you need to cook your burger well done to make sure the poultry is safe to eat, you also need to add some juicy ingredients to keep the burger moist. Add onion and some sort of sauce to the turkey, as in this recipe, and include a juicy condiment on the hamburger bun, such as the Cranberry Sauce with Caramelized Onions and Cinnamon (see Chapter 18).

Preparation time: *15 minutes*

Cooking time: *10 minutes*

Yield: *4 servings*

1¼ pounds ground turkey	Salt and pepper
¼ cup finely chopped yellow onion	Cranberry Sauce with Caramelized Onions and Cinnamon (see Chapter 18)
1 teaspoon Worcestershire sauce	
¼ teaspoon dried sage	

1 In a large bowl, combine the turkey, onion, Worcestershire sauce, sage, and salt and pepper to taste. Form into 4 patties. For a juicier burger, handle the meat as little as possible and take care not to compact the meat.

2 Cook the burgers in a hot, well-seasoned cast-iron skillet or ridged grill pan. Cook the burgers over medium heat for about 5 minutes, or until browned and crispy. Flip the burgers carefully and cook for 5 minutes longer, or until golden brown and a thermometer inserted in the center registers 165 degrees and the meat is no longer pink.

3 Serve each burger on a whole-grain hamburger bun slathered with the Cranberry Sauce with Caramelized Onions and Cinnamon.

Tip: *If the turkey meat is very lean, spray the cooking surface with oil before adding the meat, to prevent the turkey from sticking.*

Per serving (burger only): *Calories 164 (From Fat 79); Fat 9g (Saturated 2g); Cholesterol 84mg; Sodium 260mg; Carbohydrate 1g (Dietary Fiber 0g); Protein 19g.*

Chapter 13

Serving Up Great-Tasting Seafood

In This Chapter

▶ Boning up on why seafood is heart-healthy

▶ Figuring out which fish to eat regularly

▶ Selecting the best fish and treating it right

▶ Cooking fish to perfection

▶ Enjoying additional seafood dishes

Seafood deserves to be a staple of a healthy diet for all the ways it benefits heart health. The healthy fats in fish improve the balance of HDL and LDL cholesterol in the bloodstream, prevent the heartbeat from becoming erratic, thin the blood so that it's less likely to form clots and block the arteries, and reduce inflammation which plays a role in the development of atherosclerosis or hardening of the arteries.

Fish, also commonly referred to as seafood, consists of two very broad categories: fish, which are equipped with fins, and shellfish, which have shells. Got it? Fish and shellfish are delectable foods that take well to all sorts of preparations and flavorful ingredients. Yet fish cooked at home is often a poor substitute for the mouth-watering flavor of the charbroiled fish you can order in restaurants. Dining out often sets the standard for good fish eats.

But all this is about to change, as you make your way through the recipes in this chapter. You have the chance to experiment with different techniques and savor all sorts of fish made with complementary vegetables, spices, and herbs. Read on to find out how to handle fish so it's safe to eat and tasty. Relax about preparing seafood in your own kitchen. The best is yet to come.

Savoring Salubrious Seafood

Fish and shellfish are ideal foods for the heart because they offer a source of protein that's exceptionally low in saturated fat and contain only a moderate amount of cholesterol. And the fats that are in seafood are the kind associated with a lower risk of heart disease and stroke. For sure, you have lots of reasons to take advantage of seafood's salubriousness (you know, it's ability to promote health). If fish is only a sometimes food for you, here are some good health reasons to eat more.

Oh, those omega-3s and more

You want to eat fish and shellfish *because* of the fat it contains. Isn't that a great reason to enjoy these delicious foods? Fish oil (the fat in fish, which is liquid at room temperature) provides you with EPA (eicosapentaenoic acid) and DHA (docosahexaenoic acid), both omega-3 fatty acids which research has shown are healthy for the heart.

The Mediterranean Diet, associated with low rates of heart disease in that part of the world, features regular consumption of fish. And in a study of eating habits of over 50,000 U.S. male health professionals with no history of heart disease, fish again proved beneficial for heart health. A diet that included fish was associated with a lower risk of coronary heart disease while a more Western-style diet that emphasizes red and processed meats was associated with higher risk of heart disease. These results were irrespective of whether or not a person smoked, their weight and family history of heart disease. Harvard School of Public Health and Brigham and Women's Hospital, Boston, conducted this study. And in the Nurses' Health Study, also conducted by these two institutions, of the 80,000 women reporting their food intake, over a period of 14 years, those who ate 4 ounces of fish two to four times a week nearly halved their risk of stroke.

Fish oil benefits the heart in many ways. Here's what it does:

- Lowers triglycerides significantly (see Chapter 1)
- Cuts both cholesterol and LDL cholesterol somewhat
- Reduces the clotting tendency of blood
- Helps maintain a normal rhythm to the heartbeat
- Dampens chronic inflammation of the arteries (see Chapter 1)
- Reverses elevated blood pressure
- Keep arteries open by impeding atherosclerosis (hardening of the arteries)

Seafood is also a great source of minerals that function as antioxidants, maintain fluid balance, support the expansion and contraction of the heart muscle, and transport oxygen in the blood. These nutrients include selenium, potassium, magnesium, and iron. Fish is also an excellent source of B vitamins that keep homocysteine levels in check.

Counting cholesterol in fish and shellfish

Fin fish, such as salmon and cod, have about the same amount of cholesterol as white-meat chicken and turkey, foods routinely recommended for low-cholesterol diets. Even shellfish deserves a thumbs-up. Researchers at one time mistakenly warned against shellfish because of its supposed high cholesterol content, but with the development of more accurate testing, clams and other crustaceans are now known to be relatively low in cholesterol.

In addition, shellfish is ridiculously low in saturated fat. Three ounces of boiled shrimp contain less saturated fat than four dry-roasted peanuts.

Table 13-1 gives you a quick comparison of the amount of cholesterol in seafood with common high-cholesterol foods such as eggs and red meat. So, you can see there's no reason not to enjoy the recipe for Anchovy and Clam Fettuccine in this chapter.

Table 13-1 Comparing Cholesterol and Saturated Fat Content in Seafood with the Amounts in Other Foods

Food Items (3 ounces each)	Cholesterol (in Milligrams)	Saturated Fat (in Grams)
Shrimp	130	0.1
Lobster	81	0.1
Crab	50	0.1
Oysters	46	0.5
Clams	29	0.1
Scallops	28	0.1
Salmon	53	1.3
Tuna, bluefin	32	1.1
Ground beef, 15 percent; pan-broiled	73.2	4.69
Chicken breast, boneless, skinless; broiled	72.3	0.86
Pork spareribs, lean and fat; braised	103	9.45
Calf liver; braised	477	2.8

Note: The data for seafood is the amount in raw shellfish and fish.

Seafood Catch-22

Fish is a cornerstone of a heart healthy way of eating. The general recommendation is to eat fish twice a week. Although consuming fish only every three days or so doesn't sound like a lot, most Americans don't even eat this much.

However, for all the benefits of fish, you do need to select your seafood wisely. It's important to follow certain guidelines to avoid the downside of eating fish. Seafood can contain traces of industrial chemicals such as PCBs, pesticides, and toxic metals, in particular, methyl mercury. Mercury, as it accumulates, attacks nerve cells, causing loss of coordination and numbness, and impairs hearing and vision. Here's another problem: Some of the fish highest in omega-3 fatty acids (which you DO need) contain the most mercury. The fish that contain the highest amounts of mercury include the following: swordfish, shark, king mackerel (also called wahoo and appropriately, ono), tilefish, fresh and frozen tuna steaks, and canned white albacore tuna.

For more information about mercury, go to the U.S. Environmental Protection Agency's Web site at www.epa.gov/mercury.

Knowing which fish to favor

There are still plenty of fish and shellfish in the sea that are healthy and safe to eat, despite the concerns about polluted waters. You just need to know which fish contain the most omega-3 fatty acids, vitamins, and minerals and at the same time are the cleanest. For help in selecting fish, consult the following list for a good idea of which are good, better and best. I've added the name of the recipe or the section heading where you can find the cooking suggestions for the fish featured in this chapter.

Here's the A+ list, which includes seafood with high amounts of omega-3s:

- Anchovy (see the recipe for Anchovy and Clam Fettuccine)
- Herring
- Lake trout (see the section "Simple fish dishes to dive for")
- Oysters
- Salmon (see the recipe for Broiled Alaskan Wild Salmon with Chinese Vegetables)
- Sardines (see the section "Slapping together a sardine sandwich")
- Sea bass (see the recipe for Baked Sea Bass with Aromatic Vegetables)
- Small mackerel
- Whitefish

The A list includes seafood with moderate amounts of omega-3s:

- Flounder
- Perch
- Pompano
- Red snapper, also known as rockfish (see the recipe for Fish Tacos with Sweet Peppers)
- Sole
- Shellfish: scallops (see the recipe for Grilled Scallops and Vegetables Marinated in Herbs), clams (see the recipe for Anchovy and Clam Fettuccine), shrimp, king crab, and crawfish
- Tilapia (see the recipe for Tilapia with Jalapeño-Tomato Ragout)
- Turbot

The B list includes fish with somewhat higher amounts of toxins. If you eat a fish from the B list, the next time you have fish, choose one from the A list. The FDA advises that women of childbearing age eat from this B list no more than once a week.

- Bluefish
- Haddock
- Halibut (see the recipe for Halibut with Cilantro Lime Salsa)
- Shellfish: lobster and crab

Many of these fish are widely sold in supermarkets and are easy to prepare. (If you're hesitant about shucking oysters, order them in restaurants.) Make a point of having some of all of these various kinds of seafood over three months. That way, you'll be more likely to minimize your intake of toxins such as mercury, while giving yourself plenty of omega-3s and a full range of the nutrients that seafood has to offer.

Salmon: The new chicken of the sea

Salmon used to be a seasonal delicacy, but now it's cheap and always available because it's farm-raised. Such expediency has its price: This salmon is often given doses of antibiotics, colored artificially, and exposed to pollutants that can cause cancer later in life. In addition, farmed salmon are much fatter than wild salmon, yet they're lower in the good omega-3 fatty acids. Invest in the real thing and shop for salmon labeled "wild," which you can find fresh, frozen, and in cans.

To reduce exposure to mercury and other toxins that accumulate in fatty tissue, before cooking fish, trim away the skin, the fatty belly flap, and any dark meat. Certain cooking techniques, such as broiling and baking, also remove fat.

Tuna is a special case because different varieties contain different amounts of mercury and the healthy omega-3 fatty acids. Large tuna, which comes to the table as tuna steaks, contains the most mercury but also the highest amounts of healthy oils. Albacore tuna contains moderate amounts of both mercury and omega-3s while canned light tuna, from smaller fish, have the least. Opt for the canned, light tuna packed in water (which is called for in the recipe Canned Light Tuna Fish Cakes in this chapter), and give yourself fish oils by eating the A-list fish.

The FDA advises women who are pregnant or may become pregnant and nursing mothers to not eat shark, swordfish, king mackerel, or tilefish. The mercury in these fish can cause harm to an unborn child. The advocacy Environmental Working Group goes one step further, adding such fish as tuna steaks, sea bass, Gulf Coast oysters, and halibut to the warning list.

Bringing Home Beauties: Shopping for and Storing Fish

Do yourself a favor and find a place that sells really fresh, great-tasting fish, even if it charges a little more for its seafood than your local supermarket. Locate a reliable place to buy fish to make sure you give yourself quality fish you can really enjoy. You'll be more likely to eat seafood regularly and reap the health benefits.

Considering the source

Of course, the taste of absolutely fresh fish and shellfish has no match. I still remember the sublime flavor of a caught-that-day rainbow trout I purchased at a farmers market years ago and the delectable crab in garlic sauce I ordered in a Chinese restaurant where the live crab was on display just a half-hour before.

But such choice offerings are rare. When shopping for fish, the usual options are fresh, frozen, and farm-raised. Keep the following in mind when fish shopping:

✔ Upscale supermarkets and fish shops are likely to sell fresh seafood. You can find wonderful quality, but the fish may have lost texture and flavor during its hours of transport between the sea and the store.

✔ Look for blast-frozen fish (called IQF in the trade), which is filleted or cut into steaks and then specially frozen within hours of catching. This fish can taste as fresh or fresher than "fresh" fish.

✔ Often the freshest fish is precut and prewrapped. But do avoid fish sold as fresh but actually once frozen and then defrosted — fish that's definitely the worse for wear. Fish that is in a watery package and discolored, with whitish edges, is a telltale sign.

Keeping fish fresh after purchasing it

To make sure you bring the freshest fish possible to your table, after you've bought your seafood, give it your full attention. It needs to be refrigerated quickly and correctly to keep from spoiling, and handled carefully during preparation. But don't worry; all the attention will pay off in terms of flavor and texture as well as safety. In this section, you find what to do and what not to do when handling seafood.

Storing seafood safely

After you purchase seafood, you're in charge of its care, just like if you were buying a plant or adopting a puppy. It will soon let you know if you haven't given it proper care. Here's the drill:

✔ After you buy your fish, immediately take it home and put the fish in the refrigerator. Plan your errands so that you have no excuse not to come right home.

Bring an ice chest filled with ice to the store to transport your seafood home.

✔ To store fresh fish in the fridge, wrap it tightly in foil or plastic and seal it in an airtight plastic bag. Store it in the coldest part of your refrigerator, down toward the bottom. (Heat rises.)

If you purchase packaged fish, before you put it in the fridge, remove the fish from its package, rinse the fish under cold water, and pat it dry with paper towels. Then wrap it in foil or plastic and keep it in an airtight plastic bag near the bottom of the fridge.

✔ Fish held at normal refrigerator temperatures of 35 degrees to 40 degrees will stay fresh only a few hours. You can double the holding time for fish by storing it at 31 degrees. If you can't adjust the temperature of your refrigerator to the low 30s and you don't want your lettuce to freeze, fill a lidded container with crushed ice, cover the ice with a layer of wax paper, and place your fresh fish on this. Then seal the lid and store this on a shelf in the fridge.

Handling seafood properly

For safety, you need to handle fish with respect when you're prepping it for cooking. Make sure to take these steps:

✔ Cook fish the day you purchase it. If you do need to keep it one day, store it on ice.

✔ When making a fish dish with several ingredients that need prepping, finish the chopping and mixing of the other ingredients and then take out the fish from the refrigerator and add it to what you've prepared, such as a marinade or poaching broth.

✔ To trim a fish, place it on a brown paper bag or in the plastic bag, cut open, that the fish came in. After you're done prepping, you can throw away the bag, which may harbor bacteria. Don't use a cutting board — wood, plastic, and acrylic can harbor bacteria.

Fishing for Compliments: Using the Right Cooking Method

You can wow family and friends with great-tasting seafood dishes simply by observing a few basic guidelines and by choosing the right cooking method for the specific type and cut of fish.

Fish has little connective tissue, unlike meat, so it doesn't require long cooking to tenderize it. However, fish cooks quickly and tends to dry out. Techniques such as poaching, basting, and marinating help solve this problem. Your fish is done when it's no longer translucent, it easily flakes when you break it apart with a fork, and the internal temperature is 145 degrees.

Suiting the fixing to the fish

Match the seafood with the right method, and you're on your way to producing great results. The recipes in this chapter give you a chance to experiment with these techniques.

- ✔ Grilling is ideal for fish steaks such as halibut and thick fillets like flounder. The high heat cooks the seafood quickly, helping to prevent it from drying out. Cooked grilled shrimp or scallop kebabs are delicious too. Place the fish on a greased grill. To keep fish moist, baste the fish with a marinade as it grills and turn the fish once, about halfway through cooking.

   Using a special basket that holds the fish makes it easy to turn it over. Look for this utensil in barbecue stores and gourmet cookware shops.

- ✔ Broiling is the right choice for thick fillets such as salmon and fish steaks, which take well to the high direct heat of this easy cooking method. Arrange fish in a single layer on a well-greased broiler rack set about 4 inches from the heat. Season the fish if you like and baste it during cooking. Turn thick cuts once about halfway through cooking. Try the Broiled Alaskan Wild Salmon with Chinese Vegetables or Halibut with Cilantro-Lime Salsa (see the recipes in this chapter).

- ✔ Baking provides a drying heat, so it's good for small steaks and fillets such as flounder and sole, which cook very quickly. Place the fish in a greased dish and drizzle with lemon juice, wine, and/or broth plus a sprinkling of herbs. Cook in a preheated 400- to 450-degree oven. You can also bake a whole fish that's sitting in plenty of savory liquid such as in the recipe for Baked Sea Bass with Aromatic Vegetables in this chapter.

   A simple guideline in baking fish, developed by the Canadian Department of Fisheries, is to allow 10 minutes per inch of thawed fish at its thickest point.

- ✔ Sautéing is ideal for preparing thin fillets such as rex sole, sand dabs, snapper, and whiting. In this cooking method, the fish is dried, lightly floured, and sautéed over medium heat. The classic technique involves sautéing in butter, but you can use cooking oil to avoid the saturated fat.

- ✔ Poaching works well for whole fish, but steaks and even fillets can also be cooked by simmering them in liquid, which can be fish broth, vegetable broth, wine, or a combination of wine and water. Poached fish is often served cold or at room temperature with an accompanying sauce, such as a dill-mayonnaise or a sweet red pepper sauce.

Whole fish can also be dressed up in a variety of ways. The most versatile fish accessory is probably fresh lemon, which can be easily cut to garnish fish and add a bit of flavor. Figure 13-1 shows many ways that whole lemons can be prepared to make your fish more stylish and also add a flavor accent.

Of course, you can use many other foods to garnish your whole fish, including fresh vegetables, fresh herbs, and types of fruit. Figure 13-2 shows how you can garnish cooked whole fish in many different ways with a variety of garnishes.

LEMON CUTS

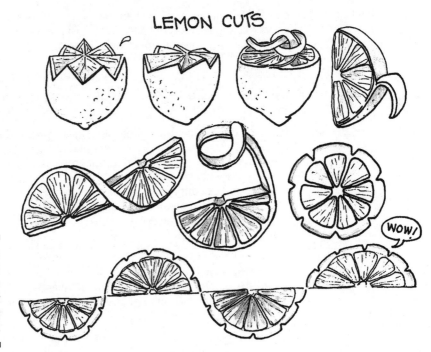

Figure 13-1:
Fancy and
easy lemon
cuts for
garnishing
fish.

DECORATING WHOLE FISH

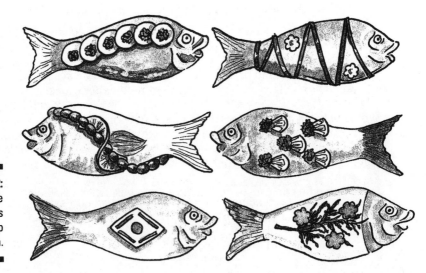

Figure 13-2:
Some of the
many ways
to dress up
a fish.

Simple fish dishes to dive for

Here are pointers on some basic ways to prepare fish that are useful to have in your repertoire. They don't really require measuring, and you probably have most of the ingredients on hand.

Dredging trout in bread crumbs and more

If you're frying trout, or such fish as fillet of sole, flounder, or cod for that matter, and the recipe calls for bread crumbs, dredge the fish in one of these alternatives instead:

- Fine ground cornmeal

- Almond meal mixed with bread crumbs

- A mixture of 1 cup all-purpose flour, 2 teaspoons toasted and ground fennel seeds, salt, and white pepper

Brewing a quick fish stew

When I don't have time to cook, I buy some halibut or flounder and a few shrimp. Then I fix a stew, following this simple recipe:

1. **Sauté some onion and garlic.**

2. **In a large pot, combine a 28-ounce can of tomatoes, a 49-ounce can of chicken broth (rather than clam juice which would make the stew taste too fishy), a bay leaf, some red pepper flakes, a few sprigs of parsley, and the onion and garlic. Bring to a boil over medium-high heat and then reduce to a simmer.**

3. **Cut a couple of potatoes into bite-size chunks and cook them in the tomato sauce for about 15 to 20 minutes.**

4. **When the potatoes are almost done, add the fish and cook for 10 minutes on medium.**

5. **Toward the end of the cooking time, add the shrimp and cook about 3 minutes, until the shrimp turn opaque.**

Serve this with French bread, a green salad, and chilled Mexican beer.

Slapping together a sardine sandwich

Start with a ½ cup of canned sardines, bones and all for the calcium. Add a splash of malt vinegar and black pepper. Mash together and mound on a slice of fresh bread. Add lettuce, tomato, cucumber, and so forth, if you wish; close with another slice of bread; and open wide.

Fabulous Whole-Fish and Filet Recipes

Well, here we go, with some lip-smacking fish dish inventions that are easy to cook and real crowd pleasers. Start with the freshest fish possible and add a few tasty ingredients for a mid-week evening meal or a weekend dinner party. The flavors of these dishes speak of Mexico, Italy, France, and Japan, and you also have the chance to do some good old American grilling.

Halibut with Cilantro-Lime Salsa

As I was cleaning up after testing this recipe, along with its variation, I found myself licking spoons that still had a trace of the purée and then dipping a piece of bread into the sauce left in the food processor and enjoying that too. If this is health food, bring it on!

Specialty tool: *Food processor*

Preparation time: *10 minutes*

Cooking time: *10 minutes*

Yield: *6 servings*

8 tablespoons extra-virgin olive oil	3 tablespoons chopped parsley	6 halibut fillets (6 ounces each), or flounder
4 tablespoons lime juice (2 limes)	2 tablespoons coarsely chopped yellow onion	Salt and pepper
3 tablespoons chopped cilantro	1 whole jalapeño chile, sliced	Cilantro sprigs for garnish

1 Place 6 tablespoons of the olive oil, the lime juice, cilantro, parsley, onion, and jalapeño in a food processor.

2 Purée the ingredients until the mixture is smooth. Set aside.

3 Preheat the broiler. Brush the halibut with the remaining 2 tablespoons olive oil. Sprinkle the fish to taste with salt and pepper.

4 Broil the halibut about 5 minutes per side, just until the center of the fillet is opaque.

5 To serve, spoon a pool of the sauce on each dinner plate. Place a portion of halibut on each plate and garnish the fish with a sprig of cilantro. Yummy accompaniments are oven-roasted potatoes and fresh corn cooked on a grill.

Vary It! *Try a Basil Lemon Sauce variation. Start with 6 tablespoons extra-virgin olive oil and add 4 tablespoons freshly squeezed lemon juice. Add 3 tablespoons basil leaves, 3 tablespoons parsley, and 3 tablespoons chives, all coarsely chopped. Purée in a food processor. To serve, spoon the sauce over the broiled halibut and garnish with a dollop of lowfat sour cream and a slice of black olive.*

Per serving: Calories 332 (From Fat 190); Fat 21g (Saturated 2g); Cholesterol 53mg; Sodium 190mg; Carbohydrate 2g (Dietary Fiber 0g); Protein 35g.

Tilapia with Jalapeño-Tomato Ragout

I started out to recipe test an elaborate recipe for red snapper Veracruzana, decided I didn't have time, and threw together this fish dish for dinner instead. The results were so tasty that I decided to give you the recipe, which makes a great main course for a weeknight dinner. Tilapia is usually inexpensive compared with other fish.

Preparation time: *15 minutes*

Cooking time: *25 minutes*

Yield: *4 servings*

1 medium yellow onion, peeled and sliced very thin (1 heaping cupful)

1 teaspoon extra-virgin olive oil

2 cloves garlic, peeled and minced

1 can (14.5 ounces) stewed tomatoes (no added salt, and flavored with onions, celery, and green bell pepper)

½ to 1 jalapeño, seeds and veins removed, chopped

1 tablespoon chopped cilantro

1 tablespoon chopped parsley

Salt and pepper

1 pound tilapia fillets

Lowfat chicken broth or tomato juice (optional)

1 In a large, 12-inch skillet, heat the onions in the olive oil on medium heat, 7 to 10 minutes or until translucent. Stir occasionally. Toward the end of this cooking process, add the garlic.

2 Add the stewed tomatoes, jalapeño, cilantro, and parsley to the onions and garlic. Stir the mixture and simmer, covered, for 15 minutes to combine the flavors. Season to taste with salt and pepper.

3 Place the tilapia filets in the skillet and spoon the tomato sauce over these. If there's not enough sauce to cover the fish, add a small amount of liquid, such as water, lowfat chicken broth, or tomato juice. Cover and cook on medium-low until the flesh of the fish is opaque, about 10 minutes. Add additional liquid if necessary while the fish is simmering to prevent it from sticking to the bottom of the pan. Serve immediately.

Tip: *If you don't have a 12-inch skillet, put the fish in a baking dish, pour the sauce over the fish, and bake at 350 degrees for 15 to 20 minutes.*

Per serving: Calories 123 (From Fat 18); Fat 2g (Saturated 1g); Cholesterol 41mg; Sodium 190mg; Carbohydrate 9g (Dietary Fiber 2g); Protein 17g.

Broiled Alaskan Wild Salmon with Chinese Vegetables

This easy dish gives you a gourmet treat even when you think you don't have time to cook. When you have this dish, you boost your intake of omega-3 fatty acids, which promote heart health in many ways, and sneak in some green vegetables, too.

Preparation time: *20 minutes, plus 1 to 2 hours to marinate the salmon*

Cooking time: *15 minutes*

Yield: *4 servings*

¼ cup white miso (fermented soybean paste)

2 tablespoons unseasoned rice vinegar

2 teaspoons soy sauce

1 tablespoon minced fresh ginger

1 scallion, trimmed and finely chopped

1 pound Alaskan wild salmon fillets, skin and bones removed

1 clove garlic, minced

1 tablespoon unrefined sesame oil

4 shiitake mushrooms, quartered

4 miniature bok choy, roughly chopped, about 4 cups

2 cups Chinese pea pods

2 teaspoons toasted sesame oil (optional)

1 In a shallow baking dish, make a marinade by whisking together the miso, rice vinegar, soy sauce, ginger, and scallions.

2 Place the salmon in the marinade and turn to coat. Cover and chill for 1 to 2 hours.

3 Preheat the broiler. Using a rubber spatula, gently scrape any excess marinade from the salmon and discard. Oil a shallow baking pan and arrange the salmon fillets in the pan.

4 Place the salmon under the broiler and cook until the edges turn golden brown, 7 to 10 minutes. Gently turn the fillets over and broil an additional 3 minutes. Cook the fish until it is opaque in the center. Cooking times may vary depending upon the type of broiler used.

5 Meanwhile, in a large skillet or wok, cook the garlic in the sesame oil 30 seconds. Add the mushrooms and bok choy. Cook on medium-high, stirring frequently, for 5 to 7 minutes, until the vegetables begin to soften. Then add the pea pods for the last 3 minutes of cooking. If desired, finish with a splash of toasted sesame oil.

6 Divide the vegetable mixture among 4 large dinner plates. Place the broiled salmon on top of the vegetables. Serve immediately with steamed brown rice.

Per serving: Calories 214 (From Fat 70); Fat 8g (Saturated 2g); Cholesterol 53mg; Sodium 267mg; Carbohydrate 10g (Dietary Fiber 3g); Protein 26g.

Baked Sea Bass with Aromatic Vegetables

Use this technique to prepare fillets of fish as well as whole fish. With miniature vegetables as a garnish, this dish dresses up for company but is also a great solution for a quick, high-protein, midweek meal.

Preparation time: *10 minutes*

Cooking time: *20 to 25 minutes*

Yield: *4 servings*

1 cup white wine

1 cup bottled clam juice

1 bulb fennel, stem and fronds trimmed, and sliced horizontally

1 bag (12 ounces) baby carrots, or 12 ounces of regular carrots, tops removed, peeled, quartered lengthwise, and cut into 2-inch lengths

¼ ounce chives, cut in 1-inch lengths

1 teaspoon dried marjoram

2 tablespoons tarragon vinegar

2 tablespoons extra-virgin olive oil

Salt and pepper

2-pound whole sea bass (see the tip at the end of the recipe)

1 Preheat the oven to 450 degrees. Put the white wine and clam juice in a medium-size pot. Add the fennel and carrots and cook over medium heat for 5 minutes. Remove from the heat and add the chives, marjoram, tarragon vinegar, olive oil, and salt and pepper to taste.

2 Place the sea bass in a shallow baking pan. Pour the vegetable and broth mixture over the fish, making sure some vegetables are also in the fish cavity.

3 Bake the fish 10 minutes per inch in the thickest part of the fish, about 15 to 20 minutes. To test for doneness, insert a thermometer at an angle into the thickest part of the flesh. The fish is edible at 140 degrees. Because fish tissues begin to break down at 150 degrees, allowing both juices and flavor to escape, remove the fish from the oven when it is no hotter than 145 degrees. The fish will continue to cook a little after it's removed from the oven. Alternatively, stick a toothpick into the thickest part of the fish. When the fish is done, the pick will meet with little resistance and come out clean. Serve immediately on a platter, with the vegetables scattered over the whole fish for decoration. Cut serving portions at the table.

Tip: Leaving the head on the fish while it cooks helps to seal in juices and keep the fish moist.

Per serving: *Calories 194 (From Fat 83); Fat 9g (Saturated 2g); Cholesterol 40mg; Sodium 379mg; Carbohydrate 9g (Dietary Fiber 2g); Protein 19g.*

Additional Sensational Seafood Recipes

The following recipes struck me as good ones to have for a quick meal at home or for an informal get-together with friends. From the taco and pasta numbers to the simple fish cakes, these are the making for good times ahead. In this section, I also give you the chance to prepare some scallops, shellfish that are perfectly fine to have on a cholesterol-controlling diet because they're low in saturated fat and cholesterol. I haven't given you a recipe for shrimp because they do contain a lot of cholesterol, and as for lobster and crab, which contain about the amount of cholesterol in chicken, prepare these by following standard recipes. But avoid those that require the shellfish to be deep-fried or served with melted butter. Alternatively, enjoy these tricky-to-cook little beasts when you're eating out.

Canned Light Tuna Fish Cakes

These cakes are double-dipped in bread crumbs to give the crunch everyone likes, but without the fat. Start with these cakes to make great fish sandwiches or assemble a green salad topped with these cakes. They also make a handy main course when you need dinner fast. Try them garnished with a wedge of lemon and an easy sauce you can whip together in an instant made with lowfat mayonnaise and wasabi, the Japanese version of horseradish.

Preparation time: *15 minutes*

Cooking time: *Approximately 35 minutes total*

Yield: *8 to 10 patties, approximately 3 inches each*

1½ cups fine, dry, unseasoned bread crumbs, preferably whole grain

1 teaspoon paprika

Salt and pepper

1 pound potatoes, with skins, cut into equal chunks

2 large shallots, finely chopped

3 tablespoons extra-virgin olive oil

2 cloves garlic, finely chopped

2 teaspoons dried thyme, or lemon thyme if available

2 cans (6 ounces each) light tuna (packed in water and no added sodium), drained of liquid

1 level tablespoon petite nonpareil capers

2 tablespoons chopped fresh parsley

2 egg whites

Lemon slices

Lowfat mayonnaise

Wasabi

1 In a small bowl, mix the bread crumbs, paprika, and salt and pepper to taste. Toast in a small dry skillet over medium heat, stirring until golden brown, about 5 minutes. Transfer the bread crumbs to a flat plate and set aside. Fill a large pot with water. Add a dash of salt and bring to a boil.

2 Cook the potatoes in boiling, salted water until tender, 15 to 20 minutes. Drain, mash, and set aside.

3 Use a paper towel to wipe out the skillet used to toast the bread crumbs. Cook the shallots in 1 tablespoon of the olive oil over medium heat for 5 minutes. Add the garlic and thyme, and cook another minute.

4 Place the tuna in a large bowl and flake it. Add the potatoes, shallot mixture, capers, and parsley. Combine and form into patties about 3 inches in diameter.

5 Put the egg whites and ¼ cup of water in a shallow bowl and beat together with a fork. Dredge the fish cakes in the bread crumbs. After each fish cake is covered, next gently dip the cake in the egg white solution and again in the bread crumbs. Your hands will get covered with crumbs and egg whites while you do this, so I suggest putting the cakes either directly in the heated pan or on a piece of waxed paper between dips. This double-dip procedure seals the cake and ensures a moist interior.

6 Again, wipe out the same skillet. Add another tablespoon of the oil and heat. Add a batch of the fish cakes and cook over medium heat, about 5 minutes per side, until the bread crumb crust is golden brown. Transfer the cooked fish cakes to a platter and cover loosely with aluminum foil to keep warm or place in the oven and turn the oven temperature to warm. To make a second batch of fish cakes, put 1 tablespoon of oil into the skillet and proceed as with the first batch. Serve with lemon slices and lowfat mayonnaise that you've seasoned with wasabi.

Per serving: Calories 176 (From Fat 49); Fat 6g (Saturated 1g); Cholesterol 13mg; Sodium 236mg; Carbohydrate 21g (Dietary Fiber 1g); Protein 11g.

Grilled Scallops and Vegetables Marinated in Herbs

Scallops are one of the many shellfish that easily fit into a heart-healthy diet because they're low in cholesterol and contain only a trace of saturated fat. Their mild flavor with a hint of the sea takes well to the flavor of fresh herbs.

Grilled Scallops

Specialty tools: 4 lightly oiled, 15-inch metal skewers or bamboo skewers (see the tip under Grilled Vegetables)

Preparation time: 15 minutes, plus 2 hours for marinating the scallops

Cooking time: 5 minutes

Yield: 4 dinner-size servings

2 tablespoons extra-virgin olive oil	1 clove garlic, minced
2 tablespoons fresh lemon juice	Pepper
2 tablespoons finely chopped basil	12 large sea scallops
2 tablespoons finely chopped parsley	Lemon wedges

1 Preheat the grill. In a medium-size, nonmetallic bowl, whisk together the olive oil, lemon juice, basil, parsley, garlic, and pepper for the marinade.

2 Add the scallops to the herb marinade and toss well. Cover and refrigerate to marinate 2 hours.

3 Using 2 skewers, thread 6 scallops through the center rather than crosswise. Repeat with the remaining scallops. Reserve the remaining marinade for use in the preparation of the Grilled Vegetables.

4 Lay the scallop skewers on an oiled grill or on an oiled grill rack set over the grill, keeping the skewers about ½-inch apart. Cook 2 minutes per side, removing from the grill as soon as the scallops become opaque. Using the blunt side of a knife, slide the scallops onto the vegetable platter.

Grilled Vegetables

Specialty tools: 4 lightly oiled, 15-inch metal or bamboo skewers (see the tip at the end of the recipe)

Preparation time: 10 minutes

Cooking time: 15 minutes

Yield: 4 dinner-size servings

8 cherry tomatoes

8 slices of zucchini, ½-inch thick, about 1 cup

½ medium yellow onion, peeled and cut into 8 wedges

1 Toss the vegetables with some of the marinade from the scallops. Using 1 skewer, thread the onion wedges on this. Leave a few inches of skewer free of vegetables so that the handle-end of the skewer can extend beyond the edge of the grill, allowing the skewer can be maneuvered easily. Next, skewer the zucchini slices, threading the skewer through the length of the slice. Then, using 2 skewers, double-skewer the tomatoes to keep them from twirling.

2 Place the onion skewer on a medium-hot oiled grill or on an oiled grill rack made for vegetables set over the grill. (See the second tip at the end of this recipe for how to test the heat of the grill.) Cook 10 minutes, turn over, and cook an additional 10 minutes. Transfer to a bowl some of the marinade used to marinate the scallops, and occasionally brush the onions with the marinade.

3 When the onions have cooked 5 minutes, put the zucchini on the grill, flat side down. Grill each side about 7 minutes. Brush with marinade as they cook.

4 When the zucchini has cooked 5 minutes and it's time to turn the onions, add the skewer of tomatoes to the grill. Cook all the vegetables together an additional 10 minutes or less, until they're cooked through.

5 Remove the vegetable skewers from the grill and place on a platter. Using the blunt edge of a knife, gently slide the vegetables onto the plate. Serve the scallops and vegetables on a bed of rice pilaf or Quinoa Italiana (see the recipe in Chapter 17). Garnish with lemon wedges.

Tip: Bamboo skewers need to be soaked in water overnight before using to prevent them from burning. They are a better choice than thick metal skewers for grilling small pieces of delicate foods that a thick metal skewer may split.

Tip: To check the temperature of a grill, hold your hand about 5 inches above the cooking surface. When you have low heat, you can hold your hand over the grill for 5 to 6 seconds; with medium heat, 3 to 4 seconds; and high heat, 1 to 2 seconds.

Per serving: *Calories 135 (From Fat 44); Fat 5g (Saturated 1g); Cholesterol 30mg; Sodium 178mg; Carbohydrate 7g (Dietary Fiber 1g); Protein 16g.*

Fish Tacos with Sweet Peppers

Here's a much more fun way of giving yourself a dose of fish oils and antioxidants than swallowing pills. Take your omega-3s and lots of selenium, an important trace mineral, in the red snapper, and phytonutrients in the vegetables. Even the corn tortillas are good for your heart, with 42 mg of calcium and 20 mg of magnesium in each. The only challenge is fitting all this good stuff into a 6-inch folded pancake. So I ask you to cut all the vegetables into narrow strips.

Preparation time: *20 minutes*

Cooking time: *20 minutes*

Yield: *6 servings (2 tacos each)*

1 tablespoon extra-virgin olive oil, plus extra to coat the skillet

1 medium yellow onion, peeled and sliced

1 chile pepper, such as jalapeño, minced (seeds and veins removed, optional)

½ teaspoon ground cumin

½ teaspoon mixed Italian dried herbs

3 sweet red peppers (or 1 yellow, 1 orange, and 1 red), cut into thin 1-inch-long strips

2 tablespoons minced fresh cilantro

2 cloves garlic, minced

1 medium zucchini, trimmed and cut into 1-inch lengths and then cut into strips

Salt and black pepper

1½ pounds red snapper or fillet of sole

12 corn tortillas (6-inch size)

Fresh salsa

Avocado slices

Lime wedges

1 Heat the 1 tablespoon olive oil in a large sauté pan and add the onion, fresh chile pepper, cumin, and dried herbs. Cook over medium-high heat for 2 minutes, stirring occasionally. Add the sweet peppers, cilantro, and garlic. Continue to cook for 15 minutes, until the vegetables soften. In the last 5 minutes of cooking, add the zucchini. Season to taste with salt and pepper.

2 Meanwhile, cook the fillets on a grill pan or in a skillet sprayed with olive oil. Grill until opaque, about 3 minutes per side, depending on thickness. When cooked, cut into ½-inch chunks.

3 After the fish and vegetables are cooked, set aside and keep warm while heating the tortillas. Microwave the tortillas in batches of 6 each. Stack the tortillas on a dinner plate and microwave for 1 minute. Alternatively, steam the tortillas in a pot, using a collapsible steamer that fits inside the pot. However, microwaving works best.

4 Assemble the fish tacos by laying a tortilla flat and placing about ¼ cup (2 ounces) of fish in the middle. Spoon ¼ cup vegetables over the fish. Fold the tortillas in half and transfer to a heated platter. Proceed until all tortillas are filled. Serve with fresh salsa, avocado slices, and wedges of lime.

Per serving: Calories 272 (From Fat 47); Fat 5g (Saturated 1g); Cholesterol 40mg; Sodium 232mg; Carbohydrate 30g (Dietary Fiber 5g); Protein 27g.

Anchovy and Clam Fettuccine

The robust flavor of this pasta is just waiting for Chianti. What a lovely way to have your antioxidants in the red wine and meet your weekly quota of seafood. Make this dish with top-quality imported pasta, such as De Cecco and Delverde brands, or fresh pasta made locally, which you can find in some upscale stores and Italian markets. Or use the recipe to experiment with whole-grain pastas; their rich flavors are a match for the gutsy ingredients in this sauce. Canned clams make this dish quick and easy, but you can dress it up for company and use fresh instead.

Preparation time: *15 minutes*

Cooking time: *15 minutes*

Yield: *4 servings*

8 ounces fettuccine

2 tablespoons extra-virgin olive oil, plus extra for cooking the fettuccine

3 cloves garlic, minced

½ cup white wine

1 can (6.5 ounces) clams, drained and juice reserved, or 2 pounds fresh clams

1 can (2 ounces) anchovies, chopped

2 tablespoons minced Italian parsley, plus extra for garnish

1 teaspoon mixed Italian dried herbs

Hot pepper flakes (optional)

1 Fill a large pot with salted water and bring to a rolling boil. Add the fettuccine slowly enough to maintain the boil, and add a splash of olive oil. Cook the pasta for about 10 minutes, until the fettuccine is almost al dente, or a few minutes less than the instructions on the package indicate for cooking the pasta.

2 Meanwhile, heat the oil in a large 12-inch skillet or a small Dutch oven-style pot. Add the garlic, cooking until the garlic begins to turn golden and immediately add the wine and reserved clam juice. Add the anchovies, parsley, dried herbs, and, if desired, the pepper flakes.

3 Bring the wine mixture to a boil as the pasta finishes cooking. Drain the pasta and add, tossing constantly until the pasta absorbs the liquid, about 3 minutes. Add the clams and toss with the pasta for 30 seconds. Serve garnished with more parsley.

Warning: *Adding more than a dash of pepper flakes will obscure the seafood flavors.*

Vary It! *Add 2 seeded and diced Roma tomatoes to the sauce when you add the anchovies. Finish the dish with a grinding of black pepper.*

Per serving: *Calories 359 (From Fat 90); Fat 10g (Saturated 1g); Cholesterol 43mg; Sodium 712mg; Carbohydrate 43g (Dietary Fiber 3g); Protein 23g.*

Chapter 14

Managing Meats in a Healthy Diet

Meat can still show up in a meal designed to lower cholesterol. Yes, you have options beyond chicken breast in one of its many disguises! Beef, pork, and lamb, as well as exotics such as buffalo, can show up in meals several times a week, especially when served along with plenty of whole grains, legumes, and vegetables that have virtually no saturated fat and zero cholesterol.

In this chapter, you find out which cuts of meat are the leanest and how many ounces are in a heart-healthy portion. You're introduced to cooking techniques that reduce fat and keep the meat juicy. I give you specifics of time and temperature and guidelines on ways to prepare various meats in your own kitchen. Now it's your turn to experiment with the recipes, which are designed to minimize fat while maximizing flavor.

Finding Healthy Ways to Eat Meat

To include meats in a cholesterol-controlling diet, there are several strategies that work very well:

✔ Choose leaner cuts that are lower in saturated fat.

✔ Reduce your usual portion sizes if you're accustomed to large servings.

✔ Cook the meat in a way that eliminates some of the fat.

The following sections give you the details.

Starting with the leanest cuts of meat

Believe it or not, certain cuts of beef and pork can hold their own when compared with lean chicken and fish. Take a look at the USDA figures in Table 14-1 to see how these items compare in terms of total fat, saturated fat, and cholesterol. The numbers refer to the amount in 3 ounces of cooked, trimmed meat.

Table 14-1	Cholesterol Content in Lean Meat, Poultry, and Fish		
Item	*Total Fat (in Grams)*	*Saturated Fat (in Grams)*	*Cholesterol (in Milligrams)*
Beef			
Beef eye of round	4.0	1.5	59
Beef top round	4.3	1.5	76
Beef tip round	5.0	1.8	69
Beef top sirloin	5.8	2.2	76
Beef tenderloin	8.1	3.0	71
Pork			
Pork tenderloin	4.1	1.4	67
Pork boneless loin roast	6.1	2.2	66
Pork loin chop	6.9	2.5	70
Pork boneless rib roast	8.6	3.0	70
Chicken			
Skinless chicken breast	3.1	0.9	73
Skinless chicken leg	7.1	2.0	80
Skinless chicken thigh	9.3	2.6	81
Fish			
Cod	0.7	0.1	40
Flounder	1.3	0.3	58
Halibut	2.5	0.4	35
Salmon	11.0	2.1	54

Later in this chapter, I give you tips on how to select the best cuts of meat and prepare them for a healthy diet and cutting cholesterol.

As long as you're being particular about the cuts of meat you purchase, consider upgrading to meat that's been fed organic feed and is free of the toxic residues of pesticides, antibiotics, and added hormones. Such substances have an impact on your body chemistry, stressing the immune system, affecting hormone balance, and possibly promoting cancer.

Practicing portion control

As you begin to alter the way you eat to lower your cholesterol, Texas-size steaks, if you ever ate them at all, are destined to become a distant memory. You need to reduce portion sizes if you've become accustomed to he-man servings. This isn't to say you have to go short on your protein intake, just on sources of protein that also deliver a lot of saturated fat and cholesterol.

Dietitians consider a portion size of cooked meat 3 ounces. This translates into a not-too-thick hamburger patty the size of the palm of your hand. (No cheating! If you have large hands, then think of a serving as the size of a deck of cards.)

A recipe that calls for a pound of meat yields about five 3-ounce servings.

Tips from Asian cooking

At first glance, a 3-ounce portion may seem appallingly skimpy, but there are ways to make it stretch. The Chinese have been doing this for centuries. In a culture where meat was scarce and plant foods plentiful, Chinese cooks invented all sorts of dishes in which meat is secondary. Many stir-fry dishes fall into this category, including the Steak Stir-Fry with Chinese Vegetables recipe in this chapter.

You can also make a small portion of beef or pork stretch by serving the meat skewered, which can make it seem like more. Start with the recipe for Grilled Marinated Chicken with Creamy Peanut Sauce in Chapter 12, but use red meat instead.

Meaty sauces

Small portions of meat can seem larger when mixed into sauces. For example, spaghetti bolognese from the north of Italy, made with a rich meat sauce, can be yours to enjoy even as you watch your cholesterol. Start with a bottled tomato sauce. You can find all sorts of delectable versions in standard markets. Cook some ground beef, 2 ounces to every 1 cup of sauce. Thoroughly drain the fat from the cooked meat. Pour the tomato sauce into a pot, and add the cooked meat. Simmer to combine flavors and serve over pasta.

Using precooked ground beef to make meat loaf also cuts the fat in this dish. Meat loaf is often made with bread crumbs that will soak up fat from the raw meat as it cooks.

The soy switcheroo

If you're still worried about eating meat, you can try substituting meat with soy protein in your recipes. Researchers have come up with lots of evidence that eating soy foods can lower cholesterol. However, a meta-analysis of many smaller studies, conducted by the University of Kentucky and published in the *New England Journal of Medicine* in 1995, found that to achieve this effect, you need to consume 2 to 3 servings of high-protein soy foods per day. This amount is equivalent to 31 to 47 grams of soy protein. Translating this into soy foods, ¾ cup of firm tofu plus 1½ cups of soy milk gives you 40 grams of soy protein. Many vegetarians may already be consuming this much soy, but if you're accustomed to the taste of meat, switching to eating this much soy could be a challenge.

One way to incorporate more soy in your diet might be to eat vegetarian one or two days a week and feature soy foods in your meals to increase your intake. The accompanying table shows the amount of soy protein in some common soy foods.

You might also try using soy coupled with other foods known to lower cholesterol. In a study conducted in cooperation with the University of Toronto and St. Michael's Hospital in Toronto, Ontario, one group of participants consumed a diet that included margarine enriched with plant sterols, foods rich in soluble fiber, almonds, and over 20 grams of soy protein from soy milk and soy meat substitutes per 1,000 calories consumed. The diet protocol also included a small amount of butter and eggs. This way of eating resulted in a reduction of the "bad" LDL cholesterol of over 28 percent in one month, about the same effectiveness produced by participants who ate a very low-saturated-fat diet and took a cholesterol-lowering statin drug. A third group of participants in the study, who simply followed a very lowfat diet, experienced a drop in LDL cholesterol of only 8 percent.

Protein in Common Soy Foods

Item	Quantity	Grams of Protein
Soy milk	1 cup	4 to 10
Fresh soybeans	3 ounces	10
Tofu, firm	4 ounces	13
Tempeh	4 ounces	17
Soy flour, defatted	½ cup	24

Preparing meats in ways that reduce fat

You can do several things to help cut down on the fat in meat. First trim away any visible fat. You don't need to do this with the precision of a neurosurgeon, but do take a moment to remove the most obvious bits. Eating this fat can double the amount of fat you consume.

Cutting away fat doesn't remove much cholesterol. Most of the cholesterol in meat is incorporated in the muscle tissue. Very little cholesterol is in the fat. However, trimming bits of solid fat is still important because this is the kind that contains saturated fat that can lead to clogged arteries. Healthy, desirable vegetables oils are liquid at room temperature (see Chapter 3).

Next, choose a cooking technique, such as grilling or broiling, that lets fat drain away as the meat cooks. Roasting meat set in a rack works the same way. When sautéing meat, after the meat is cooked, transfer it to a platter while you skim some of the fat from the pan juices.

Make sure you save some of the pan juices to serve with the meat. They contain all sorts of B vitamins, including vitamin B6, B12, thiamin, riboflavin, and niacin. These nutrients are water-soluble and leach out as meat cooks. Minerals can also make their way into cooking liquid. Meat is an excellent source of zinc that helps antioxidants do their job, as well as iron, which transports oxygen in the blood. Don't miss out on all these. Serve your steaks and chops au jus.

Rounding Up Healthy Red Meats

Sometimes, there's nothing like a piece of red meat to make you feel well fed. Perhaps it's the minerals in the meat, or, gosh, the fat, particularly if you've been eating lots of plant foods. Red meat seems to satisfy a particular hunger, and there's no reason not to have some occasionally, even if you are watching your cholesterol.

Lassoing lean beef

Beef cattle in general is leaner these days than in the 1950s and '60s because it's been bred to meet the demand of health-conscious customers. The leanest cuts of beef include top round, sirloin tip, sirloin, New York strip, and beef tenderloin.

The leanest meat is the kind that the USDA labels Select grade. Choice and Prime meats contain more fat, but they are also the tastiest. If you want Choice or Prime, make the portions smaller to cut fat.

In cooking lean beef, the challenge is to produce a tender, moist piece of meat. Fat normally does the trick. But lean meat doesn't give you this break. Instead, to keep meat tender you need to choose the right cooking method, depending upon how well done you want the meat.

✔ For medium-rare meat, heated to 130 to 140 degrees, use a dry heat method of cooking, such as grilling or broiling, for the juiciest results.

As meat is cooked with dry heat to medium-rare, the tangled molecules of protein unfold, and the meat becomes tender.

✔ If you want lean meat well done, moist heat is your best choice. Make sure the meat reaches temperatures above 160 degrees to produce tender meat.

Moist heat converts the connective tissue in meat to tender gelatin after a period of time. This is what's happening in the pot when you make the Vegetable Beef Stew in this chapter.

Counting on sheep

Some cuts of lamb are fine to include in a heart-healthy diet. Trimmed, lean leg of lamb favorably compares with pork loin chops and skinless chicken leg in terms of the amount of total fat, saturated fat, and cholesterol it contains. But not all cuts of lamb are lean. Take a look at Table 14-2.

Table 14-2	Cuts of Lamb Compared with Other Meats in 3-Ounce Servings		
Item	*Total Fat (in Grams)*	*Saturated Fat (in Grams)*	*Cholesterol (in Milligrams)*
Roasted Australian leg of lamb, lean only	6.89	2.8	75.7
Broiled loin lamb chop, lean and fat	19.6	8.36	85
Pork loin chop	6.9	2.5	70
Skinless chicken leg	7.1	2.0	80

If you long for the flavor of lamb, fix yourself some of this lamb dish inspired by the flavors in Greek cooking in which lamb is a staple food:

1. **Place the following ingredients in a pot: 1 can (32 ounces) plum tomatoes that you've chopped, 2 cloves crushed garlic, 1 teaspoon dried oregano, ½ teaspoon cinnamon, and 6 ounces shredded, roasted leg of lamb, trimmed of visible fat.**

2. **Cook over medium-low heat until the tomatoes soften and the flavors combine, about 20 minutes.**

3. **Pour over orzo pasta with a sprinkling of feta cheese to make 4 servings.**

Braving buffalo

Something inside you may be holding you back from trying a mouthful of buffalo meat — perhaps worries that the meat will taste too wild or remorse over their near-extinction from hunting by settlers. But happily, it's a new day in the buffalo world. Buffalo herds are being raised in a natural environment, free of such modern manipulations as growth hormones, on ranches in the United States and Canada.

The flavor of buffalo is sweeter and richer than beef. And compared with beef, the meat is higher in protein and lower in fat and cholesterol, as you can see in Table 14-3.

Table 14-3	A Comparison of Cooked Buffalo, Beef, and Poultry		
Meat (3 ounces)	*Protein (in Grams)*	*Total Fat (in Grams)*	*Cholesterol (in Milligrams)*
Buffalo tenderloin	21.5	2	70
Beef tenderloin	19.5	8	72
Chicken breast	26	3	73

Upscale supermarkets sell frozen buffalo patties. The recipe in this chapter for buffalo meatballs starts with these. But your butcher should be able to order all manner of cuts from special purveyors. You can check out one such source at www.broadleafgame.com, which sells everything from caribou to kangaroo to turtle. A friendly, informative Web site full of buffalo info is www.thebuffaloguys.com.

Going in search of ostrich and emu

Unlike chicken and turkey, ostrich and emu are red-meat birds, but much lower in fat than red meats such as beef. Meat from these birds is becoming increasingly popular as a healthy alternative to beef, and the birds are raised on farms all over the United States specifically for this reason.

The ostrich is the largest bird in the world, weighing over 300 pounds and reaching up to 8 feet tall. There is no breast meat on an ostrich, only meat from the tenderloin, thighs, and legs. Ostrich is similar to red meat, but with a unique, mild flavor.

Emus are the second-largest birds in existence. They weigh between 90 and 150 pounds and are between 5½ and 6 feet tall. They can jump 4 feet straight up and are able to run up to 40 miles per hour. Like ostrich, emu has no breast meat. Emu is lower in cholesterol than ostrich or beef. The American Heart Association includes emu in its listing of heart-healthy meats. To find out more about emu, visit the Web site www.aea-emu.org.

You can find ostrich sold as ground meat patties in the frozen foods section of upscale supermarkets. Emu meat is not a standard item in markets yet. It comes to market as steaks, larger cuts for roasting, and as ground meat.

Strike up a friendship with your local butcher. Ask for guidance on cuts of meat and, if you don't see what you want in the meat case, request special cuts. Asking your butcher for emu could make his day!

Because ostrich and emu meats are lean, be careful not to overcook them. An internal temperature of 150 to 160 degrees indicates the meat is done but not dry. They are best prepared on high heat and quickly cooked by broiling, pan broiling, grilling, or sautéing.

Preparing Pork That's Lean and Mean

Pork earns its place as a meat of choice in cholesterol-controlling cooking for flavor and fat content. For starters, the meat makes a remarkably versatile ingredient, adapting well to all sorts of flavorings and preparations. Pigs and hogs have also been bred to be far leaner than their counterparts of 50 years ago. However, pork these days still has one problem. What kept the pork of yore so moist and succulent was all that fat. Now pork, especially the leaner cuts you want to favor, can quickly dry out during cooking.

Keeping pork juicy

Choose a method of cooking that uses dry heat, such as grilling, broiling, sautéing, or roasting. Moist heat cooking, such as stewing and braising, draws juice out of the pork. Next, decide on a cooking temperature.

✔ When preparing thick chops, first brown them in a skillet and then finish them in the oven on moderate heat of 350 degrees to cook them through without drying the exterior. See Juicy Pork Chops with Rosemary for an example.

✔ When roasting a pork loin, start the oven at 400 to 450 degrees, roasting the meat for 15 minutes. Then lower the temperature to 325 degrees to keep the juices in the meat.

A digital instant-read thermometer gives you an accurate temperature even if inserted only ¼ inch. Consequently, you can use it to take the temperature of chops and meat patties as well as roasts. This inexpensive thermometer displays the temperature to two decimal points and is powered by a small watch battery.

I've learned through the years to proceed with caution when cooking pork chops. I approach cooking lean pork like I would an egg, paying close attention to timing and temperature.

Don't buy those very thin chops that supermarkets sell in quantity packages. The meat toward the edge will be overcooked by the time the meat next to the bone is done. Instead, start with a chop that is 1¼ to 1½ inches thick. Such a chop amounts to about two 3-ounce servings. Share it with someone or have the rest in a sandwich for lunch the next day.

Knowing when pork is done

The main worry that people have about cooking pork is that undercooked pork can result in the infection called *trichinosis*. Cases of trichinosis poisoning are rare, but prevention is still of utmost importance. The good news is that trichinosis is killed off at 137 degrees, a temperature much lower than once thought. Here are some tips to assure properly cooked pork:

✔ Cook loin pork chops until they reach an internal temperature of 145 to 150 degrees. Then cover the chops loosely with aluminum foil, and let them rest 5 minutes to absorb juice and equalize the temperature, which will rise another 5 degrees.

✔ Heat a loin roast to 145 to 155 degrees. Then cover the meat and let it rest for 20 to 30 minutes, while the temperature rises another 10 degrees.

✔ When pork is sufficiently cooked, the meat is likely to still be slightly pink.

Meaty Recipes for Healthy Eating

Try these recipes for beef, pork, and buffalo the next time you want red meat. The beef recipes include lots of vegetables. The pork recipes are designed to keep the meat moist. And the recipe for meatballs gives you a way to sample some buffalo, one bit at a time.

Steak Stir-Fry with Chinese Vegetables

This recipe gives you an experience in stir-frying, a very useful technique for turning small amounts of meat into a satisfying meal. In stir-frying, food is cooked at very high temperatures, using a small amount of fat. While the ingredients cook, they are constantly stirred and tossed to prevent burning. The shiitake mushrooms in this dish give rich flavor, but as an alternative, use the more exotic wood ear mushrooms sold dried in Chinese grocery stores. Wood ear mushrooms contain blood-thinning compounds also present in garlic and onions.

Preparation time: 20 minutes, plus 2 hours for the meat to marinate

Cooking time: 8 minutes

Yield: 4 servings

¼ cup low-sodium soy sauce

2 tablespoons hoisin sauce

1 tablespoon sherry (optional)

12 ounces round steak, cut across the grain in ¼-inch slices, cut into 1½-inch lengths (see Figure 14-1)

2 tablespoons unrefined safflower oil

1 clove garlic, crushed and minced

1 tablespoon minced fresh gingerroot

1 tablespoon roasted sesame oil

½ pound bok choy, cut crosswise in 1-inch pieces

2 ounces fresh mushrooms, shiitake or wood ear

2 scallions, trimmed and cut crosswise into ¼-inch slices

½ pound Chinese peapods, washed and trimmed

Cutting Across the Grain

Figure 14-1:
Cutting
meat across
the grain.

1 Mix the soy sauce, hoisin sauce, and, if desired, the sherry in an 8-inch square baking dish. Place the beef in the dish and turn to coat with the marinade. Cover the dish with plastic wrap and set the beef in the refrigerator to marinate for 2 hours.

2 Remove the meat from the refrigerator and transfer it to a plate where excess marinade can drain. Turn the heat on under a wok or large frying pan. Put the safflower oil in the wok, and when it's very hot, add the meat. Stir and toss continuously, cooking no more than 2 minutes. Halfway through, add the garlic and ginger. Transfer the meat to a bowl and cover with a plate to keep warm. Set aside the leftover marinade in the baking dish to add to the stir-fry later.

3 Add the roasted sesame oil to the wok, along with the bok choy and mushrooms. Stir-fry for 2 minutes and then add the scallions and peapods. Stir-fry for 1 minute. Add the marinade and continue to stir the vegetables for an additional 3 minutes, making sure the marinade comes to a boil to cook any meat juices in the liquid. Add water if necessary.

4 Remove the wok from heat. Add the meat and combine with the vegetables. Serve immediately with regular brown rice or aromatic brown basmati rice.

Tip: *If you want large portions, add more vegetables.*

Per serving: *Calories 250 (From Fat 122); Fat 14g (Saturated 2g); Cholesterol 49mg; Sodium 1,107mg; Carbohydrate 8g (Dietary Fiber 2g); Protein 23g.*

Vegetable Beef Stew

One way to continue to enjoy red meat while watching your saturated fat and cholesterol is to eat small portions coupled with lots of vegetables. This stew follows this formula, with about 3 ounces of meat per serving. But this dish is still substantial thanks to the barley, which gives you soluble fiber.

Preparation time: *15 minutes*

Cooking time: *About 2¼ hours*

Yield: *6 servings*

1¼ pounds top round or top sirloin, cut into 1-inch to 1½-inch pieces

1 tablespoon unrefined safflower oil

1 medium yellow onion, trimmed and chopped

1 tablespoon paprika

5 carrots, peeled and cut into 1-inch lengths

1 stalk celery, cut into 1-inch lengths

⅔ cup pearl barley, rinsed

1 clove garlic, minced

1 bay leaf

¼ teaspoon red pepper flakes

Salt

1 cup red wine

3 cups fat-free, low-sodium beef broth or homemade beef stock

¼ head cabbage, cut into 3-inch chunks, about 3 cups

1 In a large pot, cook the beef in the oil on medium heat, 5 to 10 minutes, stirring occasionally so all sides brown.

2 Add the onion and paprika. On medium heat, cook the onion until it softens and begins to brown, about 5 minutes.

3 Add the carrots, celery, barley, garlic, bay leaf, pepper flakes, salt, red wine, and broth. Stir to combine and bring to a boil.

4 Lower the heat so that the mixture simmers and cook, covered, for 1½ hours. Add the cabbage and cook until the meat is fork tender, about an additional half-hour. Remove the bay leaf before serving.

5 Serve the stew in bowls with a glass of red wine.

Per serving: *Calories 273 (From Fat 54); Fat 6g (Saturated 1g); Cholesterol 54mg; Sodium 409mg; Carbohydrate 29g (Dietary Fiber 7g); Protein 26g.*

Roasted Pork Tenderloin with Hazelnut-Marmalade Glaze

Tenderloin is remarkably simple to cook and takes well to all sorts of marinades and glazes. Try this recipe and make up your own variations, such as adding some dark rum to the marmalade mixture. Baked sweet potatoes and cauliflower go well with this dish.

Preparation time: *15 minutes*

Cooking time: *Approximately 40 minutes*

Yield: *4 servings, 4 ounces each*

½ cup orange marmalade (preferably an all-fruit brand such as Sorrell Ridge)

2 tablespoons Dijon mustard

½ cup chopped hazelnuts

¼ teaspoon crushed black peppercorns

1½ teaspoons apple cider vinegar

¼ teaspoon sage

2 to 2½ pounds pork tenderloin (sold as 2 pieces), trimmed of visible fat

Salt and pepper

1 tablespoon extra-virgin olive oil

1 Preheat the oven to 400 degrees. Put the marmalade, mustard, hazelnuts, peppercorns, and vinegar in a bowl. Stir to combine and set aside.

2 Rub the sage into the pork and season to taste with the salt and pepper.

3 Heat the olive oil in a skillet over medium-high heat. Put the tenderloin in the pan and lightly brown on all sides, turning frequently, for 3 minutes.

4 Transfer the meat to a baking dish. Spread the marmalade mixture over the meat. Roast in the oven for 30 minutes, or until the internal temperature is 145 to 150 degrees.

5 Remove the meat from the oven and loosely cover with aluminum foil. Let rest for 5 minutes to allow the meat to absorb juices and equalize the temperature. Serve immediately.

Per serving: *Calories 334 (From Fat 152); Fat 17g (Saturated 3g); Cholesterol 63mg; Sodium 389mg; Carbohydrate 21g (Dietary Fiber 3g); Protein 26g.*

Juicy Pork Chops with Rosemary

This is an attractive and easy-to-make recipe that's been very popular with my guests. This recipe uses several strategies for keeping the meat moist: searing, breading, and roasting with a wine reduction at a low temperature. It also requires that you start with loin pork chops about 1½ inches thick. However, one of these chops makes for quite a large portion, about a half pound. Consequently, in this recipe, I am asking you to forsake appearance in deference to juiciness, and carve up 2 chops to serve 3 persons. The portions may seem modest, but the point here is to retain the juiciness of the meat and cut down on total meat consumption. Enjoy it with your favorite side dishes.

Preparation time: *15 minutes, plus 15 minutes for the chops to refrigerate after breading*

Cooking time: *About 45 minutes*

Yield: *4 servings*

⅓ cup whole-wheat flour

¼ teaspoon salt

¾ cup whole-grain bread crumbs

2 egg whites, lightly beaten with 1 tablespoon water

2 bone-in loin pork chops (at least a half pound each), 1¼ to 1½ inches thick, trimmed of extra fat

1 clove garlic, sliced in half

Pepper

3 tablespoons extra-virgin olive oil

½ red onion, peeled and diced

2 teaspoons fresh chopped rosemary

1 bay leaf

½ cup dry white wine

½ cup water or chicken broth

1 Mix the flour and salt and spread out on a large plate. Cover a second plate with the bread crumbs. Put the egg whites in a shallow bowl and lightly beat until frothy. Using a paper towel, pat the chops dry. Rub the meat with the garlic and season to taste with pepper.

2 Dredge each chop in the flour, shake off excess, and dip the chop in the egg white. Coat each side of the chops with bread crumbs, pressing the crumbs into the meat. Set the chops aside on a platter. Refrigerate the chops at least 15 minutes before cooking.

3 Preheat the oven to 350 degrees. Put 2 tablespoons of the oil in a large skillet. Place the chops in the skillet and cook on medium-high heat until browned, about 3 minutes per side.

4 Transfer the chops to an 8-x-8-inch baking dish. Reduce the heat under the skillet and add the remaining 1 tablespoon oil along with the onion and rosemary. Cook until the onions soften and begin to brown, about 5 minutes. Add the bay leaf and wine, reducing the liquid to 2 tablespoons. Add the water or chicken broth and simmer an additional 5 minutes. Remove the bay leaf.

5 Pour the onion mixture over the chops. Cover tightly with foil and bake the chops about 30 minutes. When done, the internal temperature should be 145 degrees. Transfer to a platter and cover loosely with aluminum foil. Let the chops rest 5 minutes. The meat will still be slightly pink. To have 3 portions out of the 2 chops, make the third serving by cutting away a third of the meat from each chop and combining these to make one portion. Serve the chops immediately, along with assorted side dishes such as roasted potatoes, cauliflower, and carrots.

Tip: You find whole-grain bread crumbs sold in natural foods stores.

Per serving: Calories 249 (From Fat 124); Fat 14g (Saturated 3g); Cholesterol 31mg; Sodium 229mg; Carbohydrate 16g (Dietary Fiber 3g); Protein 16g.

Buffalo Meatballs

Surprise your friends by serving them these buffalo meatballs. Make them tiny, as in this recipe, to eat as hors d'oeuvres dipped in ketchup, barbecue sauce, or any number of gourmet relishes sold in upscale markets. Or make large ones to prepare spaghetti and meatballs.

Preparation time: 20 minutes

Cooking time: 15 minutes

Yield: 24 cocktail-size meatballs

1 pound ground buffalo	1 teaspoon mixed Italian herbs
⅓ cup finely chopped yellow onion	½ teaspoon salt
2 egg whites	½ teaspoon pepper
1 clove garlic, minced	Unrefined safflower oil to coat baking dish
1 tablespoon finely chopped fresh parsley	2 tablespoons chopped fresh parsley

1 Preheat the oven to 400 degrees. In a large bowl, put the buffalo, onion, egg whites, garlic, parsley, herbs, salt, and pepper. Mix until thoroughly combined.

2 Line a 9-x-12-inch baking dish with foil and lightly coat with oil.

3 Shape the buffalo mixture into meatballs about 1 inch in diameter, placing these in the baking dish as you finish each one. Space these to keep the meatballs separate.

4 Place the meatballs in the oven and bake for 15 minutes, until the meat is cooked to your liking. Serve with toothpick skewers and tomato or barbecue dipping sauce.

Tip: Ground buffalo meat is sold as frozen patties. Let these thaw and then use this meat to shape the meatballs for this dish. An increasing number of markets are selling frozen buffalo meat. If you don't see it, ask the store manager to order some.

Per serving: Calories 22 (From Fat 6); Fat 1g (Saturated 0g); Cholesterol 7mg; Sodium 60mg; Carbohydrate 0g (Dietary Fiber 0g); Protein 3g.

Part V

A Harvest of Cholesterol-Controlling Veggies, Beans, and Grains

The 5th Wave   By Rich Tennant

Because of his parents' practice of serving low—cholesterol meals by carving melons into the shapes of high—cholesterol foods, it wasn't until college that Dennis discovered that fried chicken didn't come with seeds.

AND WHAT THE HECK IS THIS...?

In this part . . .

How about cooking up some vegetables, legumes (you know, like beans and lentils), and whole grains? In the three chapters in this part, I show you how to prepare these foods and explain why they belong in a cholesterol-conscious diet. (I want you to be inspired to eat lots of them.)

I accompany you to the market to point out which vegetables are best and outline how to store and cook them to retain the most nutrients. Next, I share with you my favorite bean recipes. Finally, I make a big to-do over eating whole grains, which do so much more for your heart than refined products. I introduce you to the large variety of grains available and explain how to keep them fresh and cook them.

Chapter 15

Welcoming Heart-Friendly Veggies into Your Kitchen

Despite the fact that vegetables don't have any cholesterol in them, they usually aren't mentioned in talk about lowering cholesterol. In fact, they can play a significant part in controlling cholesterol because of the nutrients and soluble fiber that lots of them contain. The only trick is, you do have to eat them!

The American Heart Association Eating Plan for Healthy Americans recommends having five or more servings a day of fruits and vegetables. A serving of vegetables is a half cup, not much given that a medium-size tomato wouldn't fit in this. It's estimated that only about 20 percent of Americans manage to swallow this much. Of course, if you're vegetarian, you're probably already ahead of the pack. How many servings of vegetables did you eat yesterday?

Whether eating vegetables is a sometimes event or you're already devoted to plant foods and just want to fine-tune your eating habits, this chapter is for you. I calculated which vegetables are especially good for heart health and give you a shopping list for the top ten. Other veggies, such as cauliflower and winter squash, were contenders, but these ten are a good place to start. Information about the nutrients they contain follows. I also offer cooking tips and suggested salt-free seasonings.

The chapter concludes with recipes that call for each of the featured veggies. Some are treated to full-flavored, gutsy seasonings such as the Kale with Onions, Garlic, and Greek Olives and the Roasted Carrots with Walnuts, baked with a dusting of nutmeg and allspice. Such combinations are certain to convince the most reluctant of vegetable eaters that these plant foods are for lions and tigers and not just for rabbits. I also include some more subtle concoctions such as the Asparagus with Mustard Vinaigrette, which features the very green flavor of this succulent relative of the lily.

The Veggie VIP List

Several very large studies have confirmed that vegetables, along with fruit, are essential to ensure cardiovascular health. The first National Health and Nutritional Examination Survey Epidemiologic Follow-up Study, conducted at Tulane University and involving over 9,500 men and women, found that eating three or more fruits and vegetables a day resulted in a reduction of risk of fatal heart attack compared with people who are eating less than one serving a day. And in the Women's Health Study, conducted by Brigham and Women's Hospital and Harvard Medical School, which involved nearly 40,000 women, those eating an average of 5 to 10 servings a day of fruits and vegetables had 20 to 30 percent less cardiovascular disease.

In another large study, involving the Nurses' Health Study and the Health Professionals' Follow-Up Study, that analyzed data collected from over 75,000 women and over 38,000 men, fruit and vegetable intake was inversely related to the risk of stroke. Each additional serving per day resulted in a 7 percent lower risk in women and a 4 percent lower risk among men. Cruciferous vegetables, such as broccoli, cabbage, cauliflower, and Brussels sprouts, were most protective, but green leafy vegetables and vitamin C-rich fruits and vegetables also proved beneficial. So eat your broccoli! This chapter gives you a tasty way to do this with the recipe for Broccoli-Shiitake Stir-Fry.

To eat less red meat and the saturated fat it contains, be a sometimes vegetarian, eating only plant foods, for instance, two full days a week.

Writing your vegetable shopping list

The produce section is the prettiest part of the supermarket. It's full of color, and the air feels filled with life. But walk down the aisle where canned vegetables are on display, and you won't get the same buzz. In supermarkets, shop where you can see the color.

Does corn count?

Vegetables can be divided into two groups — starchy and nonstarchy. Corn, winter squash, and root vegetables such as parsnips are considered starchy because they're more concentrated in carbohydrates and calories than other vegetables. The nonstarchy vegetables include leafy greens, celery, mushrooms, okra, peppers, and tomatoes. A healthy diet includes both kinds, with an emphasis on the nonstarchy type. These are lower in calories and supply several phytonutrients that control cholesterol and protect arteries. Another reason to opt for nonstarchy is that these vegetables digest slowly and have a lower glycemic index, causing less of a rise in blood sugar.

When you must have a vegetable that's out of season and not on display, go ahead and buy it frozen. First, it's better to eat vegetables that have been frozen than none at all, and frozen ones happen to be quite nutritious. The produce is flash frozen within 24 hours of harvesting and is likely to contain good amounts of nutrients at least equal to a "fresh" vegetable that has traveled long distances to market and sat around in storage a few days. However, canned vegetables don't hold such promise, because in the heating process used in canning, vitamins and phytonutrients are damaged. But items such as canned pureed pumpkin and canned beans seem to hold up well.

Farmers markets offer an array of fresh produce, picked usually only the day before. You can tell how extra fresh the fruits and vegetables are when you bring them home and are pleasantly surprised at how long they stay fresh and edible in your kitchen, often much longer than store-bought produce.

Certain vegetables in particular belong on your cholesterol-controlling shopping list. They contain more of the nutrients that keep the heart functioning and the arteries clear and many have some form of soluble fiber that can lower cholesterol, just like oat bran does. I've worked out a list of ten. Buy these regularly, and you'll be off to a great start! Later in this chapter, you find a recipe for each vegetable.

- ✔ Artichokes
- ✔ Asparagus
- ✔ Broccoli
- ✔ Cabbage
- ✔ Carrots

 ✔ Kale

 ✔ Mushrooms

 ✔ Okra

 ✔ Spinach

 ✔ Sweet potatoes

This list consists of vegetables that are pretty much as nature made them, with skin and some stem and seeds — a whole food that has all of its parts. This is the same idea as eating a whole grain, a subject I discuss in Chapter 17. Whole vegetables give you a natural and complete balance of nutrients. In the recipes, I don't ask you to peel the vegetables or remove membranes and seeds. I may tell you to "trim," but that simply means to cut away tough tops and stems as well as damaged bits — that's all. You fungus-lovers out there may have noticed that I included mushrooms in this list of vegetables. They are, after all, from the plant kingdom. Furthermore, mushrooms are a source of B vitamins and chromium, needed to manage cholesterol and control blood sugar.

Dishing potatoes

Potatoes have taken a bad rap because they're thought to be fattening. But it's the butter and sour cream you put on the potato that is much more likely to add pounds, as well as raise cholesterol thanks to all the saturated fat these yummy toppings contain. Actually, an unadorned, average baked potato, with skin, is only 220 calories and without skin just 145 calories. (However, please eat the skin for the fiber.) Spuds such as russets, the standard baking potato, and the all-purpose white boiling potato are also excellent sources of potassium, which helps keep blood pressure normal. And sweet potatoes have sky-high amounts of beta carotene, an antioxidant and an important nutrient for maintaining the tissue that lines the digestive tract.

Now check out this stunning statistic: According to the United States Department of Agriculture, in 1999, potatoes accounted for one-third of all vegetables consumed. And two-thirds of these potatoes were French fries, potato chips, and other forms of processed spuds. These potatoes are cooked in oils that contain trans fatty acids. Trans fats act like saturated fat in the body. However, you always have the option of savoring a freshly baked potato, steaming and hot, and topped with lowfat yogurt and chives or nonfat sour cream and freshly ground black pepper. Roasted round red potatoes are delightful drizzled with olive oil and sprinkled with rosemary, baked in the oven. Or try the Hash Browns with Veggie Bacon in Chapter 7 and the recipe for Sweet Potato and Parsnip Purée with Toasted Pecans in this chapter. I promise you'll like how they taste. Delish!

Loading up on vitamins and minerals

Think over the vegetables you've eaten in the last few days — maybe carrots, peas, corn, and some potatoes. For many people, variety has come to mean adding string beans to your diet, but so many other vegetables are out there waiting for you, including important ones for heart health. The ten vegetables featured in this chapter provide a wide range of nutrients that play a role in controlling cholesterol and are good for the heart (see Chapter 2). These include antioxidants such as beta carotene, vitamin C and vitamin E, several B vitamins such as vitamin B6 and folic acid, and important minerals like magnesium and potassium.

Asparagus, broccoli, spinach, and sweet potatoes supply some of all of these nutrients, with spinach taking the cake for providing especially good amounts. And both carrots and sweet potatoes provide loads of beta carotene. Include all ten vegetables in your diet, and you're sure to have some of all of these nutrients. You've never tackled cooking artichokes or asparagus before? Don't worry! The recipes in this chapter guide you through the steps, in case cooking these veggies is new to you.

While vegetables are rich in nutrients, refined and processed foods are not. Refined white sugar supplies no minerals, no fiber, and no vitamins at all. And ketchup contains only a smidgeon of vitamin C. When you're tallying your vegetable intake for the day, don't try to sneak in ketchup.

Stocking up on plant power: The potent phytonutrients

The ten vegetables featured in this chapter also contain phytonutrients, which are explained in Chapter 2. Besides fighting cancer, these compounds also protect the heart. Here are some of the specific phytonutrients that these vegetables contain:

- Rutin, a flavonoid, strengthens capillary walls, working in combination with vitamin C. Asparagus is one source of rutin.

- Cynarin, a phytonutrient found in artichokes, lowers the "bad" LDL, improving the ratio of LDL to HDL cholesterol. Cynarin removes cholesterol from the body by increasing the liver's production of bile, which requires cholesterol to produce. Bile is then excreted from the body.

- Silymarin, a flavonoid used to treat liver disease, is also an antioxidant. Artichokes are a source as well as an herb called milk thistle, from which silymarin supplements are produced.

✔ Lutein is found in broccoli and prevents the progression of atherosclerosis, or hardening of the arteries.

✔ Alpha-lipoic acid and glutathione are extra-powerful antioxidants that guard against stroke and heart attack. Spinach has these and lutein, too.

The top ten vegetables include three cruciferous vegetables — broccoli, cabbage, and kale — but all of the cruciferous vegetables are good for the heart. Cruciferous vegetables are members of the mustard family, which includes cabbages, broccoli, cauliflower, Brussels sprouts, and mustard greens. No, putting more mustard on your ballpark hot dog doesn't count as a serving of cruciferous vegetables. Cruciferous vegetables such as broccoli also contain sulforaphane, a compound that boosts antioxidant activity in several ways as well as stimulating detoxification processes in the body, helping prevent cancer. Be sure to include cruciferous vegetables on your shopping list!

Supping on soluble fiber

Certain vegetables also provide a modest amount of soluble fiber, the kind that lowers cholesterol. You find about 2 grams or so of soluble fiber in around a half to a cup's worth (about 4 ounces) of vegetables. Admittedly, the amount of soluble fiber in veggies is significantly less than in oats, but every little bit counts.

Here's how vegetables, assessed in a 1992 study by Judith A. Marlett, PhD, RD, and published in the *Journal of the American Dietetic Association,* ranked in terms of soluble fiber content, with the best sources at the top. Many are included in your cholesterol-controlling vegetable shopping list and the recipes.

1. Green beans and baked potatoes with the skin

2. Brussels sprouts and pumpkin

3. Asparagus, beets, broccoli, and sweet potato

4. Cauliflower and boiled potato without the skin

5. Carrots, green peppers, and mushrooms

Other vegetables that have some soluble fiber content include okra, cabbage, and nopales, or cactus paddles (which, come to think of it, might make interesting ping pong paddles).

Readying Vegetables for the Table

Cooking vegetables is easy because they take well to all sorts of preparations, from steaming, roasting, and stir-frying to stewing and puréeing. You find all these techniques in the recipes in this chapter. Use these recipes to experiment with the techniques. I worked all of the top ten vegetables for heart health into these dishes, but feel free to substitute vegetables and make up your own combinations. I also suggest some trimmings for plain, steamed vegetables that add flavor but not salt.

Pampering veggies in the pot

Cook your vegetables by using a method that still preserves the nutrients. When a vegetable is subjected to heat, the cell walls eventually break down, releasing juices and the nutrients inside. When you boil a vegetable to death, the good stuff ends up in the water, and you eat the depleted vegetable, a shadow of its former self. Instead, lightly steam or bake your vegetables, and much more of the nutrients will reach your plate.

If you're determined not to fuss over cooking vegetables and must boil them, just make vegetable soup and drink the nutrient-rich broth. Use the Leek and Mixed Vegetable Soup recipe in Chapter 9 as your guide.

Steaming basics

To steam vegetables, use a collapsible steamer insert. Set it inside a large pot with a tight-fitting lid. Steaming is cooking over, not in, liquid, so you don't want to fill the pot with so much water that it rises above the bottom of the steamer where the vegetables sit. Lacking one of these steamers, invert a bowl or a couple of cups and place a plate on top of this to make a platform in the bottom of the pot. When steaming the vegetables, keep the water simmering, not boiling.

If you see steam escaping from the pot and you no longer hear the water moving, check if the water has boiled away. If needed, add more water, which should be boiling when you add it to the pot.

Smartening up steamed vegetables with healthy toppings

While steamed vegetables are very healthy, their simplicity can be boring. Make steamed vegetables more interesting by adding some toppings. If you've been diagnosed with hypertension and your physician has warned you against consuming too much sodium, these add-ons fit the prescription because they're all designed to enhance flavor without adding salt:

- ✔ A squeeze of lemon juice, plus freshly ground pepper

- ✔ A drizzle of special oil, such as rich olive oil or walnut or hazelnut oil, perhaps mixed with minced herbs, such as parsley or basil

- ✔ A scattering of seasoned bread crumbs, along with a drizzle of oil

- ✔ A sprinkling of gourmet vinegar, such as an aged balsamic or tarragon, maybe combined with oil

- ✔ A splash of hot sesame oil or pepper flakes to add some punch to a dish that's bland

- ✔ A toss of toasted nuts — whole, slivered, or ground — to add some crunch

- ✔ A dash of one of the salt-substitute herbal seasonings available in all food stores — one that I like is Spike

Sometimes, vegetarian main courses served in restaurants or included in veggie cookbooks have a slathering of melted cheese on top. Don't delude yourself into thinking that a dish is low in calories or saturated fat just because a dish is labeled vegetarian. If you can't resist eating such a dish, your body may be starved for fat. Increase your intake of nuts and seeds and cook with healthy vegetable oils.

Because steamed vegetables have no camouflage, be sure to use top-quality, very fresh produce.

A Diversity of Delicious Veggie Recipes

After you try these recipes, you'll never again have reason to assume that a vegetable dish need be tasteless and boring. I packed these recipes with exuberant flavors, topped some with toasted nuts and sweetened others with onions. And some are so substantial, such as Okra Mediterranean Style and Broccoli-Shiitake Stir-Fry, that you can use them as a vegetarian main course and build a meal around them.

☺ *Antipasto Artichoke*

The steaming broth that cooks and scents the artichoke contains the best of Italian flavors — garlic, onion, wine, and basil. It's too good to throw away after the artichokes are cooked, so strain it and use as a dipping sauce as you eat the artichoke leaves. Once you remove all the leaves, you'll come to the fuzzy inner choke. Remove this with a spoon and then proceed to enjoy the artichoke heart, which you can eat with a knife and a fork.

Preparation time: 15 minutes

Cooking time: 45 to 60 minutes

Yield: 4 servings as a first course

4 large artichokes

4 cups water

1 cup white wine

¼ cup extra-virgin olive oil

½ cup onion, minced

4 cloves garlic, minced

3 sprigs flat-leaf parsley, stems removed and minced

2 sprigs fresh basil, stems removed and minced

1 Using a serrated knife and kitchen shears, prepare your artichokes as shown in Figure 15-1. (The V-shaped cuts add a decorative touch.)

Figure 15-1: Cutting an artichoke before cooking it.

2 Put the water, wine, oil, onion, garlic, parsley, and basil in a large pot. Stir to mix. Place the artichokes, stem side down, on the bottom of the pot and cover with a tight-fitting lid.

3 Steam the artichokes on medium heat for 45 minutes to 1 hour, depending on the size of the artichokes. Add additional water if necessary while the artichokes cook. An artichoke is done when you can easily remove the bottom leaves by pulling them and the flesh is tender.

Per serving: Calories 190 (From Fat 123); Fat 14g (Saturated 2g); Cholesterol 0mg; Sodium 116mg; Carbohydrate 15g (Dietary Fiber 7g); Protein 5g.

☞ Asparagus with Mustard Vinaigrette

The flavor of fresh asparagus is so fine that fancy preparation is beside the point. Simply poaching it in a little water is all that's needed. Prepping the asparagus for cooking is the only thing that takes some time. First remove the tough base of each spear by holding it in one hand. Next, take the stem end in the other hand. Gently bend the asparagus until it snaps, leaving you with a tender spear and a woody portion to discard. If thick skin still remains at the base of the spear, pare this away with a vegetable peeler. To clean the asparagus, which is grown in sandy soil, set the vegetable in a large pan filled with cool water for at least 10 minutes to loosen any sand. Repeat if necessary.

Preparation time: *15 minutes*

Cooking time: *6 minutes*

Yield: *4 servings*

2 tablespoons extra-virgin olive oil	*½ teaspoon Dijon-style mustard*
1 tablespoon balsamic vinegar	*Salt and pepper*
1 tablespoons minced shallots or more if desired	*1 large bunch asparagus, about 1 pound, trimmed and cleaned*
1 clove garlic, minced	

1 To make the vinaigrette, put the olive oil, vinegar, shallots, garlic, and mustard in a small bowl. Whisk to combine the ingredients. Season to taste with salt and pepper. Set aside.

2 Fill a large, wide skillet with 1 inch of water. Bring the water to a boil.

3 Add the asparagus and a pinch of salt to the water. Cover and cook the asparagus on medium heat until just tender, about 3 to 6 minutes.

4 Drain the asparagus. Using a wide spatula, transfer the asparagus to a platter. Drizzle with the mustard vinaigrette.

Tip: *Asparagus is sometimes daintily eaten by hand, each spear picked up and dipped into sauce, such as this vinaigrette. Once in the dining room of a fancy New York hotel, I overheard two waiters arguing, nearly coming to blows over which way the asparagus should be pointing on the plate. One would turn the plate so the asparagus pointed toward the person eating, and the other turned the plate so the asparagus pointed away. Back and forth it went. Asparagus tips pointing toward the diner finally won. It's easier to reach across the plate for the thicker end of the asparagus and pick up this end to dip the asparagus point.*

Per serving: Calories 81 (From Fat 63); Fat 7g (Saturated 1g); Cholesterol 0mg; Sodium 169mg; Carbohydrate 4g (Dietary Fiber 1g); Protein 2g.

⌕ Broccoli-Shiitake Stir-Fry

The succulent texture of the buttery shiitake mushroom will have you coming back for more, but there's another reason to eat shiitakes: A Japanese study showed that shiitake mushrooms lowered cholesterol, possibly because of a protein compound they contain. This is a stir-fry dish, which means that you need to briskly "stir" the food by lifting up portions with a spatula and flipping these over so that all the ingredients at various times are directly exposed to the hot heat of the surface of the wok or skillet.

Preparation time: *15 minutes*

Cooking time: *15 minutes*

Yield: *6 servings*

3 tablespoons hoisin sauce

1 teaspoon hot sesame oil, or 1 teaspoon sesame oil plus 3 or 4 drops chili oil or to taste

¾ cup water

2 tablespoons unrefined safflower oil

6 fresh shiitake mushrooms, stems removed, quartered

1 pound bok choy, stems cut crosswise in ½-inch slices and leaves cut into strips (reserve separately)

½ pound broccoli florets, cut into 1½-inch pieces

Salt

1 In a small bowl, whisk together the hoisin sauce, sesame oil, and water. Set aside.

2 Heat the safflower oil in a wok or a large, deep skillet over medium-high heat.

3 Add the shiitake mushrooms and bok choy stems and raise the heat to high. Cook, stir-frying with a spatula for two minutes and then add the broccoli. Cook the vegetables for an additional 3 minutes, until the broccoli is bright green and begins to soften. Add the bok choy leaves and continue to stir-fry for 3 minutes.

4 Add the hoisin sauce mixture. Stir-fry and continue to cook the vegetables until almost all of the liquid evaporates and the broccoli is tender, about 5 minutes more. Add salt to taste. Serve immediately.

Per serving: *Calories 97 (From Fat 52); Fat 6g (Saturated 1g); Cholesterol 0mg; Sodium 262mg; Carbohydrate 10g (Dietary Fiber 3g); Protein 4g.*

🍅 Roasted Carrots with Walnuts

This recipe gives you a savory accompaniment for meats and poultry. It also offers the chance to experiment with a very useful method for cooking vegetables — baking — which takes little effort on your part and preserves nutrients. The addition of walnuts and walnut oil adds cholesterol-lowering essential fatty acids to this dish.

Preparation time: *15 minutes*

Cooking time: *45 to 55 minutes*

Yield: *6 servings*

8 medium carrots	*1 teaspoon ground nutmeg*
4 parsnips	*½ teaspoon allspice*
2 heads celery root	*½ cup walnut pieces*
⅓ cup walnut oil or unrefined safflower oil	*1 teaspoon salt*
10 shallots, with skins	*½ teaspoon pepper*
8 garlic cloves, with skins	

1 Preheat the oven to 400 degrees.

2 Trim the carrots, parsnips, and celery root, leaving a little of any green tops. Wash in cold water and dry thoroughly.

3 Pour the oil into a large roasting pan. Add the vegetables as you cut them. Slice the carrots and turnips lengthwise in quarters. Cutting vertically, quarter each celery root and cut each quarter in half.

4 Add the shallots and garlic cloves.

5 In a small bowl, combine the nutmeg, allspice, walnuts, salt, and pepper. Sprinkle this mixture evenly over the vegetables. Mix well until the vegetables are well coated with the seasonings and oil.

6 Cover the baking pan with foil. Roast the vegetables until they're tender and browned, 45 to 55 minutes. Stir occasionally so that the vegetables brown more evenly. Before you serve the vegetables, pop the shallots and garlic out of their skins and enjoy them with this savory vegetable medley.

Per serving: Calories 338 (From Fat 172); Fat 19g (Saturated 2g); Cholesterol 0mg; Sodium 486mg; Carbohydrate 40g (Dietary Fiber 9g); Protein 6g.

🍎 Kale with Onions, Garlic, and Greek Olives

These greens are so dressed up with mouth-watering ingredients that even the most timid will dare to sample them. Kale gives you a heaping serving of beta carotene and contains lutein, which protects your arteries.

Preparation time: *10 minutes*

Cooking time: *20 minutes*

Yield: *4 servings*

3 tablespoons extra-virgin olive oil

1 onion, halved vertically and each half cut crosswise into ¼-inch slices

1 teaspoon dried oregano

1 teaspoon dried thyme

4 cloves of garlic, skins removed and minced

1 pound kale, thoroughly washed and woody portions of stems trimmed, roughly chopped

½ cup marinated Greek olives, pitted

Juice of 1 lemon

Salt

1 Heat a heavy-bottomed sauté pan with 2 tablespoons of the olive oil. Add the onion, oregano, and thyme. Cook, stirring occasionally, 3 minutes. Add the garlic and cook the seasonings an additional minute.

2 Add the kale. Cover the pan and bring to a boil over medium-high heat. Reduce the heat and continue to cook the kale until it wilts, about 15 minutes.

3 Transfer the kale to a serving bowl. Add the remaining 1 tablespoon olive oil, the olives, lemon juice, and salt. Serve hot or at room temperature.

Vary It! *For even more flavor, add a pinch of red pepper flakes to the onion and garlic when cooking this dish.*

Tip: *Store-bought marinated Greek olives sometimes have an overpowering taste if they have been cured too long or contain too much salt or vinegar. To tame them, store them in water, which will leach out the flavors. If the olives are still too strong-tasting after a day or two, change the water and repeat. Store marinated olives in the refrigerator.*

Per serving: Calories 182 (From Fat 136); Fat 15g (Saturated 2g); Cholesterol 0mg; Sodium 443mg; Carbohydrate 12g (Dietary Fiber 3g); Protein 3g.

○ Okra Mediterranean Style

When you eat a range of colors, you consume a variety of nutrients because many phy-tonutrients are also pigments. A bonus of such colorful foods is that, when combined, they make a gorgeous dish. Cook this okra recipe for a look at its artful shapes and hues. Serve this mixture as a side dish with chicken or fish, or as a topping for pasta to create a vegetarian meal. By the way, okra is a great source of soluble fiber.

Special tool: *Collapsible metal steamer*

Preparation time: *20 minutes*

Cooking time: *30 minutes*

Yield: *8 servings*

3 tablespoons extra-virgin olive oil

3 cloves garlic, peeled and minced

1 yellow onion, outside skin removed and cut crosswise into ¼-inch slices

2 bell peppers (1 pound), preferably orange or yellow, trimmed and cut into 1-inch pieces

3 medium-size zucchini (1 pound), trimmed, cut crosswise into ¼-inch slices

4 Roma tomatoes (1 pound), trimmed, quartered vertically and each section cut crosswise into thirds

1½ teaspoons dried Italian herbs

½ cup water

1 pound okra, washed and thoroughly dried, tops of caps removed

Salt and pepper

1 In a large pot, heat the oil over medium low heat. Add the garlic and onions and cook, stirring occasionally with a wooden spoon, until the onions are translucent and the garlic is golden, about 7 minutes.

2 Add the bell peppers and cook over medium heat for 5 minutes.

3 Add the zucchini, tomatoes, herbs, and water. Bring nearly to a boil on medium-high. Cover, reduce to medium, and cook for 20 minutes, stirring occasionally with a wooden spoon, until the vegetables have softened.

4 Meanwhile, set a collapsible metal steamer in a medium-size pot filled with an inch or two of water. Make sure the water doesn't rise above the flat bottom of the steamer. Add the okra and cook over medium heat, steaming the okra for 3 to 5 minutes, until it is tender but still holds its shape. Transfer to a bowl and cover to keep warm.

5 Add the okra to the vegetable mixture. Stir to combine and heat the vegetables an addi-tional 2 or 3 minutes. Salt and pepper to taste. Serve hot or at room temperature.

Tip: *For the vegetables in this recipe, trim tough stems and any damaged parts, but keep as much of the skins, membranes, and seeds as possible. The more complete a food is, the more health giving.*

Per serving: *Calories 102 (From Fat 50); Fat 6g (Saturated 1g); Cholesterol 0mg; Sodium 82mg; Carbohydrate 13g (Dietary Fiber 4g); Protein 3g.*

☙ *Red Cabbage Braised in Red Wine*

Red cabbage, but not green, contains red anthocyanin pigments. Anthocyanins are antioxidants that have a positive effect on cholesterol, preventing the build-up of arterial plaque. This benefit aside, after you taste this savory dish, you'll need no encouragement to eat it again. This recipe also gives you experience in braising, a cooking technique in which a food (usually meat or vegetables) is first browned in fat and then cooked, tightly covered, in a small amount of liquid for a lengthy amount of time. It's an easy yet handy cooking skill to have for many different recipes.

Preparation time: *15 minutes*

Cooking time: *1 hour and 45 minutes*

Yield: *6 servings*

1 tablespoon unrefined safflower oil	*2 green Granny Smith apples, peeled, cored, and thinly sliced*
2 medium onions, 1 thinly sliced and one halved	*2 whole cloves*
1 red cabbage, shredded	*¼ cup red wine vinegar*
½ teaspoon salt	*2 cups dry red wine*

1 In a large skillet, heat the oil over medium-high heat. When the oil is hot, add the sliced onion and cook over medium heat until translucent, about 7 minutes.

2 Add the cabbage, salt, and apples. Stir to mix the ingredients.

3 Stick 1 clove in each of the onion halves. Add the onion halves, vinegar, and wine to the cabbage mixture.

4 Cover and braise the cabbage over very low heat, stirring occasionally, until the cabbage is soft, the flavors combine, and most of the liquid has been absorbed, about 1½ hours. Remove the onion halves. Serve warm.

Per serving: *Calories 93 (From Fat 25); Fat 3g (Saturated 0g); Cholesterol 0mg; Sodium 211mg; Carbohydrate 17g (Dietary Fiber 4g); Protein 2g.*

♻ Spinach with Peanuts and Ginger

Even for people who won't eat their vegetables, this spinach is easy to swallow, full of lip-smacking flavors. The spinach is cooked quickly to preserve nutrients. Consider chopping the spinach after it's cooked to make it even easier for your body to get at the nutrients.

Preparation time: *10 minutes*

Cooking time: *5 minutes*

Yield: *4 servings*

1 tablespoon extra-virgin olive oil

2 cloves garlic, minced

1 tablespoon peeled and grated fresh gingerroot

1 pound fresh spinach, trimmed, well rinsed and with some of the water still clinging to the leaves

1 tablespoon plus 1 teaspoon flavored rice wine vinegar, a brand such as Marukan

1 tablespoon plus 1 teaspoon soy sauce

¼ cup chopped roasted peanuts

1 In a heavy pot, heat the oil over medium heat until hot but not smoking.

2 Add the garlic and gingerroot and cook, stirring, until golden, about 15 seconds.

3 Add the spinach by handfuls, stirring continuously, and cook until the spinach leaves soften, about 3 minutes. Depending upon the size of the pot, the spinach may need to be added in batches. However, it cooks down quickly.

4 Add the rice wine vinegar and soy sauce. Toss the ingredients together and serve warm or at room temperature, topped with roasted peanuts.

Tip: *The only challenge in preparing spinach is the cleaning, which must be thorough. Crinkly spinach carries sand and grit from the fields, so follow these instructions. Fill your sink with cold water. Add a couple tablespoons of vinegar (apple cider vinegar is good). Hold the spinach by the stems as you immerse the leaves and swirl the spinach around. You'll see the sand that settles to the bottom of your sink. Remove the spinach, refill the sink, and repeat the procedure. One more time should do it. Dry in a salad spinner or on paper towels.*

Per serving: *Calories 116 (From Fat 74); Fat 8g (Saturated 1g); Cholesterol 0mg; Sodium 528mg; Carbohydrate 7g (Dietary Fiber 4g); Protein 6g.*

○ Sweet Potato and Parsnip Purée with Toasted Pecans

Sweet potatoes sound fattening, but they contain no more calories than white potatoes. They're also loaded with beta carotene and contain potassium and soluble fiber. This dish is just sweet enough without the addition of sugar — or marshmallows — and the pecans add just the right crunch.

Special tools: *Food processor, vegetable steamer*

Preparation time: *15 minutes*

Cooking time: *45 minutes*

Yield: *8 servings*

1 pound sweet potatoes (about 2 medium), peeled

1 yellow Golden Delicious apple, peeled, cored, and seeds removed

1 pound parsnips (about 3 small or 2 medium)

½ cup lowfat milk

½ teaspoon salt

¼ teaspoon allspice

1 teaspoon unrefined safflower oil

½ cup pecan halves (about 20)

1 Slice the sweet potatoes and apple into ½-inch slices. Slice the parsnip into ¼-inch slices. Put the sweet potatoes, apple, and parsnips in a vegetable steamer over simmering water. Cover and cook 15 minutes. Drain and cool.

2 Preheat the oven to 325 degrees. Combine the steamed ingredients with the milk, salt, and allspice in a large bowl. Purée in batches in a food processor fitted with a metal blade.

3 Transfer the purée to a 2-quart casserole coated with vegetable oil. Bake at 325 degrees until thoroughly heated, about 30 minutes.

4 Meanwhile, heat the oil in a small skillet. Add the pecans and cook on medium-high heat until you can smell them toasting, about 2 minutes.

5 Serve the heated sweet potato mixture topped with the toasted pecans.

Per serving: *Calories 149 (From Fat 53); Fat 6g (Saturated 1g); Cholesterol 1mg; Sodium 162mg; Carbohydrate 24g (Dietary Fiber 4g); Protein 3g.*

Chapter 16

Betting on Beans and Other Legumes for Lower Cholesterol

In This Chapter

▶ Looking to legumes for controlling cholesterol

▶ Getting to know different varieties of legumes

▶ Shopping for and storing beans

▶ Soaking beans and cooking them to perfection

▶ Incorporating legumes into tasty dishes

*I*f you had to invent ideal foods for controlling cholesterol and supporting heart health, it would be beans, lentils, and peas, otherwise known as *legumes*. These foods are very low in fat and a good source of protein, and they're loaded with the right vitamins and minerals. In addition, they digest slowly because of their high fiber content and have only a mild to moderate effect on blood sugar levels. A good amount of this fiber is soluble, known to cut cholesterol.

The only problem with beans is that most people don't eat enough of them. It's estimated that in the United States, the consumption of nuts, beans, and other legumes together amounts to, on average, only 0.3 servings per person per day.

The recipes in this chapter are designed to entice you into eating more beans and other legumes without giving you ingredients you don't need. Most recipes are often dressed up with bacon, ham hocks, and cheese. Brown sugar or molasses is then added to the mix. Before you know it, your beans are the nutritional equivalent of a hot fudge sundae! The recipes in this chapter avoid this unhealthy trap, but I promise they're still delicious.

I also provide you with a wealth of cooking tips for beans, the type of legume you'll probably be cooking most often, but the advice for beans applies to peas and lentils as well. Read on to find out how to cook all these legumes the heart-healthy way.

Reasons to Love Legumes

Plenty of evidence shows that beans and other legumes are good for the heart. The NHANES I Epidemiologic Follow-up Study, conducted at Tulane University and published in 2001, which tracked the health of over 9,000 men and women over 19 years, confirmed the benefits of legumes. According to this study, participants who ate legumes four times a week or more had a 22 percent lower risk of coronary heart disease than individuals who ate legumes less than once a week. No wonder, given the many ways that legumes protect the heart. Consuming just 1 cup of beans a day can lower the "bad" LDL cholesterol 15 to 20 percent in a month or so and, over a couple of years, also raise the "good" HDL cholesterol about 10 percent, thereby improving the important HDL:LDL ratio. Considering the dozens of ways that beans can fit into a meal, many of which are suggested in this chapter, eating the recommended quantity of beans this regularly isn't hard to do.

Liking legumes for their protein and low fat content

Legumes contain nearly as much protein as steak, ounce for ounce, but with a small fraction of the saturated fat. Just one cup of cooked kidney beans provides as much as 16 grams of protein, 25 percent of the recommended daily intake, and only 1 gram of fat, almost none of it saturated. Combine legumes with a grain and you have a high-quality protein that provides all the amino acids your body needs to build and repair tissue. While grains are good sources of many amino acids, they're low in or missing others. However, legumes are a good source of the needed ones. As a result, because these two foods provide complementary proteins, vegetarians have a reliable source of high quality protein equivalent to that provided by meat. Spoon the Red Lentil Dal with Caramelized Onions in this chapter over brown basmati rice for a protein-rich main course.

What, exactly, is a legume?

Legume is the species of plant that beans, peas, and lentils grow on. The beans, peas, and lentils are the mature seeds found inside the pods of the legume plants. A dried pod is called a _pulse._ There, that was easy. So this is why a dried bean, for instance, is sometimes also called a legume or a pulse. Now, in addition, some peas are called beans, and some beans are called peas. And the garbanzo bean, which is also called chickpea, is both a bean and a pea, and of course, it's also a legume. Got all that?

Legumes are also excellent sources of folate, the B vitamin that helps keep homocysteine levels low. Homocysteine is an amino acid in the blood. When a lab test detects high levels in the bloodstream, this indicates an increased abnormally elevated risk of heart disease. One serving of lentils gives you over 40 percent of your daily requirement of folate. You also find good amounts of magnesium, potassium, thiamin, riboflavin, and zinc throughout this category of food. Their benefits for heart health are outlined in Chapter 2.

When you eat a variety of legumes, you're far more likely to consume good amounts of all the needed vitamins and minerals these foods contain. A nutrient will be high in some legumes but lower in others.

Serving up soluble fiber

Soluble fiber lowers the amount of cholesterol circulating through the body, and legumes are a great source. A serving of kidney beans has significantly more soluble fiber than a serving of cooked oatmeal, in itself an excellent source of this form of fiber. Lima beans, black-eyed peas, and green peas also provide good amounts.

The recommendation for total fiber, both water-soluble and water-insoluble forms, is 25 to 35 grams of fiber a day. Just a cup of pinto or black beans gives you 16 grams, half of what you need. The body doesn't digest either form of fiber, but they do have their differences. Soluble fiber forms a gel when mixed with liquid. In the intestine, it acts as a sponge, soaking up cholesterol, which the body then excretes along with the fiber. Oats, apples, and legumes are good sources. In contrast, insoluble fiber passes through the digestive system for the most part unchanged. This fiber is often referred to as roughage and promotes regularity. It doesn't seem to affect cholesterol levels. Insoluble fiber is in wheat brans, the skins of fruits and vegetables, and in legumes.

Legumes by Many Other Names

As you become more familiar with legumes in all their variety and how easy they are to keep on hand for cooking, they do become more approachable, and you're likely to be eating more. There are more than 70 different varieties of legumes, and they've been an important part of the cuisine of every known culture. This section introduces you to all sort of legumes — beans, peas, and lentils — and gives you some coaching on how to shop for and store them so they stay fresh. The following list helps you sort through the varieties available, and Figure 16-1 shows what some legumes look like.

✔ **Black beans:** Also called turtle beans, black beans are a staple of Caribbean, Mexican, and Central and South American cooking. Their flavor is sweet, making them a perfect complement to spicy dishes. Try the Sweet and Spicy Refried Black Beans for a taste.

✔ **Black-eyed peas:** This small, beige bean is easy to spot, with its deep black dot on the inner curve. In the southern United States, where these are a staple ingredient in many dishes, they're called cowpeas.

✔ **Cannellini:** In Italy, kidney beans are white and called cannellini. They're delicious used in salads and soups. But never substitute them for dishes such as chili con carne that need the full-bodied flavor of red kidney beans. Try the Cannellini and Tomato-Parmesan Ragout in this chapter for a taste of these beans, Italian-style.

✔ **Chickpeas:** These buff-colored, round, irregular-shape legumes have a firm texture and a mild, nutlike flavor. You also find them sold under the names garbanzo and, in Italian, ceci. This bean is the primary ingredient in hummus and is used in minestrone soup. Chickpeas also show up in all sorts of Middle Eastern, Indian, and Mediterranean dishes.

✔ **Fava beans:** Resembling lima beans only larger, these tan, rather fat legumes are sold dried (called habas), cooked in cans, and fresh in spring and summer. Also known as broad beans, they have a pealike flavor and a tender texture that is not starchy. Favas are widely eaten in Europe, Africa, South America, and China.

✔ **Great Northerns:** Similar to lima beans in appearance, the Great Northern is a large white bean often used in baked bean dishes. Its flavor is distinctive but delicate, making it a good substitute for white beans in most recipes.

✔ **Green beans:** This is what I still call string beans, named so because of the fibrous string that in olden times ran down the pod's seam. The string is now bred out of the bean. Like other legumes, green beans consist of a pod and seeds, both edible. Another name is snap bean, and the yellow version is wax bean.

✔ **Kidney beans:** This bean, curved like a kidney, is a firm, medium-size legume with a cream-colored flesh and skin that may be dark red, light red, or pink. Its gutsy flavor makes it a top choice for chili con carne and the Louisiana specialty, red beans and rice. Cannellini are white kidney beans, and French kidney beans are a tiny, tender version known as flageolets.

✔ **Lentils:** These tiny, oval pulses are consumed on a daily basis in the Middle East, India, and some parts of Europe. They come in a variety of colors: the common brown lentil, the grayish-brown French lentil, the Egyptian red lentil, and a yellow lentil that you can find in Middle Eastern specialty food stores.

✔ **Lima beans:** Yes, they're named after the city in Peru where this bean was found as early as 1500. Savored for their rich, butter flavor, they're also called butter beans, a name used in the American South. You find two distinct varieties: the small baby lima and the larger Fordhook.

Fresh limas are available June to September and are pale green and plump and have a slight kidney shape. Used in side dishes, soups, and salads, they're a classic ingredient in succotash, a mixture of lima beans, corn, and sometimes sweet red and green peppers.

✔ **Navy beans:** A staple of the U.S. Navy since the mid-1800s, this is the bean in canned pork and beans. This small, white legume requires lengthy, slow cooking.

✔ **Pinto beans:** This medium-size bean is painted with reddish-brown streaks on a pale pink background. A staple in Spanish-speaking countries, pinto beans are often served with rice or added to soups and stews. This is the bean of refried beans and chili con carne. Pink bean and pinto are interchangeable. They're also referred to as red Mexican beans.

✔ **Soybeans:** Soybeans are available in many forms: whole, in custardlike cakes called tofu, as fermented tempeh, and as liquid soymilk. The subject of much scientific study, soybeans have been shown to lower cholesterol and, thanks to a powerful phytoestrogen that soy contains, improve cholesterol composition in ways that protect the arteries. You find sweet, immature green soybeans, frozen and called _edamame,_ in most supermarkets these days. This type of soybean is featured in the recipe for Edamame and Corn Succotash Scented with Butter and Chives in this chapter. (See Chapter 14 for more on soy's benefits.)

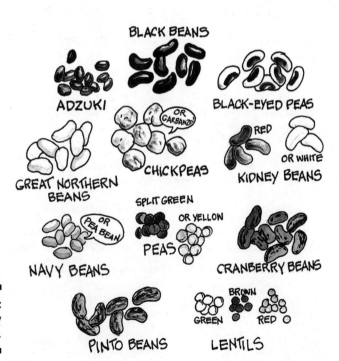

Figure 16-1:
A variety
of beans.

Shopping for Beans and Storing Them at Home

You can find a good assortment of beans in supermarkets these days. Standard stores have all the favorites, from pinto and black beans to black-eyed peas and Great Northerns, dried versions sold in cellophane bags, and cooked legumes in cans. Frozen lima beans, both baby limas and Fordhooks, and soybeans, called by their Japanese name, edamame, are also widely available. Look in the produce section for fresh legumes, such as fava beans in season.

Buy beans in glass jars rather than canned if you, er, can, for fresher, cleaner flavor. Too often, the flavor of canned beans ranges from bland to metallic. Bottled beans are often sold in upscale natural foods stores.

You need to visit a natural foods store for a broader variety of beans. Hungry for cranberry beans or French lentils? Need some dried soybeans? These are the stores for you. Middle Eastern and Indian food shops are also great resources for lentils and chickpeas used in these cuisines.

And for more exotic beans, you can turn to food catalogs, such as Indian Harvest. Look them up at www.indianharvest.com. You find legume varieties with tantalizing names such as Black Calypso, Butterscotch Calypso, Nightfall Beans, Good Mother Stollard, Cave Beans, and Southern Checker Peas.

When shopping for beans, shop only in stores where the turnover is high so that you're sure to bring home the freshest dried legumes.

Picking the freshest (but it's okay if they're dry!)

If you're buying dried beans, you still need to know how to spot ones that are fresh. Dried doesn't mean stale. Here's what to look for:

- ✔ Fresh dried beans have a consistent, deep, and somewhat glossy color.
- ✔ Beans should not look faded or dry. Neither should they have wrinkles, a lot of cracks, or tiny pinholes, which are a sign of insect damage.
- ✔ Don't buy beans from a batch that contains a lot of broken beans.

Buy beans that have a uniform size so that all the beans will finish cooking at about the same time.

Buying fresh legumes is another matter. For these, head for the produce section of the market. There you find fresh green beans and yellow wax beans. Green beans are sold fresh year-round, but the peak of their season is May to October. Look for slender beans that are bright colored, crisp, and free of blemishes. Yellow wax beans are available in summer.

Also in the produce section, you find fresh favas, lima beans, and cranberry beans and, of course, fresh green peas, depending on the season. These legumes are usually sold in their pods, which are not edible. The only exceptions are Chinese pea pods, which soften quickly when cooked.

Fresh fava beans require special handling because they have a very tough skin that should be removed before you cook the beans. (Dried favas are the beans with the skins removed.) To loosen the skin, cook the beans briefly in boiling water and then plunge them into cold water to stop the cooking process. Manually remove the skins before cooking the beans. Some fresh beans are now considered gourmet foods and can be pricey, but their just-picked taste is worth the extra expenditure.

A sign that bean pods are no longer fresh is that they look lumpy, the beans beneath having grown large, producing the bulges.

Storing legumes after you bring them home

Dried legumes will keep 12 months stored in tightly sealed containers in a cool, dry place. Put them in glass jars to decorate the kitchen and so you can find them easily. Or keep legumes in resealable plastic bags closed with a paper-wrapped wire twist. For tidiness, you can store several of these in an airtight plastic storage box.

Keep newly purchased and older legumes separate. Store fresh dried beans in their own container, not added to beans that have been around awhile.

Fresh green beans keep up to 5 days, tightly wrapped in a plastic bag, in the refrigerator. Fresh beans in their pods can be refrigerated for up to a week, stored in a plastic bag. Shell pod beans, such as lima beans, just before using.

Just because beans are canned doesn't mean they stay edible forever. The limit of freshness for canned beans is 12 months, that is, if the can has not been opened!

If you're debating with yourself whether to cook up some dried beans instead of just opening a can, you have no reason to hesitate. They're not that much trouble to prepare, if you plan ahead. Home-cooked beans surpass commercial beans in taste, texture, and appearance. And beans can be made quite digestible by cooking them the right way. So what's stopping you? It's time to start cooking!

Doing the prep work

If you haven't cooked beans in ages, don't start by being thrifty and trying to use up the beans that have been sitting around in your kitchen for as long as you can remember. Older dried beans have less flavor and nutrients and take forever to cook. Toss them out and buy fresh ones.

Beans are harvested in late summer and make their way to markets by fall. This is the best time to buy dried beans because they're at their freshest. Purchase a year's worth because they keep 12 months, and then stock up again the next fall.

After you purchase the beans you want to cook, the next step is to ready them for cooking. Here's when most people decide that canned beans will do. The prep stage has several parts that at first may seem daunting. But after you know the drill, you can whiz through the steps:

1. **Scatter the beans on a large white plate and sort through these for pebbles and stray matter to discard.**

2. **Put the beans in a pot filled with water and swish them around, removing any broken, discolored, or shriveled beans.**

3. **Dump the beans in a colander and rinse for a minute or two.**

4. **Return the beans to the pot, which you have first rinsed out.**

5. **Add cold water, 10 cups for each 2 cups of beans (5 cups of water for 1 cup of beans).**

6. **Soak the beans, refrigerated, overnight or for at least 8 hours. (Lentils, black-eyed peas, and split peas do not need to be soaked.)**

7. **After soaking, rinse the beans by emptying them into a colander and then running cold water over the beans, moving them around with your hands.**

Now the beans are ready to cook!

Always drain and thoroughly rinse canned beans before adding them to a recipe to remove the salt brine they're processed with.

Taking a shortcut

Yes, there is an alternative to the overnight soaking procedure for beans:

1. **Scatter the beans on a large white plate and sort through these for pebbles and stray matter to discard.**

2. **Put the beans in a pot filled with water and swish them around, removing any broken, discolored, or shriveled beans.**

3. **Dump the beans in a colander and rinse for a minute or two.**

4. **Return the beans to the pot, which you have first rinsed out.**

5. **Put them in a pot and add 10 cups of HOT water for each pound of beans.**

6. **Heat to boiling and let boil for 2 to 3 minutes.**

7. **Remove from the heat, cover, and set aside for at least 1 hour.**

   The beans will be tenderized as if they had soaked while you slept. At this point, the beans still need to be cooked.

Skipping the soak

Soaking dried beans in advance shortens cooking time about a half hour. If you would rather cook the beans a little longer, then all you need to do is sort them, rinse them, plunk them into a pot of water, and cook them. When they're done, drain the beans in a colander. This method produces beans with more flavor and more, er, side effects. (See the sidebar "Taming beans by various means" in this chapter.)

Don't be surprised if you hear that beans must be prepared in some way that contradicts the advice I give you. You can find a range of bean truths out there, including different cooking procedures developed over hundreds, even thousands, of years. Give other methods a try and see what works for you. The way of preparing beans that you find easiest is the best way to prepare them, especially if doing it your way means that you eat heart-healthy beans more often.

Bean-cooking basics

The easiest part about preparing beans is cooking them. They go into the pot, you turn on the heat under the pot, and then you wait. Figure 16-2 shows the steps to follow when cooking your beans.

COOKING DRIED BEANS

1. PLACE BEANS IN A COLANDER. RINSE WELL WITH COLD WATER. HEY!

PICK OUT ANYTHING THAT DOESN'T BELONG!

2. AFTER YOU CLEAN AND DRAIN THE BEANS, DUMP THEM INTO A POT.

3. ADD WATER TO THE POT (3 CUPS OF WATER TO 1 CUP OF BEANS). 1 CUP

4. BRING BEANS TO A ROLLING BOIL. BOIL FOR A MINUTE OR 2.

REMOVE THE POT FROM HEAT. COVER WITH A TIGHT FITTING LID.

5. SOAK THE BEANS.

FOR AT LEAST 2 HOURS. AT MOST FOR SEVERAL HOURS OR OVERNIGHT.

6. RINSE AND DRAIN ONCE MORE. HERE WE GO AGAIN!

☆ OPTIONAL

7. COOK THE BEANS! ON THE STOVETOP....

....BRING TO A GENTLE BOIL AND COOK UNTIL TENDER.

☆ TIP:
IF YOU KEEP A LID ON THE POT, LEAVE IT SLIGHTLY ASKEW SO THE STEAM CAN ESCAPE, SO THE WATER DOESN'T BOIL OVER THE TOP.

8. WHEN THE BEANS ARE FINISHED COOKING, REMOVE FROM HEAT AND LET THEM COOL.

Figure 16-2:
Basic steps for cooking dried beans.

Don't stir beans while they're cooking, especially toward the end of their cooking time. Stirring breaks them up. If you must stir, use a wooden spoon, scooping the beans from the bottom of the pot as gently as if you were folding egg whites.

For guidelines on how long to cook your beans, consult Table 16-1. The cooking times are estimates only for beans that have been soaked and vary depending on the age of the beans and how you have prepped them.

Table 16-1	Cooking Times for Soaked Legumes	
Type of Legume	*Top of Stove*	*Pressure Cooker*
Black beans	1 to 1½ hours	30 minutes
Black-eyed peas	45 minutes to 1 hour	20 minutes
Cannellini	1 hour	30 minutes
Chickpeas	2 to 3 hours	40 minutes
Great Northern beans	1½ to 2 hours	30 minutes
Green lentils	45 minutes	20 minutes
Green split peas	1 to 1¼ hours	25 minutes
Lima beans (large)	1 to 1½ hours	Not recommended
Navy beans	2½ to 3 hours	35 to 40 minutes
Pinto beans	1½ to 2 hours	30 minutes
Red kidney beans	1½ to 2 hours	30 to 35 minutes
Red lentils	20 to 25 minutes	Not recommended
Soybeans	3 hours	Not recommended
Yellow split peas	1 to 1¼ hours	25 minutes

The shorter cooking times for using a pressure cooker may inspire you to finally buy this handy piece of cooking equipment. These days, they're engineered to be easier to handle than the early models from the 1950s. However, in using pressure cookers, be aware of the following points:

✔ Certain legumes, such as lima beans, favas beans, and chickpeas, generate a lot of foam when cooked. To prevent this foam from jamming the valves, just fill the pressure cooker only half way up.

✔ Legumes such as lentils and split peas are so quick cooking that they are likely to overcook in a pressure cooker. You can use the pressure cooker, but I recommend cooking them in a pot on the stove instead.

✔ You'll need to check the progress of legumes two or three times as they cook to decide if they're done. Overcooked beans in the pressure cooker may disintegrate.

✔ A basic formula for pressure cooking beans is to use 1½ cups dried beans, 6 cups of water, and 1 tablespoon of oil.

Counting beans

When I used to cater and hummus was on the menu, I would invariably make much more than I needed. It's amazing how a few handfuls of dried beans can multiply into bowls of the finished product.

You can keep track of the quantity of cooked legumes you'll end up with if you do the math in advance. Here are some handy bean formulas to remember:

- ✔ 1 pound beans = 2⅓ cups dried beans = 6 cups cooked beans = 4 to 6 servings
- ✔ 1 cup dried beans = 2½ to 3 cups cooked beans
- ✔ 1 can (15 ounces) of beans = 1½ cups cooked beans, drained

Simmering legumes with seasonings

While your legumes are cooking, take advantage of this opportunity to let them soak up flavors. Choose seasonings that complement the recipe and you'll have a dish with deep, full flavor. Add a clove of crushed garlic, a wedge of onion, or ½ teaspoon or more of dried herbs, such as oregano, sage, or thyme. Cook the legumes in vegetable or meat broth, full strength or mixed with water, but make sure that the broth contains no salt, which toughens the beans.

Acidic ingredients such as tomatoes, lemon juice, vinegar, and wine will slow the cooking process. Do not add acidic ingredients until the beans are tender.

Drain and rinse canned beans before using them. You remove some of the hard-to-digest sugars and about 40 percent of the added salt as well.

Using your bean when it comes to freezing

With some planning, you can always have some homemade beans on hand because, fortunately, beans freeze! They keep their superior flavor and texture beautifully.

Make a large batch and freeze this in small portions. To use the beans in vegetable soups, meat stews, and mixed vegetable salads, put aside portions of 1 to 2 cups, an amount easily added to such dishes without upsetting the balance of ingredients. Freeze 3- to 4-cup portions to have beans on hand for lunch entrees and dinner side dishes. You'll thank yourself for the effort and save cooking time later.

Taming beans by various means

We all know the problem: Beans are difficult to digest and can cause gas. They contain certain sugars that require a special enzyme in order to be digested, one that we humans don't possess. (We can buy it, though! The product comes in tablet and liquid form.) To reduce this unwanted side effect of eating beans, here are some tactics to take:

✔ Eat beans more often. Start with a small amount and increase gradually.

✔ Choose beans that are easier to digest such as lentils, lima beans, white beans, chickpeas, and black-eyed peas.

✔ Soak beans and then discard the soaking water. It's full of those hard-to-digest sugars.

✔ Add one of the many herbs that traditionally have been cooked with beans to reduce gas. Experiment with thyme, bay leaf, summer savory, fennel seeds, caraway seeds, and *epazote,* a pungent, wild herb with a strong taste used in Mexican cooking. It has flat, pointed leaves and is sold dried.

Handling cooked legumes with great care

After legumes are cooked, you must handle them with care. Like grains, they provide an ideal environment for bacteria to thrive. Follow these guidelines strictly:

✔ If you cook beans and such for later use, cool them to room temperature and then immediately refrigerate. Never leave legumes unrefrigerated for longer than 4 hours. If you do, throw them out.

✔ Store cooked beans, refrigerated, in a covered container, for up to 5 days. To make sure they don't turn sour, bring the beans to a boil for a few minutes each day.

✔ Discard frozen beans after six months.

Luscious Legume Recipes

The following recipes give you ways of preparing savory bean dishes, accented with the flavors of piquant spices, appetizing vegetables, and agreeable herbs. These are far removed from the usual sugary bean dishes cloaked in carbohydrate-loaded sauce. These dishes give you a good mix of nutritious vegetables, legumes rich in protein and fiber, and healthy fats to satisfy your hunger and manage cholesterol.

Great Northern Tuna Salad Provençal

This recipe takes its inspiration from Salade Niçoise, the specialty of southern France, featuring tuna and potatoes, accented with green beans, tomatoes, sweet peppers, and hard-cooked eggs. In this version, white beans provide the starch (plus protein), and the egg garnish is omitted. For a reduced-sodium diet, omit the capers.

Special tool: *Collapsible metal steamer*

Preparation time: *30 minutes*

Cooking time: *1½ hours*

Yield: *6 servings as a side dish and 4 servings as a main dish*

1 cup dried Great Northern beans, soaked

½ medium onion, peeled and cut into 1-inch chunks

½ teaspoon herbes de Provence (see the tip at the end of the recipe)

1 small bay leaf

5 cups water

2 cups green beans

1 tablespoon chopped fresh parsley

1 clove garlic, peeled, crushed, and chopped

1 teaspoon Dijon mustard

1 teaspoon capers

1 tablespoon extra-virgin olive oil

1 can (6 ounces) tuna, packed in water

Cherry tomatoes, for garnish

Black olives, for garnish

Fresh basil leaves, for garnish

1 Place the Great Northern beans, onion, herbes de Provence, bay leaf, and water in a medium-size pot. Bring to a boil, partially cover, reduce the heat to low, and simmer the beans until tender, about 1½ hours. Once cooked, cool and drain the beans.

2 Meanwhile, in a pot fitted with a collapsible metal steamer set over water, put the green beans. Steam the beans, covered, on medium heat for 10 minutes, until they are somewhat tender. Cool and cut into 2-inch lengths. Set aside.

3 To make the salad dressing put the parsley, garlic, Dijon mustard, capers, and olive oil in a small bowl and stir with a fork to combine.

4 Put the tuna, along with the water from the can, in a large bowl. Add the green beans and dressing. Mix well, breaking the tuna into small pieces. Add the Great Northern beans. Toss the tuna-bean mixture together gently to mix all ingredients.

5 Serve the salad garnished with one or more of the following: cherry tomatoes, black olives, and fresh basil leaves. Or scoop the salad into whole-grain pita pockets and eat as a sandwich.

Per serving: Calories 228 (From Fat 47); Fat 5g (Saturated 1g); Cholesterol 15mg; Sodium 191mg; Carbohydrate 28g (Dietary Fiber 9g); Protein 19g.

⟡ Cannellini and Tomato-Parmesan Ragout

Start adding beans to your meals with this quick and easy recipe that relies on a few simple ingredients. It's half beans and half tomatoes, giving you a good helping of folate in the beans and the powerful antioxidant, lutein, in the tomatoes. And the onions in this dish thin the blood. Scatter some Parmesan cheese over the top, and you have a high protein/lowfat dish that eats like a bowl of pasta.

Preparation time: *5 minutes*

Cooking time: *25 minutes*

Yield: *4 servings as a side dish, 2 servings as a lunch entree*

2 cups diced fresh tomatoes, or 1 can (15 ounces) diced tomatoes, undrained	*Salt and pepper*
½ yellow onion, diced	*2 cups cooked cannellini beans (¾ cup dried), or 1 can (15 ounces) cannellini beans*
1 clove garlic, minced	*1 sprig parsley, finely chopped*
½ teaspoon summer savory	*¼ cup Parmesan cheese*

1 Put the tomatoes, onion, garlic, savory, and salt and pepper in a medium-size pot. Bring to a boil and cook, uncovered, on medium heat, 5 minutes, to reduce some of the liquid.

2 Meanwhile, if using canned beans, pour off the liquid and put the beans in a colander. Rinse the beans under cold water.

3 Add the drained beans and parsley to the tomato mixture. Simmer 20 minutes. Season to taste with additional salt and pepper if desired. Serve with grated Parmesan on the side.

Per serving: *Calories 124 (From Fat 6); Fat 1g (Saturated 0g); Cholesterol 0mg; Sodium 455mg; Carbohydrate 24g (Dietary Fiber 6g); Protein 6g.*

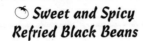 **Sweet and Spicy Refried Black Beans**

These refried black beans outclass the usual kind, offering a complexity of flavors plus a kick from jalapeño chili. The black beans are also a nice change from the kidney beans that are standard in this dish. The black beans deliver lots of folate, magnesium, and fiber, and this version is also healthier than the usual, made with unrefined oil and only a small amount.

Special tool: *Food processor*

Preparation time: *15 minutes*

Cooking time: *30 minutes*

Yield: *6 servings*

2 tablespoons extra-virgin olive oil	*2 tablespoons cider vinegar*
1 medium yellow onion, skin removed and chopped	*2 tablespoons honey*
	2 teaspoons chili powder
1 green bell pepper, seeds and core removed, chopped	*2 teaspoons ground cumin*
	4 cups canned black beans, well-drained
1 jalapeño chile, seeds and veins removed, finely chopped	*Salt and pepper*
6 cloves garlic, peeled, crushed and minced	

1 Put the olive oil in a large skillet set over medium heat. Add the onion, bell pepper, and jalapeño. Cook until the ingredients begin to soften, about 10 minutes.

2 To the onion mixture, add the garlic, cider vinegar, honey, chili powder, and cumin. Using a wooden spoon, stir to combine. Then add the beans to the skillet and stir until all ingredients are combined.

3 Working in batches, spoon the bean mixture into a food processor and process for about 30 seconds to purée.

4 Return the bean mixture to the skillet and cook over medium-high heat, stirring frequently, for 10 to 15 minutes until the mixture looks dry. Season to taste with salt and pepper. Serve with a dish inspired by Mexican cuisine, such as Halibut with Cilantro-Lime Salsa or Fish Tacos with Sweet Peppers (see both recipes in Chapter 13). Or use the beans to top brown rice for a vegetarian main course. So delicious!

Per serving: Calories 230 (From Fat 56); Fat 6g (Saturated 1g); Cholesterol 0mg; Sodium 432mg; Carbohydrate 33g (Dietary Fiber 11g); Protein 10g.

⟁ Edamame and Corn Succotash Scented with Butter and Chives

If you were wondering just how much the flavor of butter, even a little smidgeon, could permeate a dish, try this one! One teaspoon of butter is a match for 6 cups of beans and vegetables! This amount contains 4.1 grams of fat, including 2.5 grams of saturated fat. Divide 1 teaspoon of butter into six servings of nutritious succotash and butter gets the green light, used as a seasoning accent. In this recipe, whole soybeans, called edamame, are substituted for lima beans, the usual ingredient in this old-fashioned, homey dish. As always, eating a food in its whole form is the most nutritious way to go.

Preparation time: *15 minutes*

Cooking time: *35 minutes*

Yield: *6 generous servings*

7 cups water	*1 package (10 ounces) frozen sweet corn kernels*
2½ cups shelled edamame (most of a 16-ounce bag of frozen soybeans)	*¼ teaspoon paprika*
1 tablespoon unrefined safflower oil	*½ cup milk*
1 yellow onion, skin removed and diced	*1 teaspoon butter*
1 green bell pepper, seeds and core removed, cut in ½-inch pieces	*2 tablespoons chives, cut into ¼-inch lengths*
	Salt and pepper

1 Bring 6 cups of water to a boil over high heat in a large pot. Add the frozen soybeans and boil for about 8 minutes, until the soybeans soften. Drain in a colander.

2 Using the same pot, heat the safflower oil and add the onion and bell pepper. Cook over moderate heat, stirring frequently, until the vegetables soften, 7 minutes.

3 Add the cooked soybeans, corn, paprika, and the remaining 1 cup water. Simmer, covered, until the vegetables are tender, about 10 minutes.

4 Increase the heat to high and add the milk and butter. Boil, uncovered, until the liquid is reduced by half, about 3 minutes. Stir in the chives and season to taste with salt and pepper.

Per serving: *Calories 179 (From Fat 59); Fat 7g (Saturated 1g); Cholesterol 5mg; Sodium 135mg; Carbohydrate 22g (Dietary Fiber 5g); Protein 9g.*

☙ Red Lentil Dal with Caramelized Onions

Dal is a lentil dish that accompanies most meals in India, a staple food along with rice. The crowning glory of these lentils is the onions — caramelized ambrosia. Fried garnishes such as this are an integral part of Indian dishes, lending a distinct aroma, texture, and taste. Traditionally, cooking these onions requires faithfully stirring them while they cook, about 20 minutes. Do the best you can and make sure to attend to the onions the last 10 minutes of cooking. And need I mention that the lentils, onion, garlic, and seasonings are all health-enhancing ingredients.

Preparation time: _25 minutes_

Cooking time: _40 minutes_

Yield: _4 servings_

1 tablespoon unrefined safflower oil	_½ teaspoon turmeric_
1 yellow onion, skin removed and cut vertically in very thin slices	_½ teaspoon ground ginger_
	½ teaspoon ground cardamom
1 clove garlic, crushed and minced	_2½ cups water_
1 cup red lentils, sorted and washed	

1 In a medium-size saucepan, heat the oil over medium heat for 1 minute and add the onions. Stir so the onions cook evenly and don't burn. After about 10 minutes, the onions will be limp and yellow as they lose moisture.

2 Continue to stir the onions as you cook them another 10 minutes. The oil will begin to separate from the onions, a sign they're ready to brown. The onions will clump together and turn light brown. Continue frying as they turn caramel brown and begin to look shriveled up. If the onions begin to stick a little to the pan, add a little cold water, 1 tablespoon at a time, but don't lower the heat. In the last 5 minutes of cooking the onions, add the garlic.

3 After the onions are done, add 1 tablespoon of cold water to stop the cooking. Transfer to a small bowl and set aside.

4 In the saucepan used to cook the onions, put the lentils, turmeric, ginger, cardamom, and the 2½ cups water. Bring to a boil. Reduce the heat, cover, and simmer until the lentils are tender, about 15 minutes.

5 Serve the red lentil dal, topped with the fried onions, over rice for a vegetarian dish that provides high-quality protein, or as a side dish to a curry or Chicken Tandoori with Yogurt-Mint Sauce (see the recipe in Chapter 12). The spiced lentils, without the onions, are also perfumed and appealing on their own.

Per serving: _Calories 189 (From Fat 31); Fat 4g (Saturated 0g); Cholesterol 0mg; Sodium 16mg; Carbohydrate 29g (Dietary Fiber 7g); Protein 11g._

☺ Garlic Lima Beans

Sure to become a favorite, this fierce, Greek version of lima beans is just what grilled swordfish or a chicken kebab is waiting for! Both garlic and lima beans can have a positive impact on cholesterol, so dig in. This medicine is not hard to take!

Preparation time: *5 minutes*

Cooking time: *20 minutes*

Yield: *6 servings*

1 package (16 ounces) frozen baby lima beans

3 cloves garlic, crushed and minced

2 tablespoons chopped fresh parsley

2 tablespoons extra-virgin olive oil with a rich olive taste

1 cup water

Salt

1 Place the lima beans, garlic, parsley, olive oil, and water in a medium-size, heavy saucepan. Bring to a boil and cover the pot tightly.

2 Cook the lima beans on medium heat, stirring occasionally, until tender, about 20 minutes.

3 Season the lima beans with salt to taste and enjoy!

Per serving: *Calories 126 (From Fat 43); Fat 5g (Saturated 1g); Cholesterol 0mg; Sodium 121mg; Carbohydrate 16g (Dietary Fiber 5g); Protein 5g.*

Chapter 17

Quality Grains for Your Heart's Sake

In This Chapter

▶ Considering the difference between refined grains and whole

▶ Expanding your grain vocabulary

▶ Trying out whole-grain cookery

▶ Cooking pilafs and quinoa

▶ Getting a dose of healthy pasta

Making sure that your meals include nutritious, quality grains is one way to control your cholesterol. That's why this chapter focuses on whole grains, which are high in fiber and supply generous amounts of vitamins, minerals, and phytonutrients important for heart health. Refined grains — the standard white wheat flour and white rice of the Western diet — supply paltry amounts in comparison. In this chapter, you have the chance to compare the nutritional values of whole grains versus refined and see why going out of your way to eat whole grains can pay off big time in terms of your health.

In this chapter, you find out how easy it is to add whole grains, such as brown rice, wild rice, buckwheat, and hulled barley, to everyday meals. Whole grains have a reputation for being chewy and looking very brown. Yet most whole grains can fit in just fine with soups, stews, salads, and vegetables, lending richness that is very pleasing. In developing the recipes in this chapter, I started with basic grains but fiddled with the flavoring and texture to give these grain dishes some pizzazz. Sample the Herbed Wild Rice with Currants and Pecans to taste what I mean. The pasta section is also up-to-date, featuring pasta made with whole grains rather than refined wheat flour.

Refined Doesn't Mean Better: The Health Benefits of Whole Grains

You make every calorie count when you eat nutrient-dense foods that contain whole grains. Whole grains are a rich source of antioxidants such as vitamin E and selenium. The outer layer of grains, lost in refining, contains the important trace minerals copper, zinc, and manganese. The grains featured in this chapter's recipes — cornmeal, brown rice, wild rice, quinoa, and buckwheat — give you a good dose of a variety of nutrients needed for heart health.

Losing nutrients through refining

In refining grain, the bran and germ are removed from each kernel (see Figure 17-1), leaving only the large core of the grain, the endosperm. Unfortunately, while only a little of the bulk is removed, much of the nutrition goes with it.

Figure 17-1:
Cross-section of a grain of wheat. The bran and germ contain the most nutrients, but are usually removed in the refining process.

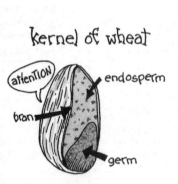

Within a kernel of grain, the nutrients are very unevenly distributed. In wheat, the bran has the lion's share of fiber plus many nutrients, including 80 percent of the niacin in the entire kernel. The tiny germ contains over 60 percent of the thiamin, vitamin E, and unsaturated fat. The endosperm is mostly carbohydrate and protein, but it contains only relatively small amounts of other nutrients. When wheat and other grains are refined, many nutrients for heart health are greatly reduced.

Yes, you're right. When flour is enriched, several nutrients are added back in equal or greater amounts — iron, thiamin, niacin, riboflavin, folic acid, and sometimes calcium. But even enriched, refined flour contains only 20 percent to 30 percent of some 20 nutrients naturally present in wheat. In addition, nutrients such as vitamin E are harmed in the bleaching process that makes flour snowy white.

What's left in those grains?

After wheat and rice are refined, only a small percent of the original amount of nutrients remain. Table 17-1 shows how you're short-changed by the nutrients that remain after refining. All these nutrients play a role in supporting heart health, and nutrients such as vitamin E, selenium, and zinc specifically help control cholesterol.

Table 17-1	Nutritional Content of White Flour and White Rice	
Nutrients	*Percentage Left in Enriched White Flour*	*Percentage Left in White Rice*
Fiber	13%	22%
Vitamin B6	17%	60%
Magnesium	18%	28%
Potassium	22%	81%
Selenium	75%	77%
Zinc	20%	78%

Giving high marks to whole grains

Scientists have put whole grains to the test in recent years and, based on the results of various studies, have concluded that whole grains offer strong protection against heart disease. Researchers at Harvard Medical School and Brigham and Women's Hospital in Boston analyzed dietary and health data of 75,000 women participating in the Nurses' Health Study and found that eating two and half servings a day of whole-grain products lowered the risk of coronary heart disease by 30 percent compared with women who consumed only 0.13 servings per day. (One serving of whole grain is equivalent to a slice of whole-grain bread.) And in another analysis of the same data, published in the *Journal of the American Medical Association* in 2000, consuming just 1.3 servings a day of whole grains significantly reduced the risk of stroke.

According to study findings, whole grains are beneficial for several possible reasons, including the following:

- They lower total cholesterol and LDL cholesterol, thanks to soluble fiber. Wheat bran in particular is beneficial.
- They provide antioxidants that slow the accumulation of cholesterol on artery walls.
- They decrease the tendency for blood to clot.

The U.S. Food and Drug Administration has found recent scientific evidence convincing enough that manufacturers are now allowed to make health claims for foods in which at least 51 percent of the ingredients are whole grains. On cereal boxes, you're likely to find such statements as "diets rich in whole-grain foods and other plant foods and low in total fat, saturated fat, and cholesterol may help reduce the risk of heart disease." Good advice!

Offering help for the carbophobic

When high-protein diets became the rage, out went grains with all their carbohydrates. The message seemed to be no more bread, cakes, or muffins. The fear is that eating carbohydrates will rapidly raise blood sugar levels, triggering weight gain.

In fact, the effect of grain on blood sugar can vary widely depending upon whether the grain is refined or whole. The more likely a food is to boost blood sugar levels, the higher its glycemic index. The glycemic index is a measure of a food's immediate effect on blood glucose levels. When the glycemic index was developed, refined wheat flour, such as that used to produce commercial white bread, was assigned a glycemic index of 100. Based on this standard, grains such as barley, oatmeal, and whole-grain rye, which elevate blood sugar much less, rate glycemic indexes in the range of 30 to 50.

High levels of blood sugar can also lead to insulin resistance (see Chapter 1) and associated high cholesterol. But eating whole grains can help prevent this condition and, according to a recent study, even protect against Type II diabetes, which can raise the risk of heart disease. Researchers from the University of Minnesota and the Harvard School of Public Health examined data from the Iowa Women's Health Study and found a strong association between the amount of whole grains a woman ate and a reduced risk of Type II diabetes. They suggest that the benefits at least in part are due to the fiber and magnesium whole grains provide.

Whole grain's fat and fiber, which take time to digest, dampen its effect on blood glucose.

The foods you eat along with the grain also affect its impact. A breakfast of white-flour pancakes with maple syrup is starch plus sugar and, metabolically speaking, behaves like a sweet dessert, while eating cornmeal with a little sausage, which contains protein and fat, moderates the effect of the carbohydrates in the cornmeal. Polenta with Turkey Sausage and Broccoli Rabe is waiting! See the recipe in this chapter.

Growing Your Grain Choices

Consider the easy-to-like whole grains on the following list as you write your next food shopping list, and cart some home to your kitchen. Each has its own distinctive character. Some grains, such as basmati rice, are sweet and fragrant, while the flavor of buckwheat is nutlike and robust. If you want a satisfying chew, try hulled barley. Or sample quinoa, which is light on the tongue. Cook these grains for novel additions to your everyday meals, and you'll significantly increase your intake of heart-healthy nutrients at the same time. (See Chapter 2 for the specific benefits of vitamins and minerals.)

- ✔ **Barley:** This grain is a good source of soluble fiber, which lowers cholesterol. Hulled barley is a whole grain that has had only the outer husk removed. You'll find it sold in bulk at natural food stores. Whole barley has four times the amount of fiber found in pearl barley, which has had the hull and bran removed. Barley supplies thiamin, copper, manganese, and selenium.

- ✔ **Brown rice:** A whole grain with a nutlike flavor, brown rice retains the germ and high-fiber bran, with only the inedible outer husk removed. Brown basmati rice is an especially fragrant variety. Brown rice supplies magnesium, vitamin B6, manganese, and selenium.

- ✔ **Buckwheat:** Not a cereal but triangular seeds of an herb related to rhubarb, buckwheat groats are hulled, crushed kernels, which cook in a manner similar to rice. Kasha is buckwheat groats that are toasted. Kasha is sold packaged in four forms: whole and in three grinds — coarse, medium, and fine. Buckwheat groats are available in bulk in natural foods stores. Kasha has a richer nutlike flavor compared with the milder, earthier flavor of unroasted buckwheat groats. The ground forms of kasha also have a more delicate texture than the whole grain. Buckwheat supplies magnesium, niacin, copper, manganese, riboflavin, and zinc.

- ✔ **Bulgur wheat:** These whole-grain wheat kernels have been steamed, dried, and cracked. This traditional grain of the Middle East has a tender, chewy texture and is used in wheat pilaf, salads, and vegetable and meat dishes. Bulgur supplies magnesium, manganese, and thiamin.

- ✔ **Corn:** Not a vegetable but a cereal grain, corn is a member of the grass family, along with barley and oats. That Italian gourmet classic, polenta, is the same as Southern cornmeal grits. Corn supplies thiamin, pantothenic acid, niacin, folate, vitamin C, magnesium, and potassium.

✔ **Millet:** Millet is a small, high-protein grain that is a staple in human diets throughout Africa and in much of Asia. We eat millet hulled, but you can also buy the unhulled version, sold in pet shops as birdseed. Treat yourself to this light, nutty grain in hot cereal and pilaf, and buy a little extra for your parakeet. Millet supplies calcium, riboflavin, and niacin.

✔ **Oats:** This grain is an excellent source of soluble fiber. Whole oats, which are the grain form fed to horses, are cleaned, toasted, hulled, and cleaned again and then called oat groats, food for humans. Oatmeal is oat groats, steamed and flattened with huge rollers. (See Chapter 6 for more information on this staple grain.)

✔ **Quinoa:** One of the newly rediscovered ancient grains, quinoa (pronounced keen-wa) was a staple of the Inca civilization. This tiny grain is light and fluffy when cooked and has a grassy, likable flavor. You can use it like you do rice in a variety of dishes. Quinoa is a quality source of protein, and it's higher in unsaturated fat and lower in carbohydrates than most grains. It also supplies vitamin E, calcium, and assorted B vitamins.

✔ **Whole-wheat couscous:** A pasta made with whole-grain wheat that includes the germ and the bran, whole-grain couscous provides manganese, selenium, magnesium, thiamin, and niacin.

✔ **Wild rice:** A long-grain marsh grass native to the northern Great Lakes area, wild rice supplies magnesium, phosphorous, copper, manganese, zinc, vitamin B6, niacin, and riboflavin.

Figure 17-2 shows you some of the many types of foods you can make using a variety of grains.

Buying whole-grain products

In a standard supermarket, you're likely to find boxed whole grains, such as rolled oats, kasha, cornmeal, and brown rice. But you have to visit a natural foods store to buy grains in bulk. However, the extra effort can be worth it. Bulk grains are significantly less expensive, and you can find a greater variety of whole grains. Millet, quinoa, and hulled barley are standard items. You can also buy just a recipe's worth to sample a grain that is new to you.

Whole grains have a shorter shelf life than refined grains because whole grains retain the germ, which contains oils that can go rancid. A good bet is to shop for grain in a store with a high turnover of these foods. Visit a health food store or an ethnic food shop where customers regularly go for staples such as Middle Eastern bulgur wheat or Indian basmati rice. Sniff the grain to judge freshness.

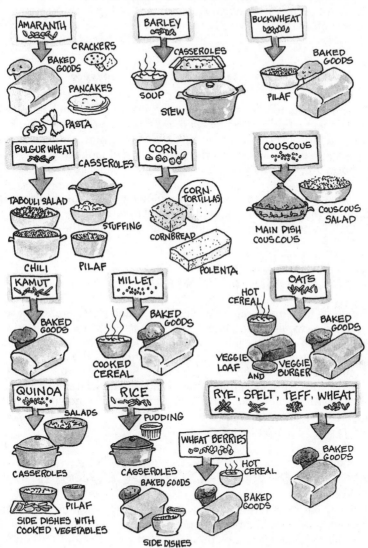

Figure 17-2:
Foods made with different types of grains.

While you're at the market, also check out all the whole-grain baked goods and other products now available. Look for breads and muffins but also pita pockets, bagels, tortillas, breakfast cereals, bread mixes, and even bread crumbs.

Look for the small loaves of thin-sliced, dense whole-grain rye and pumpernickel breads sold in the deli section of most supermarkets. The moist, rich slices are perfect with smoked salmon or toasted in the morning for a wake-up crunch.

Discovering the "whole" truth

When it comes to whole-grain bread, the word *whole* on a label tells you it's 100 percent whole grains. *Wheat bread* on the other hand is a mix of white flour and whole grain, a compromise but still a better choice nutritionally than white bread. Many brands of wheat bread look like whole-grain loaves, but don't be fooled; the color comes from caramel color or molasses.

A good general rule to follow in shopping for store-bought bread is to buy a product that contains at least 3 grams of fiber per slice to make sure the loaf contains a good amount of whole-grain flour. Check the label.

Reading the fine print

Shopping for whole-grain crackers, cereal, and pasta is another matter because — wouldn't you know? — manufacturers are permitted to use the term "whole" on these labels much more loosely. In this case, you need to read the ingredient list to find out what's really in the product. White flour of some sort is usually the first ingredient. "Enriched flour," "unbleached flour," "wheat flour," and just "flour" also mean refined white flour. Phrases such as "made with whole grains" and "all natural" are also no guarantee that the items on the ingredient list are whole wheat.

Easing Into Whole-Grain Cookery

Cooking whole grains isn't difficult. They only need more liquid and some extra time to cook than refined grains require. As you read in the following section, you can even cook them like pasta, which doesn't require you to measure the water. And preparing bulgur wheat requires no actually cooking at all. You just pour hot water over the grain and let it sit until done.

A sure-fire cooking technique

Grain can be prepared like pasta: Simply drop it into a bubbling pot of hot water and cook until tender. This technique is easy, with no need for precise measuring or timing. And cooking with plenty of water, there's no chance you'll burn the grain!

A can't-miss grain

Bulgur wheat doesn't even require cooking. Just cover it with boiling water and let the grain soak for 15 to 30 minutes and — presto — it's done. Use 1 cup of fine-grind (#1) bulgur or medium-grind (#2) to 2½ cups liquid. Now you have the prime ingredients in that famous Middle Eastern salad, *tabbouleh*. To the cooked grain, add equal amounts of minced fresh parsley leaves and tomato, half as much mint, 1 chopped onion, and the juice of 1 lemon. Serve with grilled chicken or meats, or keep your meal vegetarian and add a cucumber salad and chickpea hummus.

Here's how to make enough grain to yield about six 1-cup servings, depending upon the grain:

1. **Fill a large pot with at least 6 cups of water, add ¼ teaspoon salt, and, over high heat, bring the water to a boil.**

2. **Stir in 1½ cups grain, adjust the heat so that the water gently boils, and cook the grain uncovered.**

3. **If necessary, add additional water to keep the grains covered while cooking.**

4. **Keep testing the grain for doneness, and when it's to your taste, pour the grain into a strainer and then place the strainer in a bowl of cold water to stop the grain from cooking and drain again.**

   With whole grains such as brown rice and unhulled barley, the cooking time can be an hour or longer.

Use the boiled grain cold in a salad or as an ingredient in a dish that will be cooked. Or to eat the grain as a dish in itself, reheat it in a skillet to which you've added a tablespoon or two of oil plus seasonings if desired. Cook over medium heat, stirring occasionally, about 10 minutes, until the grain is thoroughly heated.

Grain cooking basics

While the boiling water approach to cooking grains has its advantages, using a precise amount of water in a ratio to the amount of grain gives you a way of controlling doneness that doesn't require supervision. Just follow the recommended amounts and cooking times in Table 17-2. You may have to make small adjustments to suit the pots you're cooking the grain in, but after you work out the right formula, you can rely on it time and again. While the risk in boiling grains is that they become water logged, this technique gives you fluffy grains with all the liquid evaporated. And the grains are hot and ready to eat right from the pot.

While many grains, such as brown rice and barley, can be cooked by either method, buckwheat, millet, and quinoa require the measured technique. What you don't do is as important as what you do. Here's the drill:

1. **To remove dust and pesticides, put the grain in a large bowl, add water, swish the grain around, and pour off the liquid.**

2. **Repeat Step 1 until the rinse water is clear.**

3. **Using the ratios shown in Table 17-2, put the grain of your choice and water, homemade stock, or canned broth in a small saucepan; bring the liquid to a boil; and then cover with a tight-fitting lid.**

   If the lid doesn't fit properly, cover the lid with a piece of aluminum foil, tucking the foil under the lip of the lid to prevent steam from escaping from the pot.

4. **Reduce the heat to low and cook for the times listed in Table 17-2.**

   If you see steam escaping from the pot, briefly remove the pot to a work surface and seal the top with a square of aluminum foil wrapped over the lid and tucked under the lid's lip. Then place the pot back on the stove to continue cooking the grain. You'll avoid ending up with undercooked or scorched grain.

   Don't be tempted to increase the heat to help the grains cook. They need heat, but they also simply need time in the warm liquid — think of each grain as a little sponge — to soak up moisture.

   Resist the temptation to lift the lid and peek at the grains to see how they're doing during the cooking time. You'll lose some of the liquid as steam.

5. **When the cooking time is up, for a little extra cook, turn off the heat and let the pot stand for 5 to 10 minutes before serving.**

6. **Raise the lid and fluff the grain with a fork to separate the kernels.**

7. **Test for doneness.**

   If the only grain you're accustomed to eating is white rice, which is quite soft when cooked, be forewarned that most whole grains are slightly chewy when adequately cooked. The chew comes from all that beneficial fiber in the bran, which is only minimally affected by cooking.

Whole grains take somewhat longer to cook than their refined versions because they still retain the fibrous bran, which takes time to break down. If you plan to eat whole grains as part of a dinner, start them when you would start fixing baked potatoes, about an hour before you expect to serve the meal, and they'll be done on time.

Grain is easy to cook if you add the right amount of water for the quantity of grain, and, with a measure of patience, cook them long enough. Table 17-2 gives you guidelines to follow.

Table 17-2	Grain Cooking Times	
Grain	**Grain:Liquid Ratio**	**Cooking Time**
Long-grain brown rice	1:2½	40 to 50 minutes
Hulled barley	1:3	1¼ to 1½ hours
Pearled barley	1:3	50 to 60 minutes
Wild rice	1:4	50 minutes
Buckwheat groats and kasha	1:2	20 minutes
Bulgur wheat	1:2½	Cover with boiling water and let sit 15 to 30 minutes
Quinoa	1:2	15 minutes
Millet	1:2	35 minutes
Whole-grain couscous	1:1½	Add liquid and turn off heat; let sit 10 minutes

Adding grains to all sorts of dishes

Besides the grain recipes in this chapter, many other ways of adding whole grains to your meals are scattered throughout this book. Bake a whole-wheat muffin that also includes oat flour using the recipe in Chapter 8. Turn to Chapter 6 for a basic recipe to prepare a hot porridge made with assorted whole grains starting with millet and invent your own variations. Follow the directions in Chapter 20 and bake a cracker with rye flour or make a cake with spelt flour.

Whole grains also show up in lunch and dinner dishes. Barley is added to soups in Chapter 9, salads in Chapter 10, and to beef stew in Chapter 14. Or stuff a chicken with whole-wheat couscous in Chapter 12.

Grain recipes for real meals

The two recipes that follow give you the chance to experiment with two very different grains: cornmeal, which you stir as it cooks, and barley, which you leave alone, letting it absorb its liquid in private. The cornmeal in Polenta with Turkey Sausage and Broccoli Rabe is as mouthwatering and fun to eat as popcorn. The more sober barley dish, with its portobello mushrooms, makes a fine accompaniment for pork roast or game birds.

Polenta with Turkey Sausage and Broccoli Rabe

With the great variety of lowfat sausages available in supermarkets, these succulent and savory meats can be part of a heart-healthy diet. The turkey sausage I used to test this recipe contained, per sausage, only 2.5 grams of saturated fat out of 13 grams total fat. To convert this dish to vegetarian, you have the option of substituting soy sausage for the turkey sausage. Be forewarned, though: The result is likely to be less scrumptious.

Preparation time: *15 minutes*

Cooking time: *30 minutes*

Servings: *4 for lunch*

1 tablespoon extra-virgin olive oil

4 turkey sausages

1 pound broccoli rabe

1 large clove garlic, minced

½ cup chicken stock (see the Basic Chicken Stock recipe in Chapter 9 or use canned, low sodium fat-free chicken broth)

6 cups water

1 package (13 ounces) precooked instant polenta, or 1 tube (24 ounces) precooked plain polenta

Salt

1 In a heavy skillet, heat the olive oil over medium heat. Add the sausages and cook until cooked through and browned, about 10 minutes per side.

2 Meanwhile, trim the broccoli rabe by removing the ends of the stalks. Cut the stalks crosswise in ½-inch lengths and slice the tops into bite-size pieces. Set aside.

3 When cooked, transfer the sausages to a plate and keep warm in an oven on low heat.

4 Place the garlic in the same skillet used for the sausages and cook on medium heat, stirring, for 30 seconds.

5 Add the chopped broccoli rabe and ½ cup of the chicken stock. Cover and cook until the broccoli rabe is tender, about 7 minutes.

6 To prepare the instant polenta, put the water in a heavy, large saucepan and on high heat, bring to a boil. Add the polenta and lower heat to cook the polenta at a gentle boil and then at a simmer as it becomes very thick towards the end of the cooking process, stirring continuously with a wooden spoon for 5 to 8 minutes. Add salt to taste. Alternatively, cut the tube of polenta into 16 round slices and follow the package instructions for reheating.

7 To serve, spoon a cupful of polenta in the center of a warm dinner plate. Edge one side of the polenta with broccoli rabe and cross the polenta and vegetable with one sausage.

Per serving: Calories 250 (From Fat 66); Fat 7g (Saturated 2g); Cholesterol 45mg; Sodium 907mg; Carbohydrate 25g (Dietary Fiber 4g); Protein 19g.

⟋ Sage-Scented Barley with Portobello Mushrooms

Made with unhulled barley, this gutsy side dish seems just right with game birds and beef. If you decide to wimp out and cook the recipe with more tender pearled barley, you'll miss much of barley's healing nutrients.

Preparation time: *30 minutes, plus 2 to 3 hours to soak the barley*

Cooking time: *1 hour and 15 minutes*

Yield: *6 servings*

1 cup unhulled barley, rinsed

4 tablespoons extra-virgin olive oil

6 ounces sliced portobello mushrooms, cleaned and cut into 1-inch pieces

1 medium yellow onion, coarsely chopped

1 tablespoon chopped fresh sage leaves

½ teaspoon ground allspice

½ cup white wine

4½ cups vegetable or chicken stock (see the Basic Chicken Stock recipe in Chapter 9 or use canned, low sodium fat-free chicken broth and omit salt called for in recipe)

2 tablespoons chopped parsley

Salt and pepper

1 To shorten the cooking time of the barley, soak it in water for 2 to 3 hours. Drain.

2 After the barley has soaked, heat 2 tablespoons of the oil in a heavy skillet over medium-high heat. Add the mushroom pieces and cook about 7 minutes, stirring frequently. Transfer the mushrooms to a bowl.

3 Add the remaining 2 tablespoons of the oil to the skillet, along with the onion. Reduce the heat to medium and cook until the onion is soft and translucent, about 10 minutes.

4 Add the barley, sage, and allspice to the onions and cook for 1 minute, stirring to coat the barley with the oil. Add the wine and cook 5 minutes, until nearly evaporated.

5 Add the stock to the barley mixture, bring to a boil, lower the heat to low, and cover the skillet tightly so that steam doesn't escape. When the barley has cooked for 1¼ hours, check for doneness. Add additional broth if necessary and cook for an additional 15 minutes.

6 Stir in the mushrooms. Cook, covered, an additional few minutes to combine the flavors. Add the parsley and season to taste with salt and pepper. Serve immediately.

Vary It! *To prepare the barley with homemade vegetable broth, begin by cooking 2 carrots, 1 stalk celery, 1 onion, 1 bay leaf, and 1 clove in 6 cups water for 30 minutes. Meanwhile, assemble the ingredients and prepare the vegetables for the barley recipe. If you choose to prepare this recipe with pearled barley, reduce the broth to 3 cups and cook the barley for 45 minutes.*

Per serving: *Calories 221 (From Fat 95); Fat 11g (Saturated 1g); Cholesterol 0mg; Sodium 854mg; Carbohydrate 27g (Dietary Fiber 6g); Protein 6g.*

Treasuring Grains with a History

Grains that have sustained civilizations became an integral part of the history of many cultures — rice in Asia, kamut in Egypt, and quinoa in Peru. These grains were the staple for daily meals and dressed up for feast days. Maharajahs garnished their rice pilafs with gold and silver. Grain was given divine status. Java has its rice goddess, Dewi Sri; the Greek goddess, Demeter, is symbolized by wheat or barley; and the Aztec goddess, Chicomecoatel, is represented by a double ear of corn.

In this section, you have the chance to add some delicious rice pilafs and a recipe for the ancient grain, quinoa, to your cooking repertoire. Eating grain need never be dull again.

Pilaf recipes with pizzazz

Rice pilaf, a mixture that is primarily grain with the addition of some other ingredients, such as chopped and cooked vegetables, poultry, meats, and seafood, originated in the Near East. Traditionally, a pilaf always begins with first browning the rice in butter or oil before cooking it in stock. A variation of this procedure is used in Stuffed Bell Peppers with Turkish Pilaf. In the second pilaf recipe, Herbed Wild Rice with Currants and Pecans, the grain is added directly to stock or broth, cooked, and seasoned, and then other ingredients are incorporated.

Use these pilaf recipes as a starting point to flavor your own grain mixtures. These recipes feature citrus, toasted nuts, dusky spices such as allspice and cinnamon, and refreshing mint.

◌ Stuffed Bell Peppers with Turkish Pilaf

When you eat a grain with some sort of bean or pea, you give yourself a complete protein — the equivalent of that found in meats and poultry, but without the saturated fat and cholesterol. For instance, if you start with these peppers, filled with sweet raisins and spices, and have some chickpea hummus, you have a meal with high-quality protein, all from the plant kingdom. The recipe calls for long-grain, Indian basmati rice, raised for thousands of years in the foothills of the Himalayas. The grain is aged, giving the rice a delectable nutlike, perfumed flavor. Basmati rice is sold in Indian and Middle Eastern markets and in some supermarkets.

Preparation time: *30 minutes*

Cooking time: *1½ hours*

Yield: *6 servings*

3 cups water

1½ cups brown basmati rice (which yields 5 cups cooked rice)

3 tablespoons extra-virgin olive oil

1 cup onion, chopped into ¼-inch pieces

2 tablespoons pine nuts

1½ teaspoons ground cinnamon

1 teaspoon allspice

¼ teaspoon ground nutmeg

1 large tomato, diced

2 tablespoons golden raisins

2 tablespoons fresh dill, chopped fine

2 teaspoons lemon juice

6 medium-size green bell peppers

1 Put the water in a heavy saucepan with a tight-fitting lid. Add the brown rice and bring to a boil. Cover, reduce the heat to low, and cook undisturbed, until the rice is tender, about 40 minutes.

2 Meanwhile, put the olive oil in a large skillet. Add the onions and pine nuts and cook on medium heat for 7 minutes, until the onions become translucent. Stir occasionally.

3 To the onions, add the cinnamon, allspice, nutmeg, tomato, raisins, dill, and lemon juice. Mix together. Add the cooked rice and combine with the other ingredients.

4 Fill a large pot with water and bring to a boil. Meanwhile, cut the tops off the peppers and scoop out the seeds. Add the pepper tops and bottoms to the pot and parboil for 2 minutes. With tongs, remove the peppers and arrange on a work surface.

5 Spoon the pilaf mixture into the pepper bottoms until they're filled and cap with pepper tops. Place the stuffed peppers in a baking pan with a half inch of water to prevent the peppers from burning on the bottom. Bake for 45 minutes, until the peppers are tender, and serve.

Per serving: *Calories 297 (From Fat 92); Fat 10g (Saturated 2g); Cholesterol 0mg; Sodium 11mg; Carbohydrate 50g (Dietary Fiber 6g); Protein 6g.*

Herbed Wild Rice with Currants and Pecans

This pilaf has it all: texture from the grain, sweetness from the currants and orange, a little bite from the onions, and the richness of the pecans. Made with brown rice, this recipe provides more than its share of nutrients important for heart health, including magnesium, selenium, zinc, vitamin B6, and niacin.

Preparation time: *25 minutes*

Cooking time: *1 hour 15 minutes*

Yield: *6 servings*

1 organic orange (see Warning at the end of this recipe)

2 cups chicken stock (see the Basic Chicken Stock recipe in Chapter 9 or use canned, low sodium fat-free chicken broth and omit salt for seasoning)

½ cup wild rice, well rinsed

2½ cups water

1 cup brown rice

2 scallions, cut crosswise into thin rings

¼ cup chopped Italian parsley

¼ cup chopped mint leaves

½ cup currants

½ cup pecan halves, toasted

2 tablespoons extra-virgin olive oil

Salt and pepper

1 Grate the rind of the orange to yield 1 heaping teaspoon zest. Cut the orange in half and squeeze to yield 2 tablespoons juice. Set aside.

2 Put the chicken stock in a medium saucepan with a tight-fitting lid. Bring the broth to a boil.

3 Add the wild rice and bring to a boil. Reduce the heat to low, cover the pot, and cook, undisturbed, until the rice is puffed up and quite tender, about 1 hour. The rice is done when the grains have puffed up and are quite tender, regardless of whether the liquid has been absorbed. Drain if necessary.

4 Meanwhile, in a second heavy saucepan, put the 2½ cups water and bring to a boil. Add the brown rice and bring to a boil. Cover, reduce the heat to low, and cook, undisturbed, until the rice is tender, about 50 minutes.

5 Add the brown rice to the wild rice. Add the scallions, parsley, mint, currants, pecans, orange zest, olive oil, orange juice, and salt and pepper to taste.

6 Serve as a side dish with roast turkey or chicken. The pilaf can also be served at room temperature for a lunch buffet.

Warning: *Because the rind is an ingredient, use an organic orange to avoid possible chemicals used in growing the fruit and bringing it to market.*

Per serving: *Calories 311 (From Fat 110); Fat 12g (Saturated 1g); Cholesterol 0mg; Sodium 173mg; Carbohydrate 47g (Dietary Fiber 5g); Protein 7g.*

Using grains from the distant past in recipes today

The ancient grains have made their way back into the modern diet via vegetarianism and the interest in preserving biodiversity. Buying and cooking these grains happily takes the focus off wheat. Quinoa became a staple of the Inca civilization, and amaranth sustained life in ancient Mexico and Peru for good reason. Both grains are an excellent source of high-quality protein. You too can use these as a protein source, replacing red meat, which is high in saturated fat. Shop for these grains in natural foods stores. You're more likely to find amaranth as a flour and quinoa in grain form. A recipe for quinoa with basil and tomato follows.

 Quinoa Italiana

The texture of quinoa is nicely soft and light but with intermittent grains that pop. Its delicate taste is fine on its own but also welcomes herbs and vegetables. The version here uses Italian flavorings and is especially tasty with a dusting of grated Parmesan cheese. Serve quinoa as a side dish, just as you would serve rice.

Preparation time: *10 minutes*

Cooking time: *20 minutes*

Yield: *6 servings*

1½ cups quinoa	2 Roma tomatoes	Salt and pepper
2 cups water	4 sprigs basil, stems removed and leaves cut in thin ribbons	Parmesan cheese, grated
½ teaspoon salt		

1 Rinse the quinoa in five changes of water in a bowl, while at the same time, manually sifting through the grains and moving them around. Let the grains settle before pouring off the water. If the quinoa doesn't settle, drain in a large, fine sieve after each rinse.

2 Put the quinoa in a heavy medium saucepan filled with the 2 cups of water. Add the salt. Bring to a boil and reduce the heat to medium-low. Cover the pot and simmer until the quinoa is tender and the water is absorbed, about 20 minutes.

3 Quarter the tomatoes and remove the seeds. Dice the tomatoes.

4 When the quinoa is done, toss with a fork to separate the grains. Add the tomatoes and basil and combine. Salt and pepper to taste. Serve with grated Parmesan cheese.

Per serving: *Calories 169 (From Fat 26); Fat 3g (Saturated 1g); Cholesterol 1mg; Sodium 322mg; Carbohydrate 30g (Dietary Fiber 3g); Protein 6g.*

Ciaoing Down on Healthy Pasta

Pasta became a health food when dieters were counting only calories. Dieters like the idea that spaghetti, without the sauce, is low in fat, and they feel virtuous having cold pasta salads for lunch. But if your aim is to give yourself a serving of nutrients that nourish your heart and do their part in lowering cholesterol, don't turn to the standard spaghettis. You'll see on labels that they're made out of semolina, which sounds very nutritious but is actually just a type of wheat and, in addition, refined. Most pastas on the supermarket shelf are made of refined white wheat flour, just like white bread is.

If you visit a natural foods store, however, you're sure to find an impressive variety of intriguing whole-grain pastas. Don't be surprised to find brown rice fettuccine, angel hair pasta made with whole-grain spelt (an ancient cereal grain with a mellow, nutty flavor), corn pasta, and spinach spaghetti that also contains flour made from the Jerusalem artichoke (a tuber that is a variety of sunflower). These are whole-food pastas, complete with fiber and all their original nutrients.

Figure on 2 ounces uncooked, dried pasta per serving. This quantity is enough to fill a pasta bowl, along with the sauce, but still keep calories in check. Serve with salad and add minestrone soup to satisfy bigger appetites.

Going with the grain

Whole-grain pastas have a stronger, more nutlike taste than white-flour spaghetti, calling for a sauce that can compete in flavor. Meaty portobello mushrooms, roasted vegetables, and piquant chiles are a match. Add these to homemade and bottled sauces.

Avoid diluting the sauce and its flavors with the pasta cooking liquid. Thoroughly drain the cooked pasta and return the pasta in the pot to the stove. Heat 1 minute, on medium, uncovered, so that any remaining liquid evaporates.

Splitting the difference: Pasta that's a mix of refined flour and whole food

If whole-grain pastas are just too overbearing for you, you do have some pasta options, which are featured in the two recipes that follow. Spinach pasta is made with white flour but also gives you a dose of green vegetable. Soba noodles, a staple of Japanese cooking, are a combination of refined wheat flour and whole-grain buckwheat.

You can also start with your favorite refined durum wheat pasta and beef up the sauce with the missing wheat bran and wheat germ. Natural foods stores sell bran and germ on their own. Add these to your favorite homemade or bottled pasta tomato sauce, and you have a nutritious, quick meal. Here are the proportions to use:

✔ For each pound of pasta, add 1 tablespoon wheat germ and ¾ cup wheat bran. These amounts replace about half of the wheat germ and bran lost in refining.

✔ For a half pound of pasta (8 ounces and enough for 4 servings), add 1½ teaspoons wheat germ and about ⅓ cup bran.

✔ Because you're adding more bulk to the sauce, you also need to add a few tablespoons water to retain its original consistency.

Toasted wheat germ goes rancid quickly. Store it in vacuum-sealed jars, keep it in the refrigerator or freezer, and use within 2 to 3 months.

Pasta recipes for getting your grains

These recipes are terrific on their own without any embellishments, but a fine flavored cheese is also welcome. Even though you're probably watching your fat intake, you can probably afford a sprinkling of cheese on your pasta. Because you won't need pounds of the stuff, treat yourself to the best you can find and enjoy the superior flavor. Hunt out imported Parmesan and Pecorino Romano or some mild goat cheese produced on a local farm.

Spinach Pasta with Walnut-Basil Sauce

This colorful dish in green, red, and yellow provides heaps of special nutrients for the heart. Using this spinach pasta lets you sneak leafy greens into meals, but the recipe works just as well with whole-grain pastas such as spelt, a type of wheat, and brown rice pasta. The walnut basil sauce is a match for the more robust flavors of the whole grains.

Preparation time: *15 minutes*

Cooking time: *40 minutes*

Yield: *4 servings*

1 cup walnut pieces

½ cup basil leaves, about 3 ounces

2 cloves garlic, skin removed

⅓ cup plus 2 tablespoons extra-virgin olive oil

¾ pound sweet red bell peppers, seeds removed and quartered

¾ pound yellow squash

¾ pound asparagus

6 ounces baby portobello or button mushrooms, washed

Salt

8 ounces spinach spaghetti

1 Put the walnuts, basil, garlic, and ⅓ cup olive oil in a food processor fitted with a metal blade. Blend until smooth. Pour into a small bowl and set aside.

2 On a cutting board, slice the red peppers crosswise into ¼-inch-wide slices. Cut the yellow squash crosswise into ¼-inch rounds. Cut the asparagus into 2-inch lengths. Cut each mushroom vertically into 4 slices.

3 In a large skillet filled with an inch of water, parboil the asparagus until almost tender, about 10 minutes. Drain the cooking liquid. Remove the asparagus to a bowl and set aside. Thoroughly dry the skillet with a paper towel.

4 In the same skillet, cook the peppers, squash, and mushrooms in the remaining 2 tablespoons olive oil over medium heat, until vegetables are tender, about 25 minutes. Toward the end of cooking period, add the asparagus.

5 Meanwhile, bring a pot of water to a boil, uncovered, on high heat. Add a dash of salt and a small splash of olive oil to prevent strands of spaghetti from sticking together. Add the spaghetti and cook about 12 minutes, or according to package instructions.

6 Drain the spaghetti in a colander, making sure that no liquid remains in the pot.

7 Add the walnut-basil sauce to the spaghetti and toss to coat.

8 Distribute the spaghetti in warmed pasta bowls and top with the sautéed vegetables.

Per serving: *Calories 646 (From Fat 384); Fat 43g (Saturated 5g); Cholesterol 0mg; Sodium 154mg; Carbohydrate 56g (Dietary Fiber 9g); Protein 15g.*

☺ Buckwheat Noodles in Asian Sesame Sauce

These noodles, dressed with a honeyed sesame-soy sauce, are good hot or cold. They supply magnesium, which helps maintain the heart muscle in working order, and folic acid, which keeps homocysteine levels in check (see Chapter 1 for more on homocysteine).

Preparation time: *20 minutes*

Cooking time: *30 minutes*

Yield: *4 servings*

2 quarts water	*1 tablespoon sherry*
1 package (8 ounces) soba noodles	*½ cup loosely packed cilantro leaves*
2 tablespoons sesame tahini	*2 cloves garlic, peeled and minced*
3 tablespoons soy sauce	*1 teaspoon salt*
2 tablespoons rice vinegar	*2 teaspoons hot sauce*
2 tablespoons honey	*2 scallions, minced*

1 In a large pot, bring the 2 quarts water, covered, to a boil. Add the noodles and cook, uncovered, according to package directions, about 12 to 15 minutes. Drain in a colander. Place the noodles in a large bowl of cold water to cool for 10 minutes and then drain again in the colander.

2 In a medium bowl, using a whisk, mix together the tahini, soy sauce, and vinegar until smooth. Add the honey and sherry and stir again.

3 Add a few tablespoons of water to the tahini mixture, stirring well after each addition, until the mixture is of sauce consistency.

4 Stir in the cilantro, garlic, salt, and hot sauce.

5 Place the noodles in a serving bowl and drizzle with the sauce. Toss and then garnish with the scallions. Serve immediately at room temperature.

Per serving: *Calories 280 (From Fat 4); Fat 0g (Saturated 1g); Cholesterol 0mg; Sodium 1,787mg; Carbohydrate 54g (Dietary Fiber 1g); Protein 11g.*

Part VI
Savory Accompaniments and Sweet Finishes

The 5th Wave   By Rich Tennant

"Don't blame us! The recipe clearly states, 'Add 4 tablespoons of sugar.'"

In this part . . .

This part contains recipes for bright and spicy condiments and luxurious legal desserts. To prepare sauces and salsas, you find out how to start with such nutritious ingredients as apples, onions, and chile peppers to turn out your own special concoctions. And you also discover all the good things garlic does for your heart!

Next I give you ways to assemble healthy fruit desserts to finish a meal. I explain which fruits are highest in soluble fiber and colorful, antioxidant nutrients. And for you carb watchers, I also point out which fruits raise blood sugar only minimally. Finally, I discuss how you can mix whole grains with natural sweeteners to create cookies and tea cakes healthy enough to be served as a main course for breakfast.

Noble motives aside, these recipes are so yummy that I bet you forget they're health food.

Chapter 18

Sparking Flavors with Seasonings and Sauces

In This Chapter

▶ Replacing salt with lots of herbs and spices

▶ Savoring the heart-healthy foods in salsa

▶ Stirring up homemade condiments and sauces

Recipes aimed at cardiac health are often low on fat and salt. While your heart benefits, your taste buds often lose out. Fat is a flavor carrier, helping you to taste the flavors of other ingredients, and salt is a flavor enhancer. That's why hollandaise and steak sauce are so tasty. However, as this chapter proves, it is possible to create tantalizing sauces and condiments by relying on other ingredients such as fresh herbs, exotic spices, garlic, and onions. Reducing a sauce to intensify flavor, the secret to the Sweet Red Pepper Sauce, also works.

Some of the recipes in this chapter give you updated versions of old favorites, with added healthy ingredients, such as the one for Cranberry Sauce with Caramelized Onions and Cinnamon. Others like the recipe for Asian Cucumber Relish give you a new condiment for your repertoire. You also have the chance to experiment with herb and spice pairings and come up with your own combinations. And this chapter gives you tips on shopping for herbs and spices. You can turn an ordinary dish into something special when you serve it with one of the condiments prepared from the recipes in this chapter.

Seasoning When You Want Less Salt

Heart-healthy diets that restrict cholesterol usually also include a recommendation to limit sodium intake. If you're salt-sensitive and have high blood pressure, your physician has probably recommended cutting back on salt.

This advice probably sounded like a sentence to a lifetime of eating bland food, but it needn't be. As you cut back on salt, your taste buds will adjust to this change and soon you'll find lightly salted foods salty enough.

You can bring out the flavor of food with substances other than salt. Adding fresh lemon or lime juice or a dash of vinegar can enhance flavors. Strong herbs and spices, such as garlic, ginger, cayenne, and hot pepper sauce, can also eliminate the need for salt. Or make up some herb and spice mixtures with complex flavors that will keep your mind off the missing salt. This chapter tells you how.

Another way to cut back on salt in your diet is to stay away from seasoned salts, pickle condiments, and salty commercial sauces. Here are some likely suspects:

- Garlic salt
- Onion salt
- Celery salt
- Lemon-pepper
- Seasoning blends
- Hot dog pickle relish
- Soy sauce
- Barbecue sauce

When buying seasoning blends, read the label to find out if salt is one of the ingredients. Some brands include salt in fajita seasoning, spice rubs, chili powder, and curry.

Doing the herb shuffle

Herbs are the leaves and soft stems of plants. You can buy them fresh, sold in the produce department of most markets. You can also maintain a supply of fresh herbs by growing them at home. Plant nurseries carry an assortment of these, which change with the season. Often a pot containing a living plant doesn't cost much more than a meager package of fresh herbs at the store. Just set the pot in your kitchen window and harvest a continuing supply.

When shopping for fresh herbs, select those with a healthy green color and avoid those that are limp and yellowing. An herb should have a clean scent.

Your other option is to buy dried herbs, which come whole, flaked, ground, or powdered. They're widely available and easy to measure and require no trimming. The main concern about dried herbs is whether they are old and stale. The flavor in dried herbs comes from their essential oils, which lose their strength and character when exposed to air, heat, and light.

Buy the dried herbs that are packaged in airtight jars rather than those that come in cellophane bags, which can let in air.

To cook with herbs, start out simple by adding just a single herb to a recipe you're preparing, for example basil in tomato sauce or sage in a turkey pot pie. Often one extra flavor note is all you need to elevate an ordinary dish to something special. Certain herbs are best with certain foods. Here's a list of herbs that partner well with various foods.

- ✔ **With beef:** Bay leaf, rosemary, parsley, chives, marjoram, garlic, savory, and cloves

- ✔ **With pork:** Sage, savory, cumin, coriander, garlic, rosemary, and bay

- ✔ **With poultry:** Rosemary, bay, thyme, oregano, savory, garlic, and tarragon

- ✔ **With fish:** Dill, fennel, garlic, parsley, tarragon, cilantro, and parsley

- ✔ **With grain:** Parsley, cilantro, mint, savory, garlic, dill, and sage

- ✔ **With vegetables:** Basil, chives, oregano, garlic, rosemary, tarragon, and parsley

Stepping out with spices

Spices are aromatic or pungent seasonings that come from the bark (cinnamon), the buds (capers), the berries (vanilla), the roots (ginger), the stigmas of flowers (saffron), and the seeds (coriander) of plants. They are always sold dried. Spices are at the heart of such culinary classics as Indian curry, Mexican mole sauce (which also includes chocolate), Chinese Szechwan dishes, and American pumpkin pie. For best results, cook with the freshest, highest quality spices. One of the best sources of these is the mail-order company Penzeys Spices. Browsing through their catalog of scores of spices as well as herbs is like strolling through the proverbial candy store. Have a look at www.penzeys.com.

Several spices are good for heart health. Ginger thins the blood and enhances circulation. In an animal study conducted in India, ginger was shown to lower cholesterol by stimulating the conversion of cholesterol to bile acids. And turmeric, thanks to a compound called curcumin, helps dampen inflammation that can promote atherosclerosis. Curry powder and the Moroccan spice mixture, ras el hanout, both contain turmeric. For a dose of cucumin, enjoy a serving of the Moroccan Chicken with Couscous in Chapter 12.

Saffron luxury

The rare spice saffron consists of the stigmas (that part in the center of a flower that receives the pollen when a bee pollinates the flower) of a certain small purple crocus. Obviously, harvesting and gathering a sizeable amount of these tiny bits presents a challenge. Each crocus provides only three stigmas, and 14,000 of these stigmas amount to only one ounce of spice. That's why supermarkets sell you saffron in tiny glass vials that hold only a few strands of saffron and charge you as if it were gold. Fortunately, a little of this precious spice goes a long way, a couple of strands sufficient to flavor an entire dish such as a poached sea bass.

Saffron is an essential ingredient in recipes for paella, risotto, and bouillabaisse. It is also used to impart its yellow-orange color to dishes such as rice pilaf. Saffron is sold powdered, which loses its flavor readily and can easily be adulterated, and you can buy whole saffron threads. In European cooking, saffron is added directly to stews and broths. In India, to develop the richest saffron color, cooks briefly dry roast the spice, crush it and then soak the saffron for an hour in a couple tablespoons of warm milk. Once in Egypt, at a food bazaar in Luxor, a vendor offered to sell me a whole bag of saffron for only a couple of dollars. I bet it wasn't saffron.

Certain spices are best with specific foods. Here are lists of pairings that give you guaranteed successful combinations:

- ✔ **With beef:** Onion, garlic, cloves, mustard, ginger, paprika, and pepper
- ✔ **With pork:** Ginger, garlic, onion, mustard, coriander, cardamom, and allspice
- ✔ **With chicken:** Cumin, coriander, cinnamon, anise, garlic, turmeric, and sesame
- ✔ **With fish:** Fennel, capers, onion, garlic, ginger, saffron, and celery seed
- ✔ **With grains:** Saffron, cinnamon, clove, nutmeg, turmeric, garlic, and onions
- ✔ **With vegetables:** Onions, garlic, ginger, celery seed, nutmeg, capers, and pepper

Both onion and garlic are roots, so they're technically spices, not herbs.

When more is more: A chorus line of complex herb and spice mixtures

When you combine herbs or spices, the results can be symphonic. Some mixtures have become classics, developed over the centuries:

- **Chinese five-spice powder** is a pungent mixture of equal parts cinnamon, cloves, fennel seed, star anise, and Szechwan peppercorns.

- **Herbes de Provence** is a savory blend of basil, fennel seed, lavender, marjoram, rosemary, sage, summer savory, and thyme.

- **Ras el hanout,** which comes from Morocco, means literally "head of the shop," referring to the spice shop owners who assemble their own blends. An authentic mixture may contain up to 50 ingredients, including dried rose buds.

Many upscale markets sell these spice mixtures ready-made.

You can also try blending your own spices. Grind the ingredients with a mortar and pestle or in an electric spice grinder. Here are three formulas:

- **Savory herb seasoning:** 3 teaspoons basil, 2 teaspoons summer savory, 2 teaspoons celery seed, 2 teaspoons ground cumin seed, 2 teaspoons sage, 2 teaspoons marjoram, and 1 teaspoon thyme, or better yet, lemon thyme

- **Lemon garlic seasoning:** 2 teaspoons garlic powder, 1 teaspoon dried basil, and 1 teaspoon dried lemon peel

- **Spicy seasoning:** 1 teaspoon black pepper, 1 teaspoon ground ginger, 1 teaspoon ground coriander, and ½ teaspoon dried oregano

You can make your own version of ras el hanout with just 11 herbs and spices. Here's what you need:

- 2 teaspoons black pepper

- 2 teaspoons dried ginger

- 1 teaspoon ground cumin

- 1 teaspoon ground cinnamon

- 1 teaspoon ground coriander

- 1 teaspoon ground allspice

- 1 teaspoon ground cardamom

- ½ teaspoon ground nutmeg

- ½ teaspoon turmeric

- ¼ teaspoon ground cloves

- ¼ teaspoon cayenne

Put all the spices in a small bowl and thoroughly combine. The Moroccan Chicken with Couscous in Chapter 12 calls for this spice mixture.

If you own only a couple of these spices, you may be hesitant to invest in all the others. In fact, the ingredients in ras el hanout make a great starter set for a spice cabinet. Stock up on all of these useful seasonings.

Salsa Dancing

Salsa now takes its place along side such standard condiments as ketchup and mustard. Like so many time-honored, traditional foods, salsa is naturally healthy. The standard salsa is made with tomato, onion, garlic, and chiles — all good for the heart. Here's a rundown of their specific benefits.

Twirling with tomatoes

Tomatoes are very rich in antioxidants, such as beta carotene, as well as vitamins C and E, necessary ammunition for protecting the cardiovascular system because these nutrients protect cholesterol from becoming oxidized (see Chapter 2 for more on antioxidants). Tomatoes also are very low in sodium and high in potassium, a ratio that counteracts high blood pressure. A single medium tomato has only about 35 calories.

One of the antioxidants in tomatoes is lycopene. Cooked tomatoes have more available lycopene than raw tomatoes, and fat increases its absorption into the body. Now there's a way to think of pizza as health food!

Supermarket tomatoes have a reputation for being flavorless, mushy, and underripe. But some of the problem comes from how they're handled once they come home. Here are some guidelines to follow:

- ✔ Store vegetables at room temperature. Cold arrests the ripening process of tomatoes, turns them mushy, and kills their flavor.

- ✔ Place tomatoes on the counter, stem end up, not on the "bumps," the shoulders of the tomato that are the tenderest part. If you leave them on their shoulders for a few days, the weight of the tomato itself is enough to bruise them. And once bruises appear, spoilage will eventually follow.

- ✔ Ripe tomatoes hold perfectly well for a few days at room temperature. Buy enough to last you only three or four days.

Stepping out with onions

Onions are a love song for your heart. In a study that appeared in the *India Journal of Medical Science*, total cholesterol levels declined in participants when onions were added to their high fat diet. Onions also raise HDL, the "good" cholesterol, according to research conducted in the 1980s by Dr. Victor Gurewich at Harvard Medical School. Eating one medium onion a day, preferably raw, raised HDL as much as 30 percent. Onions also act as a blood thinner, able to counteract the effects of a fatty meal and help reduce inflammation. They're even a good source of antioxidant vitamin C and small amounts of the B vitamins and trace minerals.

When you want red meat, which is high in saturated fat, eat some steak topped with lots of sautéed onions. The onions, a blood thinner, help counteract the effect of the saturated fat.

With all these benefits, onions are worth eating every day, which is easy to do because their flavor goes well with practically any food, from eggs and fish to vegetables, grains, and beans. But which kind of onion is best for each dish. The variety of onions you see at the store can be confusing. Identifying the scallions and leeks is easy, but what about all those white and brown globes? The following list explains their differences.

- **Yellow onions:** A truly all-purpose onion, good raw or cooked. They have a medium to strong flavor that stays intact even when the onion is cooked for hours.

- **Red onions:** Best eaten raw. Cooking turns red onions watery, and they lose their royal color.

- **White onions:** The most pungent onions in the market, with a sharp flavor and a strong bite. They have a shorter shelf life because of higher water content.

- **Green onions:** Most of the onion, including the white base and the green leaves, is edible except for the white roots. The bottom has a rounded base, indicating the beginning of a bulb. Select those with the most white up the stem. Eat raw or prepared like leeks, braised in stock.

- **Scallions:** Similar to green onions but with a flat base. Can be used interchangeably with green onions although scallions are milder.

- **Spanish onions:** Large, spherical onions. Their sweet taste suits all types of cooking.

- **Pearl onions:** Called for in coq au vin (chicken in wine). They're best peeled and simmered whole in casseroles and stews.

- **Shallots:** Crisp, with a refined, delicate flavor, more intense than onions but not as hot. Shallots can be eaten raw and add sophistication to oil-and-vinegar dressings. Roast or grill shallots for an elegant onion topping on chops and steaks.

- **Vidalia, Maui, and Walla Walla:** Varieties of fresh onions that are particularly succulent and not at all hot. They have thin, shiny skins and a high water content and are both juicy and sweet. Enjoy these raw in salads and on burgers.

Gamboling with garlic

For garlic lovers, you can never have too much. I was once at Carnegie Hall with a friend, listening to a concert that we decided we did not like. Plan two, at intermission, was to head for Greenwich Village, to a pizza parlor famous for its liberal use of garlic. We ordered the garlic pizza, with an order of garlic on the side, and had a thoroughly memorable evening.

If you like the taste of garlic, you're in luck because garlic happens to be one of the most medicinal of foods. Garlic gives some protection against heart disease and stroke by slightly lowering blood pressure and thinning the blood by inhibiting clotting.

There's also some scientific evidence that garlic lowers cholesterol. In one combined analysis of 12 well-designed studies from various countries, supplementation of garlic in many forms was associated with a 12 percent reduction in total cholesterol after only 4 weeks of treatment. The study was published in 1994 in the *Journal of the Royal College of Physicians.* In another meta-analysis, garlic was also found to be beneficial but to a lesser extent, reducing cholesterol by only about 6 percent. While the benefits of taking garlic supplements to reduce cholesterol is still being debated, research does suggest that regular consumption of garlic in the diet can lower total cholesterol. Indeed, garlic belongs in a cholesterol-lowering diet as part of an overall strategy. Aim for one or two average-size cloves of garlic a day, not difficult to do if you like Italian food.

Allicin, a sulfur compound in garlic, is responsible for garlic's health benefits. Heat destroys it, so it's best to eat garlic raw or only lightly cooked.

The medicinal properties of garlic develop when the bulb is crushed or chopped and the garlic juices begin to flow. Two substances are released and react with each other to form allicin. When cooking with garlic, first crush the bulbs and let them sit for 10 minutes while this alchemy proceeds. Fresh minced garlic that's sold in jars retains these active compounds, but don't expect benefits from garlic powder or garlic salt.

Stompin' with chile peppers

Chiles get your attention, a fiery addition that can enliven mild ingredients. The heat comes from *capsaicin,* the medicinal compound in chiles. It's concentrated in the seeds, membranes, and soft core of the pepper. To temper the heat of a chile, carefully remove these (see Figure 18-1).

If you chomp down on a fiery chile and can't take the heat, put out the fire with a swig of milk. Milk contains *casein,* a protein particularly effective at washing away capsaicin. When you're handling chiles without gloves, dipping your fingers in milk also helps cool fiery hands.

HOW TO SEED AND JULIENNE A CHILE

Figure 18-1: Coring a chile pepper and removing the seeds and membranes.

1. CUT FROM TOP TO BOTTOM WITH A PARING KNIFE.

2. CUT OFF THE STEMS, REMOVE THE VEINS AND SEEDS THAT RUN DOWN THE SIDES. (LEAVE THE FLESH IN TACT.) WIPE OUT ANY REMAINING SEEDS WITH A DAMP CLOTH.

3. CUT LENGTH-WISE IN STRIPS, ABOUT THE SIZE OF A MATCHSTICK!

Chiles stimulate circulation and thin the blood. Some evidence also shows that capsaicin can lower blood pressure. Chiles also are loaded with vitamins A and C. The hotter the pepper, the more capsaicin it contains. Here's how they rank.

- ✔ **Hottest:** Habanero and serrano
- ✔ **Medium hot:** Cayenne, early jalapeño, and poblano
- ✔ **Mildest:** Anaheim, Nu Mex Joe Parker, and pepperoncini

Better-Than-Store-Bought Sauces

I'm not suggesting that you should never buy a bottle of ketchup or hot dog mustard. But I do hope that you will remember that bottled sauces and condiments are loaded with salt, and often carbs. Ketchup contains high-fructose corn syrup and corn syrup (both sugars), and each tablespoon gives you 190 mg of sodium. Don't load them on your food like there's no tomorrow. In addition, some condiments, such as mayonnaise, usually contain partially hydrogenated oil, a source of trans fatty acids. Some stores sell mayonnaise without the trans fats, but you have to hunt.

Luckily, you can sidestep the search for a healthy condiment or sauce by making your own. Heart-healthy condiments and sauces are very easy to make at home, and you may find that you like them even better than the ones from the store. Try the following condiment and sauce recipes to add a healthy little zing to your meals.

Saucy recipes for piquant condiments

Sample the three condiments that follow. The first is a gourmet version of cranberry sauce with sautéed onions to update a turkey dinner.

The second is a version of salsa that replaces the tomato with fruit. Mango salsa is a winner, so popular that it's now sold fresh-made in upscale super-markets. Out of curiosity, and because I happened to have an apple on hand and not a mango, I cooked up some Apple Salsa, as in the recipe given here. My family liked the results so much that this salsa never made it to the dinner table. We ate it straight out of the bowl!

The third recipe uses many of the standard salsa ingredients, but with the addition of rice wine vinegar, it becomes an Asian relish, creating a relish that complements Asian food.

☉ Cranberry Sauce with Caramelized Onions and Cinnamon

Even though fresh cranberries are naturally very tart, this relish proves that you don't always have to add cupfuls of sugar to make them tolerable, thus saving you empty calories and carbs. The caramelized onions in this dish, and even the salt and pepper, distract the palate. The result is a relish that offers a bright balance of flavors, savory and fruity. Try this cranberry relish on the Turkey Burger in Chapter 12.

Preparation time: _10 minutes_

Cooking time: _20 minutes_

Yield: _About 2 cups_

2 cups fresh or frozen cranberries, rinsed

1 cup apple juice

1 cinnamon stick, or ½ teaspoon ground cinnamon

1 tablespoon unrefined safflower oil or other mild-flavored oil

1 medium yellow onion, cut in half vertically and each half cut crosswise into ¼-inch slices

2 teaspoons honey

Salt and pepper

_1_ Put the cranberries, apple juice, and cinnamon in a saucepan. Bring to a boil over medium-high heat.

_2_ Reduce the heat and simmer gently, cooking until the cranberries soften and begin to pop, about 5 minutes. Remove from heat and set aside.

_3_ Meanwhile, in a large, heavy-bottomed skillet, heat the oil over medium heat. Add the onions and honey. Cook, stirring occasionally, until the onion turns golden brown, about 12 minutes. Season to taste with the salt and pepper.

4 Add the onions to the cranberry mixture and combine. Season to taste with additional salt, pepper, and honey.

Per serving: Calories 13 (From Fat 4); Fat 0g (Saturated 0g); Cholesterol 0mg; Sodium 19mg; Carbohydrate 2g (Dietary Fiber 0g); Protein 0g.

🍎 Apple Salsa

The classic ingredients in this salsa — onions and chiles — stimulate circulation and counteract inflammation. Adding to the flavor and texture, the apple also provides a source of soluble fiber that lowers cholesterol.

Special tool: Food processor

Preparation time: 15 minutes, plus 1 hour refrigeration time

Yield: 2 cups

1 red apple, cored and coarsely chopped	*1 clove garlic, peeled*
½ cup coarsely chopped onion	*1 tablespoon apple cider vinegar*
¼ cup loosely packed cilantro, stems removed	*2 teaspoons chili pepper*

1 Place the apples, onions, cilantro, garlic, vinegar, and chili pepper in a food processor fitted with a metal blade.

2 Process the ingredients, pulsing on and off 2 or 3 times, until the pieces of apple and onion are cut into ¼-inch pieces.

3 Transfer mixture to a bowl. To combine the flavors, refrigerate for 1 hour before serving.

Go-With: Serve with Canned Light Tuna Fish Cakes in Chapter 13 or as a substitute for the Cranberry Sauce with Caramelized Onions and Cinnamon on the Turkey Burger in Chapter 12.

Per serving: Calories 4 (From Fat 0); Fat 0g (Saturated 0g); Cholesterol 0mg; Sodium 2mg; Carbohydrate 1g (Dietary Fiber 0g); Protein 0g.

○ *Asian Cucumber Relish*

This relish tastes just like the delicious relish that the local Thai restaurant serves, only prettier because of the red pepper and red onion. It's a truly mouth-watering way to make sure that you eat heart-healthy onions, red peppers, and ginger. Enjoy this relish with the Grilled Marinated Chicken with Creamy Peanut Sauce in Chapter 12.

Preparation time: *15 minutes, plus 1 or 2 hours refrigeration time*

Yield: *3 cups*

1 cucumber	*½ red onion*
½ sweet red pepper, prepared as in Figure 18-1	*1 tablespoon minced cilantro*
	¼ cup seasoned rice wine vinegar
1 tablespoon gingerroot, prepared as in Figure 9-2 in Chapter 9	*Salt and pepper*

1 Peel the cucumber and cut it in half lengthwise. Cut each length crosswise in very thin slices, using a knife or a mandoline. Place in a medium-size bowl.

2 Prepare the pepper as shown in Figure 18-1 and the gingerroot as shown in Figure 9-2 in Chapter 9. Place in the bowl with the cucumbers.

3 Cut the onion half in half vertically. Cut each quarter horizontally into very thin slices.

4 Place the onion, along with the ginger, cilantro, and rice wine vinegar, in the bowl with the cucumbers and red pepper.

5 Mix all the ingredients well. Season to taste with salt and pepper.

6 Refrigerate, covered, for an hour or two before serving to allow the flavors to mingle.

Per serving: *Calories 3 (From Fat 0); Fat 0g (Saturated 0g); Cholesterol 0mg; Sodium 37mg; Carbohydrate 1g (Dietary Fiber 0g); Protein 0g.*

Savory sauce and spread recipes

The two recipes that follow give you alternatives to mayo and ketchup, in the forms of a tofu-based sandwich spread and a spicy puree of sweet red peppers. They're full of flavor, without loads of added salt or sugar.

☞ Creamy Sandwich Spread

This pleasantly light tofu-yogurt mixture provides an eggless spread with the look and feel of mayonnaise. For best results, use mild-flavored tofu to act as a background for the more assertive flavors of mustard and garlic.

Special tool: *Food processor*

Preparation time: *15 minutes*

Yield: *8 servings (1 cup)*

4 ounces firm tofu, drained and pressed dry

4 tablespoons lowfat, plain yogurt

2 tablespoons white wine vinegar

1 clove garlic, peeled and chopped

1 teaspoon Dijon mustard, preferably whole grain

1 Place all the ingredients in a food processor. Process until very smooth, about 1 minute.

2 Transfer the tofu mixture to a bowl. Season with salt and pepper to taste. Store this spread in an airtight container in the refrigerator.

Per serving: *Calories 15 (From Fat 5); Fat 1g (Saturated 0g); Cholesterol 1mg; Sodium 27mg; Carbohydrate 1g (Dietary Fiber 0g); Protein 2g.*

☙ *Sweet Red Pepper Sauce*

This mouth-watering sauce is welcome just about anywhere you put it, on fish, steaks, and sandwiches and as a garnish in soups. It's even good as a dip. All the ingredients are praiseworthy, from the garlic and onions with all their healing properties, to the sweet red peppers, which are high in the antioxidant beta carotene.

Special tool: *Food processor*

Preparation time: *20 minutes*

Cooking time: *35 minutes*

Yield: *1½ cups*

6 medium, sweet red peppers, with skins and coarsely chopped	*3 green chiles, seeds and veins removed, and minced*
2 cloves garlic, peeled and chopped	*1 cup water*
6 scallions, trimmed and coarsely chopped	*Salt and black pepper*

1 Put the red peppers, garlic, scallions, chiles, and water in a large skillet. Bring to a boil over medium-high heat. Reduce the heat to medium and simmer until the vegetables are tender, about 25 minutes.

2 Season with salt and pepper, if desired. Set aside for 5 minutes to allow the red pepper mixture to cool slightly.

3 Using a food processor, purée the red pepper mixture in batches. Have a bowl nearby so that, as you purée each batch, you can transfer it to this bowl.

4 Strain the red pepper purée through a strainer, using a wooden spoon to rub the purée through the mesh. Discard the bits of pepper skin left behind in the sieve.

5 Return the purée to the skillet and simmer over medium heat, 10 to 15 minutes, stirring occasionally, until the sauce is thick enough to coat the back of a spoon. Season to taste with salt and pepper.

Tip: Use the sauce as a sandwich spread, as a garnish for soups, as a sauce for chops, and as a condiment for the Canned Light Tuna Fish Cakes in Chapter 13.

Per serving: Calories 10 (From Fat 1); Fat 0g (Saturated 0g); Cholesterol 0mg; Sodium 1mg; Carbohydrate 2g (Dietary Fiber 0g); Protein 0g.

Chapter 19

Dishing Up Fruit for Dessert

In This Chapter

▶ Choosing fruits that are good for your heart

▶ Picking fruits for their beautiful colors

▶ Squeezing fruit into a low-carb diet

▶ Discovering healthy fruit dessert recipes

"*A*n apple a day keeps the doctor away" takes on greater meaning when you consider all the ways apples and other fruit control cholesterol. Not only is fruit naturally low in fat, but it's a source of soluble fiber, just like oatmeal. Colorful melons, citrus, and berries also provide a wealth of antioxidants and phytonutrients that do their part in preventing heart disease.

Despite all the nutritional benefits of fruit, however, eating fruit is rarely emphasized in dietary advice about lowering cholesterol. To make matters worse, people on low-carb diets skip fruit because it contains sugars. So this chapter is designed to give fruit its due.

Take a fresh look at fruit and increase your intake the easiest way possible, in the form of fruit desserts. Read on for information and inspiration, and top off your meals with fruit. Try the recipes, and chop, spice, and freeze fruit, or add something creamy. You can't go wrong!

Picking Fruit to Enhance Heart Health

Whole fruit — flesh, skin, core, and all — provides fiber and an array of nutrients that have been associated with the prevention of heart disease in an abundance of research. A study published in the *American Journal of Clinical*

Nutrition compared the health of individuals who ate three or more servings of fruit and vegetables a day with that of those who ate less than one serving, and found that higher intake reduced the risk of dying from heart attack and stroke. Imagine the benefits of eating five or more servings a day, a dietary guideline developed by the U.S. Department of Agriculture for healthy eating for Americans.

Sopping up cholesterol with soluble fiber

Many fruits contain a significant amount of soluble fiber, pectin in particular. Soluble fiber in the intestinal tract acts like a sponge, absorbing cholesterol. Because the body does not digest fiber, it passes on through, taking the cholesterol with it.

Following are examples of fruits that are high in soluble fiber. The following list shows you how many grams of soluble fiber are in 100 grams of the fruits that are the best sources. Considering that 100 grams (one half a cup) of oatmeal, long promoted as an excellent source of soluble fiber, provides 0.7 grams, the amounts in these fruits come in a none-too-shabby second place finish.

- Oranges: 0.6
- Apricots: 0.5
- Banana: 0.5
- Nectarine: 0.4
- Pear: 0.4
- Plum: 0.4
- Strawberries: 0.4
- Tangerine: 0.4
- Granny Smith apple: 0.3
- Blueberries: 0.3

Figures for soluble fiber content in foods vary depending upon what method of analysis is used. This data is based on research conducted at the University of Wisconsin and published in the *Journal of the American Dietetic Association*.

Three cheers, the gang's all here: Choosing a variety of fruit

If you eat a variety of fruit, you have cause for celebration. This is the only way you can be certain that you're consuming all the different vitamins and minerals that various fruit contain. Some are great sources of antioxidants, while others are tops for certain minerals. You need the whole shebang.

Enjoy the different kinds of fruit individually or prepare a luscious bowlful of cut-up mixed fruit. Such a dish always feels like a luxury, with the fruit trimmed and cut and all the work done for you. Such a mixture even has a culinary name, macedoine, named after the republic of Macedonia, a region divided among Greece, Bulgaria, and the republic itself. Macedonia inspired the term *macedoine* because the area contains a mixture of peoples just like a bowl that is filled with mixed fruit.

Take a look at the following list of nutrients, all good for the heart, and the fruit containing them. The first fruit in each list is the richest source of that nutrient with the others arranged in descending order. (Chapter 2 gives you specifics about how these vitamins and minerals help control cholesterol.)

- **Beta carotene:** Cantaloupe, mangoes, apricots, persimmons, plantains, and papayas

- **Vitamin B6:** Mangoes, watermelon, bananas, plantains, and melons

- **Vitamin C:** Papaya, guava, kiwi, lychees, oranges, grapefruit, mangoes, cantaloupe, watermelon, strawberries, and black currants

- **Calcium:** Figs, cherimoyas, papayas, oranges, tangerines, and boysenberries

- **Folate:** Boysenberries, cantaloupe, oranges, loganberries, strawberries, and papayas

- **Magnesium:** Figs and plantains

- **Potassium:** Raisins, papayas, plantains, figs, black currants, cantaloupe, apricots, and bananas

Feel free to explore and try fruits that you've never tried before. You can also explore new ways to enjoy old standbys. Melons, in particular, are very versatile and can be enjoyed and presented in a variety of ways, including with other fruits. Figure 19-1 shows ways that you can cut and serve melons for yourself, your family, or guests.

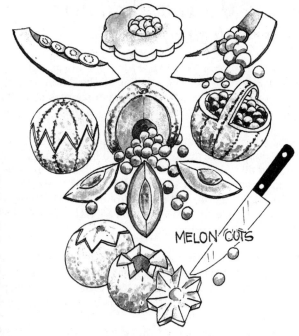

Figure 19-1:
Various
ways to cut
and serve
melons,
either by
themselves
or with
other fruits.

Don't make a habit of eating canned fruit, because vitamins and some phytonutrients are lost in the heating process used in canning. In addition, the fruit may be packed in heavy syrup that contains loads of refined sugar. Fresh fruit is best.

There's also nothing wrong with supplementing your fresh fruit intake with fruit in other forms. Dried fruit retains its minerals, although it's lower in vitamins, and is very handy to snack on when you're out and about. Just remember that eating a handful of raisins, a condensed food, is equivalent to consuming a large bunch of grapes and delivers as many calories.

Frozen fruit is another good option. After harvesting, ripe fruit is flash-frozen within 24-hours and is likely to contain at least as much nutrients as fruit picked before it has ripened and then transported long distances to market. I routinely supplement the limited variety of fresh fruit available in winter months with frozen mango and blueberries.

Also keep some fruit spreads on hand, such as apple butter or apricot conserves. You can find lots of products out there made without added sugar. The Buttermilk Crepes with Brandied Apricot Conserve are filled with a thick spread of flavored apricot.

Fruit phytonutrients that control cholesterol

Fruit is an abundant source of phytonutrients, a huge, recently discovered world of compounds in plant foods that are as important to good health as vitamins and minerals. (Chapter 2 introduces these in detail.) The various phytonutrients perform an array of functions, including controlling cholesterol.

Phytonutrients that do double-duty as pigments

Many phytonutrients are also pigments — the red in cherries, the blue in blueberries, and the orange in oranges — so they're easy to spot at the supermarket. The two main classes are *carotenoids,* which are the yellow-orange-red hues, and *anthocyanins,* which range from crimson and magenta to violet and indigo. You get the picture. Buy fruit in an assortment of colors, and you'll be bringing home a variety of phytonutrients.

In terms of cholesterol, some of these pigments function as antioxidants. They help prevent the oxidation of LDL cholesterol, which can set in motion a chain of events that can lead to heart disease. Others prevent blood clots or reduce chronic inflammation, now considered a factor in heart disease. And although the work is preliminary, in one animal study conducted in Israel and published in the *American Journal of Clinical Nutrition* in 2000, the pigments in ruby-red pomegranates prevented plaque deposits from forming and also reduced the size of existing ones.

Other fruity nutrients

All sorts of other compounds in fruit help control cholesterol in intriguing ways. The following list tells you about some of these:

- Beta-sitosterol competes with cholesterol for absorption into the bloodstream and comes in first place, lowering the level of circulating cholesterol. You get beta-sitosterol in oranges, cherries, bananas, and apples.

- D-glucaric acid is a cholesterol-lowering compound found abundantly in grapefruit and Granny Smith apples. It's in cherries, apricots, and oranges, too.

If you take calcium-channel blocker medication or statin drugs, avoid grapefruit and grapefruit juice. These medications are in part deactivated before they reach your blood stream by a certain enzyme. Prescription dosages compensate for this. However, compounds in grapefruit deactivate this enzyme. A drug overdose could result.

✔ Inulin is a fiberlike carbohydrate in raisins (but not in grapes) that signals the liver to make less cholesterol.

✔ Hesperetin in oranges and other citrus fruits reduces the liver's production of certain compounds that are essential for the formation of the "bad" LDL cholesterol.

Top picks of fruit for dessert

You can hardly go wrong no matter what fruit you decide to slice and serve up at the end of a meal. Raw, baked, or stewed fruit makes a great finish. The tartness of citrus balances the fat in an oily dinner. That's one reason Chinese restaurants serve a plate of sliced oranges along with the check. And the juiciness of melon is a refreshing end to lunch in hot weather.

Fruits are perfect desserts — low in calories and no hassle for you, so be sure to include the following fruits on your shopping lists. That way, you'll always have dessert on hand.

✔ **The usual suspects:** Apples, pears, bananas, cantaloupe, red grapes, oranges, and apricots

✔ **Berries:** Blueberries, strawberries, raspberries, blackberries, and cranberries

✔ **Special treats:** Cherries, mango, papaya, pineapple, and kiwi

Bluish red, purple, and blue fruits (such as cherries, strawberries, Concord grapes, and plums) are best eaten raw because the anthocyanin pigments that give them their color are damaged by heat when they're canned or baked in a pie. Raw fruit by itself is very colorful and versatile and can be served in a variety of ways. Figure 19-2 shows examples of how raw fruit can be arranged as single dessert servings.

Legal fruit for low-carb dieters

Losing weight lowers cholesterol and the risk of heart disease. Following a low-carb diet is one possible way to do this. Such a diet keeps you from eating a lot of sugar and other carbohydrates all at once, which can cause a spike in blood sugar that can add to your girth.

However, if you're following one of the low-carb diets that are currently so popular, you're probably not eating much fruit, which is bad. Fruit is good for the heart in so many ways. This is probably the case especially if you're in the early stages of these programs when intake of carbohydrates such as fruit sugars is severely restricted. But as you move into the next phases of these programs when consuming more carbs is okay, you can include fruit in your diet if you do it the right way. (Please don't stop eating fruit entirely and miss out on all the benefits of fruit for general and heart health!)

First, whole fruit with all its fiber is always a better choice than peeled fruit and fruit juice. And eat fruit with some protein and fat to slow absorption and prevent a spike in blood sugar. For instance, when you make baked apples, stuff the hollowed out core with walnuts. And to control blood sugar, choose fruit with a low glycemic index.

Each fruit has a glycemic index, or a number that tells you how fast a food causes blood sugar to rise. The higher the index number for a fruit, the faster it raises sugar in the bloodstream. The fruit in the following lists are those that researchers have studied so far. Each list begins with the fruit with the highest glycemic index in each category.

When you want a sweet snack, choose fruit over cakes and cookies made with white sugar. The types of sugars in fruit have a gentler effect on blood sugar than the sugars in most baked goods.

SINGLE SERVING FRUIT ARRANGEMENTS FOR DESSERT

Figure 19-2:
Attractive
ways to
serve
raw fruit.

> ✔ **Over 70:** Watermelon
>
> ✔ **60–69:** Pineapple, cantaloupe, raisins, and canned apricots in syrup
>
> ✔ **50–59:** Fresh apricots, mango, canned fruit cocktail, banana, kiwi, and orange juice
>
> ✔ **40–49:** Grapefruit juice, canned peaches, pineapple juice, grapes, canned pears, oranges, peaches, and apple juice
>
> ✔ **30–39:** Plums, apples, pear, dried apricots, grapefruit, and cherries

Fun and Fruity Recipes

Now for the sweet stuff. The following recipes include gourmet desserts such elegant French crepes, homemade sorbet and poached pears as well as a homey concoction for an apple crumble. Fruit is the perfect food to start with when inventing desserts, with its color, flavor and natural sweetness. What an easy way to add a serving of fruit to your daily intake.

🍑 Buttermilk Crepes with Brandied Apricot Conserve

This elegant dessert gives you just enough fat and protein to balance the carbs. Fill the crepes with the fruit of your choice or with conserves, which is a fruit spread (not to be confused with a fruit preserve or jam, which is fruit plus sugar).

Preparation time: 15 minutes

Cooking time: 30 minutes

Yield: 8 crepes, or 4 servings

¼ cup plus 2 tablespoons all-fruit apricot spread

1 tablespoon brandy, or ¼ teaspoon brandy extract

½ cup spelt flour (see Chapter 20)

⅓ cup whole-wheat flour

Pinch of salt

1 egg white

⅔ cup buttermilk

¾ cup water

Safflower oil for cooking the crepes

Nonfat sour cream (about ¼ cup), for garnish

Toasted almonds (about 3 tablespoons), for garnish

1 Turn the oven temperature dial to warm. In a small bowl, mix the apricot preserves and brandy. Set aside.

2 Sift the spelt flour, whole-wheat flour, and salt into a medium-size bowl. Make a well in the center of the flour and add the egg white. Slowly add the buttermilk and water, while beating hard with a whisk to incorporate all the liquid and create a smooth, frothy batter.

3 Wipe a nonstick crepe pan or skillet with shallow sides with an oiled paper towel and heat until very hot. It's reached a high temperature when a drop of water you flick into the pan skitters across the surface before evaporating. Pour in about ⅛ cup batter, enough to cover the bottom of the pan, swirling the batter around to distribute it evenly. Cook the crepe on medium about 1 minute, until it is set and golden.

4 Turn the crepe over to cook the other side for an additional 15 to 20 seconds. The crepe is finished when the edges are just beginning to brown and it is not at all crisp. Transfer to a platter and place in an oven set on warm. Proceed to make all the crepes. Keep the crepes thin and delicate by adding a few teaspoons of water if the batter thickens.

5 To serve, lay a crepe on a work surface and spread 1½ teaspoons of the apricot mixture in a stripe across the middle. Roll the crepe into a log and place on an individual desert plate. Garnish the crepe with nonfat sour cream and scatter the almonds over the sour cream and crepes. Serve immediately.

Per serving: Calories 234 (From Fat 61); Fat 7g (Saturated 1g); Cholesterol 2mg; Sodium 112mg; Carbohydrate 37g (Dietary Fiber 4g); Protein 7g.

☞ Mango Sorbet with Minted Strawberry Sauce

Make this dessert and you'll earn high marks for content — zero fat — and presentation — pretty as a picture, thanks to all the colorful and heart-healthy phytonutrients that make up the palette of this elegant summertime dessert. It's convenient to serve when you're entertaining and want time with your guests, because you can partially assemble this plated dessert in advance. Arranged the individual fruit plates, keeping them in the refrigerator and have the scoops of mango puree, ready to add to the fruit plates, stored in the freezer.

Special tool: *Food processor*

Preparation time: *15 minutes*

Yield: *4 servings*

1 heaping cup frozen mango chunks, prepared from fresh at home or commercial frozen chunks	*1 tablespoon pure maple syrup*
	3 tablespoons water or sparkling white wine, or as needed
15 medium-size strawberries	*¼ honeydew melon, cut into 4 slices, rind removed*
2 large sprigs of mint (about 1 heaping tablespoon)	

1 Have on hand a small bowl and a plate that have been chilled in the freezer. Put the mango in the bowl of a food processor and chop the fruit, pulsing until the mango is puréed. Immediately transfer the fruit to the chilled bowl and chill in the freezer section of your refrigerator for 10 to 20 minutes, so that a scoop of puree holds its shape.

2 Using a small ice cream scoop, 2 inches in diameter, scoop out some mango and somewhat flatten the top of the sorbet in the spoon. Squeeze the handle of the ice cream scoop to release the sorbet onto the chilled plate, flat side down. Repeat to make 3 more scoops. Reserve the mango sorbet in the freezer.

3 Meanwhile, put 7 strawberries, the mint, and maple syrup into the processor and blend. Add the water or wine to thin the strawberry purée to the consistency of a sauce, to make about 1 cup of sauce.

4 Assemble the fruit by placing an arc of melon on each of 4 individual dessert plates. In the curve of the melon, put one of the reserved scoops of mango. Next to the mango, place 2 strawberries.

5 With a large soup spoon, drizzle ¼ cup of the strawberry sauce over the fruit and mango sorbet, making 3 stripes that cross the melon at right angles. Garnish with a sprig of mint. Serve immediately.

Per serving: Calories 84 (From Fat 2); Fat 0g (Saturated 0g); Cholesterol 0mg; Sodium 8mg; Carbohydrate 22g (Dietary Fiber 3g); Protein 1g.

⏣ Poached Pears with Cardamom-Flavored Frozen Yogurt

I invented this recipe when I decided I wanted to make fancy flavors of ice cream and it dawned on me to start off with plain vanilla ice cream and mix in my own ingredients. I used that basic idea to then create this recipe. I used Bosc pears, which, like Anjou, are good for poaching but are more perfumed than other varieties.

Special tool: *Food processor*

Preparation time: *30 minutes, plus several hours or overnight refrigeration*

Cooking time: *20 minutes*

Yield: *4 servings*

¼ cup loosely packed candied ginger, chopped

1 pint lowfat frozen vanilla yogurt, slightly softened

½ teaspoon ground cardamom

1½ cups water

1½ cups white wine

4 Bosc pears, ripe but not mushy, peeled, cored, and sliced (see the tip at the end of this recipe)

1 lemon, sliced

2 tablespoons chopped pistachios, for garnish

1 Put the chopped candied ginger into the bowl of a food processor fitted with a metal blade and process until the ginger is in very small pieces. Spoon the frozen yogurt into the processor and add the cardamom. Briefly pulse, taking care that the frozen yogurt stays as chilled as possible. Immediately return the frozen yogurt mixture to its container and place in the freezer.

2 In a medium saucepan, bring the water and wine to a boil. Lower the heat to medium-low and add the pears and lemon. Cover the pan and simmer until the pears are very tender, at least 20 minutes. Remove the cooked lemon slices.

3 Transfer the cooked pears to a bowl, leaving the pear juice to cook over medium-high heat until reduced by half. Strain the juice over the pears and refrigerate several hours or overnight.

4 Place a scoop of the frozen yogurt in each of four shallow dessert bowls and top with slices of poached pear. Sprinkle with the pistachios. Serve immediately.

Tip: To core a pear without ruining the shape of the slices, first peel the pear with a vegetable peeler. Then cut the pear in half lengthwise. Next, using a melon baller, dig out the core in each half. Now slice the pear if you wish.

Per serving: *Calories 212 (From Fat 28); Fat 3g (Saturated 1g); Cholesterol 5mg; Sodium 66mg; Carbohydrate 42g (Dietary Fiber 3g); Protein 6g.*

⟋ *Apple-Sour Cream Crumble*

A crumble is pie the easy way, with a fruit mixture on the bottom and a flour mixture on top, but no pie crust to make. For this version, I decided on apples, oats, and walnuts, all foods that help control cholesterol. The soluble fiber in apples reduces the amount of "bad" LDL cholesterol produced in the liver, and apples' insoluble fiber latches on to LDL in the digestive tract and removes it from the body. And in a study appearing in 2003 in the *European Journal of Clinical Nutrition,* researchers combining the results of seven studies involving over 100,000 men and women, singled out apples as one of a small number of fruit that contributed to low rates of heart disease. So make this crumble and dig in!

Preparation time: *20 minutes*

Cooking time: *35 minutes*

Yield: *8 servings*

1½ cups raw rolled oats	*2 pounds Golden Delicious or Cortland apples, peeled, cored, and sliced*
½ cup plus 2 tablespoons whole-wheat flour	*Rind and juice of ½ lemon*
½ cup chopped walnuts	*½ teaspoon allspice*
½ teaspoon cinnamon	*¼ teaspoon nutmeg*
Pinch of salt	*1 egg*
¼ cup unrefined safflower oil	*½ cup nonfat sour cream*
½ cup pure maple syrup	

1 Preheat the oven to 350 degrees. In a large bowl, mix together the rolled oats, ½ cup of the flour, the walnuts, cinnamon, and salt. Add the safflower oil and ¼ cup of the maple syrup. Stir to combine thoroughly. Set the crumble aside.

2 Place the apples, the remaining ¼ cup maple syrup, the lemon rind, and lemon juice in a large bowl. Toss gently with a wooden spoon to coat the apples.

3 Put the remaining 2 tablespoons flour, the allspice, and nutmeg in a small sieve and shake the sieve over the apple mixture, occasionally stirring the apples to make sure the dry ingredients are evenly distributed.

4 In a small bowl, whisk together the egg and sour cream. Pour over the apple mixture and toss to combine.

5 Fill the bottom of an 8-x-8-inch baking pan with the apple mixture. Distribute spoonfuls of the oatmeal crumble evenly over the apples. Bake in the center of the oven until the crumble is golden, about 35 minutes.

Per serving: *Calories 327 (From Fat 124); Fat 14g (Saturated 1g); Cholesterol 27mg; Sodium 49mg; Carbohydrate 48g (Dietary Fiber 5g); Protein 6g.*

◌ *Blueberry-Lemon Mousse*

This fruit and yogurt mixture, which becomes a mousse, is a good candidate for using berries because the fruit doesn't have to be cooked, and the antioxidants in berries are damaged by heat. The blueberries in this dish contain a phytonutrient, pterostilbene, which may lower the "bad" LDL cholesterol, according to preliminary research (using lab animals) conducted in 2004 by the U.S. Department of Agriculture at the University of Mississippi School of Pharmacy. The recipe also gives you a simple technique for making yogurt cheese, which involves draining it of the watery liquid, the whey, leaving the solid parts or curds. (Of course, you don't want to do this if you're Little Miss Muffet, sitting on a tuffet, and you want to eat both the curds and whey.)

Special tools: *Cheesecloth, food processor*

Preparation time: *45 minutes, plus 6 hours or longer for the yogurt to drain and 1 hour to refrigerate the finished dessert*

Cooking time: *2 minutes*

Yield: *4 servings*

1 cup nonfat plain yogurt	*1 cup water*	*1 cup fresh blueberries, rinsed and patted dry*
1 cup nonfat lemon yogurt	*1 envelope unflavored gelatin*	*Blueberries, for garnish*

1 Line a strainer with several layers of cheesecloth and set the strainer over a large bowl. To drain the yogurt, turning it into "cheese," spoon the plain yogurt and lemon yogurt into the strainer. Cover with a spare pot lid to press down on the yogurt, to remove more liquid. Place in the refrigerator to drain for at least 6 hours, preferably longer.

2 When the yogurt has drained, put the water in a small saucepan and sprinkle the gelatin over the top. Set aside for 5 minutes while the gelatin softens. Bring to a boil over medium-high heat, stirring to dissolve the gelatin, 2 minutes. Remove the pot from the heat and pour the gelatin into a bowl. Place the bowl in the refrigerator for 10 minutes to cool the gelatin sufficiently that you can comfortably touch the gelatin.

3 Purée the blueberries in the bowl of a food processor fitted with a metal blade. Add the cooled gelatin mixture and process to blend.

4 Put the drained yogurt cheese in a large bowl. Slowly add the blueberry mixture, using a whisk to thoroughly combine. Pour into individual dessert dishes or long-stemmed glassware. Refrigerate until firm, about 1 hour. Served topped with fresh whole blueberries.

Tip: *Use nonfat yogurt cheese to add that needed touch of creaminess, but not the calories, to all sorts of fruit desserts, including baked apples and fruit tarts. Yogurt cheese is also a satisfying substitute for cream cheese smeared on a bagel.*

Per serving: *Calories 122 (From Fat 2); Fat 0g (Saturated 0g); Cholesterol 1mg; Sodium 128mg; Carbohydrate 22g (Dietary Fiber 1g); Protein 7g.*

Chapter 20

Baked Goods that Keep the Heart Ticking

*B*elieve it or not, you can enjoy cakes and cookies even though you're watching your cholesterol. The pleasure of that first bite into the tawny, rich flavors of warm gingerbread, fresh from the oven, is quite permissible! An afternoon snack of a cup of tea and a slice of Banana-Date Tea Loaf is yours! Baked goods such as these can be included in a cholesterol-controlling diet. It's all a matter of substituting ingredients.

In this chapter's recipes, whole-grain flour replaces refined. Sweeteners with redeeming qualities stand in for white sugar. The addition of nuts brings a good dose of minerals and healthy fats and, at the same time, replaces butter with its saturated fat. Admittedly, the flavor of whole-grain, unrefined flour is typically quite robust and distinctive, normally out of place in the usual baked goods because we've become accustomed to the blandness of white flour and white sugar. With this in mind, I chose recipes that take advantage of the complex flavors of natural ingredients that give a richness to the final product. When you try the recipes, you'll be pleased with how good these ingredients taste.

The added advantage of making such noble sweet things is that, because they're so nutritious, it's fine if you have them for breakfast!

Heartfelt Reasons to Bake

Homemade baked goods protect the heart as much for what they don't contain as for what healthy ingredients they do contain. By comparison, manufacturers have designed their store-bought baked products with ingredients that have a long shelf life and are well priced, good for the bottom line. However, these ingredients aren't necessarily good for the heart.

Turning out baked goods made with quality oils

One of the great health advantages of doing your own baking is that you have control over the quality of oil that goes into the baked goods. The recipes in this chapter use unrefined safflower oil, which adds richness, small amounts of various nutrients, and healthy polyunsaturated fats. (For more on this subject, see the section "Including healthy fats" in this chapter.) In contrast, so many commercial breads, cakes, cookies, and crackers are made with partially hydrogenated vegetable oils, usually soybean and corn oils. Unfortunately, in the process of hydrogenation, trans fatty acids form. Trans fats act like saturated fat in the body, increasing total cholesterol and the "bad" LDL cholesterol, too. Some products also contain refined cottonseed oil, made from a plant not even in the human diet, which is added to keep baked goods moist and seemingly fresh for days as they sit on the shelf waiting for you to buy them.

Avoiding white flour and sugar

Commercially produced baked goods are virtually synonymous with white flour and sugar. White flour, like in a piece of white bread, is low on many vitamins and minerals that keep the heart humming. Refined white sugar has no vitamins or minerals at all. Such foods are a waste of calories if you're eating to enhance your health. If you check the label on many products, you're likely to see that the first ingredient (the most abundant substance in the product) is white sugar.

Typical commercial baked goods, particularly lowfat versions, consist mostly of carbohydrates, thanks to the flour and sweeteners. Eating such foods, which have a high glycemic index, is associated with low levels of the "good" HDL cholesterol, the finding of a 1999 study that appeared in *The Lancet* and was conducted by King's College and Imperial College, London. Researchers examined the eating habits of over 1,400 men and women, using data from the 1986-87 Survey of British Adults. They found that levels of HDL were inversely associated with the glycemic index of carbohydrates consumed: lower glycemic index, higher HDL. Perhaps even more interesting, intake of total fat, type of fat, cholesterol, fiber, and alcohol showed no significant relationship to HDL levels. Low levels of HDL increase the risk of coronary artery disease. (For more about the effect of high glycemic foods on heart health, see Chapter 1.)

So here's another good reason to do some of your own baking: You get to choose the flour! Of course you'll use whole-grain flours, which, because of their fiber, you absorb more slowly than white flour. Hence, whole-grain flours have a lower glycemic index than their refined versions. They also retain all of their original nutrients just like the whole grains that you can cook with in Chapter 17. And you won't miss the blandness of white flour as you discover the authentic flavor of whole-grain flour.

Upgrading Your Ingredients

Baking without refined wheat and sugar is not a hardship when you consider all the alternative kinds of flour and sweeteners available. And face it, the refining of flour and sugar began only about 150 years ago. Before then, baking with whole grains and natural sugars was the norm.

The following sections tell you about some of the most useful and popular healthy baking ingredients, such as flour made from whole grain, natural sweeteners, and unrefined cooking oils. I include several of these nutritious staples in the recipes in this chapter so you'll bring them into your kitchen. Having these healthful products on hand means that perhaps you're more likely to use them in your cooking!

Baking with whole-grain flours

You can always find whole-wheat flour in the standard grocery store. But to shop for the full array of whole grains converted into flour these days, you need to visit one of those gorgeous new natural food supermarkets where these products are given lots of shelf space. The same stores also sell many of the items in bulk. Smaller health food stores carry these ingredients too. Have fun buying an assortment and be sure to use several at a time, like I did in the recipe for Homemade Crackers Flavored with Garlic and Herbs, which calls for oat flour, rye flour, and cornmeal. Experiment with the recipes that follow, inventing your own combinations.

Sample some of these flours:

- ✔ **Spelt flour:** This whole grain has a mellow flavor and can be substituted for wheat flour. This ancient grain has a slightly higher protein content than wheat. If you're sensitive to wheat, try baking with spelt, which can be tolerated by many individuals with wheat allergies.

- ✔ **Oat flour:** Made from hulled oats that have been ground into powder, this flour still contains most of the original nutrients. Combine it with other flours that contain gluten for baked goods that need to rise, as oats contain no gluten. Oat bran can also be added to baked goods, as I did in the Chewy Oatmeal Cookies with Currants recipe in this chapter, to add cholesterol-lowering, soluble fiber.

- ✔ **Rye flour:** In Scandinavia, rye flour is used in all sorts of baked goods, while most Americans only have some when they order a ham on rye at the local deli. This tasty flour is heavier and darker than most other flours and contains less gluten than wheat. For depth of flavor, I include some rye flour in the cracker recipe in this chapter and mix it with some cornmeal, inspired by my favorite deli rye bread that has a corn crust.

Flour spoils, like any other food, but the changes may not be obvious. Check for an off odor or flavor, a sign that the fat in the flour has become rancid. And use Table 20-1 for storage times for different types, to make sure you're baking with flour that's still fresh.

Table 20-1	Storage Times for Flour	
Types of Flour	*Months at Room Temperature*	*Months in Fridge or Freezer*
White flour and other refined flours	6 to 12	12
Whole wheat flour	1	12
Other whole-grain flour	1	2 to 3
Wheat germ	0	2 to 3

Wheat germ comes in vacuum-packed jars. These are fine to store at room temperature, but after you open the jar, the wheat germ must be refrigerated.

As soon as you bring flour home, take it out of the bag and store it in an airtight canister, or store the bag or box inside an airtight plastic bag. Keep flour cool, dry, and in the dark.

Sweetening with natural sugars

Cakes and cookies are by definition sweet, so the goal is not to eliminate all sugars completely. But you can improve the nutritional value of these goodies by making them with smaller amounts of sweetener and using those that also provide some vitamins, minerals, or fiber. You can use maple syrup, honey, and blackstrap molasses, as well as fruits such as apples and bananas to replace the white sugar, adding nutrients and distinctive flavor. For some other examples of substitutions you can try, see the section "Doing the switcheroo: Substituting for healthy ingredients," later in this chapter.

Sugar cane in its natural state contains several minerals — calcium, iron, and phosphorous — as well as B vitamins, which the body needs to metabolize sugar. When the cane is refined, the juice is squeezed from the plants and boiled, producing a syrupy mixture from which sugar crystals are extracted. The brownish-black liquid that remains is molasses. The first boiling of the sugar syrup produces light molasses, the second dark molasses, and the third boiling blackstrap molasses. Blackstrap molasses is slightly richer in nutrients.

Brown sugar isn't a health food just because it's brown. Brown sugar is just white sugar combined with molasses.

Treat yourself to unsulphured molasses, sold in natural foods stores. Other names for this are Barbados or West Indies molasses. It's a better choice for baked goods because the flavor is mellower than standard supermarket molasses, and it won't overwhelm the flavor of other ingredients. Try the recipe for Gingerbread-Applesauce Muffins in this chapter to see what I mean.

Grocery stores sometimes sell the sugar cane itself. Boil raw sugar cane and strip the light brown skin away from the white flesh. Then cut this into strips or chunks. Use this natural, unrefined sugar as a garnish on desserts.

Including healthy fats

Some recipes, such as butter cookies, just aren't themselves without you know what. But many baked goods are just as tasty and light made without the butter, using oils instead that are lower in saturated fat and don't contain cholesterol.

In this chapter, the cake and cracker recipes call for unrefined safflower oil, a minimally processed, quality oil. The results are rich and moist. Extra virgin olive oil is another nutritious oil but you probably won't want its olive flavor in most baked goods.

Oil produces a softer, more tender cookie than butter.

Saving your eggs for baked goods

Even if you're watching your cholesterol, you still need eggs in your diet, as I explain in Chapter 1. For many people, a heart-healthy eating plan can include four eggs a week — but it's up to you when you eat them! If you like, save an egg or two for baked goods such as those in the recipes in this chapter. They're loaded with nutrient and fiber-rich ingredients but require egg to hold all this together. Remember, when it comes to baked goods, you're eating only part of the recipe and a small fraction of the egg the recipe asks for.

Another option is to bake with one of the butter alternatives you find in the dairy section of markets. (See Chapter 5 for a full description of these products.) All of these are made with vegetable oils to create products with no cholesterol and less fat than butter. But not all are good for baking. You need a product in "stick" form rather than the spreadable kind, which contains ingredients that can make 'your baking too soggy, or worse. You also want to avoid products made with partially hydrogenated oils, which contain trans fatty acids. These fats behave like saturated fat and can raise cholesterol.

Read the labels of products that call themselves "natural oil blend," "buttery spread," and "vegetable oil spread." The fine print will tell you if the product is not for baking. A good product to use in baking is Smart Balance Buttery Sticks. These are made with a mixture of saturated, polyunsaturated, and monounsaturated fats, which researchers at Brandeis University found helped improve the important cholesterol ratio. Use it as the butter substitute in the recipe for Chewy Oatmeal Cookies with Currants.

Including nuts and seeds

Throughout this book, I talk about the health benefits of eating nuts every chance I get, and here I go again! Adding some nuts to baked goods is an easy way to increase the amount you eat.

✔ Whole and chopped nuts give a needed crunch to cakes and cookies.

✔ Use almond meal, which is simply ground almonds, to augment or substitute for a portion of the flour. The delicate flavor of almonds is welcome in all sorts of cakes. Their heart-healthy monounsaturated oils replace the saturated fat of butter. Almond meal is a must staple for baking. It's one of the ingredients in the Banana-Date Tea Loaf in this chapter.

Look for almond meal, sold packaged, in the section of natural food stores and health food stores where whole-grain flour is displayed. The brand I use for the almond meal, and for that matter, all the flour, is Bob's Red Mill. Its Web site is `www.bobsredmill.com`.

Almonds contain beta-sitosterol, a phytonutrient that has a structure similar to cholesterol. Because of this, beta-sitosterol competes with cholesterol for absorption into the body and comes in first place! Consequently, less cholesterol enters the system, lowering cholesterol levels in the bloodstream.

✔ Garnish baked goods with nuts you have roasted in the oven set at 450 degrees. Toss 2 cups of nuts with 1 tablespoon of oil and roast them on a baking sheet, shaking this occasionally. Roast the nuts for 10 minutes, until lightly browned. Alternatively, toast them in a dry skillet on medium-high heat, stirring frequently, for about 3 to 5 minutes, until they begin to brown.

Nuts and seeds are little packets of fuel. Be sure to include these nutritious foods here and there to round out your diet. They make special additions to all sorts of dishes. Sprinkle chopped pistachios on basmati rice pilaf and toasted slivered almonds over mixed fruit. Scatter sesame seeds on a Chinese vegetable stir-fry and add poppy seeds to baked goods, as I do in the recipe for Homemade Crackers Flavored with Garlic and Herbs.

Peanuts can cause an acute and dangerous allergic reaction in people who are sensitive to proteins these nuts contain. If you're allergic to peanuts and you want to try a recipe that calls for them, substitute cashews or pecans for the peanuts. Cashews and pecans provide similar richness and mellow flavor.

Converting recipes to switch to healthier ingredients

Cooks over the years have worked out many types of substitutions, such as how much honey you need to replace a cup of sugar, and so forth. This is handy information to have when you want to convert an old recipe to fit into your current way of healthy eating, or when you discover a new recipe that sounds yummy but forbidden. The trick is improving the nutrition without ruining the flavor and texture. Who hasn't sampled one of those whole-wheat, no anything, super sweet cookies you could use as a doorstop?

To create the recipes in this chapter, I started with white flour and white sugar versions, substituting flours, sweeteners, and fats. I chose types of baked goods — loaf cakes, cookies, and crackers — that take well to changes

Going crackers over crackers

When you prepare your own homemade crackers, you control the amount of added salt and the quality of the flour and oil. The basic formula for making crackers — just flour, a source of fat, and some liquid — is very forgiving, so you can experiment with all sorts of ingredients. In developing the Homemade Crackers Flavored with Garlic and Herbs recipe in this chapter, I tried various flours, all whole-grain, and produced some very sober numbers. One hard-to-forget version was made exclusively with oat flour, and I'm sure a horse would have loved it.

But do experiment, adding fresh and dried herbs, spices, minced garlic, a sprinkling of Parmesan cheese, or just freshly ground black pepper. Tailor your cracker invention to what you'll be serving it with — such as a garlic cracker with minestrone soup, or an herb cracker with salad.

If you have a child who wants to learn to bake, start with cracker making, a quick and easy process just one step beyond playing with dough.

in ingredients, and selected the variations I thought were the tastiest (I admit, I don't like things too sweet). But please make your own substitutions of my substitutions if you wish! Start with the following formulas, fiddling a bit with the amounts, depending upon how the dough handles and the final baked good tastes.

- ✔ **1 cup white flour:** Substitute 1 cup minus 2 tablespoons whole-wheat flour. Then, per cup of flour replaced, reduce the oil by 1 tablespoon and increase the liquid (such as buttermilk or apple juice) by 1 to 2 teaspoons.

- ✔ **1 cup sugar:** Substitute ¾ cup honey or ¾ cup maple syrup. Then, per cup of sugar replaced, decrease the liquid ingredients in the recipe by ¼ cup, or add ¼ cup flour.

- ✔ **1 cup butter, lard, or other solid shortening:** Substitute 1 cup vegetable or nut oil minus 2 tablespoons.

- ✔ **1 cup liquid butter:** Use 1 cup vegetable oil.

Guilt-Free Recipes for Baking

Are you feeling inspired to bake? Even if you haven't turned out a batch of homemade cookies for years or have never been near a stove, give it a try, starting with the easy recipes that follow.

✸ Homemade Crackers Flavored with Garlic and Herbs

If you've never baked, this is the recipe to start with! Making crackers is as much fun as baking cookies and definitely worth the time. You prepare a dough mixture, moisten it, and roll it out. The process is quick and easy, and you have crackers made with the healthiest of ingredients. Serve them to guests, who are sure to be impressed by your attention to detail.

Special tool: *Parchment paper*

Preparation time: *15 minutes*

Cooking time: *15 minutes*

Yield: *About 18 crackers*

½ cup oat flour

½ cup rye flour

¼ cup cornmeal

1 clove garlic, crushed and minced

1 teaspoon dried mixed Italian herbs

¼ teaspoon baking soda

¼ teaspoon salt

¼ cup warm water

3 tablespoons unrefined safflower oil, plus oil to brush the cracker dough

1 tablespoon cider vinegar

½ teaspoon poppy seeds

1 Preheat the oven to 400 degrees. Put the oat flour, rye flour, cornmeal, garlic, Italian herbs, baking soda, and salt in a large bowl. Mix together with a fork.

2 To the flour mixture, add the water, oil, and vinegar and mix thoroughly.

3 Place the dough on a work surface. Knead until the dough is stiff, 1 to 2 minutes.

4 Cut a length of parchment paper about 18 inches in length. Place the paper on a work surface and transfer the dough to the paper. With a floured rolling pin, roll the dough into a flat sheet about ⅛ inch thick and 12 inches in diameter. Toward the end of the process, sprinkle with the poppy seeds and press these into the dough as you continue to roll out the crackers.

5 Score the dough, marking out square or rectangular crackers. Brush with oil.

6 Place the parchment with the dough on a cookie sheet and bake for about 15 minutes, until the crackers begin to crisp and turn golden. Transfer the crackers to a cake rack to cool. Break the cracker dough into pieces and serve immediately, or when cooled, store in an airtight container. The crackers will stay fresh 2 to 3 days.

Per serving: Calories 26 (From Fat 11); Fat 1g (Saturated 0g); Cholesterol 0mg; Sodium 0mg; Carbohydrate 3g (Dietary Fiber 1g); Protein 1g.

◌ *Gingerbread-Applesauce Muffins*

The virtues of these satisfying muffins are many. They provide soluble fiber, an array of heart-healthy vitamins and minerals, and healing spices. They dress up nicely, too! Top them with a dollop of lowfat sour cream or yogurt and more candied ginger. Serve with baked apples or poached pears. (You can find a recipe for poached pears in Chapter 19.) If you plan to serve the muffins with poached pears, substitute pear nectar for the applesauce in the recipe. Or just drizzle the little darlings with some rum or bourbon and add lowfat frozen yogurt. Right now, as I write, I'm eating one of these muffins, spread with marmalade, for breakfast. Yummm.

Preparation time: *20 minutes*

Cooking time: *20 minutes*

Yield: *12 muffins*

2 cups whole-wheat flour

1½ teaspoons baking soda

1 teaspoon ground ginger

1 teaspoon cinnamon

½ teaspoon allspice

¼ teaspoon ground cardamom or nutmeg

¼ teaspoon salt

½ cup raisins

¼ cup chopped candied ginger

¼ cup unsulphured Barbados molasses

½ cup unsweetened applesauce

½ cup 2 percent cultured, reduced-fat buttermilk

6 tablespoons unrefined safflower oil

1 Preheat the oven to 350 degrees. Using a muffin pan for 12 muffins, place a paper cupcake liner in each muffin cup.

2 In a medium-size bowl, put the whole-wheat flour, baking soda, ground ginger, cinnamon, allspice, cardamom, and salt. Whisk together to blend. Briefly mix the raisins and candied ginger with the flour mixture.

3 Put the molasses, applesauce, buttermilk, and safflower oil in a bowl and whisk to combine.

4 Slowly pour the molasses mixture into the flour mixture, combining with a spoon. Make sure that all the flour has been incorporated, but don't overmix.

5 Spoon the batter into the muffin cups, distributing it evenly among the cups. The muffins are done when the top surface is springy to the touch, or when a toothpick inserted into the center comes out clean, about 20 minutes.

Vary It! *You can also bake the gingerbread in an 8-inch square pan. The baking time is 30 to 35 minutes.*

Per serving: *Calories 188 (From Fat 66); Fat 7g (Saturated 1g); Cholesterol 0mg; Sodium 222mg; Carbohydrate 30g (Dietary Fiber 3g); Protein 3g.*

☙ Banana-Date Tea Loaf

This moist, rich cake is full of nutritious ingredients, a substantial food that tastes like a treat. The ample sweetness comes from the ripe bananas, which are a source of potassium, and from the smooth-textured dates, a source of fiber and vitamin B6. And instead of using butter to supply fat, the recipe calls for almond meal and safflower oil, sources of healthy oils that won't clog arteries. This recipe also gives you a chance to bake with spelt flour, which you can buy in natural foods stores.

Special tool: *Food processor*

Preparation time: *20 minutes*

Cooking time: *45 minutes*

Yield: *12 slices*

3 very ripe bananas

¼ cup lemon juice (juice of 1 lemon)

¼ cup unrefined safflower oil, plus extra for oiling the loaf pan

1½ cups spelt flour

½ cup almond meal

½ teaspoon baking soda

½ teaspoon baking powder

¼ teaspoon nutmeg

½ teaspoon salt

½ cup dates (about 4), pitted and chopped

1 Preheat the oven to 350 degrees. In a food processor fitted with a metal blade, pulse the bananas, 15 seconds, until they're smooth. Add the lemon juice and safflower oil and process briefly to combine.

2 In a medium-size bowl, put the spelt flour, almond meal, baking soda, baking powder, nutmeg, and salt. Whisk together.

3 To the flour mixture, add the banana mixture and the dates. Using a spoon, mix until ingredients are thoroughly combined.

4 Grease a 9-x-4-inch loaf pan with safflower oil. Turn the dough into the pan and bake for 45 minutes. The cake is done when a knife inserted into the loaf comes out clean. Serve with afternoon tea or with sliced oranges for dessert after dinner, or start your day with a piece of it rather than cereal.

Per serving: Calories 165 (From Fat 45); Fat 5g (Saturated 1g); Cholesterol 0mg; Sodium 167mg; Carbohydrate 25g (Dietary Fiber 4g); Protein 4g.

☙ *Chewy Oatmeal Cookies with Currants*

If you're curious about substituting ingredients, play with this recipe. I tucked in all sorts of ingredients to lower cholesterol and protect the heart. The fat is a butter substitute (not margarine) made from vegetable oil, with no trans fats or cholesterol. But give unrefined safflower oil a try, too. You may decide to use raisins rather than currants, which I chose because they contain flavonoids that strengthen capillary walls. You can also make the cookies even chewier by using thick-cut, rolled oats rather than regular oats. Have fun.

Special tool: *Parchment paper*

Preparation time: *15 minutes*

Cooking time: *15 minutes*

Yield: *30 cookies*

½ cup Smart Balance Butter Sticks butter substitute or unrefined safflower oil	*1½ teaspoons vanilla*	*½ cup oat bran*
	½ teaspoon cinnamon	*1 teaspoon baking powder*
½ cup maple syrup	*½ teaspoon salt*	*¾ cup currants*
1 egg, slightly beaten	*1½ cups rolled oats*	*½ cup chopped walnuts*
	1 cup whole-wheat flour	

1 Preheat the oven to 375 degrees. In a medium bowl, use an electric mixer to cream together the butter substitute and maple syrup. Add the egg, vanilla, cinnamon, and salt and mix until well blended. (If using oil, add the oil and the other ingredients to the bowl at the same time and mix.)

2 Put the rolled oats, whole-wheat flour, oat bran, and baking powder in a bowl and stir together with a fork. Mix in the currants and walnuts.

3 Slowly add the maple syrup mixture to the oat mixture, combining until all the dry ingredients are moistened. If necessary, add a tablespoon or two of water to hold the dough together.

4 Cover 2 cookie sheets with parchment paper. On the paper, place the dough by tablespoons. Flatten the dough slightly. Bake for 15 minutes, until the cookies are lightly browned. Cool for 2 minutes on the baking sheet before using a spatula to transfer the cookies to a wire rack to finish cooling. Store in an airtight container to preserve freshness.

Per serving: Calories 108 (From Fat 6); Fat 6g (Saturated 1g); Cholesterol 7mg; Sodium 42mg; Carbohydrate 13g (Dietary Fiber 2g); Protein 2g.

Part VII
The Part of Tens

The 5th Wave   By Rich Tennant

"Jane finally teach Boy how to cook.
Before that, him just eat cheetah.
Too much fast food not good."

In this part . . .

In this part, I explain why certain beverages protect the heart from disease and wave you off high-sugar drinks that can trigger body chemistry that may raise cholesterol.

The other chapter in this part offers advice on buying healthy ingredients that don't have to be expensive if you know how and where to shop. I want to help you make sure that your kitchen is filled with quality foods forevermore!

Chapter 21

Ten Beverages That Say, "Here's to Your Health!"

*Y*ou've been told about the importance of drinking water over and over, and now I'm going to tell you one more time. There's no substitute for the plain stuff, which flushes the system and refreshes the body. Water is essential for nutrient absorption, chemical reactions, and proper circulation in the body. In these many ways, drinking sufficient water supports the health of the heart.

But what about the other liquids you drink from morn till night? This chapter gives you an overview of some of the most common beverages and takes a look at the health benefits of these, as well as some of the drawbacks. Why not sit with a glass of your favorite drink right now as you read about some of the healthier ways to quench your thirst?

Benefiting from Black Tea

If you don't already drink tea, give it a try. Yes, it has less of a kick than coffee, but the body does adjust. Soon you'll be humming along on tea just as you did on the high-octane stuff. To make the transition from coffee to tea easier, start with a complex, richly flavored tea, such as Earl Grey, which is perfumed with bergamot oranges.

But these pleasures aside, tea benefits the heart in many ways. Here are some reasons, based on the results of many large studies, to brew a pot full of tea:

✔ Antioxidants in tea help prevent LDL cholesterol from oxidizing, an early stage in the development of atherosclerosis. In fact, tea contains even higher levels of antioxidants than many fruits and vegetables.

- ✔ Heart disease is now considered an inflammatory process, and phytonutrients in tea have an anti-inflammatory effect.

- ✔ Tea helps keep blood vessels functioning normally.

If this section has inspired you to try some tea, don't start with tea that you've had in the cupboard forever. When you buy tea in the market, it's probably already a year old, so keep tea no longer than six months to a year. Black tea stays fresh longer than green tea.

Enjoying Green Tea

The delicate flavor of green tea, suggestive of twigs and herbs, is a refreshing change from the richer flavor of black tea. It begs to be sipped, to savor its subtle flavor, as is the practice in the traditional Japanese tea ceremony. The flavor of green tea is also the perfect complement to Japanese specialties such as sushi and tempura. In additional, green tea is a healing beverage for the heart.

Green tea contains more beneficial nutrients than black tea, which is fermented, a process that destroys some of these compounds. The nutrients in green tea most important for heart health are the polyphenols, some of which are antioxidants and others anti-inflammatory substances (see Chapter 1). Many studies, although not all, have shown that green tea also mildly lowers total cholesterol, increases the "good" HDL cholesterol while lowering the "bad" LDL, and protects LDL from oxidation. Green tea may also help prevent the formation of blood clots that can cause heart attack and stroke.

One of the polyphenols in green tea, epigallocatechin gallate (EGCG), is a mouthful and an antioxidant 20 times stronger than vitamin E.

Considering Chamomile Tea

Chamomile tea earns its place in a heart healthy diet because of its anti-inflammatory properties. A form of inflammation that is systemic can set the stage for heart disease. Very mild but chronic inflammation of body tissues such as those lining the arteries can set the stage for heart disease. You can find chamomile tea bags in most supermarkets. Steep in a cup of hot water for 5 to 10 minutes.

Chamomile also has a mild relaxing effect, so it's the right drink when you're feeling stressed.

Curbing coffee to cut cholesterol

The latest word on whether coffee raises cholesterol is that it does, when you drink too much. The recommendation is to drink not more than one to two cups a day.

Earlier research suggested that the brewing method was the deciding factor. Boiled coffee, the kind favored in Scandinavia, raised cholesterol levels, but filtered coffee did not. However, conclusions of a recent Norwegian study, conducted by researchers at the University of Oslo and published in 2001 in the *American Journal of Clinical Nutrition,* question the safety of drinking even filtered coffee. When participants who had been drinking an average of 4 cups of filtered coffee daily for the past year abstained for the test period of six weeks, they experienced a drop in total cholesterol and homocysteine levels, both risk factors for heart disease. (See Chapter 1.)

Experiment with coffee alternatives, which are much healthier drinks than actual coffee because of what they do not contain, specifically, caffeine and alkaloid compounds. These compounds are cardiac stimulants that can stress the heart muscle and lead to heart palpitations. Coffee substitutes consist of clever mixes of ingredients such as roasted barley, chicory, figs, orange peel, rye, and roasted soy. The result is a surprisingly satisfying, pleasantly bitter, and rich drink. Gourmet versions are scented with hazelnut and Mexican chocolate. Good brands to look for are Pero, Roma, Cafix, and Teeccino.

Winning with Red Wine

The civilized habit of having a couple swallows of wine with lunch and dinner, an established part of meals in Europe, is considered one of the main reasons that the French have a low incidence of heart disease, despite having high cholesterol and eating a diet that includes cream sauces, cheese, and pâté.

Flavonoids, also known as polyphenols, in red wine are thought to be responsible for these benefits. One important flavonoid, quercetin, has antioxidant and anti-inflammatory properties. Tannins, which are found in the skin and seed of grapes and give red wine its color, protect the body from harmful cholesterol. Red wine raises "good" HDL cholesterol levels and promotes the breakup of "bad" LDL cholesterol. It may also help keep arteries open.

Choose red wine over white and rosé, both of which contain only relatively small amounts of heart-protective tannins.

Alcohol itself is now thought to reduce the risk of coronary artery disease. But of course, abusing alcohol increases the chance of life-threatening liver disease as well as heart disease. Having one to three drinks a week is considered light drinking. Moderate drinking covers the range of four drinks a week to two drinks a day.

Enjoying a Drop of the Grape

Drinking purple grape juice, just like red wine, benefits the heart in many ways such as inhibiting the formation of blood clots. In a study conducted at the University of Wisconsin Medical School and published in *Circulation* in 1999, grape juice was also shown to prevent LDL cholesterol from oxidizing and help keep arteries elastic. The 15 adults with coronary artery disease who participated in this study consumed 12 to 16 ounces (about 2 cups) of purple grape juice daily for two weeks. Admittedly this quantity of juice adds calories but it certainly is a better choice than a sugary cola.

If you decide to start drinking lots of grape juice, have only about a half cup or 4 ounces at a time. And sip it slowly, preferably with food, to avoid quickly swallowing a lot of sugar, which can rapidly elevate blood sugar levels. (See Chapter 1.)

Like red wine, purple grape juice protects the heart in the following ways:

- ✔ Reduces the stickiness of blood to help prevent blood clots
- ✔ Protects LDL cholesterol from oxidation which promotes the accumulation of plaque on artery walls
- ✔ Triggers the arteries to dilate when necessary to respond to an increased flow in blood

Read the label and make sure that you buy juice made with Concord grapes, the dark purple-blue grape with the highest levels of antioxidants. White and red grape juice has far less. (I have new respect for the 70-year-old Concord grape vine that edges one side of my yard. The juice is very sweet while the tannin-rich skins are super tart, which doesn't stop the raccoon from spending his nights eating all the grapes.)

For a nonalcoholic treat, look for gourmet brands of grape beverages that are designed to taste like wine.

Going for the Orange

Buy some juice oranges, such as smooth, thin skin Valencias, and give them a squeeze. Oranges are full of nutrients, especially when juice is fresh-made. While mineral content remains the same, the amount of the more fragile vitamin C and B vitamins in orange juice can decline. For instance, vitamin C is destroyed when exposed to air, and thiamin is lost to heat. So it's best to squeeze and quickly drink your OJ for the most benefits. Here is a list of nutrients in orange juice that are good for the heart.

✔ All sorts of antioxidants, including vitamin C

✔ Vitamin B6 and folic acid, both associated with lower levels of homocysteine (see Chapters 1 and 2 for more on homocysteine)

✔ Potassium in good amounts, an important mineral for preventing high blood pressure (over 80 percent of Americans do not consume enough)

Including Other Fruit Juices (but Not Too Much!)

Besides grape and orange juice, how about other good-for-you juices such as apple, apricot, pear, pineapple, papaya, and watermelon — great mixed with orange juice. And don't forget such exotics as pomegranate and cherry juice. (See Chapter 8 to find out their benefits.) Just as eating a variety of fruit lets you take in an assortment of nutrients, drinking their juice does the same thing.

However, juice also has its downside. You can quickly add a surprising amount of calories to your daily intake as you guzzle glassfuls of juice to quench your thirst. Take a look at Table 21-1:

Table 21-1	Calories in 1 Cup (8 ounces) of Fruit Juice
Type of Juice	*Calories*
Fresh orange juice	111
Cranberry juice cocktail	147
Canned pear nectar	149
Bottled grape juice	155

Drinking a cup of orange juice is equivalent to eating two oranges. While the bulk of actual oranges prevent you from quickly taking in all the sugar in this amount of fruit, you can gulp a cup of juice in 5 seconds and cause your blood sugar to rapidly rise. Making this a habit can contribute to weight gain and even lead to insulin resistance, and consequently high cholesterol (see Chapter 1.)

To reduce calories and concentrated sugars, cut fruit juice with plain water, club soda, or herbal tea. Try these combinations:

✔ Pear nectar and ginger tea

✔ Peach nectar and mint tea

✔ Concord grape juice and sparkling water

Most commercial fruit juice is missing the soluble fiber that is in the whole fruit. But you can remedy this by making your own juice. Use a blender that liquefies the entire peeled fruit, rather than a juice extractor, which removes all the pulp and fiber.

Lifting a Stein

Imagine! A beer a day can keep the doctor away. Researchers gave hamsters with atherosclerosis the equivalent of one beer a day and observed a 50 percent reduction in fatty deposits in the arteries. Like red wine, proven to be good for the heart, beer is full of flavonoid antioxidants that can slow aging and help prevent heart disease. Dark beers contain more flavonoids than light.

The prescription for beer is one a day. Drinking more than this does not produce additional benefits, and you can end up with a genuine beer belly, which can stress the heart.

Sipping Healthy Sparkling Beverages

Instead of regular commercial soft drinks, enjoy some of the sparkling alternatives now on the market. Try some carbonated apple juice such as Martinelli's Sparkling Cider or Izze's sparkling grapefruit juice, both winners. Sample Steaz's root beer made with organic ingredients and a shot of green tea. You can find such soda alternatives in both supermarkets and natural food stores.

But be sure to read labels. Manufacturers have come up with all sorts of specialty fruit juice-sparkling water-herbal tea mixtures, ready-made and in fancy bottles, elegant-looking enough to serve on special occasions. These are healthier than colas but not necessarily health foods as they often contain non-nutritive sweeteners.

Lassi Come Home

In India, a *lassi* is a popular chilled yogurt drink. The yogurt is mixed with water and/or crushed ice and can be flavored with salt, or it can be served sweet by mixing it with sugar, fruit, and fruit juices. Mint and cumin are also common additions. All Indian restaurants serve lassi, but it's easy to make in your own kitchen. For a delightful treat, put 1 cup plain, lowfat yogurt and 1 cup chopped mango in a blender. Add a pinch of cumin and blend until light and frothy. Enjoy this drink at room temperature, chilled in the fridge, or simply poured over ice. Serve with Indian food such as the Chicken Tandoori with Yogurt-Mint Sauce in Chapter 12.

Chapter 22

Ten Ways to Trim Your Food Bill

Saving money on food is easy, because prices for meals can vary so much depending upon whether you eat at home or out and how cleverly you shop for groceries. Here are ten ways to cut food expenditures that are just a matter of thinking ahead and being willing to try new places to shop and eat. If you save just $3 a day, that comes to $1,095 a year — and that's not chicken feed!

Shopping More Often but Buying Less

When you shop for perishable items, buy only as much as you think you'll really eat before it goes bad. In our household, we do as Noah did and allow into the kitchen kinds of fruit, two by two. We can always finish two avocados before they go rotten, but not three or four.

Freezing the bread isn't recommended. It doesn't freeze that well, and the texture and flavor deteriorate.

Showing Up at Farmers Markets

Buy seasonal; buy local. Why pay a cantaloupe's travel expenses from Central America or Peru when you can purchase a melon that's grown closer to home instead? At farmers markets you also find reasonably priced specialty items such as baby lettuces, heirloom tomatoes, white peaches, and specialty cheeses produced on a small scale. Produce at farmer's markets often costs about as much as the same fruits and vegetables at the supermarket, but you can trust farmers market produce to be fresher and of higher quality.

Buying Produce in Season

Take advantage of fruit and vegetables in season, when the supply is plentiful, prices drop, and flavor is at its peak. In-season produce is also likely to contain more of the antioxidants and phytonutrients that help control cholesterol. (Of course, you've probably become accustomed to seeing strawberries for sale at Christmas, but despite their holiday colors, these berries are actually not winter fruit.)

Going Grocery Shopping with a Plan

The experts advise you to have a written shopping list and stick to it when you head out to the mall to do your Christmas shopping. The same advice applies when you're on your way to the grocery store. This way, you aren't as likely to pick up gourmet and exotic foods you don't really need. Alternatively, your plan could be to have no plan at all. Wander the aisles and look for special bargains the store is offering. If you see that pork loin, apples, and cabbage are on sale, you've nearly written your complete dinner menu.

Scouting Out Neighborhood Food Shops

In my own neighborhood, I can shop at a newly remodeled, snazzy supermarket and buy dates that are nothing special for $5 a pound. Or I can go around the corner to a little Armenian store and buy gorgeous dates for $2.75. The same goes for feta and marinated olives. Taking the time to find new places to shop can save you money.

Wising Up about How to Keep Food Fresh

Storing your food properly will prevent it from spoiling before you can use it. If you have to toss out food that you didn't store or freeze properly, it's like tossing out your hard-earned money. Know the special storage requirements of all sorts of foods, from flour and nuts to basil and filet of sole. Here are some suggestions:

✔ Collect storage containers of various sizes and with airtight lids, and keep plastic freezer bags on hand.

✔ Make room in your refrigerator or freezer for whole grain flour and nuts. These should be stored in tightly lidded containers or sealed in airtight plastic bags. Whole grain flour stays fresh for 2 to 3 months and most nuts keep at least 6 months.

✔ Put perishables such as avocados and mangoes on display in your kitchen where you'll see them every day and be more likely to eat them.

✔ Resist the temptation to keep cooking oils in clear glass bottles in a kitchen window. Light causes oil to go rancid even faster then exposure to air.

Stocking Up on Stock

Always have on hand some sort of stock — vegetarian or meat and poultry-based — frozen in 1-quart portions. Use these to create a quick soup (see Chapter 9 for some ideas) made with trimmings and leftovers, a thrifty way to use up all sorts of foods in your fridge. At last, a free lunch!

Traveling with Snacks

Don't leave home without something to munch on, whether on a cross-country trip with your family or just an outing for the day in your hometown. You're sure to eat healthier and far cheaper than if you rely on fast food outlets and coffee shops when you feel peckish. If you're looking for snacks that are low in cholesterol and high in healthy fats and fiber, try these:

✔ Peanuts and a banana, which is great for traveling because it comes with its own handy package and doesn't drip juice

✔ Cut, raw veggies in a plastic bag and yogurt dip stored in the yogurt container

✔ Keep perishable snacks such as yogurt dip in a small cooler. Large drug stores sell these.

✔ Ready-made hummus, sold as party food in small containers, and whole-wheat pitas

✔ Cracker sandwiches made with almond butter (using crackers that don't contain partially-hydrogenated oil) and an apple

Bring along something to drink. Whether in the car or at work, be sure to have fresh, bottled water handy. Then, when you feel tired and thirsty, reach for what you really need — a refreshing glass of water — instead of making a pit stop for a $3.50 frozen mocha latte.

Finding Cheap Restaurant Eats

Many times the best restaurant meals, and the best deals, are in those modest restaurants that feature the cooking of various cultures. Poke your nose in some intriguing joint and sample the cooking smells. Be willing to make some mistakes. Find your favorites and then be sure to make a habit of going to these places once a week to save on your dining-out budget.

If you only want a smallish meal, try ordering one or two appetizers rather than a pricy main course. Ordering this way also lets you put together a creative vegetarian meal; for instance, a salad with bean soup.

Cooking at Home More Often

Food prepared at home is usually a fraction of the cost of eating out. Even when you spend the same amount, the dollars that give you wild salmon and fresh pineapple in a supermarket will buy only fish and chips in a restaurant. And if there are leftovers when you cook for yourself, you have two meals for the price of one. Cooking at home also gives you control over the ingredients. You can fashion meals with all those ingredients that help control cholesterol.

Appendix

Metric Conversion Guide

• •

*N**ote:* The recipes in this cookbook were not developed or tested using metric measures. There may be some variation in quality when converting to metric units.

Common Abbreviations

Abbreviation(s)	What It Stands For
C, c	cup
g	gram
kg	kilogram
L, l	liter
lb	pound
mL, ml	milliliter
oz	ounce
pt	pint
t, tsp	teaspoon
T, TB, Tbl, Tbsp	tablespoon

Volume

U.S. Units	Canadian Metric	Australian Metric
¼ teaspoon	1 mL	1 ml
½ teaspoon	2 mL	2 ml
1 teaspoon	5 mL	5 ml
1 tablespoon	15 mL	20 ml

(continued)

Volume *(continued)*

U.S. Units	Canadian Metric	Australian Metric
¼ cup	50 mL	60 ml
⅓ cup	75 mL	80 ml
½ cup	125 mL	125 ml
⅔ cup	150 mL	170 ml
¾ cup	175 mL	190 ml
1 cup	250 mL	250 ml
1 quart	1 liter	1 liter
1½ quarts	1.5 liters	1.5 liters
2 quarts	2 liters	2 liters
2½ quarts	2.5 liters	2.5 liters
3 quarts	3 liters	3 liters
4 quarts	4 liters	4 liters

Weight

U.S. Units	Canadian Metric	Australian Metric
1 ounce	30 grams	30 grams
2 ounces	55 grams	60 grams
3 ounces	85 grams	90 grams
4 ounces (¼ pound)	115 grams	125 grams
8 ounces (½ pound)	225 grams	225 grams
16 ounces (1 pound)	455 grams	500 grams
1 pound	455 grams	½ kilogram

Measurements

Inches	Centimeters
½	1.5
1	2.5

Inches	Centimeters
2	5.0
3	7.5
4	10.0
5	12.5
6	15.0
7	17.5
8	20.5
9	23.0
10	25.5
11	28.0
12	30.5
13	33.0

Temperature (Degrees)

Fahrenheit	Celsius
32	0
212	100
250	120
275	140
300	150
325	160
350	180
375	190
400	200
425	220
450	230
475	240
500	260

Index

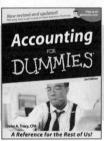

FOR DUMMIES®

A world of resources to help you grow

HOME, GARDEN & HOBBIES

0-7645-5295-3

0-7645-5130-2

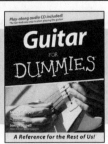

0-7645-5106-X

Also available:

Auto Repair For Dummies
(0-7645-5089-6)

Chess For Dummies
(0-7645-5003-9)

Home Maintenance For Dummies
(0-7645-5215-5)

Organizing For Dummies
(0-7645-5300-3)

Piano For Dummies
(0-7645-5105-1)

Poker For Dummies
(0-7645-5232-5)

Quilting For Dummies
(0-7645-5118-3)

Rock Guitar For Dummies
(0-7645-5356-9)

Roses For Dummies
(0-7645-5202-3)

Sewing For Dummies
(0-7645-5137-X)

FOOD & WINE

0-7645-5250-3

0-7645-5390-9

0-7645-5114-0

Also available:

Bartending For Dummies
(0-7645-5051-9)

Chinese Cooking For Dummies
(0-7645-5247-3)

Christmas Cooking For Dummies
(0-7645-5407-7)

Diabetes Cookbook For Dummies
(0-7645-5230-9)

Grilling For Dummies
(0-7645-5076-4)

Low-Fat Cooking For Dummies
(0-7645-5035-7)

Slow Cookers For Dummies
(0-7645-5240-6)

TRAVEL

0-7645-5453-0

0-7645-5438-7

0-7645-5448-4

Also available:

America's National Parks For Dummies
(0-7645-6204-5)

Caribbean For Dummies
(0-7645-5445-X)

Cruise Vacations For Dummies 2003
(0-7645-5459-X)

Europe For Dummies
(0-7645-5456-5)

Ireland For Dummies
(0-7645-6199-5)

France For Dummies
(0-7645-6292-4)

London For Dummies
(0-7645-5416-6)

Mexico's Beach Resorts For Dummies
(0-7645-6262-2)

Paris For Dummies
(0-7645-5494-8)

RV Vacations For Dummies
(0-7645-5443-3)

Walt Disney World & Orlando For Dummies
(0-7645-5444-1)

Available wherever books are sold. Go to www.dummies.com or call 1-877-762-2974 to order direct.